Contested Eden

Contested Eden

CALIFORNIA BEFORE
THE GOLD RUSH

Editors

RAMÓN A. GUTIÉRREZ and RICHARD J. ORSI

Illustrations Editor
ANTHONY KIRK

Associate Editor
MARLENE SMITH-BARANZINI

Published in association with the California Historical Society

UNIVERSITY OF CALIFORNIA PRESS
Berkeley · Los Angeles · London

University of California Press
Berkeley and Los Angeles, California

University of California Press, Ltd.
London, England

LIBRARY OF CONGRESS CATALOGING-IN-PUBLICATION DATA

Contested Eden: California before the Gold Rush / edited by
    Ramón Gutiérrez, Richard J. Orsi.
        p.   cm.   (California history sesquicentennial series ; 1)
        Includes bibliographical references and index.
        ISBN 0-520-21273-8 (cloth : alk. paper).—ISBN 0-520-21274-6
    (pbk. : alk. paper)
        1. California—History—to 1846. 2. California—History—
    1846–1850. 1. Gutiérrez, Ramón A., 1951–   . 11. Orsi, Richard J.
    111. Series.
    F864.C735   1998
    979.4—dc21   97-23057
                                                             CIP

Printed in the United States of America
9 8 7 6 5 4 3 2 1

Contents

Maps

Preface

As the twenty-first century dawns, it is incumbent on Californians to take stock of their civilization. Over centuries, indeed millennia, through the application of human intelligence and organization, they have built monumental productive systems, sophisticated associations, flexible governments, and creative and vigorous, if somewhat untamed, cultures. On the other hand, Californians continue to be troubled by contradictions, debates, and conflicts, ironically often stemming from those same successes. While, for example, the people benefit from perhaps the most diverse and profitable regional economy in the world, resource exhaustion renders the continuation of that affluence problematic. Whereas California has always been a land of immigrants, ever refreshing the state with their ideas, skills, and energies, some contemporaries now challenge the wisdom, and even the viability, of a multicultural society. Although the complex, modern California way of life, with its gargantuan infrastructure and environmental management systems, has been made possible only because of the evolution of powerful government agencies to further the common interest, in the last two decades those governments have been crippled by dwindling finances, a stalemate of contending interests, and growing doubts among some of the populace regarding their efficiency and representativeness. Private interest has, for many Californians, replaced community well-being as the state's driving principle. As it has been in the past, California remains a "contested Eden."

The victories and torments of modern California, which actually reflect those of much of the rest of the nation and world, though perhaps in bolder relief, can be understood only in the context of the state's history. The origins of an ambiguous present lie not simply in yesterday, but also in pioneer days. Demonstrating this is the great opportunity, and the challenge, presented by the California Sesquicentennial between 1998 and 2000.

It is with pleasure and a sense of obligation that, in conjunction with the University of California Press and many other partners, the California Historical Society—the officially designated "state historical society"—launches the California History Sesquicentennial Series as its principal contribution to the statewide commemoration. Four topical, but interrelated, volumes, one published in each year from 1997 through 2000, will reexamine the meaning, particularly from today's perspective, of the founding of modern California in the pre-1848 and gold-rush era experiences. Each of the volumes will collect essays by a dozen authors, drawn from the ranks of leading humanists, social scientists, and scientists, reviewing the best, most up-to-date thinking on major topics associated with the state's pioneer period through the 1870s. The authors have been asked to consider, within their area of expertise, the general themes that run through all four volumes: the interplay of traditional cultures and frontier innovation in the creation of a distinctive California society; the dynamic interaction of people and nature and the beginnings of massive environmental change; the impact of the California experience on the nation and the wider world; the shaping influence of pioneer patterns on modern California; and the importance and legacy of ethnic and cultural diversity as a major dimension of the state's history.

The Sesquicentennial California History volumes will be published simultaneously as double issues of *California History*, the quarterly of the Historical Society, and as books for general distribution. This volume, Volume 1 in the series, *Contested Eden: California before the Gold Rush*, co-edited by Ramón A. Gutiérrez, Professor of Ethnic Studies and History at the University of California, San Diego, deals with the social, economic, cultural, political, and environmental patterns of Native American, Spanish, and Mexican California through 1848. Volume 2 (1998), being co-edited by James J. Rawls, member of the history faculty at Diablo Valley College, will focus on the pioneer industry of gold mining, its discovery and its impact on the state, the West, and the national and world economies. Volume 3 (1999), being co-edited by Kevin Starr, State Librarian of California, will focus on the Gold Rush and the migration and settlement of peoples, cultures, organizations, and institutions. Volume 4 (2000), being co-edited by John Burns, Chief Archivist of the California State Archives, will investigate the inception of government and politics—statehood, early constitution-building, law, bureaucracy, and civil rights.

The California Historical Society's issuing of these major sesquicentennial publications is made possible through the contributions of all the Society's members, as well as a host of direct and indirect supporters. Chief among the helping agencies are the University of California Press, the California State Archives, California State University, Hayward, which furnishes ongoing support for editing the quarterly, and the Mericos Foundation of South Pasadena, which has provided a generous grant specifically for the Sesquicentennial Series.

Many individuals have also shared their time, knowledge, energy, and resources. The Historical Society's particular appreciation goes to Lynne Withey, associate director of the University of California Press, who has been an indispensable part of the project from the beginning; Ramón A. Gutiérrez, the pioneering co-editor of the first series volume, who not only contributed immeasurably to conceptualizing the volume, selecting authors, and evaluating and editing manuscripts, but also established a very high standard for subsequent editors; Anthony Kirk, illustrations editor, who applied his unequaled knowledge and appreciation of California iconography to discover and edit a stunning series of images, many of them never before published; and Marlene Smith-Baranzini, associate editor of *California History* and true partner-editor in every facet of the Sesquicentennial History Series. Other important contributors include graduate assistants Sandra DeSalles and Mary-Jo Wainwright, and Liz Ginno, historian and member of the library faculty at California State University, Hayward. Our thanks also go to all the institutions and individuals who made it possible to use images from their collections in this work or who provided other valuable assistance. Although space precludes listing all their names, special mention should be made of Mina Jacobs, assistant archivist at the Anchorage Museum of History and Art; Barbara Allgaier, lecturer in the Department of History at California State University, Hayward; Dace Taube, curator of the California Historical Society/Title Insurance and Trust Photo Collection, Department of Special Collections, University of Southern California Library; Peter Blodgett at the Huntington Library; Richard Ogar and William Roberts at the Bancroft Library; John Cahoon, Seaver Center for Western History Research, Natural History Museum of Los Angeles County; Linda Agren, Santa Barbara Museum of Natural History; David Bisol, Santa Barbara Historical Society; Joy Tahan, Oakland Museum; Robin Inglis, director of North Vancouver Museum and Archives; Iris Engstrand, professor of history at the University of San Diego; and Larry Campbell, Patricia Keats, Katherine Holland, Emily Wolff, Bo Mompho, and other members of the professional staff of the California Historical Society, San Francisco.

Michael McCone
Executive Director
California Historical Society

Richard J. Orsi
Professor of History
California State University, Hayward
Editor, *California History*

1

Contested Eden

An Introduction

Ramón A. Gutiérrez

History, as the study of change over time, always requires that we stop periodically to take stock. Whether we measure by years, decades, or centuries, by regions, cohorts, or generations, the goal is identical: to assess what has transpired and what still remains to be done. California became part of the United States of America a century and a half ago. On the event of the state's sesquicentennial we commemorate our genealogies and complex pasts, acknowledging the debts of knowledge and interpretation we owe to previous generations, fashioning our present with distinct questions and concerns, charting a course toward a richer, more complex understanding of the past.

In the years since 1850, when statehood was won, California has gone from a space sparsely populated to the most populous place in the Union. Once a largely isolated backwater where Native Americans subsisted on hunt products, on plantings, and what could be gathered, California has been continuously and radically transformed, and periodically renewed. Spanish-speaking settlers arrived febrile with dreams of gold. But on finding none, they settled for lordship over the land and over its native labor. Gold was eventually discovered by Anglo-Americans in 1848. Gold fever truly gripped the national imagination then, and in California that fever has never completely cooled.

In the Golden State, one generation after another has found a tangible place on which to project its myths and fantasies of utopic possibility. Eden, Arcadia, lands flowing with milk and honey, gardens grander than Nebuchadnezzar's—in California such dreams have taken form. Parched deserts have been turned into verdant fields of plenty. The sea constantly yields its bounty. The aerospace industry has given us mastery over our universe. And our edifices scrape the sky and color the horizons.

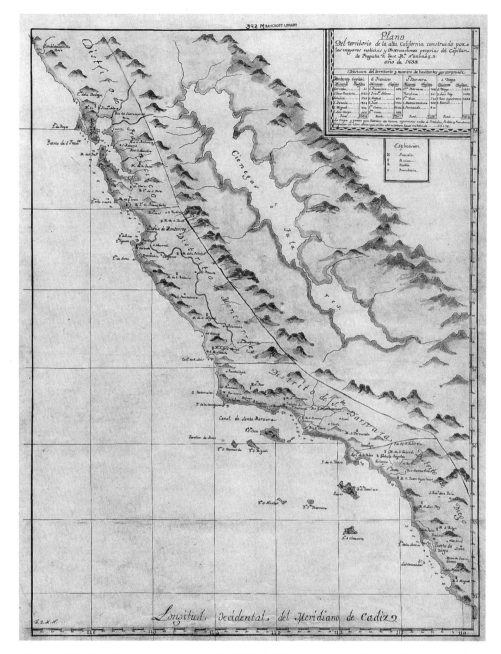

A map of California drawn in 1830 by José María Narváez, showing the missions, presidios, pueblos, and ranchos strung along the coast, and the massive wetlands—the *ciengas* or *tulares*—that filled the Central Valley. Though not many years would pass before topographers came to understand more fully the great complexity of the California landscape, it is relatively recently that historians have begun to explore some long-neglected aspects of the Golden State's storied past, working to create a history that is more comprehensive, more inclusive, and more subtle than older accounts. *Courtesy Bancroft Library.*

California's is today the sixth largest economy in the world because of its incredible human and natural resources. Since the earliest days of human occupation, California has been home to numerous linguistic, ethnic, racial, and national groups. If in ancient times the first natives of this land were Asians from Siberia, Asian presence today is much more diverse and of even grander import. If from central Mexico came the Spanish impetus for settling California, over the centuries Mexican presence has only grown. The Anglo-Americans who first visited California under Mexican rule were a diverse lot. The boom towns they and the forty-niners fueled were often cosmopolitan sites for feasting and hosting diplomats and plenipotentates, raiders and traders, and just plain folk. California, a state blessed by numerous microclimates, has also been cursed by virulent climates of hate, genocide, and intolerance for differences born of blood, faith, and race.

California is today the product of these multiple and diverse pasts. Still vibrant and alive today are many human memories of feast and famine, joy and pain, centrality and marginality, power and powerlessness. These memories are the potent stuff of history, for they fuel conflicting narratives of how it was in the "olden days." Call them golden days of yore or hurtful times that remain tender and sore, they are, nevertheless, wellsprings of historical imagination and the breeding ground of historians. Communities of memory and interest in the present cannot advance a trajectory toward the future without a commonly accepted origin and useable past. This is even more the case today, as California's population is renewed by immigrants from every corner of the globe.

Historians and the histories they write have always been the imaginative products of the period in which they were produced. Each generation turns to the past with different questions, with new concerns, with different hopes and anxieties. Since the 1960s there has been a revolution in historical writing about the United States, and about California's past more specifically. The exact causal lineages for this profound transformation are complicated and remain open to debate. Obviously, such change was born of generational tensions, fueled by the war in Vietnam, and intensified in the late 1950s and early 1960s by the massive social movements for civil rights, women's equality, lesbian and gay freedom, and the full extension of personhood to the very young, the very old, the disabled, and the transgendered. Eventually the force of state was given to the reaffirmation of our egalitarian constitutional principles, and as this occurred, educational institutions were desegregated and the American mind was opened to different ways of thinking and to perspectives on the past that were situated in relationship to power.

The impact of these changes on contemporary historical writing has been a heightened body ethic. Greater attention and importance is given to the human body, particularly to those physical aspects by which the status inequalities of gender, sexuality, race, and ethnicity are read. Now, for history-as-written to be deemed a good depiction of history-as-lived, it must acknowledge that it is but a very small slice or limited perspective on a whole as viewed from a specific locale, rather than a transcendent total perspective. For a social whole to be represented, a matrix of society's status groups must be systematically addressed. No longer is it considered adequate to write the history of men without acknowledging the presence of women, and vice versa. Power and its relational dyads—conqueror and conquered, master and slave, white and Indian, male and female, rich and poor, old and young—are similarly the focus of new and sustained attention.

Much of what is considered new in historical writing stems from profound epistemological shifts, most notably an attack on positivism and empiricism as truths, and the feminist critique of modernism's transcendent, universal "Man." Modernity was that extraordinary intellectual effort on the part of Enlightenment thinkers to develop objective science and a universal morality and law. The idea was to use the accumulation of knowledge, generated by many individuals working freely and creatively, for the pursuit of human emancipation and the enrichment of daily life. The scientific domination of nature promised freedom from scarcity, want, and the arbitrariness of natural calamities. Rational forms of social organization and thought would liberate humanity from irrationality, myth, religion, and superstition.

History as a university discipline and profession was born out of this modernist impulse.[1] Historians sought objective, universal truth, laws of human progress, and ways to liberate citizens and subjects. In the late nineteenth century, objectivity and the quest for truth became the collective myths of the historical profession. By reading sources in a detached and dispassionate manner, historians of that era assumed, one could reveal and discover the truth of the past. That knowledge, gained in an "objective" manner, enhanced its scientific value. If scientific rules were imposed on documentary bodies of evidence, the past would be reflected in written history.

Postmodern critics have retorted that consciousness has always been, and always will be, embodied. Can historians detach themselves from their bodies and their social participation in class-, gender-, and race-inflected ways? No. Are archives neutral and systematic collections of documents that record everyone's past? No. Can history-as-written exactly represent history-as-lived? No. The selection process, the mental filters and prisms through which events, people, and theories are refracted to create historical narratives, are always supremely subjective acts rooted in bodily experiences. Bodies are alive at particular times, in specific contexts, and in unique warps of power. In the writing of history, such realities cannot be ignored.

The implications of these epistemological and interpretive shifts for writing about early California's history heighten our awareness of how each generation has interpreted its past differently. Those pasts have always been partial views, rendered from highly partisan economic and political sites. When the Spanish arrived in California and pronounced that Native Americans were savages, ensnared by Satan and re-

In 1806 the German-born physician and naturalist Georg Heinrich von Langsdorff portrayed a ceremonial dance of mission Indians that he observed near the shores of San Francisco Bay. Decorating their bodies with red clay, chalk, and charcoal, the natives moved to the accompaniment of singing and the clapping of sticks, attempting, thought Langsdorff "to represent battles, or scenes of domestic life." *Courtesy Bancroft Library.*

quiring instruction in civilization, they concluded that these people had a history, but one that had to be obliterated. By calling them "Indians," the incredible complexity and diversity of native peoples and cultures in California was erased; henceforth Native Americans would share a subjective legal identity as "Indians." When Anglo-Americans conquered California at the end of the U.S.-Mexico War in 1848, they too rewrote history to fit the designs of conquerors. From the perspective of the new lords of California, the land was vacant, the Indians a meaningless race that would soon disappear, the Mexicans an inferior, indolent breed in whose command California had wasted.

The essays collected in this volume significantly revise the history of California from prehistoric times to 1848. The historians, scientists, anthropologists, and social ecologists chosen to write for this volume represent the best of interdisciplinary work in their scholarship. Readers familiar with California's traditional history writing will note that the missions, as the main institutions of mythology, fantasy, and romance, have receded into the background, and are analyzed here instead as institutions not only with religious, but with economic, social, and political functions. Where generals, friars, soldiers, adventurers, and merchants as individual actors used to dominate the narrative of Spanish and Mexican California's history, here the essays focus less on persons and personalities and more on the complex social networks of society. And while some familiar and well-known terrain is addressed—European exploration, the U.S.-Mexican War—these essays assess what has been learned over the last thirty years about these topics and what still remains to be investigated. Long ignored, California's indigenous peoples here take center stage. Rarely mentioned until recently, California's ecology and changing natural environment here gain sustained attention. Women, the family, the nature of Californio society, these are all themes of the vibrant scholarship over the last thirty years that is represented here.

One of the most troublesome aspects of histories of California written between the 1880s and 1960s is that they largely ignored the Indians. When Indians were mentioned, they were, more often than not, set in an endless stream of blood—nameless, and usually faceless, victims of atrocities. Indian prehistory was found mainly in archaeology and anthropology books, but rarely in history books. If and when Indian history gained attention, it was only as a prelude to the larger narrative of American triumphalism. Indian voices were rarely heard, and the categories of thought and action they were given to respond to their own conquest and colonization were those of ventriloquists. Bit players in morality plays about assimilation, noble savages who had disappeared—this is how Native Americans were primarily represented in early writing on California history.

The essays collected here not only offer a very different starting point for Native American history, but also give agency to California's Indians. This is not the history of white expansion and Indian responses to it; it begins with the complex dimensions of indigenous prehistory. Beginning Indian history before contact allows us to understand how leaders and followers responded to invasion and the changing circumstances of various tribes over time.

M. Kat Anderson, Michael Barbour, and Valerie Whitworth's rich essay on the natural environment surveys the state's great climatic, geological, floral, and faunal arrays, the complicated natural history of its vegetation, and the abundant, creative new scholarship about it. This information forms the foundation for a brilliant discussion of the intimate relationship Indians had with the natural world, structured around complex methods of plant conservation and use. Anderson, Barbour, and Whitworth urge us to view Indians as active agents in the use and modification of their environments and to abandon long-held stereotypes about a sharp divide between Indians who practiced agriculture and those who subsisted on hunting and gathering.

William Simmons's essay, "Indian Peoples of California," provides a succinct discussion of indigenous linguistic diversity. California was and remains geographically diverse. California Indian communities reflected that diversity in the resource base on which their economies and cultures were structured. Drawing on native categories and indigenous memories, Simmons brings attention to the centrality of human-animal relations and by so doing allows us to understand better why Indians thought that the first Europeans they encountered were beings from the spirit world.

Indian agency and the logic of native cultural categories forms the substance of Antonia Castañeda's essay, "Engendering the History of Alta California, 1769–1848: Gender, Sexuality, and the Family." Here readers will learn how California's Indians organized their gender and sexual systems, and particularly how those systems were assaulted, resisted, and transformed. Attention is given to the resistance strategies Indian women crafted to protect their status in native society and to assure that their cultures endured despite Spanish assaults. Castañeda also asks us to reassess the nature and extent of biological mixing that occurred when Spanish men raped Indian women, thus creating the beginnings of mestizo California.

Indigenous resistance strategies are also at the core of James Sandos's essay, "Between Crucifix and Lance: Indian-White Relations in California, 1769–1848." Seeking to understand how California's Indians resisted and often subverted their own domination, Sandos explores the "hidden transcripts" of Indian life, those often overt and covert folktales, graffiti, rumors, and actions that reveal native agency in the darkest moments of colonial domination. As readers will note from this and other essays, California's Indians both before and after conquest were not passive, silent observers of their own conquest and subordination. In the history presented here, they are historical actors; the complexity of their cultures before and under colonial rule is explained; and their long-silent voices are heard with particular clarity.

A second set of essays addresses the complex motivations that led to the conquest and colonization of California, the structure of the colonial economy, church-state conflicts over the place of the Indians in that scheme, and the tenor of daily life in Spanish and Mexican California. American exceptionalism often colored previous interpretations of the Spanish/Mexican past. Here, California is examined as one of many colonial outposts of imperial Spain, and thus a part of a much larger whole, encompassing both Europe and the Western Hemisphere, with all that entailed with respect to church-state relations, government, fiscal reform, and the institutions of daily life. For much too long, historians have wrongly assumed that the Enlightenment and the Bourbon Reforms had no impact on Spanish California. These essays profoundly revise that mistaken impression.

Iris Engstrand's essay, "Seekers of the 'Northern Mystery': European Exploration of California and the Pacific," begins the section of this volume that addresses the

Vaqueros at Mission San José lasso cattle with their *reatas* in an engraving based on a
watercolor made in the 1820s by William Smyth, an admiralty mate who visited California with a British exploring expedition. Expert horsemen, legendary for their skill
in working cattle, the California vaqueros captured the imagination of travelers and
became a symbol of provincial Hispanic life on a distant Pacific shore. From Frederick
W. Beechey, *Narrative of a Voyage to the Pacific and Beering's Strait* (London, 1831).
Courtesy California State Library.

European arrival and its impact on California as a land and on its native inhabitants.
Engstrand explains the complicated motivations that brought Europeans to California. First were the dreams of wealth and discovery, then came population movements motivated by defensive concerns, reconnaissance, and scientific discovery.
Extensive attention is given to the scientific journeys, which originate in Enlightenment curiosities and Bourbon economic imperatives. Each of these types of exploration devoted attention to geographic features, fauna and flora, native languages
and cultures, and natural products that eventually became coveted trade items.

William Preston's essay, "Serpent in the Garden: Environmental Change in Colonial California," studies the devastating impact of European diseases on Native Californians through human and nonhuman vectors, such as lice, mosquitoes, and fleas.
Preston also documents the spread of foreign seeds and weeds and the impact of European livestock on indigenous flora and fauna, which together worked a literal
revolution in California's life forms. Since Californians, both native and European,

depended on the natural environment for their existence, Preston's account of the intended and unintended consequences of biological exchanges is a particularly important one.

Bourbon defensive policy in New Spain, most notably the protection of northern Mexico's silver mines from possible British and Russian encroachment, was the motive for colonizing Alta California, according to Steven Hackel in his essay, "Land, Labor, and Production: The Colonial Economy of Spanish and Mexican California." Since this was Spain's primary interest in California, Spanish desire to invest in the area was marginal, never amounting to more than meager military salaries and church subventions. California's colonial economy thus developed a self-sufficiency through agricultural and livestock production and ancillary products, some of which found their way to markets in central Mexico. Production depended on Indian labor, and on this topic Hackel brings our attention to several forms that are rarely mentioned: the compensated use of non-mission Indians for prearranged tasks and the periodic contracting of mission Indians. After 1821, the Californios believed that Mexican independence would bring greater governmental attention to their province, but it did not. Under Mexican rule, California prospered somewhat, nonetheless, primarily because the lifting of trade restrictions quickened mercantile activities in local products, especially cattle hides.

Douglas Monroy's essay, "The Creation and Re-creation of Californio Society," begins with an insightful analysis of the politics of previous interpretations of the Californio past, colored as they were by the preoccupations of each age. Whereas early romanticizers characterized the Californios as Spanish Europeans, Monroy's own interpretation highlights the fundamentally hybrid, or mestizo, nature of the society created when Indians and Spanish colonists came together in California. Particularly important is Monroy's analysis of the caricatures of Indians the colonists crafted, which bore little relationship to the complex spiritual and productive lifeways Native Americans created even under the harshest conditions on the missions and on their ancestral lands. Unlike the Indians, who imagined a relationship of reciprocity between themselves and the natural environment, the Spanish attitude toward land was one of ownership and command. Monroy describes the culture and customs that such attitudes encouraged, including how life was produced and reproduced.

Church-state conflict over Indian labor forms the core of Michael González's essay, "The Child of the Wilderness Weeps for the Father of Our Country." This is an intellectual and political history of imperial Spanish debates about the place of the Indian in the Americas, and more specifically, how those contests were played out on the bodies of Indians for whom California's friars and soldiers competed. Like Steven Hackel, whose essay ends with the secularization of the missions under Mexican rule in the 1830s, González addresses secularization in the context of central Mexican intellectual currents.

The final two chapters of this volume chronicle the changes that transpired under Spanish and Mexican rule because of growing foreign influences. The essays address how foreigners entered California in larger numbers after 1821, how some of them intermarried with the Californios, how their economic activities profoundly shifted the direction and geography of trade, and finally, how the U.S.-Mexico War was fought and lost.

Doyce B. Nunis, Jr., in his essay, "Alta California's Trojan Horse: Foreign Immigration," displaces standard interpretations about the role of Manifest Destiny in bringing California into the American republic. Nunis describes the nature and motivations behind the initial visits to Spanish California by French, Russian, and British travelers. With Mexican independence after 1821, the pace of visitation quickened, led increasingly by Anglo-American traders who married Californio women to gain access to large amounts of land and business opportunity. Indeed, the presence of many citizens of Britain and the United States in an enclave distant from Mexican military control created the conditions for secessionist movements that culminated in the U.S.-Mexico War from 1846 to 1848.

The acquisition of California from Mexico was one of the largest spoils of that war. Lisbeth Haas's essay, "War in California, 1846–1848," provides a sweeping overview of the personages, motives, and war campaigns in California. What is particularly noteworthy in her essay is the discussion of Californio responses to their displacement by Anglo-Americans both before and after 1848. What is still sorely needed to reach a fuller understanding of the war and its impact is more study of how the Indians allied themselves, and what thoughts and actions may have shaped the reactions of ordinary Californios. We know the details of the war and its aftermath primarily from the perspective of the victors. The voices of the vanquished have still not been heard in their polyphonic complexity. This is one of the challenges Haas offers us in her essay.

In addition to the innovative historical research gathered in these pages, this volume is also extensively illustrated with some of the earliest and rarest images of California. Anthony Kirk gathered the illustrations for this volume, and in his essay, "Picturing California," he draws our attention to California's iconographic history before 1848. Beginning with Native American pictographs, Kirk shows just how important the natural environment has been in shaping human perceptions of California. From the early Spanish maps to drawings of the area's flora and fauna by French explorers, from Russian watercolors of Fort Ross to the American drawings of the Klamath River, the objective has been the same: to depict California as a land of abundant wealth and natural variety awaiting human exploitation.

The thirteen essays collected in this volume represent a full range of interpretations about California's past from prehistoric times to 1848. Natural and human ecology are given equal weight. California's long historiographic traditions and its uncharted terrains are all laid bare. Our hope is that by examining what is new in California history and what still remains to be studied and written, this volume will be generative, giving readers the leading questions and historiographic resources necessary to pursue these topics further on their own.

NOTES

1. Peter Novick, *That Noble Dream: The "Objectivity Question" and the American Historical Profession* (New York: Cambridge University Press, 1988).

2

A World of Balance and Plenty

Land, Plants, Animals, and Humans
in a Pre-European California

M. Kat Anderson, Michael G. Barbour,
and Valerie Whitworth

California has environmental diversity and richness unparalleled anywhere in the world. The state's geographic undulations encompass the lowest and the highest points in the conterminous United States. Spanning more than ten degrees of latitude and extending over one hundred million acres, California is a bridge between cool-temperate, foggy, dimly lit rainforests and open, parched, hot, sun-bathed subtropical deserts. This astounding array of California vegetation exists in close juxtaposition, spilling and swirling in patterns created by elevation, climate, soil, and bedrock.

From a distance—as from a jet aircraft flying over the state at great elevation and speed—California's vegetation cover today might still appear continuous and healthy and relatively unchanged from 1848. However, only isolated areas of pre-European vegetation types in oak woodlands, desert scrub, montane forests, chaparral, woodland, and grassland still exist. Urban areas, agriculture, clearcuts, weeds, and pavement have replaced much of the former vegetation. Except for small areas that are rare examples of prior landscapes, the vegetation types that remain are not the same as the ones that Native Californians lived in 150 years ago.

Many factors have influenced the land over the last 150 years. Desert scrub is degraded by overgrazing and off-road sport vehicles. Because of fire suppression and weakened overstories from drought, insects, and atmospheric pollutants, montane forests have flammable, dense understories. Once, small lowburning fires cleared this underbrush out, keeping firehazard low and forests healthy. Many square miles of chaparral have been converted to grassland or homesites, coastal scrub to suburbs, and perennial grasslands to weedy annual pastures or farmland. Only a small per-

A sailing ship glides past the old Mexican presidio and into San Francisco Bay in Richard Beechey's charming watercolor of coastal California, executed in 1826, when the talented young English midshipman first visited the province. Contributing to the Golden State's complex mosaic of diverse landscapes, the San Francisco peninsula enjoys a temperate climate of cool, wet winters and warm, dry summers, with the long sunny days of May through September subject to the rhythmic incursion of chilling sea fogs. *Courtesy Mr. and Mrs. Henry Dakin. Photograph courtesy North Point Gallery.*

centage of old-growth forests such as riparian, coast redwood, mixed conifer, and Douglas fir remains. Less than a fragmented 10 percent of coastal wetlands and a meager 2 percent of interior wetlands are still intact. Furthermore, the quality of remaining fragments has been compromised by adjacent development, which turns the fragments into unstable islands. About six hundred plants (10 percent of the native species) and three hundred vertebrates (30 percent of the native species) are declining in numbers and are in danger of extinction. Some 17 percent of all plants in California are non-native, most of which were introduced after 1848, and some 40 percent of our inland fish species are similarly non-native.[1]

This decline did not occur because California was suddenly overwhelmed with human inhabitants. For millennia before Europeans arrived, California was an inhabited land. Every part of the region had long been discovered, walked, or settled by native people by the time Spaniards first landed on the shores of San Diego Bay in

1542.[2] At the time of Euro-American contact, California was more densely populated than any area of equal size in North America, north of central Mexico. Long before Europeans mapped the region, California's tallest mountain peaks, its largest lakes, its longest rivers, and its oldest trees all had names. The state's promontories, declivities, and unusual rock formations were infused with human meaning. What is labeled as "wilderness" in today's popular imagination and on current topographic maps actually harbored human gathering and hunting sites, burial grounds, work sites, sacred areas, trails, and village sites. Today's wilderness was then human homeland.

Native American manipulations in California were conducted in a manner that allowed certain plants to regenerate so completely that virtually every Euro-American explorer, gold miner, and missionary was fooled into thinking that the land was a wilderness—unaffected by humans. Environmental historian William Cronon says that "one of the most striking proofs of the cultural invention of wilderness is its thoroughgoing erasure of the history from which it sprang."[3] In California, that history is rich with cultural phenomena: the long-term interactions between Native Americans and landscapes.

Ironically, the adjectives and adverbs used by the first non-Indian visitors and settlers in describing the countryside often hinted of human intervention. Analogies early commentators used to describe California landscapes were human-modified environments—such as gardens, parks, or orchards. For example, William Bryant, an emigrant and newspaper editor from Kentucky, wrote in his journal in 1846 of the landscape near San Luis Obispo: "The hills and plains are verdant with a carpet of fresh grass, and the scattered live-oaks on all sides appearing like orchards of fruit-trees, give to the country an old and cultivated aspect."[4] J. D. Borthwick in the early 1850s described the countryside near Placerville: "gradually ascending . . . we came upon a comparatively level country, which had all the beauty of an English park. . . . The oaks of various kinds, which were here the only tree, were of an immense size, but not so numerous as to confine the view; and the only underwood was the mansanita, a very beautiful and graceful shrub, generally growing in single plants to the height of six or eight feet. There was no appearance of ruggedness or disorder; we might have imagined ourselves in a well-kept domain. . . ."[5]

Behind these awe-inspiring landscapes, unseen by the culture-bound foreigners, were native gardeners. They tended the land in ways that often mimicked nature—similar to the changes caused by floods, fires, gopher activity, and tree windfalls. For example, when the Western Mono lit hillsides on fire to encourage the growth of young redbud shrub shoots for basketry, they simulated lightning fires. When the Washoe pruned willow, they mimicked the natural pruning caused by river flooding. Deliberate burning was the major management tool used to shape California's landscapes. Natives frequently lit surface fires in many areas, effectively precluding the kinds of holocaust fires that regularly devastate large areas of California today. Fire

Based on a watercolor made in 1794 by John Sykes, a master's mate on George Vancouver's great voyage of discovery, *A Remarkable Mountain near the River of Monterrey* testifies to the land-management techniques of California Indians two hundred years ago. The natives maintained the open foothill woodlands through systematic burning, which promoted the growth of useful plants and kept the ground free of woody underbrush. Vancouver first encountered a cultivated California woodland such as this while riding horseback from San Francisco to Santa Clara and compared it to "a park" that had been "planted with the true old English Oak." From George Vancouver, *A Voyage of Discovery* (London, 1798). *Courtesy California Historical Society, FN-30521.*

scientists Robert Martin and David Sapsis estimate that between 5.6 and 13 million acres of California burned annually under both lightning and indigenous fire regimes.[6] By a host of other horticultural methods—including weeding, pruning, irrigating, sowing, selective harvesting, and tilling—native peoples influenced the land in more subtle dimensions.

Cultivating favored plants in different patches was common among all of the tribes. Through different methods, Native Americans augmented plant populations and reshaped the boundaries of various types of plant communities, in some cases creating anthropogenic landscapes of unique form and character. Pomo women weeded sedgebeds to loosen the soil and remove impediments to rhizomes radiating from each plant, promoting the untangled, long underground stems desirable for basketry material.[7] The Owens Valley Paiute artificially irrigated love grass, wild rye, and blue dicks to encourage their growth and abundance.[8] The Pomo, Cupeño,

Diegueño, Kumeyaay, and other tribes burned fields of edible seed plants to improve their productivity.[9] The Cahuilla planted the seeds of the desert fan palm and other plants at various desert oases in southern California.[10] Gathering sites were subjected to the same competitors as a modern-day orchard, agricultural monoculture, or vineyard: insects, diseases, and weeds. Human management kept these competitors in check and stimulated qualities that were culturally valued. The Choinumni Yokuts and Indians along the Klamath River fired older stems of shrubs to encourage thick berry crops and reduce insects;[11] beargrass and hazelnut (highly valued by Northwest coast basketmakers) were fired to encourage proper growth;[12] the Karok lit annual fires in forests to curtail tree diseases.[13]

GATHERING THE MOUNTAINS, VALLEYS, DESERTS, AND COASTS

The Native Californians were not simply *in* California; they *were* California. They were an integral and essential agent in the creation of a balance of land, vegetation, and animal life. When modern landscapes, climates, and biological communities began to emerge, with the close of the Ice Age about ten to fifteen thousand years ago, the people had arrived and were interacting with and shaping the land, plants, and animals. By listening to the land's daily rhythms, scheduling activities according to its seasonal cycles, and always adjusting to California's continually changing environment, Native Americans transformed their status from newcomer to native and in doing so transformed the land and lifeforms as well. Being native to the land also meant taking the time to understand all of nature's denizens and tapping the latent potential usefulness of California's flora and fauna—valuable in as yet undreamed of dimensions. Native American men fished for amphibians, fish, and mollusks in California's crystal streams.[14] They hunted birds, small and large mammals, and reptiles in fertile forests, shrublands, and grasslands. Native women's hands gathered juicy fruits, pinched leaves, snipped pods, and plucked flower stalks in an intimate relationship with individual plants.[15] Animal and plant parts were transformed into beautiful and useful objects, attesting to the ingenuity of indigenous cultures.

Tribal territories often spanned several elevational zones, encompassing a variety of plant communities. Every plant community type was visited by gatherers—from beach and dune to coastal scrub, evergreen forest, sagebrush steppe, valley grassland, and pinyon-juniper woodland. A diversity of plant and animal resources was obtained by following an annual cycle of population movements that coincided with seasonal availability of specific resources.[16] The repertoire of subsistence activities included gathering, hunting, fishing, firewood use, and toolstone quarrying. Hundreds of plant and animal species were useful in the economies of each tribal group.

Gathering sites had very old usage. For example, acorn-bearing oaks were pri-

Working from a field drawing made about 1847 by the expeditionary artist Edward Kern, Seth Eastman several years later produced this handsome watercolor of a Sacramento Valley Indian, probably an Eastern Miwok, fashioning an ornately designed seed-gathering basket. Through the burning and pruning of shrubs, native women promoted to the growth of long, straight, flexible shoots, which allowed them to produce basketry of the highest distinction. *Courtesy W. Duncan MacMillan.*

vately owned by the Coast Miwok. Bark was peeled off in a special pattern to indicate ownership.[17] Subsistence foods of the Yurok were gathered in family-owned
plots or the same location year after year.[18] Many places were comfortably inhabited
because of the sensory and memory ties to those special areas. A cordage gathering
site, a pinyon collection area, or a fishing rock would be known through use, and represented in song, ceremony, and stories.

Gathering in a place where your grandmother, great-grandmother, and great-
great-grandmother had gone before showed deep respect for the old ways and was
a poignant commentary on the sustainability of human harvesting practices. Knowledge of the natural history of places grew out of watching those places for hours,
days, years, lifetimes, and generations. A gatherer, hunter, or fisherman carried the
inherited memory of an ancient, organic, incalculably valuable body of knowledge
that was passed down, added to, and then passed again through many generations of
elders.[19]

Because the California Indian cultures were oral-tradition cultures, this passing of
knowledge occurred through social interaction and custom. The rapid European
intrusion and the destruction that accompanied it splintered the native knowledge
of the local landscapes. The native population of perhaps three hundred thousand in
1769 plummeted to thirty thousand by 1860.[20] Introduced diseases, starvation, relocation, and outright homicide caused this decline.[21] The decline of population created a decline of knowledge that was accompanied by a steady intrusion of non-
native plants, activities that devastated local plants, and people who failed to
appreciated the role the native population had played in maintaining the landscape
before. The landscape we know today is well removed from the landscape the native
population tended 150 years ago. To appreciate the previous landscapes, it is necessary to understand the climates, soil composition, and zonation that supports the
vegetation of California.

UNCOMMON ENVIRONMENTS: DRY SUMMERS,
NATURAL WILDFIRE, AND DIVERSE SOIL TYPES

Most of California has a climate called *Mediterranean*, similar to that of lands bordering the Mediterranean Sea.[22] Winters are cool and wet; summers are hot and dry.
Hard frost and snow in winter are rare, and summer temperatures may approach one
hundred degrees, one cloudless, arid day after another. More than two-thirds of the
ten to thirty inches of annual rain falls in the winter months of October through
March, which is the beginning of the growing season. The end of the growing season occurs late in the summer period of drought. California's low elevation landscapes are typically green in winter, brown in summer.

It is a rare climate found in only three other parts of the world besides California and the Mediterranean rim: central Chile, the Cape region of South Africa, and southern and western parts of Australia. Only certain types of vegetation are associated with it. These types—chaparral, foothill woodland, coastal scrub, montane evergreen forest—recur in every Mediterranean climate region.

Within California, the Mediterranean climate is moderated along three gradients: one from west to east, another from north to south, and a third from low to high elevations. Along the immediate coast there is little temperature change from day to night or from season to season. This is because the ocean releases heat to the air in the winter and absorbs it in the summer. In addition, a cold offshore current cools summer air, forming fog banks that shield the land and its vegetation from direct sunlight. Coastal climate is a maritime version of the Mediterranean climate. If one moves inland less than one hundred miles, the moderating effect of the ocean is lost. Daily and seasonal oscillations of temperature become much greater and rainfall declines markedly.

In a second gradient, rainfall declines from north to south. Crescent City, in the northwest, is drenched by six feet of rain a year, but San Francisco receives only twenty-five inches, and San Diego in the southwest gets merely ten inches. The length and intensity of the summer-dry period also increases to the south.

Both temperature and rainfall are affected by the third gradient, elevation. Mountain ranges force air moving east to rise, cooling as it does so and dropping moisture in the form of rain in summer or snow in winter. Temperatures fall about three degrees for every one thousand feet of elevation rise. Annual precipitation (the sum of rain and snow), in contrast, increases about seven inches for every one thousand feet of rise, up to eight thousand feet elevation. Above this, most of the moisture has been wrung out of the air and precipitation lessens. The high peaks of California mountains, then, are cold deserts. Patches of snow and ice remain there all summer because of cold summer temperatures, not because of heavy precipitation. Finally, the westerlies clear the mountain tops and descend along eastern flanks, heating and drawing moisture from soil and vegetation. Eastern California lies in a dry rain-shadow cast by the mountains. This is the region of desert scrub; elevations below five thousand feet receive less than ten inches of moisture a year.

An important component of Mediterranean climates is fire. Mediterranean climates are fire climates characterized by lightning strikes not followed by rain. A fraction of these strikes set fire to the vegetation because air humidity is low, fallen twigs and leaves on the ground are dry, and winds are sufficiently strong to carry the flames forward. Until Californians adopted a fire-suppression policy eighty years ago, late summer and early fall fires were an expected natural event in many California vegetation types below six thousand feet elevation. The same acre of ground could be expected to burn every ten to fifty years. Fire was uncommon only in wetlands, deserts, and at high elevations. California plants evolved with fire as a natural

environmental factor over millions of years. As a result, not only do many Californian species survive fires, but some require fire in order to complete their life cycle or
to remain vigorous. Native Californians knew this and, prior to the European intrusion, set low cool ground fires to maintain the understory plants in forests and the
grasses in meadows.

California has all eleven of the world's major soil groups and 10 percent of all of
the named soil types in the United States.[23] The bedrock of California has come
from many sources: volcanic ejections of lava and ash; wind-blown sand; faulting and
uplift, which brought ocean-floor sediments and deformed crustal rock to the surface; glaciers that carved valleys and dropped loads of rock; and erosion that left deposits of coarse sand and fine clay. Each substrate has its own chemical and physical characteristics, so the soils that weather from them are diverse.

Some of these soils are exceptionally old, up to half a million years. Many are
chemically unique, being high in toxic elements, low in essential nutrients, or extremely acid or basic. A number of well-known California plants are endemic to special soils. Examples include the small but colorful herbs gold fields (*Lasthenia*
species) and meadow foam (*Limnanthes* species) on hardpan soils of the Central Valley where vernal pools fill with water in winter and spring, the pygmy bolander pine
(*Pinus contorta* subspecies *bolanderi*) of Mendocino County on ancient, acidic sandstone, shore pine (*Pinus contorta* subspecies *contorta*) on the far north coast on
droughty coastal sand dunes, picturesquely twisted Sierran mountain junipers (*Juniperus occidentalis* var. *australis*) on solid granite outcrops, massive valley oaks (*Quercus lobata*) in the Central Valley on deep, well-drained, structureless sediment within
thirty feet of groundwater, and stands of oddly branched ghost pine (*Pinus sabiniana*) on island-like outcrops of chromium- and nickel-laden serpentine soil amidst
a sea of foothill brush.

LANDSCAPES ARE COMPOSED OF VEGETATION TYPES

Not only do individual species faithfully follow their substrates, but so do entire
groups of species. These groups make up the vegetation type of which each species
is a part. For example, shrubby, fire-prone foothill chaparral—consisting of dozens
of species of shrubs—typically grows on coarse, shallow soils; valley grassland—
with a hundred species of grasses and forbs—occurs on finer, deeper soils; high elevation conifer forest—with a rich suite of tree, shrub, and herb species—occupies
young, relatively unweathered soils; coastal marshes and mountain meadows are on
anaerobic, organically rich soils; and lowland riparian forests cover natural levees
built from centuries of flood-deposited loam.

Each of these groups of species—each vegetation type—occupies a distinct habitat, with its own soil and local climate. Climate and soil interact in California to cre-

ate the mosaic of vegetation types that characterizes each of the regional landscapes. California has some fifty types of vegetation.[24] Vegetation can be likened to the clothing over the land. This thin cloth is at once durable and fragile, able to repair and reproduce itself for centuries if the environment remains stable, but subject to ir-reversible unravelling when environmental stresses become too severe. When vege-tation is disrupted, its integrity is fractured. The degraded cover loses ecological re-lationships, nutrients, and plant and animal diversity.

CALIFORNIA'S VEGETATION HAS ALWAYS BEEN CHANGING

California's landscapes have changed dramatically over the vast panorama of geologic time. The topography and shape of California were modified by sea level fluctua-tions, periods of mountain building and faulting, advances and retreats of glaciers, and movement of the earth's continents.[25] Sixty million years ago, for example, Cal-ifornia was less mountainous and the climate was more tropical. Its location on the globe was approximately where Cuba is today. Rainfall then peaked in the summer, and average annual precipitation near sea level was about fifty inches. About ten mil-lion years ago, a semi-arid flora became dominant in the fossil record—close relatives of modern madrone (*Arbutus mensiezii*), live oak (*Quercus* species), pinyon (*Pinus* species), and chaparral and desert shrubs that apparently moved into California from Mexico as our modern Mediterranean climate became more pronounced. To-day, descendants of this flora dominate lowlying vegetation throughout much of the state.

Within the past two centuries, explorers and colonists accidentally or purposely brought with them plants from their countries of origin. Approximately one thou-sand of these species now grow naturally in California, some in such high numbers that they have changed forever the face of the landscape.[26] There is hardly a plant community or habitat left in California unaffected by some introduced plant species.

The pace of recent change is one reason why ecologists have a difficult time re-constructing the California landscape prior to 1848. The earliest detailed accounts of the Californias—diaries of Juan Crespi and Junípero Serra (1769), Juan Bautista de Anza and Gaspár de Portolá (1771–1776), Winceslaus Linck (1776), José Longino-Martinez (1792), and José Joaquin de Arrillaga (1796)—were for the most part botanically naive because they were encountering a flora almost totally different at the genus level from that of the Mediterranean rim.[27] Euro-American influences at low elevations were so enormous and rapid that by the time trained botanists and plant geographers arrived in the late nineteenth century to take photographs, many landscapes had been greatly modified. Ecologists have speculated about the past vegetation of the state, but their reconstructions are based on inferences from climate, soil, known history of land use, and personal intuition. Will Kuchler published a map of pre-contact vegetation of California that remains our best state-wide guess, but many of its suppositions are still argued about, twenty years after its publication.[28] Paying special attention to landscapes most changed since 1848, we begin our survey of California vegetation with the humid western shore and move eastward to the arid desert.

COASTAL MOSAIC OF DUNE, MARSH, GRASSLAND, SCRUB, AND FOREST

California's western edge is a restless interface between land and sea. Landforms along the 1,100-mile coastline are spectacular and diverse: graceful sandy bays, muddy tidal flats, precipitous cliffs, undulating dunes, terraced grasslands, steep shrub-covered hillsides, and dense forests fringing riverine bottomlands. The coastal mosaic of vegetation types covers about 15 percent of California's area.

Beach plants at the leading edge of vegetation must be tough enough to withstand the violent coastal environment—saline salt spray, abrasive sand blast, droughty sand substrate, low soil nitrogen, and high light intensity. As a result, beach vegetation is open and prostrate, made up of only a handful of species at any one location. In 1848, the dominant plant was American dune grass, which formed a scattering of tall leafy stems over the sand surface. Today, the dunes north of Big Sur are dominated by European beachgrass, brought here in 1869 to stabilize sand dunes in San Francisco. This grass has had a drastic effect on dune topography and vegetation. It traps more sand than native Pacific beachgrass (*Elymus mollis*), creating much taller foredunes covered with dense stands of beachgrass instead of open vegetation with many more species. Few Californian plant species can tolerate the shade and competition within European beachgrass stands, thus biotic diversity plummets as the European grass continues to extend its dominance. Native Pacific beachgrass has retained a hold only along small stretches of Point Reyes National Seashore and within the privately protected Lanphere-Christensen Dunes near Arcata.[29]

Prior to 1848, between four and five million acres of wetlands existed in California. The term "wetland" does not stand for a single vegetation type nor a single plant community. It is a legal term that presently applies to any habitat where the soil surface is saturated with water to within eighteen inches of the surface for a period of at least one week a year. Today, less than a fragmented 10 percent of coastal wetlands and a meager 2 percent of interior wetlands survive, and much of what remains is degraded. It is no coincidence that 25 percent of all plant and 55 percent of all animal species designated by state agencies as either threatened or endangered have wetlands as their essential habitat.[30]

Cliffs, terraces, and rolling hills have surfaces away from tide, surf, and moving sand. This is the region of coastal prairie and coastal scrub. North of Big Sur, uplifted marine terraces provide deep, moist, well-drained soils that once supported a rich assortment of perennial grasses and showy, broad-leaved herbs, some of which extend well north of California. Prior to 1848, Oregon hairgrass (*Deschampsia cespitosa* subspecies *holciformis*), Idaho fescue (*Festuca idahoensis*), California oatgrass (*Danthonia californica*), and as many as twelve other grass species formed a two- to three-foot-tall canopy that glistened with droplets of summer fog. These native perennials are called bunchgrasses because they do not have spreading rhizomes and they tend to grow in clumps. Today they are rare and can be found only occasionally, usually in protected areas.

The arrival of Euro-Americans brought fire suppression, invasive weeds, and heavy, year-round grazing by cattle and sheep. The coastal prairie was in most places transformed into a grassland of introduced species such as velvet grass (*Holcus lanatus*), sweet vernal grass (*Anthoxanthum odoratum*), soft chess (*Bromus mollis*), Italian ryegrass (*Lolium multiflorum*), wild oats (*Avena* species), and wild barley (*Hordeum* species). In the absence of fire, weedy herbs, particularly those such as thistles, which cattle find unpalatable, spread indiscriminantly over millions of acres of former coastal prairie.[31] Efforts to revegetate some grasslands with bunch grasses have started in several locations in northern and southern California.

Shrub-dominated vegetation (scrub) covers steep slopes and invades some margins of coastal prairie on terraces and in valleys. Northern coastal scrub extends north of Big Sur. It is a dense, two-storied assemblage of shrubs, vines, herbs, and grasses. Dominant plants are coyote-brush (*Baccharis pilularis* subspecies *consanguinea*), salal (*Gaultheria shallon*), California coffee berry (*Rhamnus californica*), cow parsnip (*Heracleum lanatum*), and bush lupines (mainly *Lupinus arboreus*). This vegetation has also been modified in the past century by introduced plants, especially pampas grass, gorse, Scotch broom, and *Eucalyptus*. Southern coastal scrub extends south of Big Sur. A simpler, more open community than northern scrub, it is dominated by pungent-smelling, drought-deciduous sage (*Salvia* species) and sagebrush (*Artemisia californica*). Near the Mexican border, succulent plants become an added element. In this century, many gentle hills and terraces of this vegetation have been converted into housing and commercial developments, and invasive grasses have contributed to a further decline in shrubs.[32]

A series of coastal forests that include redwood and Douglas fir occupy lowland pockets and mountain slopes somewhat away from the ocean. These are unique forests, relicts from ancient climates, coddled by the moderated maritime environment in a pool of fog. Conifer trees here have the fastest growth rates of any in the world. The most famous of these is the redwood forest, which forms the southern tip of a magnificent conifer forest that blankets a strip of coastal slopes and flats from Alaska to Monterey County.

Though the forest seems placid, violent episodes of fire and flood sweep through it every century.[33] Mature redwoods (*Sequoia sempervirens*) survive such trauma, thanks to a unique root system and an insulating layer of bark. Seedlings germinate on the fresh, flood-deposited soil; redwoods are also capable of stump-sprouting should the above-ground portion of the tree burn or topple, and in this way the parent plant is survived by a clone of genetically identical offspring. In the absence of fire and flood, saplings of Douglas fir (*Pseudotsuga menziesii*), tanbark oak (*Lithocarpus densiflorus*), Sitka spruce (*Picea sitchensis*), and grand fir (*Abies grandis*) will grow beneath the redwood canopy and eventually replace the redwoods. Management of redwood parks now must permit or even create fire and flood, in order to maintain the pre–European-contact forest landscape. Old-growth redwood forests are uncommon today. Only 5 percent of an original two million acres still remain, mainly in state and federal parks. The rest has been logged once or twice and supports second-growth redwood forest or young forests converted to faster-growing Douglas fir.

Above the redwood forest, on steeper, warmer, and higher slopes, is a mixed evergreen forest. It grows at elevations of one thousand to four thousand feet in northwestern California and 3,500 to 5,700 feet in southwestern California. Dominant trees include conifers and broad-leaf evergreens. Conifer species change with latitude: typically they are Douglas fir in the north and Coulter pine (*Pinus coulteri*) and big-cone Douglas fir in the south. The conifers form an incomplete canopy one hundred to two hundred feet tall that allows full sun to reach down between the trees. The sunlight is intercepted by a continous layer of broad-leaved trees, standing forty to sixty feet tall, including evergreen tanbark oak, madrone, bay (*Umbellularia californica*), coast live oak (*Quercus agrifolia*), interior live oak (*Q. wislizenii*), and canyon oak (*Q. chrysolepis*). Some winter-deciduous species are also members of this understory layer. Most of the original old-growth Douglas fir phase of the mixed evergreen forest has been cut for timber, because Douglas fir is an important lumber species. The results of a century or more of such harvest are a post-contact landscape of dense stands of pole-size hardwoods, especially tanbark oak and madrone, since they are capable of stump-sprouting following disturbance. Thus, young second-growth modern forests are not ecologically the same as old-growth pre-contact forests. They create, for example, an insufficient habitat for such animals as spotted owls, marbled murelets, and red tree voles that nest in or on large Douglas firs or dead snags.

INTERIOR MOSAIC OF GRASSLAND, CHAPARRAL, AND WOODLAND

Inland from the fog fence—the Coast Ranges—summer heat becomes more extreme and a typical Mediterranean climate prevails. The texture of interior foothills

By the mid-1870s, when William Hahn captured a characteristic California wheat-ranching scene in *Harvest Time*, the Central Valley had undergone astounding environmental alterations. Beginning early in the century, wild oats and other exotic annuals had spread through the interior with astonishing swiftness, supplanting the native perennial bunchgrasses of the vast inland prairies. Then in the decades following the Gold Rush, as much of the valley was planted to wheat, the landscape was once again transformed. *Courtesy The Fine Arts Museums of San Francisco; gift of Mrs. Harold R. McKinnon and Mrs. Harry L. Brown.*

and valleys is a mosaic of woodland with scattered trees of pine and oak, or chaparral with densely rigid shrubs, or open grassland that collectively covers one-third of California's area. The borders between vegetation patches are often narrow and abrupt, capable of being walked across in a few paces.

While all three vegetation types occur within the same climatic and elevational zones, they sort themselves out according to such local variations as soil depth, soil texture, slope face, and fire history.[34] Grassland tends to occupy the gentlest slopes with deepest and finest-textured soils, and, under natural conditions, it would burn every several years. Chaparral tends to cover the steepest slopes, with shallowest and coarsest soils, and it would burn with an intermediate frequency of fifteen to twenty-five years. Foothill woodland grows on intermediate slopes and soils and would burn at intervals of twenty-five years or more.

The original interior grassland blanketed much of the Central Valley and low elevations along the central and southern coast. It covered more than thirteen million acres and an additional nine to ten million acres underneath oaks in the foothills, for a total area representing one-fourth of California. Before European colonization, that grassland supported large herds of pronghorn, deer, tule elk, and an extensive native human population. The interior grassland was dominated by several species of bunchgrasses—in particular, purple and nodding needle grasses (*Stipa pulchra* and *S. cernua*). Between the grasses were some annual and perennial herbs that grew lush and colorful in spring. In summer, most grazing animals moved upslope, out of the grassland, and returned only when winter rains brought new germination and growth. Natural fires ignited by dry-lightning strikes and fires purposely started by Indians were probably an annual event. Both types of fire favored the native grass-land vegetation. Fires stimulated regrowth in the following wet season and also pre-vented woody plants from invading.

This grassland no longer exists, except in tiny preserves that show only a portion of the pre-1848 panorama. Beginning in the nineteenth century, livestock were kept at high numbers, year-round, in fenced pastures; some grassland was plowed and farmed; fire was controlled; and weed seeds were accidentally and intentionally in-troduced. In a dramatically short time, the bunchgrass prairie was converted to an annual grassland of introduced European species such as filaree (*Erodium* species), soft chess, wild oat, ripgut (*Bromus diandrus*), ryegrass, foxtail (*Hordeum* species), fes-cue (*Vulpia* species), and bur clover (*Medicago polymorpha*).[35]

To the majority of Indian groups in 1848, the foothill woodland was the most im-portant vegetation type. It was home to a greater number and density of humans than any other vegetation type. The acorn was a critical dietary staple of these peo-ples, its abundance and storability permitting the establishment of large, year-round settlements. The foothill woodland is a two-storied vegetation, with an open tree canopy partially shading a carpet of grasses and forbs beneath. Close to the coast, the dominant trees in the north are Oregon white oak (*Quercus garryana*) and Califor-nia black oak (*Q. kelloggii*), and in the south, the coast live oak (*Quercus agrifolia*), mesa oak (*Q. engelmannii*), and California walnut (*Juglans californica*) Along interior, drier foothills, the dominant trees are blue oak (*Quercus douglasii*), interior live oak (*Q. wislizenii*), foothill pine (*Pinus sabiniana*), and buckeye (*Aesculus californica*). The large trees are a mix of evergreens and deciduous hardwoods. Some of the de-ciduous species seem to be in decline. Few young trees have become established in the last century.[36] If this pattern continues for another century, mature oaks will have reached the end of their natural life spans, and these oak woodlands will either be-come grasslands or denser woodlands dominated by evergreen oaks. The causes for this decline may include exploding populations of root-eating pocket gophers, browsing deer and cattle that devour seedlings, competitive, introduced annual plants, and modern fire suppression. In addition to the decline in reproduction, about 10 to 20 percent of the woodland has been converted since 1848 into treeless pasture and range or into urban housing.

Chaparral comes from Spanish words for "low-growing, treeless vegetation."

Early Spanish explorers were impressed with the tightly intertwined and close-fitting canopy that covered the hills as uniformly as a shirt over the human torso, and they were reminded of a similar scrub in the hills of Spain. Chaparral vegetation is a single layer of impenetrable shrubs, four to eight feet tall, with intricately branched, interlacing evergreen canopies. The most common shrubs in northern California are chamise(*Adenostoma fasciculatum*), scrub oak (*Quercus dumosa*), Christmas berry (*Heteromeles arbutifolia*), California coffeeberry, and more than twenty species each of manzanita (*Arctostaphylos*) and *Ceanothus. Yucca*, red shank (*Adenostoma sparsifolium*), laurel sumac (*Malosma laurina*), and lemonade berry (*Rhus integrifolia*) are additional elements in southern California. The ground is nearly bare of plants, and only an occasional bay tree, clump of cypress, or pine rises above the shrub layer.

Chaparral is a fire-dependent vegetation that burns very hot in all-consuming crown fires expected to occur naturally every twenty to twenty-five years.[37] It is rare to find an unburned chaparral stand older than sixty years. After fire, only the skeletons of shrubs and trees remain above-ground, together with a thick layer of ash on the soil surface. Shrub seeds and roots deeper than a few inches below the surface survive the fire, however, and these germinate and sprout during the following wet season. Shrub growth is rapid for a few years, then slows for the next thirty to forty years. With time, most of the nutrients essential for growth become locked up in the woody biomass and so are unavailable to support new growth. Fire releases the nutrients as ash, triggering a renewal of growth.

MOSAIC OF MONTANE VEGETATION TYPES

California mountains are not uniformly covered with one continuous, monotonously unvarying forest. Instead, the landscape is a mosaic of oak-filled canyons, brushy ridges, meadows in wet flats, riparian woods, and conifer-forested slopes. Only about half of the montane region, which covers 20 percent of California, supports conifer forest. Four zones of climate and vegetation exist in California mountains, sequentially replacing each other with increasing elevation: lower-montane, upper-montane, subalpine, and alpine. Every thousand-foot climb in elevation is equivalent to moving three hundred miles north, and the vegetation varies accordingly.[38]

The mixed conifer forest occupies much of the lower-montane zone, which lies between two thousand and five thousand feet elevation in northern mountain ranges and five thousand to eight thousand feet elevation in southern ranges. Six conifers—ponderosa pine (*Pinus ponderosa*), sugar pine (*P. lambertiana*), white fir (*Abies concolor*), Douglas fir, incense cedar (*Calocedrus decurrens*), and giant sequoia—coexist and shift in importance from stand to stand, and for this reason the community is not named for any one of them, but is instead called the mixed conifer forest.

John Muir, among other early naturalists, commented on "the inviting openness"

A tourist party enjoys a leisurely moment by the Merced River in Virgil Williams's 1863 painting of Yosemite Valley, *Along the Mariposa Trail*. The rich riparian growth portrayed by Williams composes one of several typical plant communities associated with what is perhaps the most famous of the state's geomorphic provinces, the Sierra Nevada. *Courtesy California Historical Society; gift of A. K. Browne. Photograph by M. Lee Fatherree.*

of this forest, where trees "stand more or less apart in groves, or in small irregular groups, enabling one to find a way nearly everywhere, along sunny colonnades and through openings that have a smooth, park-like surface."[39] The forests that Muir saw, and that Native Americans lived in prior to 1848, are rare today because of 150 years of logging and 100 years of fire-suppression. Three-fourths of the original acreage of the mixed conifer forest has been clear-cut or select-cut at least once. Second-growth forests are more crowded, with smaller overstory trees.

Furthermore, in the absence of ground fire, white fir has grown up densely beneath the older trees, creating potential fire ladders that convert ground fires into destructive crown fires. Ponderosa pine, in contrast, has few juveniles because its seedlings require bare mineral soil to establish themselves on—and only fire clears the litter and provides such a surface. This modern second-growth forest casts a denser shade, and no longer has the park-like atmosphere Muir described. Adoption of a prescribed burning policy by the U.S. Forest Service, the California Departments of Forestry and of Parks and Recreation, and the National Park Service has had some success in reversing the trend. The success is limited, however, because the practice remains controversial and managers must be overly cautious in controlling fire, thus the kind of fire produced is unusually cool-burning. Too few young white fir trees are killed in such fires, and the pristine openness of the forest is not reclaimed. Furthermore, the number of acres actually burned by prescribed fire so far has only been a small fraction of the total acreage of the forest. Another stress affecting the lower-montane zone, unknown in 1848, is air pollution,[40] which damages conifer needles and slows tree growth in mixed conifer forests (particularly the ponderosa pines) that lie many miles from and thousands of feet above the sea-level cities that produce this smog.

The upper-montane is the zone of maximum snowfall throughout California. About 80 percent of all precipitation during the year falls as snow, which builds snowpacks eight to thirteen feet deep that stay on the ground for two hundred days of the year. Saplings successful in the upper-montane must tolerate winter burial under snow for decades until they are tall enough to reach above the snowpack.[41] Upper-montane forests are simple, with just two canopies: an overstory tree layer and a scattered herb layer. Common trees are lodgepole pine (*Pinus contorta* subspecies *murrayana*) and Jeffrey pine (*P. jeffreyi*) throughout the state, joined by red fir (*Abies magnifica*) and western white pine (*P. monticola*) in northern California. Ancient, twisted mountain juniper trees (*Juniperus occidentalis* subspecies *australis*) seem to spring full-grown out of solid ridge rock. Quaking aspen (*Populus tremuloides*) and black cottonwood (*Populus balsamifera* subspecies *trichocarpa*) cover narrow riparian corridors. Fire plays a less important role in this zone than in the lower-montane. The trees, shrubs, and herbs are neither especially tolerant of fire, nor is their survival enhanced by fire. Fires occur, but at intervals twice as long as in lower-elevation forests.[42]

Forests thin with elevation, just as the air itself thins. Groves of trees in the sub-alpine zone (above nine thousand feet elevation in the south, above eight thousand feet in the north) become restricted to patches protected from the sweep of cold air and drying wind. Pruned by winter ice blast, trees are stunted, twisted, and multiple-trunked. This is a place of short, open forest at the very limit of tree growth. As one moves higher, even these bonsai-like remnants fail to grow, and the herbaceous alpine tundra replaces the land of wood.

Few tree species are able to tolerate the special stresses of the subalpine zone.[43] Lodgepole pine and western white pine continue upslope from the upper-montane, and are joined by mountain hemlock (*Tsuga mertensiana*) and the five-needled whitebark (*Pinus albicaulis*), limber (*P. flexilis*), foxtail (*P. balfouriana*), and bristlecone pines (*P. longaeva*), which are found only in the subalpine. Not all of these species occur together on the same mountain. In some places, a single species will dominate; in others they mix together. For this reason the vegetation is called mixed subalpine woodland.

Not much is known about the climate of this zone because few long-term weather stations are located here. Average precipitation is less than in the upper-montane, probably averaging thirty inches, mostly as snow. Average temperature over the entire year is just a few degrees above freezing. Soils are shallow and rocky, so they hold little moisture. Because the growing season is so stressful, subalpine trees rarely become established as seedlings. Once established, however, they grow slowly for centuries. Average tree life spans are five hundred to one thousand years. Foxtail pines attain ages greater than three thousand years, and the well-known bristlecone pines of the White Mountains of far east-central California can exceed five thousand years.

The alpine zone is a thin fringe of green near the limits of all forms of plant life. The growing season is measured in weeks and days, not months: six to ten weeks long, or forty to seventy days. Even during the growing season, frost can occur nightly. Plants tend to hug the ground and to sequester most of their stored food underground in root or rhizome systems.

Alpine tundra is a meadow-type of vegetation rich in sedges (*Carex* species), rushes (*Juncus* species), grasses, and perennial broad-leaf herbs. Woody dwarf willows (*Salix* species) and white and mountain heather (*Cassiope mertensiana* and two *Phyllodoce* species) are present, but not dominant. Away from wet basins and snowmelt areas, the environment becomes drier, and tundra gives way to a fell-field of scattered bunchgrasses and "cushion plants"—herbs with tiny, densely arranged leaves pressed against the soil surface. Alpine plants are small, but they are tenacious and their life spans are twenty to fifty years.[44]

In California, about 40 percent of the total number of alpine species are widespread, ranging north into other North American mountain chains or all the way to the polar tundra. Another 15 percent are endemic to California, and so must have evolved in place as the mountains rose during the past ten million years. These endemics probably evolved from desert plants downslope.

Alpine tundra is relatively intolerant of disturbance from humans and their grazing animals. Trampling along trails rapidly thins out the vegetation, and plants are slow to recover from over-grazing. During the nineteenth century, heavy, uncontrolled grazing by sheep (John Muir called them "hoofed locusts") permanently degraded many alpine meadows. Grazing by sheep, cattle, and pack horses continues today, although it is much more carefully regulated, and environmental damage persists.[45]

A GRADIENT OF DESERT VEGETATION: COLD, WARM, AND HOT

Eastern, desert-facing slopes of California mountains are steep, rocky, and more arid than western slopes at the same elevation. The eastern rainshadow intensifies as elevation drops, and by the six-thousand-foot elevation, trees reach a second kind of timberline—a low-elevation timber line. This timberline, the last gasp of montane trees before the aridity and desert scrub below, is an open woodland of Utah juniper (*Juniperus osteosperma*) and several pinyon pines (*Pinus edulis, P. monphylla, P. quadrifolia*). Despite the pinyon pine's short stature, slow growth rate, and small cone size, its seeds are large and produced in great numbers. Pinyon seeds ("nuts") were an important food of Native Californians before the European conquest, and some native families continue to harvest them today. Flour made from pinyon seeds has a higher fat content and caloric value than modern wheat flour and a protein concentration higher than corn flour. Annual fall trips were made to the pinyon woodlands by many mountain and desert tribes.

Beyond the pinyon-juniper woodland is desert scrub vegetation, occupying about one-fourth of California's land area. Desert climate and vegetation are not uniform within such a vast region, and as a result there are three types of desert in California: cold, warm, and hot. The cold desert, or Great Basin Desert, is a high desert lying above the four-thousand-foot elevation between the Sierra-Cascade axis on the west and the Wasatch Mountains of Utah on the east. Winters are cold, with most precipitation falling as snow; summers are dry and hot. It is a land characterized by dark volcanic rock, pronghorn, and pungent sagebrush (*Artemisia tridentata*).

Associated plants include several small shrubs, a diversity of bunchgrasses, and a number of annual plants. The annuals germinate in wintertime, grow slowly to spring, then bolt, flower, and set seed by early summer. Cacti are uncommon because most succulent species are frost-sensitive, thus winter temperatures are too cold for them here. Cottonwood trees (*Populus fremontii*) line intermittent waterways, and saline basins support such salt-tolerant shrubs as fourwing saltbush (*Atriplex canescens*) and greasewood (*Sarcobatus vermiculatus*). Cold desert vegetation has been significantly modified since 1848 by overgrazing, the accidental introduction of aggressive weedy species such as cheatgrass (*Bromus tectorum*), and an increased frequency of wildfire.[46] Enormous populations of sheep and cattle selectively removed most bunchgrass cover, and purposeful burning killed sagebrush. Sagebrush does not stump sprout. In order to reestablish itself, it must germinate from seed, and as a seedling it is a poor competitor with cheatgrass and other introduced annuals whose numbers may exceed one thousand plants per square yard.

The warm Mojave Desert lies just south of, and at elevations below, the cold Great Basin Desert. The meeting ground of the two deserts is the place of Joshua tree woodland and blackbrush scrub, east and northeast of the Los Angeles basin. Farther east, as elevation drops, the landscape becomes dominated by creosotebush (*Larrea tridentata*), burrobush (*Ambrosia dumosa*), brittlebush (*Encelia farinosa*), more than twenty species of cacti, and a great diversity of winter annual wildflowers. Localized habitats such as sand dunes, saline basins, and desert washes support rarer plant species.

The hot Colorado Desert occupies the southeastern corner of California at elevations below one thousand feet. The region is far enough east to escape the California rainshadow, far enough south to receive summer rains from subtropical storms and low enough in elevation to be frost-free. As a result, the Colorado Desert is home to a greater variety of plant growth forms and species than the other two desert types. Winter-deciduous small trees, arboreal cacti, evergreen and drought-deciduous shrubs, rosette-shaped leaf succulents, subshrubs, small cacti, and winter- and summer-active annual wildflowers all grow here. The overwhelmingly dominant species are creosotebush and burrobush.[47] Wash vegetation is also rich, with fifteen-foot-tall desert willow (*Chilopsis linearis*), palo verde (two species of *Cercidium*), and honey mesquite (*Prosopis juliflora* variety *torreyana*) as scattered individuals or as woodland thickets. Oasis stands of California fan palm (*Washingtonia filifera*) occur along faultlines where breaks in the bedrock allow natural springs to surface.

Even here, in the hottest and most arid part of California, invasive plants have modified the pre-European landscape. Salt cedar, native to Europe and Asia, was introduced by Spanish explorers and settlers of the seventeenth and eighteenth centuries. Today it colonizes washes, river banks, and basin margins, sometimes forming impenetrable thickets hundreds of yards deep. Springs and subterranean water sources can literally be sucked dry by such thickets, exterminating wetland habitats previously occupied by native plants and animals. Another post-conquest disturbance to the warm and hot deserts has been soil compaction and vegetation destruction by off-road vehicles (ORVs). Long-term studies of ghost town streets, homesteads, military exercise routes, utility service roads, and ORV trails indicate that significant vegetation recovery requires more than sixty years.[48]

When examined at a closer proximity and in some detail, pre-contact landscapes, like the deserts, have been profoundly and permanently changed. Without the tradition and understanding derived through observation and traditional practice, there has been little intervention and much destruction of the formerly highly useful and sustainable landscapes. How were those pre-contact landscapes lived in, interpreted, used, and managed by Native Californians?

CONSERVING THE EARTH

There were types and scales of human harvesting that meshed with wilderness. Sophisticated taxonomies, taboos, and harvesting strategies for key resources evolved and were widespread among native communities. Conservation practices were developed to combat scarcity of resources. Two overarching maxims that dictated Native American resource use were "do not waste resources" and "do not hoard resources." Indigenous folklore is rich with messages concerning the dire ecological consequences of excessive consumption of resources. According to many tribal legends, inappropriate human behavior toward nature through greed, wastefulness, or disrespect for other lifeforms causes the world to go out of balance. Signs of this imbalance were natural catastrophes such as enormous wildfires, droughts, floods, and twisters.[49]

Native Americans skillfully gathered plants over long periods in different habitats without depleting their populations to the point of extinction. This required intimate knowledge of each species' life characteristics. Plants were gathered with regard to at least six variables: season, frequency, appropriate tool, pattern, scale, and intensity.[50] If plants were gathered too often, or at an inappropriate season, or at an extreme intensity without sparing individual plants, the population could easily be extinguished, even with low levels of technology. For example, natives gathered edible mushrooms while being careful not to disturb the soil mycelia in order to ensure future production;[51] basketry shrubs were pruned in the late fall or winter during the dormant period, when such disturbance is least detrimental to the plants' vital processes. Subterranean foods such as lilies, wild onions, yampah, and blue dicks were harvested in great quantities, but bulblets and cormlets were deliberately left behind in the loosened earth to grow the following year.[52]

CALIFORNIA: AN ENGENDERED LAND

Through interacting with nature for millennia, Native Americans left their signature in the vegetation. That imprint is still visible in the scars on juniper trees in eastern California harvested sustainably by the Paiute and Western Shoshoni for bow staves.[53] Certain creosote bushes in the Colorado Desert, now thousands of years old, were picked centuries ago by Indian hands to treat nausea, intestinal discomfort, and chest infections. Four-hundred-year-old sugar pines (*Pinus lambertiana*) in Sequoia National Park are marked with fire-scars from fires set by Indians. These trees were harvested by Native Americans for their delectable sugar, oozing from fresh wounds caused by the fires. Humans also acted as dispersal agents carrying seeds from place to place, deliberately or inadvertently. This is obvious in the clusters of useful plant species that populate Indian middens, graves, temporary camps, and other archaeological sites.

Scholars have more recently produced more accurate reconstructions of interactions between indigenous people and the natural environment in California through interdisciplinary research that combines knowledge of social, physical, and biological sciences as well as the humanities.[54] For instance, nature keeps a historical record of environmental changes in the growth rings of trees, plant remains in a preserved packrat's nest, plant and animal fossils and charcoal in the soil, and plant pollen laid down in layers in bog sediments. Scientists using microscopes, molecular dating methods, and other techniques can retrieve this information, incorporating it into a comprehensive framework for interpretation and giving us a remarkably clear window to the past. Finally, a recognition among university scholars that Native American elders are the keepers of ancient knowledge and remember details of former burning and other horticultural practices of their ancestors has resulted in an integration of this information into university sources.

Only recently have scientists ceased to pigeonhole Native Americans into one of two limited categories: hunter-gatherer *or* agriculturalist. To earlier scholars, Mohave and Yuman tribes in southeastern California grew domesticated plants—corn, beans, and squash—and were labeled "agriculturalists," while the myriad of other tribes were tagged "hunter-gatherers." Modern scholars, on the other hand, maintain that both stereotypes are merely opposite ends of a continuum of human-nature interactions that represent a much more complex and rich set of interactions than that portrayed in older history books and ecology and anthropology texts. The vast knowledge and understanding that the traditional Indian people had of the California landscape prior to the European contact is only beginning to be fully recognized. Most likely, however, we will never completely recover all the information lost during the destructive post-contact years.

The sustainability of native practices allowed natural vegetation and human inhabitation of the landscape to exist and continue over hundreds of years. From the coastal prairies of northwestern California to the palm oases in the southeastern part of the state, indigenous traditional management systems have influenced the size, extent, pattern, structure, composition, and genetics of the flora within select areas of a multitude of vegetation types.[55] Native-induced changes, however, unlike those of the last two hundred years dominated by European attitudes, sustained the vegetation and allowed generational use of the same species.

Mosaics of Vegetation and Location of Ecotones

Native peoples played a major role in the maintenance and enhancement of biological diversity by introducing disturbances that promoted mosaics of vegetation found
within different landscapes in California. They enhanced ecosystem diversity in
California through the maintenance of heterogeneous vegetation that would have
disappeared in the absence of human influence, including coastal prairies, freshwater marshes, and dry montane meadows. Forest ecologist Susan Bicknell has recently been involved in a series of studies of particular locales along the northern
California coast, and has utilized opal phytoliths in conjunction with other evidence to demonstrate that much of the coastal aboriginal prairie habitat was anthropogenic in nature, maintained with frequent fires set by local tribes and that it
reverted to woody vegetation after Euro-American settlement of the area and with
the cessation of fire and ungulate grazing.[56]

Similarly, to encourage growth and harvest of a smorgasbord of plant species, the
Wukchumni Yokuts and the Timbisha Shoshone burned freshwater marshes to remove old growth, provide emergent plants for animal forage, and stimulate the production of long, straight, new tules.[57] Burning cleared out reed-choked marshlands,
reducing the density and creating an edge effect, allowing space for waterfowl movement and nesting activities and increased light to the soil floor at the peripheries of
marshes and springs, thereby heightening plant species diversity.[58] Studies have
shown that controlled burning can reduce the invasion of woody vegetation and
enhance wetland habitats for wildlife.[59] Native Americans understood that fires in
conjunction with the recurrent changes in water level blocked plant succession and
were the basis for these enduring systems.

Strings of meadows in the Sierra Nevada, the Cascades, and other California
mountain ranges formed the resting places, pantry, and trade grounds for numerous
tribes. These open spaces with grasses and forbs break up the monotonous mixed-
conifer forests. Ecotones, where forest and meadow merge, also contain unique plant
life and attract animals as well. Native Americans set fires in the ecotone areas
surrounding the meadows to decrease the more wet-tolerant lodgepole pine or other
conifers and keep them from encroaching into meadow areas, thus maintaining and
perhaps, in some cases, enlarging meadow areas. Periodic purposeful burning also occurred within the meadow boundaries, influencing the composition, density, and frequency of native plant and animal populations. Certain meadow plants such as deer-
grass, yampahs, and clovers were favored through burning.[60] Natives also set fires in
and around meadows to drive game and catch grasshoppers.[61] In recent times,
cessation of Native American burning and the modern policy of suppressing lightning fires have caused forest and brush to encroach on meadows throughout the
mountains.

Costanoan (Ohlone) men use double-bladed paddles to negotiate the waters of San Francisco Bay in a balsa, or boat, constructed of tules bound together with vines. Based on a watercolor made in 1816 by Louis Choris, this lithograph is from the artist's *Voyage pittoresque autour du monde* (Paris, 1822). *Courtesy California Historical Society, FN-30512.*

Indian burning also opened up forests and woodlands so the sun could fall free to the earth in many places. Pre-contact California had abundant park-like forests of oaks and conifers, with large-diametered trees that were widely-spaced, unlike the overstocked, disease- and insect-infested second-growth forests of today. Frequent Indian-set fires in lower and mid-elevation mixed-conifer forests favored fire-tolerant species such as black oak, giant sequoia, and ponderosa pine, and a biologically diverse understory vegetation of native grasses and forbs.[62] An uncluttered coniferous forest or oak woodland could also be walked through by Native Americans with ease, without hacking vegetation, and without being scratched by shrubbery. The people could see far ahead in all directions and avoid surprise by grizzlies, black bears, mountain lions, or human enemies. The earth between the trees fostered many blooming and edible plants, rather than a seemingly lifeless mass of thick layers of decomposing leaves and twigs, characteristic of many forests today.[63] This rich understory vegetation attracted small and large mammals, birds, and many types of insects. The interior of the human-tended forest was full of life. Journalist Stephen Powers took note of this bounty: "In the mountains they [Yokuts] used to fire the forests, and thereby catch great quantities of grasshoppers and caterpillars already

Wintu Indians Rosa Charles and Billy George pause from gathering yampah to pose
for the legendary ethnographer John P. Harrington, who made this photograph in 1931.
Yampa fields were regularly burned by Native Californians in order to recycle nutrients,
reduce plant competition, and prevent the encroachment of forests on meadows. *Courtesy
Santa Barbara Museum of Natural History.*

roasted, which they devoured with relish, and this practice kept the underbrush
burned out, and the woods much more open and park-like than at present. This was
the case all along the Sierra."[64]

Human-tended plant gathering sites dotted the land, creating a quiltwork pattern
of openings within different plant communities. The visual effect of encouraging
populations of plant species at numerous gathering sites was a high degree of "patchi-
ness" reflecting plant species in varying successional stages within more homogeneous naturally occurring plant community types. When the Europeans arrived in
California, many populations of plants and associated animals persisted in different
areas as a result of the Native Americans' clearing the engulfing vegetation by hand-
weeding and burning.

The Range and Distribution of Plant and Animal Species

Native Americans also widened the ecological amplitude of native animal and plant
species by introducing them to new areas. Dispersal through human agency often
took place over relatively short distances and thereby gave the appearance that the

normal distribution was somewhat more extensive than was actually the case. This appearance may have influenced, in turn, the conclusions of later plant and animal scientists, leading them to consider the extended range as the normal range.

Some authorities have noted plants established in association with historical sites of human occupation, but for the most part, this topic has not been explored. Native American protection of volunteer plant species, actual sowing of seed, or transplanting of valuable or preferred plants are all possible explanations for the occurrence of uncharacteristic native plant populations and the repeated appearance of the same plant species at former sites of human occupation. The native tobacco (*Nicotiana clevelandii*) may have been planted or established itself in the enriched soils of the Indian middens around the camps of the Chumash in Santa Barbara. Tobacco also occurs on Santa Cruz Island and is often associated with midden deposits,[65] and ethnobotanist Jan Timbrook believes that it was probably brought there by the Chumash. Archaeologist Schumacher noted that he always found elderberry shrubs in the neighborhood of ancient settlements or near graves.[66] Jimsonweed, an important ceremonial plant to many tribes, is often associated with aboriginal habitation sites in San Diego County. Willis Jepson in the 1920s noted that California black walnut trees occurred readily on "old Indian camps-sites" in central California in what are now Walnut Creek, Walnut Grove, and Napa Range above Wooden Valley.[67] Vertebrate zoologist Paul Collins, using the archaeological record and morphometric analysis, has concluded that Indians were responsible for establishing island foxes on San Clemente, Santa Catalina, and San Nicolas islands from northern Channel Island populations.[68]

RESTORATION OF THE ABORIGINAL LANDSCAPE WITH HUMANS INCLUDED

As a truer picture of California's first human inhabitants comes into clearer focus, a very different world emerges—a world where humans were more than mere external visitors to nature. California was not "wild." The tribal territories were filled with places that were comfortably inhabited and stewarded. Judicious gathering, hunting, and fishing deepened human interactions with the land. Using nature sustainably, Indians inhabited that middle ground between true wilderness and the domesticated garden. Early settlers' diaries, missionaries' notes, and explorers' logs describe California as unsurpassed in beauty and biological wealth. But, unknowingly, Euro-Americans were in many cases really describing the successful results of the stewardship of Native Americans in fostering this fecundity. What is compelling about this shift in perception of California Indians from hunter-gatherers into wildland managers is its demonstration that it is possible for humans to tend and use wildland resources *and* coexist as part of sustainable and diverse ecosystems.

Native American tribes of today have endured threats to their cultural survival for over two hundred years. Yet with the influx of large human populations from outside the region and the steady degradation of California's landscapes, native gatherers, hunters, and fishermen have increasingly faced barbed-wire fences, "no trespassing" signs, scarce resources, water pollution, and pesticide residues in their attempts to continue their traditions.[69]

The decline of natural systems in the state is intimately tied with the diminishment of the native cultural heritage. This cultural wealth—the vast experience of native cultures in how to use, manage, respect, *and* coexist with these other lifeforms— is valuable and could be part of serious conservation and restoration efforts towards nature.[70]

Among public lands agencies, there is increasing interest in Native American traditional ecological knowledge. Those professionals who are most interested in restoration of California's fire-type natural landscapes are finding that knowledge of past land management—indigenous burning, for example—is imperative before alternatives for preservation and management of plant communities can be designed. Scholarship by ecologists, archaeologists, and biologists, in partnership with Native Americans, is beginning to unravel the complexities of these former wildland management systems.

Simulating some native practices in a series of long-term field experiments will give scientists and managers a more accurate sense of the impact of aboriginal activities on vegetation in different regions. Such experimentation will also disclose the extent to which ecosystem health in the areas of soil productivity, gene conservation, biodiversity, landscape patterns, nutrient cycling, and an array of ecological processes is tied to former indigenous economic and management activities.[71] Contemporary tribal cultures are still practicing some of these traditional techniques. These ongoing traditional practices may serve as analogs for testing alternative wildland management strategies. They may be used to restore endangered ecosystems and species, as well as to enhance the productivity and biodiversity of wildlands, while maintaining culturally significant plant resources for the perpetuation of indigenous cultural traditions and future scientific endeavors.[72]

NOTES

1. D. A. Jensen, et al., *In Our Own Hands: A Strategy for Conserving California's Biodiversity* (Berkeley: University of California Press, 1993); M. W. Skinner and B. M. Pavlik, *Inventory of Rare and Endangered Vascular Plants of California,* 5th ed. (Sacramento: California Native Plant Society, 1994); and C. G. Thelander, ed., *Life on the Edge: A Guide to California's Endangered Natural Resources: Wildlife* (Santa Cruz: Biosystems Books, and Berkeley: Heyday Books, 1994).

2. Men Sailing under Juan Rodríguez Cabrillo were the first documented Europeans to

set foot in California. See Harry Kelsey, *Juan Rodríguez Cabrillo* (San Marino: Huntington Library, 1986).

3. William Cronon, "The Trouble with Wilderness," in *Uncommon Ground: Toward Reinventing Nature*, William Cronon, ed. (New York: W. W. Norton and Company, 1995), 69–90. Other important articles that question the authenticity of the traditional "wilderness" idea include Paul Faulstich, "The Cultured Wild and the Limits of Wilderness," in *Place of the Wild*, D. C. Burks, ed. (Washington D.C.: Island Press, 1994), 161–74; A. Gomez-Pompa and A. Kaus, "Taming the Wilderness Myth," *Bioscience* 42 (1992): 71–279; and S. M. Wilson, "That Unmanned Wild Countrey," *Natural History* (1992):16–17.

4. Edwin Bryant, *What I Saw in California* (Lincoln: University of Nebraska Press, 1985), 377.

5. J. D. Borthwick, *Three Years in California* (Oakland: Biobooks, 1948), 114.

6. Robert E. Martin and David B. Sapsis, "Fires as Agents of Biodiversity—Pyrodiversity Promotes Biodiversity," in *Proceedings of the Symposium on Biodiversity of Northwestern California, October, 1991,* Richard R. Harris and Donald C. Erman, eds., Division of Agriculture and Natural Resources, University of California, 1992.

7. David W. Peri and Scott M. Patterson, "The Basket Is in the Roots, That's Where It Begins," in *Before the Wilderness: Environmental Management by Native Californians,* T. C. Blackburn and K. Anderson, eds. (Menlo Park, Calif.: Ballena Press, 1993), 175–94.

8. Harry W. Lawton, et al., "Agriculture Among the Paiute of Owens Valley," in Blackburn and Anderson, *Before the Wilderness,* 329–78.

9. Philip Drucker, "Culture Element Distributions, V: Southern California," *University of California Anthropological Records* 1, no. 1 (1937):1–52. Florence C. Shipek, "An Example of Intensive Plant Husbandry: The Kumeyaay of Southern California," in *Foraging and Farming: The Evolution of Plant Exploitation,* David R. Harris and Gordon C. Hillman, eds. (London: Unwin Hyman, 1989), 159–70.

10. Biologist James Cornett has spent twenty years studying desert fan palms, and his research elucidates indigenous people's major role in shaping the ecology of the palms in California. See his publications: James W. Cornett, *Desert Palm Oasis* (Santa Barbara: Palm Springs Desert Museum and Companion Press, 1989); "The Desert Fan Palm—Not a Relict," abstract, in *Mojave Desert Quaternary Research Center, Third Annual Symposium Proceedings,* C. A. Warren and J. S. Schneider, eds., San Bernardino County Museum Association, 1989; "Indians and the Desert Fan Palm," *Masterkey* (1987): 12–17; "A Giant Boring Beetle," *Environment Southwest* (1987): 21–25; James W. Cornett, "Reading Fan Palms," *Natural History* 94 (1985):64–73.

11. K. R. Jack, "An Indian's View of Burning, and a Reply," *California Fish and Game Journal* 2 (1916): 194–96; M. Kat Anderson, "Indian Fire-Based Management in the Sequoia–Mixed Conifer Forests of the Central and Southern Sierra Nevada," paper submitted to the Yosemite Research Center, Yosemite National Park, July 1993, United States Department of Interior, National Park Service, Western Region, Cooperative Agreement Order Number 8027-002.

12. Kathy Heffner, "Following the Smoke: Contemporary Plant Procurement by the Indians of Northwest California," paper submitted to Six Rivers National Forest, Eureka, 1984.

13. Sara M. Schenck and Edward W. Gifford, "Karok Ethnobotany," *University of California Anthropological Records* 13 (1952):377–92.

A WORLD OF BALANCE AND PLENTY 41

14. For an overview of fishing techniques, see Alfred L. Kroeber and Samuel A. Barrett, "Fishing Among the Indians of Northwestern California," *Anthropological Records* 22 (1960): 1–156; and Sean L. Swezey and Robert F. Heizer, "Ritual Management of Salmonid Fish Resources in California," in Blackburn and Anderson, *Before the Wilderness*, 299–328.

15. For a compendium of indigenous plant uses of the California flora, see Sandra S. Strike, *Ethnobotany of the California Indians: Aboriginal Uses of California's Indigenous Plants* (Champaign, Illinois: Koeltz Scientific Books, 1994), vol. 2; George R. Mead, *The Ethnobotany of the California Indians: A Compendium of the Plants, Their Uses and Their Users* (Greeley, Colorado: University of Northern Colorado Press, 1972). For an ethnobotanical bibliography, see Beatrice M. Beck, *Ethnobotany of the California Indians, Volume 1: A Bibliography and Index* (Champaign, Illinois: Koeltz Scientific Books, 1994).

16. Michael J. Moratto, *California Archeology* (Orlando: Academic Press, 1984).

17. Mary E. T. Collier and Sylvia Barker Thalman, *Interviews with Tom Smith and Maria Copa* (San Rafael, Calif.: Miwok Archaeological Preserve of Marin, 1991), 37.

18. Arnold R. Pilling, "Yurok," in Robert F. Heizer, ed., *Handbook of North American Indians*, Volume 8, *California* (Washington, D.C.: Smithsonian Institution, 1978), 137–54.

19. The eminent biologist E. O. Wilson maintains that indigenous ecological knowledge is in fact "true scientific knowledge." See E. O. Wilson, *The Diversity of Life* (Cambridge: Belknap Press of Harvard University Press, 1992), 44. In a cover article for *Time* magazine, the author E. Linden likens the loss of this knowledge to the burning of the great library of Alexandria. See E. Linden, "Lost Tribes, Lost Knowledge," *Time*, 138, no. 12 (1991):46–56.

20. For a review of California Indian population estimates, consult Sherburne F. Cook, "Historical Demography," in *Handbook of North American Indians, Vol. 8: California*.

21. Albert L. Hurtado, "Introduction," in *The Destruction of California Indians*, ed. Robert F. Heizer (Lincoln: University of Nebraska Press, 1974). Other graphic descriptions of harsh treatment of Native Americans by Europeans include George H. Phillips, *Indians and Intruders in Central California, 1769–1849* (Norman: University of Oklahoma Press, 1993); Van H. Garner, *The Broken Ring: The Destruction of the California Indians* (Tucson: Westernlore Press, 1982); and Rupert Costo and Jeannette H. Costo, *The Missions of California: A Legacy of Genocide* (San Francisco: Indian Historian Press, 1987).

22. H. H. Aschmann, "Distribution and Peculiarity of Mediterranean Ecosystems," in *Mediterranean Type Ecosystems: Origins and Structure*, F. di Castri and H. A. Mooney, eds. (New York: Springer, 1973), 11–19; Aschmann, "A More Restrictive Definition of Mediterranean Climates," *Bulletin, Botanical Society of France, Actual Botany* 2, 3, and 4 (1985):21–30. Fire is included by ecologists as a component of the California climate, as most completely described by *Proceedings, California Tall Timbers Fire Ecology Conference*, ed. E. V. Komarek (Tallahassee, Florida. Tall Timbers Research Station, 1968).

23. California has about 11,000 soil series, an unusually high diversity for the state's area. H. Jenny, R. J. Arkley, and A. M. Schultz, "The Pygmy Forest Podzol Ecosystem and its Dune Associates of the Mendocino Coast," *Madrono* 20 (1969):60–74; A. Kruckeberg, "California Serpentines," *University of California Publications in Botany* 78 (1984): 1–180. A more general reference on geologic substrates is R. M. Norris and R. W. Webb, *Geology of California*, 2nd ed. (New York: Wiley, 1990).

24. There have been several efforts to map and classify California vegetation. These have divided California into as few as 29 and as many as 375 units. Full references are as follows:

Anonymous, *California Vegetation* [a map] (Sacramento: Teale Data Center, 1991); W. L. Colwell, Jr., "The Status of Vegetation Mapping in California Today," in *Terrestrial Vegetation of California, M. G. Barbour and J. Major, eds. (Sacramento: California Native Plant Society, 1988), 195–220; C. B. Goudey and D. W. Smith*, Ecological Units of California: Subsections (Albany: USDA Forest Service, PSW-map, 1994); R. F. Holland, *Preliminary Descriptions of the Terrestrial Natural Communities of California* (Sacramento: California Resources Agency, California Department of Fish and Game, 1986); S. C. Hunter and T. E. Paysen, *Vegetation Classification System for California* (Berkeley: USDA Forest Service, Gen. Tech. Rep. PSW-94, 1986); H. A. Jensen, "A System for Classifying Vegetation in California," *California Fish and Game* 33 (1947):199–266; A. W. Kuchler, "The Map of the Vegetation of California," in *Terrestrial Vegetation of California*, ed. M. G. Barbour and J. Major, 909–38; W. J. Matyas and I. Parker, *CALVEG, Mosaic of Existing Vegetation of California* (San Francisco: USDA Forest Service, Regional Ecology Group, 1980); K. Mayer and W. Laudenslayer, *A Guide to Wildlife Habitats of California* (Sacramento: California Resources Agency, Department of Forestry and Fire Protection, 1988); P. A. Munz and D. D. Keck, *A California Flora* (Berkeley: University of California Press 1959); J. O. Sawyer and T. Keeler-Wolf, *A Manual of California Vegetation* (Sacramento: California Native Plant Society, 1995).

25. We recommend four reviews of the climate and vegetation of California during the past 2 to sixty million years: D. I. Axelrod, "Evolution of Madro-Tertiary Geoflora," *Botanical Review* 24 (1958):433–509; D. I. Axelrod, "History of the Coniferous Forests, California and Nevada,"*University of California Publications in Botany* 70 (1976):1–62; D. I. Axelrod, "Outline History of California Vegetation," in *Terrestrial Vegetation of California*, 2nd ed., M. G. Barbour and J. Major (Sacramento: California Native Plant Society, 1988), 139–92; A. Graham, "History of the Vegetation," in *Flora of North America*, vol. 1, Flora of North America Editorial Committee (New York: Oxford University Press, 1993), 57–70.

26. According to James Hickman's recent state flora, California encompasses 5,862 species and 1,169 subspecies or varieties, for a total of 7,061 taxa. Some 1,023 of these taxa have been introduced but now grow wild (that is, they are called "naturalized"). This list does not, then, include introduced plants that only survive where tended in gardens, orchards, farms, etc. About 30 percent of our native taxa are endemic to California, found nowhere else in the world except where they have been introduced. J. C. Hickman, ed., *The Jepson Manual* (Berkeley: University of California Press, 1993).

27. Richard A. Minnich and E. Franco-Vizcaino, *Land of Chamise and Pines: Historical Descriptions of Northern Baja California* (Berkeley: University of California Press, in press for 1997 publication).

28. Kuchler, "Map of Vegetation of California."

29. Barbour and Johnson, "Beach and Dune," in Barbour and Major, *Terrestrial Vegetation of California*, 223–61; B. M. Pavlik, "Nutrient and Productivity Relations of the Dune Grasses *Ammophila arenaria* and *Elymus mollis*, I: Blade Photosynthesis and N Use Efficiency in the Laboratory and Field," *Oecologia* 57 (1983):227–32, "II: Growth and Patterns of Dry Matter and N Allocation as Influenced by N Supply," 233–38, and "III: Spatial Aspects of Clonal Expansion with Reference to Rhizome Growth and the Dispersal of Buds, "*Bulletin of the Torrey Botanical Club* (110):271–79. See also Pavlik, "Water Relations of the Dune Grasses *Ammophila arenaria* and *Elymus mollis* on the Coast of Oregon, USA," *Oikos* 45 (1985):197–205.

30. Jensen, et al., *In Our Own Hands.*

31. H. H. Heady, T. C. Foin, M. M. Hektner, D. W. Taylor, M. G. Barbour, and W. J. Barry, "Coastal Prairie and Northern Coastal Scrub," in Barbour and Major, *Terrestrial Vegetation of California*, 733–60.

32. W. E. Westman, "Factors Influencing the Distribution of Species of Californian Coastal Sage Scrub," *Ecology* 62 (1981):439–55, and "Diversity Relations and Succession in Californian Coastal Sage Scrub," *Ecology* 62 (1981):170–84; Richard A. Minnich and R. J. Dezzani, "Historical Decline of Coastal Sage Scrub in the Parris Plain, California," in *Proceedings of the Symposium on the California Gnat Catcher,*ed. T. A. Scott and J. T. Rtenberry, (San Francisco: Cooper Ornithological Society, in press for 1997 publication).

33. Redwood trees tolerate floods by generating new roots near the soil surface, within the layer of flood-deposited silt that suffocates the deeper roots of other species. Redwood seedlings also survive much better when they germinate on bare mineral soil (flood-deposited silt) than when they germinate on litter. Redwood trees tolerate ground fires because their thick bark insulates the living cambium from high temperatures. Fires and floods recur in redwood forests on the average of once a century. See P. J. Zinke, "The Redwood Forest and Associated North Coast Forests," in Barbour and Major, *Terrestrial Vegetation of California*, 679–732. Also Jerry Franklin, "Pacific Northwest," in *North American Terrestrial Vegetation*, 2nd ed., eds, M. G. Barbour and W. D. Billings (New York: Cambridge University Press, in press for 1997 publication), ch. 4. A more recent, lay-oriented summary of coast redwood ecology is *The Coast Redwood: A Natural and Cultural History*, ed. J. Evarts (Los Olivos: Cachuma Press, in press for 1997 publication).

34. The mosaic of woodland, grassland, savanna, and chaparral seems to be caused by differences in topography, soil depth, and fire frequency. M. G. Barbour, B. M. Pavlik, F. R. Drysdale, and S. A. Lindstrom, *California's Changing Landscapes* (Sacramento: California Native Plant Society, 1993), and Elna Bakker, *An Island Called California*, 2nd ed. (Berkeley: University of California Press, 1984).

35. Vegetational, floristic, and land-use changes in California's central prairie have been described by W. J. Barry, *The Central Valley Prairie* (Sacramento: California Department of Parks and Recreation, 1972); H. F. Heady, "Valley Grassland," in Barbour and Major, *Terrestrial Vegetation of California*, 491–514; and L. T. Burcham, "Historical Background of Range Land Use in California," *Journal of Range Management* 9 (1956):81–86.

36. M. G. Barbour and R. A. Minnich, "Californian Upland Forests and Woodlands," in Barbour and Billings, *North American Terrestrial Vegetation*, ch. 5; M. I. Borchert, F. W. Davis, J. Michaelsen, and L. D. Oyler, "Interactions of Factors Affecting Seedling Recruitment of Blue Oak (*Quercus douglasii*) in California," *Ecology* 70 (1989):389–404; D. R. Gordon and K. J. Rice, "Competitive Effects of Grassland Annuals on Soil Water and Blue Oak (*Quercus douglasii*) Seedlings," *Oecologia* 79 (1993):533–41; P. C. Muick and J. W. Bartolome, *An Assessment of Natural Regeneration of Oaks in California* (Sacramento: California Department of Forestry and Fire Protection, 1987); B. M. Pavlik, P. C. Muick, S. Johnson, and J. Popper, *Oaks of California* (Los Olivos: Cachuma Press, 1991); and J. M. Welker and J. W. Menke, "The Influence of Simulated Browsing on Tissue Water Relations, Growth, and Survival of *Quercus douglasii* (Hook and Arn.) Seedlings Under Slow and Rapid Rates of Soil Drought," *Functional Ecology* 4 (1990):807–817.

37. T. L. Hanes, "California Chaparral," in Barbour and Major, *Terrestrial Vegetation of California*, 417–69; and J. Keeley, "Chaparral," in Barbour and Billings, *North American Terrestrial Vegetation*, ch. 6.

38. A lapse rate is the rate of change in some environmental factors in relation to elevation. Jack Major, "California Climate in Relation to Vegetation," in Barbour and Major, *Terrestrial Vegetation of California*, 11–74. The mean elevational displacement of all tree species between Lassen and Yosemite national parks is steeper than for any other temperate zone mountain range. A. J. Parker, "Latitudinal Gradients of Coniferous Tree Species, Vegetation, and Climate in the Sierran-Cascade Axis of Northern California," *Vegetatio* 115 (1994):145–55.

39. John Muir, *The Mountains of California* (New York: Dorset Press, 1988), 141–42. The impact of natural ground fires on the structure and species composition of mixed conifer forest has been discussed by many authors, most recently Chi-ru Chang, "Ecosystem Responses to Fire and Variations in Fire Regimes," in *Status of the Sierra Nevada*, vol. 2, ed. SNEP Science Team (University of California, Davis: Wildland Resources Center Report 36, 1996), ch. 39; B. M. Kilgore, "Fire in Ecosystem Distribution and Structure: Western Forests and Scrublands," in *Fire Regimes and Ecosystem Properties*, ed. H. A. Mooney (Washington, D.C.: USDA Forest Service, General Technical Report WO-26, 1981), 58–80; R. A. Minnich, M. G. Barbour, J. H. Burk, and R. F. Fernau, "Sixty Years of Change in California Conifer Forest of the San Bernardino Mountains," *Conservation Biology* 9 (1995):902–14; R. A. Minnich, M. G. Barbour, J. H. Burk, and J. Sosa-Ramirez, "Californian Conifer Forests under Unmanaged Fire Regimes in the Sierra San Pedro Martir, Baja California, Mexico," *Ecological Monographs* (in review for 1997 publication); P. W. Rundel, D. J. Parsons, and D. T. Gordon, "Montane and Subalpine Vegetation of the Sierra Nevada and Cascade Ranges," in Barbour and Major, *Terrestrial Vegetation of California*, 559–99; and T. W. Swetnam, "Fire History and Climatic Change in Giant Sequoia Groves," *Science* 262 (1993):885–90.

40. Air pollutants that affect vegetation in the mountains are primarily those released in automobile exhaust or that result from exhaust fumes interacting with oxygen in the presence of sunlight. Major phytotoxicants are ozone, nitrogen oxides, hydrocarbons such as PAN, and sulfur dioxide. Ozone appears to be the most important phytotoxicant in this complex. G. G. Bradford, A. L. Page, and J. R. Straughan, "Are Sierra Lakes Becoming Acid?" *California Agriculture* (May–June 1981):6–7; T. A. Cahill, J. J. Carroll, D. Campbell, and T. E. Gill, "Air Quality," in *Status of the Sierra Nevada*, vol.2, ch. 48, and P. R. Miller, "Biological Effects of Air Pollution in the Sierra Nevada," in *Status of the Sierra Nevada*, vol.3, ed. SNEP Science Team (University of California, Davis: Wildland Resources Center, 1996), 885–900.

41. M. G. Barbour, N. Berg, T. Kittel, and M. Kunz, "Snowpack and the Distribution of a Major Vegetation Ecotone in the Sierra Nevada of California," *Journal of Biogeography* 18 (1991):141–49.

42. Very little is known about fire behavior and fire frequency in upper montane forests. M. G. Barbour and J. A. Antos, "Age Structure and Fire History of Old-Growth Red Fir Stands in the Northern Sierra Nevada, California," *Conservation Biology*, in press for 1998 publication; C. B. Chappell and J. K. Agee , "Fire Severity and Seedling Establishment in *Abies magnifica* Forests, Southern Cascades, Oregon," *Ecological Applications* 6 (1996):628–40; D. C. Pitcher, "Fire History and Age Structure in Red Fir Forests of Sequoia National Park, California," *Canadian Journal of Forest Research* 17 (1987):582–87; A. H. Taylor and C. B. Halpern, "Structure and Dynamics of *Abies magnifica* Forests in the Southern Cascade Range, USA," *Journal of Vegetation Science* 2 (1991):189–200; and A. H. Taylor, "Fire History and Structure of Red Fir (*Abies magnifica*) Forests, Swain Mountain Experimental Forest, Cascade Range, Northeastern California," *Canadian Journal of Forest Research* 23 (1993):1672–78.

43. M. G. Barbour and R. A. Minnich, "Californian Upland Forests and Woodlands," in Barbour and Billings, *North American Terrestrial Vegetation*, ch. 5; and *Forest Cover Types of the United States and Canada*, F. H. Eyre, ed. (Washington, D.C.: Society of American Foresters, 1980); the upper limit of tree distribution—that is, the limit between subalpine woodland and alpine tundra—appears to be linked with warmth during the growing season. H. A. Mooney, R. D. Wright, and B. R. Strain, "Field Measurements of the Metabolic Responses of Bristlecone Pine and Big Sagebrush in the White Mountains of California," *American Midland Naturalist* 72 (1964):281–97. Timberline elevation has shifted up and down with warm and cold centuries during the past 6,000 years. R. S.Anderson, "Holocene Forest Development and Paleoclimates Within the Central Sierra Nevada, California," *Journal of Ecology* 78 (1990):470–89; L. J. Graumlich, "Subalpine Tree Growth, Climate, and Increasing CO_2: An Assessment of Recent Growth Trends," *Ecology* 72 (1991):1–11; and L. J. Graumlich, "A 1000-Year Record of Temperature and Precipitation in the Sierra Nevada," *Quaternary Research* 39 (1993):249–55.

44. W. D. Billings, "Adaptations and Origins of Alpine Plants," *Arctic and Alpine Research* 6 (1974):129–42; and B. F. Chabot and W. D. Billings, "Origins and Ecology of the Sierran Alpine Flora and Vegetation," *Ecological Monographs* 42 (1972):163–99.

45. Grazing damage to alpine areas has been the subject of considerable attention by conservationists from the time of John Muir, as recently summarized by W. Menke, C. Davis, and P. Beesley, "Rangeland Assessment," in *Status of the Sierra Nevada*, vol. 3, 901–72.

46. J. A. Young, R. A. Evans, and J. Major, "Sagebrush Steppe," in Barbour and Major, *Terrestrial Vegetation of California*, 763–69; N. West, "Intermountain Deserts, Shrub Steppes, and Woodlands," in Barbour and Billings, *North American Terrestrial Vegetation*, 209–30; and J. A. Young, R. A. Evans, and J. Major, "Alien Plants in the Great Basin," *Journal of Range Management* 25 (1972):194–201.

47. J. A. MacMahon, "Warm Desert Vegetation," in Barbour and Billings, *North American Terrestrial Vegetation*, ch. 14; and J. A MacMahon and F. H. Wagner, "The Mojave, Sonoran, and Chihuahuan deserts of North America," in *Hot Deserts and Arid Shrublands*, ed. M. Evenari, I. Noy-Meir, and D. W. Goodall (Amsterdam: Elsevier, 1985), 105–202.

48. The damaging effect of ORVs on California desert ecosystems is dramatically captured by Robert Stebbins in a lay-oriented review, R. C. Stebbins, "Off Road Vehicles and the Fragile Desert," *The American Biology Teacher* 36 (1974):203–34. The lengthy, decades-long course of vegetation recovery following vehicle traffic is described by D. E. Carpenter, M. G. Barbour, and C. J. Bahre, "Old-Field Succession in Mojave Desert Scrub, *Madrono* 33 (1986):111–22.

49. Jaime de Angulo, "Pomo Creation Myth," *Journal of American Folk-Lore* 48 (1935):203; Edwin M. Loeb, "The Creator Concept among the Indians of North Central California," *American Anthropologist* 28 (1926):489.

50. M. Kat Anderson, "The Sustainable Harvesting and Horticultural Practices of California Indian Tribes: Linking Plant Homelands and Human Homelands," in *Raise the Stakes* (San Francisco: The Planet Drum Review, 1994).

51. M. Kat Anderson, "Native Californians as Ancient and Contemporary Cultivators," Blackburn and Anderson, in *Before the Wilderness*.

52. M. Kat Anderson and Gary P. Nabhan, "Gardeners in Eden," *Wilderness Magazine* 55 (1991):27–30.

53. Philip J. Wilke, "Bow Staves Harvested from Juniper Trees by Indians of Nevada," in Blackburn and Anderson, *Before the Wilderness,* 241–77.

54. Carole L. Crumley, "Historical Ecology: A Multidimensional Ecological Orientation," in *Historical Ecology: Cultural Knowledge and Changing Landscapes,* ed. C. L. Crumley (Santa Fe: School of American Research Press, 1994).

55. M. Kat Anderson, "Tending the Wilderness," *Restoration and Management Notes* 14 (Winter 1996): 154–66.

56. Susan Bicknell and colleagues at Humboldt State University have done the seminal research that shows the human origins of California's formerly vast coastal prairies. A series of unpublished reports was done for California Department of Parks and Recreation and conclusions appear in two abstracts: Susan H. Bicknell et al., "Late Prehistoric Vegetation Patterns at Six Sites in Coastal California," *Supplement to Bulletin of the Ecological Society of America,* Program and Abstracts, 73, no. 2 (1992):112. Susan H. Bicknell et al., "Strategy for Reconstructing Presettlement Vegetation," *Supplement to Bulletin of the Ecological Society of America,* Program and Abstracts, 70, no. 2 (1989):62.

57. For addition on native uses of tule, consult Frank F. Latta, *Handbook of Yokuts Indians* (Bakersfield: Kern County Museum, 1949); Alfred L. Kroeber, *Handbook of the Indians of California* (Washington: Smithsonian Institution, 1925).

58. Hector Franco, "That Place Needs a Good Fire," *News from Native California* (1993):17–19. Catherine S. Fowler, "Historical Perspectives on Timbisha Shoshone Land Management Practices, Death Valley, California," *Case Studies in Environmental Archaeology,* ed. Elizabeth J. Reitz, Lee A. Newsom, and Sylvia J. Scudder (New York: Plenum Press 1996), 87–101.

59. D. P. Warners, "Effects of Burning on Sedge Meadow Studied," *Restoration and Management Notes* 5 (1987):90–91; G. Schlichtemeier, "Marsh Burning for Water-fowl," *Proceedings Sixth Annual Tall Timbers Fire Ecology Conference,* March 6–7, 1967, Tallahassee, Florida.

60. Anderson, "Native Californians as Ancient and Contemporary Cultivators," 167–70.

61. S. A. Barrett and E. W. Gifford, *Miwok Material Culture* (Yosemite National Park: Yosemite National History Association, ca. 1959) 179.

62. For a good overview of indigenous burning in different vegetation types, see Henry T. Lewis, "Patterns of Indian Burning in California: Ecology and Ethnohistory," in Blackburn and Anderson, *Before the Wilderness,* 55–116. For an annotated bibliography of indigenous fire use in California, see C. Kristina Roper Wickstrom, *Issues Concerning Native American Use of Fire: A Literature Review* (Yosemite Research Center, Yosemite National Park: National Park Service, U.S. Department of Interior Publications in Anthropology, No. 6, 1987).

63. Barrett and Gifford, *Miwok Material Culture,* 151–58; John W. Duncan III, "Maidu Ethnobotany" (M.A. thesis, California State University, Sacramento, 1961).

64. Stephen Powers, *Tribes of California* (Berkeley: University of California Press, 1976), 379.

65. Steve Junak et al., *A Flora of Santa Cruz Island* (Santa Barbara: Santa Barbara Botanic Garden and the California Native Plant Society, 1995).

66. Paul Schumacher, "Ancient Graves and Shell-Heaps of California," in *Annual Report of the Smithsonian Institution for 1874* (Washington, 1875), 335–50.

67. Willis L. Jepson, *The Trees of California* (San Francisco: Independent Pressroom and Williams Printing Company, 1923), 109.

68. Paul W. Collins, "Interaction between Island Foxes *(Urocyon littoralis)* and Indians on Islands off the Coast of Southern California, I: Morphologic and Archaeological Evidence of Human Assisted Dispersal," *Journal of Ethnobiology* 11 (1991): 51–82.

69. For current information regarding current threats to Native American gathering activities, consult back issues of the *California Indian Basketweaver Association Newsletter* and *News from Native California.* For information on California basketweavers and herbicides, consult Michael Garitty, "Direct Effects: California Indian Basketweavers, Herbicides, and National Forest Lands," *Native Americas* 12 (1995):42–9.

70. The Society for Ecological Restoration has recognized that indigenous peoples must be a part of any serious efforts at restoring and preserving ecosystems. Within the organization, the Indigenous Peoples' Restoration Network (IPRN) was formed in 1995 for the purposes of utilizing indigenous knowledge in contemporary land management and restoration projects that consider both long-term ecosystem health and the cultural well-being of indigenous people.

71. M. Kat Anderson and Michael J. Moratto, "Native American Land-Use Practices and Ecological Impacts," in *Status of the Sierra Nevada,* vol. 2, ch. 5.

72. Jim T. Birckhead, Terry De Lacy, and Laurajane Smith, eds., *Aboriginal Involvement in Parks and Protected Areas* (Canberra: Aboriginal Studies Press, 1993), Australian Institute of Aboriginal and Torres Strait Islander Studies; Dennis Martinez, "Native American Forestry Practices," in *The Status and Future of Pesticide Use in California,* California Forest Pest Council Proceedings of the 41st Annual Meeting, Redding, 1992.

3

Indian Peoples of California

William S. Simmons

INTRODUCTION

This chapter provides a glimpse of certain key aspects of California Indian life shortly before and after the beginning of European colonization. Although it includes the entire area encompassed by the present-day state of California, the focus primarily is on the peoples who inhabited the north and south Coast Ranges, the Sacramento and San Joaquin river valleys, and the western Sierra. In selecting and depicting the topics to be emphasized, I have tried to present a balance between a comparative approach that suggests the great diversity of native California peoples, certain shared characteristics of their cultures, and specific details of particular local communities. In constructing this account, I have given substantial attention to the actual voices of those Native Californians, missionaries, anthropologists, linguists, and others whose testimonies have shaped the understanding of California Indian life at the threshold of the historic period.

Native Americans had been living in what is today known as California for perhaps fifteen thousand years before explorers from New Spain first visited by ship and gave the area its present name. In the three centuries between 1542, when the expedition of Juan Rodríguez Cabrillo reconnoitered the California coast, and 1849, when immigrant gold miners flooded the remote waterways of the Sierra, all California Indians had been exposed to and overwhelmed by colonists seeking labor, land, furs, and gold. According to the most reliable estimates, the indigenous population numbered around 310,000 persons who spoke perhaps as many as one hundred mutually unintelligible languages. By the late nineteenth century the native population had declined to a low point of some twenty thousand survivors, and many language communities had begun to disappear. While the California Indian population has been growing steadily through the twentieth century, the number of spoken languages has declined to perhaps half of the original figure, and most of these persist only among a few elderly people.

The faces of five native men drawn by Louis Choris at San Francisco in 1816 compose
a poignant and powerful image of California mission Indians in the final years of Spanish
rule. Choris, who served as the official artist of a Russian exploring expedition commanded
by Otto von Kotzebue, created the most sensitive and significant pictorial record of
California Indians under Hispanic rule extant. *Habitants de Californie,* one of a dozen
lithographs made from Choris's watercolors, appeared in the artist's *Voyage pittoresque
autour du monde,* published in Paris in 1822. *Courtesy California Historical Society,
FN-30510.*

An understanding of California Indian life before European colonization is complicated by at least four factors. First, California has an unusual history in the sense
that it was colonized in different areas at different times in the course of four frontier expansions: Spanish, Russian, Mexican, and American. For those natives who
lived in the path of initial Spanish settlement, the colonial period began in 1769 with
the establishment of the mission and presidio at San Diego. For groups that lived
outside the orbits of Spanish, Russian, and Mexican influence, in the foothills and
remote valleys of the Sierra, colonization began in the American period after the discovery of gold in 1848. The second factor is the extreme geographical diversity of native groups, which makes it difficult to generalize about their many cultures. The
speakers of the approximately one hundred languages lived in as many as five hundred autonomous land-owning communities, often referred to as tribelets, which
differed regionally in their environments, material cultures, myths, and social practices. The third factor is that, prior to colonization, Native Californians did not

possess knowledge of writing and therefore did not document their own experiences through the written word. Modern interpreters of pre-colonial life have drawn heavily upon accounts written about Indians by others such as missionaries, soldiers, miners, journalists, travelers, historians, linguists, and anthropologists, and upon the independent work of archaeologists. Fourth, the written sources pertain mainly to the period after colonization, when the native peoples had been influenced to varying degrees by their relationships with the foreigners who settled in their territories. Although a few sources directly reflect the perspectives of Native Californians who were living at the time of initial colonization, most are "downstream" accounts, written at a later date and based on the experiences, memories, and traditions of persons who lived after the Spanish, Mexicans, Russians, and Americans had long been present. Such downstream accounts, taken with appropriate caution, and combined where possible with archaeological testimony, are an important key to deciphering and envisaging the "upstream" world of California Indian life as it existed in the pre-colonial period.[1]

RESEARCH TRENDS

The Spanish, Mexicans, Russians, and Americans who initially colonized California represented the final stage of their respective frontier movements. All had encountered and subdued many native peoples (some wealthier, some more powerful than the Native Californians) in the course of their territorial expansions. They also brought with them a legacy of increasing disinterest in the cultural lives and languages of native peoples, which contributed to a widely shared belief that Native Californians were among the world's least cultured people. This negative cultural stereotype of California Indians, which originated in rationalizations of the various outsiders who displaced them, persisted throughout the historical period and is still commonplace today. Hubert Howe Bancroft, for example, saw California's natives as almost without culture by comparison with other North American Indians: "The missionary Fathers found a virgin field whereon neither god nor devil was worshiped."[2]

Historians, anthropologists, and linguists interested in pre-colonial Indian life in California long ago discarded the evolutionary framework evident in Bancroft's work and in the assumptions of numerous late-nineteenth- and early-twentieth-century writers, in favor of more ethnographically descriptive and less evaluative approaches based on the analysis of material data, field research, and the firsthand testimonies of living people. Even Bancroft, to his considerable credit, was responsible for the collection of important personal testimony from former mission Indians. The earliest ethnographers and linguists, such as Roland B. Dixon, Pliny Earle Goddard, Alfred L. Kroeber, C. Hart Merriam, Constance G. Du Bois, John Alden Mason, John Peabody Harrington, Samuel A. Barrett, and Edward Winslow

The Chumash Indian Kitsepawit, better known by his Hispanic name, Fernando Librado, was born early in the nineteenth century and lived well into the following century. It was from natives such as Librado, who spent his early years at Mission La Purísima, that Alfred Kroeber, John Harrington, and other pioneer anthropologists learned much about California Indian language, history, and culture. *Courtesy Lompoc Valley Historical Society, Lompoc, Calif.*

Gifford, focused intensively on the "memory culture" of those individuals who were thought to be most knowledgeable about life as it existed before colonization or during the initial historic period. Interest in the past, what Kroeber once described as "the purely aboriginal, the uncontaminatedly native," dominated research on Native Californians until the 1930s, when anthropologists in general turned away from "conjectural history" to the study of how communities functioned in the present and how they fared in the course of change.[3] Although the value of memory culture research among present-day Native Californians has by no means been exhausted, its potential for illuminating pre-colonial or early colonial Indian life becomes more attenuated with succeeding generations.

The cumulative early ethnographic achievement in California, largely inspired by the influence of Alfred L. Kroeber, and published in the *University of California Publications in American Archaeology and Ethnography* and in the *Anthropological Records,* is a remarkable source for Native Californian personal testimony, particularly by comparison to what is available for other regions of North America. These earlier monographs and the associated unpublished fieldnotes continue to reward anthropologists, historians, natives, and others in their ongoing efforts to better understand the character of indigenous life in California. An array of recent work demonstrates the sophisticated ways in which California hunter-gatherers managed their diverse plant and animal habitats to sustain population densities extraordinary for hunting-gathering societies, including those with limited agriculture. In a recent overview of complex hunter-gatherer societies of the Pacific coastal region, including California, Kent Lightfoot suggested that the "late prehistoric and early contact period societies in the Pacific represent the upper range of sociopolitical development supported by hunter-gatherer economies."[4] Scholars continue to explore and debate the actual levels of political hierarchy and extents of territorial authority that formerly existed. Other new work advances the interpretation of such topics as the long-term development of craft specialization, gender identities and relationships, population health and disease, mythical and other oral narratives, religious belief and organization, and world-view, in late prehistoric and early historic times.[5]

CULTURE AREAS

Early, as well as recent, scholars, in their attempts to describe the geographical diversity of California Indian communities, have tended to follow a "culture area" approach that originated in the theoretical interests of late-nineteenth- and early-twentieth-century anthropologists. Kroeber, for example, proposed six such areas (northwest, northeast, central, southern, Great Basin, and lower Colorado) based on language groupings and what he described as culture element distributions.[6]

Central California, considered by Kroeber to be the most distinctively Californian culture area, included a vast expanse of the north and south coasts, as well as the adjoining Coast Ranges, the Sacramento and San Joaquin river valleys, and the foothills and high valleys of the northern and southern Sierra. Although the hunting and gathering economies of this area varied according to the availability of local resources, most communities had access to salmon, acorns, deer, elk, pronghorn, rabbits, and waterfowl, as well as to insects, roots, berries, and seeds. Coastal groups depended on a variety of marine resources, including shellfish and sea mammals, in addition to fish. Languages indigenous to this area included Pomo, Miwok, Wintun, Maidu, Yana, Yuki, Ohlone (also known as Costanoan), Esselen, Salinan, Western Mono or Monache, and Yokuts. The rich ceremonial life of the central California area centered on the roundhouse, a large wood-framed structure that was built of posts and rafters over an excavated pit and then covered with earth. As noted by Robert Heizer and Albert Elsasser, family dwellings over much of central California were essentially small versions of the larger ceremonial houses. Villages of such houses, warm in winter and cool in summer, looked like little clusters of hills with smoke rising from openings at the top. Another widespread dwelling type, particularly in mountainous and forested areas, was the conical house constructed of redwood or pine boards and bark slabs. Although women throughout Native California made fine basketry, specific groups differed in their weaving techniques and decorative styles. The Pomo, Coast Miwok, and Ohlone of central California were particularly distinguished for the feather and shell bead decorating techniques they

Native men play a game of chance in their ceremonial roundhouse near the head of the Sacramento Valley. Henry B. Brown, who made the field sketches for this composition near Tehama in the spring of 1852, relied on traditional aesthetic principles in turning his original studies into finished drawings, as did other artists of the day. "I procured two portraits there," he wrote of the creative process that produced the image, "and an interior of a large council house 39 feet in diameter and twelve feet high, into which I shall put a group gambling from studies taken on the spot, a singular & striking scene with a Rembrandt effect of chiar'oscuro." *Courtesy John Carter Brown Library, Brown University.*

applied to the exteriors of their baskets. Knowledge of pottery vessel manufacture, while not widespread, had diffused from the eastern Sierra to the Western Mono and to a few foothill Yokuts tribelets, and to the ancestors of the Plains Miwok in the lower Sacramento Valley.[7]

The southern area from north to south includes the Chumash, Gabrielino; Luiseño, and Kumeyaay (or Diegueño) of the coast, and the Serrano, Cupeño, and Cahuilla of the interior. Earliest explorers along this coast, particularly in the Santa Barbara Channel area, found large, populous villages of hunters and gatherers with sea-going plank canoes, who harvested sea mammals and ocean fish in addition to abundant shellfish. Recent archaeological research in this region suggests a tendency toward sociopolitical ranking and increasingly larger chiefdoms, as well as craft specialization, shortly before the arrival of Europeans in the sixteenth cen-

A typical Konkow Maidu village in the upper Sacramento Valley as depicted in 1852 by Henry B. Brown. Scattered about the subterranean dwelling houses are acorn granaries, where the natives stored the nuts that composed one of their basic food sources. *Courtesy John Carter Brown Library, Brown University.*

tury.[8] Acorns, while less available than they were in some moister areas of central California, were nevertheless an important staple. The Chumash, in addition to being capable mariners, also perfected the skill of stoneworking to produce elegant flat-bottomed sandstone mortars, graceful long stone pestles, steatite animal effigies, and steatite bowls. The southernmost groups in this area (Kamia, Kumeyaay, and Cahuilla) made pottery vessels, a culture element that they shared with the greater Southwest culture area of Arizona, Colorado, and New Mexico. These same groups and their immediate neighbors may have practiced a limited "kitchen garden" type of agriculture that appears to have originated from more developed practices among Colorado River peoples.[9]

In the northwest area, which included such language groups as Hupa, Yurok, Karok, and Wiyot, riverine and coastal food resources and heavy redwood timber abounded. Their rich material culture included an array of fishing and sea hunting technologies as well as woodworking tools such as adzes, mauls, and wedges for constructing dugout canoes and substantial houses. Wealth and status differences were more pronounced here than in most other areas of California, and local leaders tended to be the wealthiest men, but their influence was mainly over their own kin, and a village might have several such leaders. The peoples of northwest California shared a number of cultural affiliations with their coastal hunting and gathering neighbors to the north and for this reason are generally considered to be a periphery of the Pacific Northwest Coast culture area that extends from northwest California to Alaska.

The northeast culture area of California, home to speakers of the Modoc, Achomawi, and Atsugewi languages, was considered by Kroeber and others to be a periphery of the interior Columbia-Fraser Plateau culture area to the north. Economic life in this area centered on hunting, fishing, and gathering of wild roots and seeds. Late prehistoric inhabitants of the Pit River drainage are known to have manufactured pottery bowls, most probably for serving food.

The Great Basin culture area of California extended along the eastern watershed of the Sierra and included some of the interior regions of southern California. Here lived mainly desert hunting and gathering groups such as the Northern Paiute, Washo, Mono, Owens Valley Paiute, and Chemehuevi, who are considered to be a western periphery of a much larger culture area that extends into Nevada and Utah. Although the economy of Great Basin peoples was heavily dependent on rabbit hunting and gathering seed and root crops (particularly pine nuts, but also acorns), the Owens Valley Paiute developed a distinctive agricultural practice that required communal labor to prepare ditches and dams to irrigate and thus increase the productivity of wild plants.[10]

The lower Colorado River groups included the Yuma, Mohave, and Halchidhoma, who were the primary California hunters and gatherers to also practice subsistence farming. Situated at the western periphery of the greater Southwest culture area, with its agricultural peoples such as the Hopi, Pima, and Havasupai, they regularly cultivated several varieties of maize and beans, as well as pumpkins, on the floodplains of the Colorado River. The Yuma and Mohave were also among the few California groups to manufacture pottery vessels, another element that they shared with cultures of the greater Southwest.

Kroeber and others who initiated the culture-area classifications did so in part to better understand the prehistoric formation of and relationships among California native cultures. Prior to the discovery of accurate dating techniques such as carbon-14, obsidian hydration, and tree-ring dating, scholars tried to determine the relative antiquity of specific cultural elements by investigating their distributions among contemporary people. The more widespread an element, for example, the more ancient it might be. Their efforts to map culture element distributions also reflected early interest in the relationship between cultural adaptation and environment.

While the relation of material culture to environment continues to be an essential interest, much of the theoretical purpose to constructing culture-area classifications has passed out of fashion in anthropology. The regional classifications that Kroeber formulated, however, remain in widespread use as a conventional, if imprecise, way to talk about and summarize the regional diversity of California peoples. The boundaries of such units are nevertheless often blurred. The Achomawi people of the northeast culture area of California are considered to be a fringe of the Columbia-Fraser Plateau area, yet they intermarried with and shared elements of material culture and mythology with their Maidu neighbors of the central California area to the south. Again, the several groups such as the Yurok and Hupa in the northwest culture area of California, considered to be the southern fringe of the Pacific Northwest Coast area, shared mythological elements with central and northeastern California.

LANGUAGES

California is one of the most linguistically diverse areas in the world. Linguists tend to classify California languages by means of a four-level system of stock, family, language, and dialect.[11] When anthropologists and linguists speak of California "tribes," they generally mean language families or languages, not actual social groups with territorial boundaries and unifying political leadership. Recent classifications suggest that all California languages derive from one of seven stocks known to linguists as Hokan, Penutian, Utian, Algic, Na-Dene, Uto-Aztecan, and Yukian. The Hokan stock, for example, includes several families, one of which is Pomoan, which in turn includes seven distinct languages (Northern, Northeastern, Eastern, Central, Southeastern, Southern, and Kashaya Pomo). To speak of the Pomo "tribe," therefore, is really to speak of a large family of languages, not of an actual social group with a leadership structure. The Penutian stock divides into the Wintun and Maidun families, the latter of which includes Northeastern Maidu, Konkow, and Nisenan. Utian comprises such well-known families as Miwokan (eight languages: Lake Miwok, Coast Miwok, Bay Miwok, Plains Miwok, Northern Sierra Miwok, East Central Sierra Miwok, West Central Sierra Miwok, Southern Sierra Miwok), Costanoan or Ohlone (eight languages: Karkin, Chochenyo, Tamien, Ramaytush, Awaswas, Rumsen, Mutsun, Chalon), and Yokutsan (seven languages: Choynumni, Chukchansi, Dumna, Tachi, Wukchumne, Yowlumni, Gashowu). Languages may in turn be divided into dialects. The northeastern Maidu, for example, lived in four regions, Susanville, Big Meadows, Indian Valley, and American Valley, each with its local dialect.

TRIBELETS

Most California native people, particularly in the central, northeastern, and southern areas, lived intimately with perhaps two to five hundred persons in small well-defined territories under the traditional authority of a leader who almost always was a male. Kroeber and others since have referred to these autonomous land-owning groups as "tribelets," or as village-communities.[12] In most cases, the residents of such communities lived independently of any authority other than that of the local chief or headman, whose primary responsibilities were to oversee the economic

Drawn by José Cardero, an artist with the Spanish voyage of discovery
that visited California in 1791 under the command of Alejandro Malaspina,
India y Indio de Monterey depicts Esselen or Rumsen Costanoan natives
encountered at the presidio or Mission Carmel. One of the earliest images
of California Indians derived from direct observation, it shows the woman
wearing the traditional native costume of braided tule skirt, buckskin rear
apron, and sea-otter skin robe. *Courtesy Museo Naval, Madrid. Photograph
courtesy Iris Engstrand.*

life of the group, assist in settling disputes, and represent the group to outsiders. Among the Ohlone or Costanoan of the San Francisco Bay Area, these tribelet territories extended some eight to twelve miles in diameter and contained populations of some two hundred to four hundred individuals. Where resources were particularly abundant, as in the Pomo territories around Clear Lake, and in the coastal Chumash areas, population densities tended be high and the overall territory claimed by the tribelet might be relatively compact. The entire Pomo-speaking population lived in some seventy-two tribelets, ranging in population from about 125 to about 1,500 persons each and occupying an average territory of perhaps one hundred square miles. Achomawi tribelet communities of northeast California needed larger territiories to support their more dispersed hunting and gathering activities.

Although a great deal of regional variation existed, tribelets tended to include a central village where the headman lived and that served as the political and religious center for several smaller settlements nearby. Headmen had more power, and in general status differences tended to be more pronounced, in tribelet areas particularly favored by abundant food resources and materials sought by other groups in trade. Yet there was variation. The Yokuts and Western Mono of the San Joaquin Valley and Sierra Foothills lived in an area of abundant food resources, but appeared to Anna Gayton as egalitarian in their social and property relationships:

> Though wealth was regarded as desirable, and a wealthy man was respected for his possessions, the actual range of financial extremes was not great. There was no wealthy class. The annual mourning ceremonies at which much property was destroyed and more distributed among the attendants, dispossessed a bereaved family of such wealth as it might have accumulated.[13]

Among the Yurok of the northwest, an area characterized by abundant maritime resources and large, sedentary villages, an aristocratic social stratum existed, and property differences between the *peyerk,* or "aristocrats," and the "commoners" were pronounced.

Given the smallness of many tribelet territories, the lower end of the range being around fifty square miles, the inhabitants knew each other, their terrain, resources, and boundaries exceedingly well. Robert Heizer once commented that "California Indians, while perhaps knowing individuals in neighboring tribelets, for the most part lived out their lives mainly within their own limited and familiar territory. Nothing illustrates more the deep-seated provincialism and attachment to the place of their birth . . . than the abundantly documented wish for persons who had died away from home to have their bodies (or their ashes . . .) returned for burial at their natal village."[14] In some cases, as among the Pomo and Yokuts, tribelet boundaries appear to have been somewhat flexible. Among the Maidun peoples of the Sacramento Valley and the Sierra, wrote Roland Dixon, "the area owned by each

community was very definite, and its exact limits were known and marked. . . . Each
tribe or group of communities kept its boundary-lines constantly patrolled by men,
who were to see that no poaching took place, and that the rights of each tribe were
respected."[15] Stephen Powers recorded an extraordinary early account of how Mat-
tole mothers of northwest California imparted the significance of tribelet boundaries
and geography to their children:

> Besides the coyote stories with which gifted [women] amuse their children, and
> which are common throughout all this region, there prevails among the Mattoal a cus-
> tom which might almost be dignified with the name of geographical study. In the first
> place, it is necessary to premise that the boundaries of all the tribes on Humboldt Bay,
> Eel River, Van Dusen's Fork, and in fact everywhere, are marked with the greatest pre-
> cision, being defined by certain creeks, canyons, bowlders, conspicuous trees, springs,
> etc., each one of which objects has its own individual name. It is perilous for an Indian
> to be found outside of his tribal boundaries, wherefore it stands him well in hand to
> make himself acquainted with the same early in life. Accordingly the [women] teach
> these things to their children in a kind of sing-song. . . . Over and over, time and
> again, they rehearse all these bowlders, etc., describing each minutely and by name, with
> its surroundings. Then when the children are old enough, they take them around to
> beat the bounds . . . and so wonderful is the Indian memory naturally, and so faithful
> has been their instruction, that the little shavers generally recognize the objects from
> the descriptions of them previously given by their mothers.[16]

Although tribelet communities knew their boundaries and often were protective
of them, neighboring groups had many customary understandings by which they
could visit nearby areas for hunting, gathering, and trade. Thomas Jefferson
Mayfield, a white man who was raised in a Choynumni Yokuts tribelet in the 1850s,
recalled two long tule rafting trips to the territory of a Tachi Yokuts tribelet on Tulare Lake, where they hunted ducks and rabbits and caught fish:

> After I had been with the Indians periodically several months the time came for
> them to make one of their annual pilgrimages to Tulare Lake. I am sure that it was their
> habit to go there yearly. The lake shore was held by the Tachi tribe, but the tribe I was
> with was quite friendly with the Tachis, and they made no objection to our using the
> lake shore. . . .
> Occasionally we met or saw Indians from other tribes along the river. They were all
> friendly and seemed to take our trip as a matter of course. I remember that once a party
> of three of these Indians rode with us all day.
> At the lake we made a permanent camp on some high ground along a slough. I be-
> lieve that they had used this place before, as one of the mokees [women] dug up a mor-
> tar and pestle that had been buried there previously.

We found the lake Indians near us living in some ways quite differently from the Indians at Sycamore creek. They talked enough of our language that we could understand them readily, but the rest of their life differed more than the language.[17]

POLITICAL LEADERSHIP

The chief or headman throughout most of California was generally responsible for overseeing the production, distribution, and conservation of food and other material resources in his kinship, village, or tribelet domain. Although most such leaders were male, exceptions did occur, one of which Cabrillo reported among the Chumash in November of 1542: "The chief of these towns is an old Indian woman who came on board the ships and slept two nights . . . many others doing the same."[18] The chieftainship was usually hereditary, passing generally from father to son but, as in the case of the Northern Sierra Miwok, sometimes to a daughter in lieu of a son, or in the case of the Central Pomo of the Yokaya tribelet, "from a man to his sister's son."[19] In some cases, including the Central Pomo and Eastern Coastal Chumash, several chiefs might exercise authority in a particular territory. All groups, even those that emphasized hereditary succession, allowed room for the selection or de-selection of particular individuals.

Particular headmen were known to invite the members of nearby tribelet communities for special occasions such as the completion of a new roundhouse, but despite gatherings initiated by tribelet chiefs for celebrations, for ritual events, and for trade, leadership was primarily local, without formally structured political alliances like the famous League of the Iroquois, which extended over a vast area centered in northern New York. Nevertheless, Lowell Bean and others have cautioned against overlooking the degree of intertribelet organization that could be documented in the post-contact period: "Two or more tribelets were sometimes federated under a single political authority," as among the Shasta, Miwok, Chumash, Gabrielino, Tipai-Ipai, and Salinan, although local groups generally "were interconnected by temporary, nonformalized economic exchanges and by formal secular associations such as the trade feast partners."[20] When Lieutenant José María Estudillo visited the Yokuts headman, "Captain" Joasps, in 1819, he found at least 2,600 people from numerous surrounding tribelets who had assembled in his village for a mourning feast:

I was urged many times to remain with them over night, which was that of the weeping, and for the dance on the following day. . . . Their captain Joasps, as I have said, is making the funeral celebration which was carried out . . . in the following way. They gathered in little groups with faces blackened, and giving most lamentable wails with exaggerated grief, so they passed the night. On the day following they washed themselves, and painted, and formed dancing groups by rancherias. The master of the fiesta, after giving them a feast of fish caught in the river, deer meat, venison . . . and antelope . . . that there are in abundance, flour and mush, concluded by paying them all with beads and baskets, and they left for their homes.[21]

By such gatherings, influential local chiefs cultivated good relations with their counterparts in other autonomous tribelets, thus raising their currency at home while also facilitating marriage and trade relations and therefore neighborliness between these groups.

SHAMANS

Throughout California, as elsewhere in North America, communities recognized individuals, generally men but often women, who had particularly strong rapport with spirits that in turn imparted distinctive abilities to their human allies, such as the power to cure or to cause illness or death, to predict the future, to influence outcomes in hunting and war, to control weather, plant production, and natural events, and to transform themselves into spirit forms. Such individuals, referred to by anthropologists as shamans, helped reinforce conformity to community expectations through their ability to cause and cure illness. To behave poorly was to invite misfortune. Gayton's account of Yokuts shamanism describes beliefs and practices known throughout most of California:

> The most common cause of illness was believed to be the intrusion into the body of some foreign object which had been projected by the evil magic of a doctor. The extraction of this object by cutting and sucking theoretically constituted a cure. The intruding object was always exhibited upon its extraction by the curing shaman; it might be a few hairs, finger-nail clippings, insects, a blood clot, the moustache of a mountain lion, and so on.[22]

Roland Dixon wrote of the Maidu in 1905 that "the shaman was, and still is, perhaps the most important individual. . . . the word of the shaman has great weight: as a class they are regarded with much awe, and as a rule are obeyed much more than the chief."[23]

All shamans owed their power to a dream helper, often perceived as an animal, who came invited or uninvited in a dream or vision to give them a particular mandate and who also could take it away. Depending upon the particular tribe, the ability to become a shaman could be more or less influenced by a hereditary predisposition. In the case of the Northern Maidu, for example, "if either of a man's parents is a shaman, he must inevitably be one also," typically after the parent died.[24] Maidu women also could inherit this predisposition. The dream spirits that appeared to both male and female shamans had been dreamed of by their parents and stayed in

A Pomo shaman conducts a curing ceremonial in a watercolor executed at Bodega Bay in 1818 by the Russian artist Mikhail Tikhanov. One of a series of drawings produced by Tikhanov while serving on a round-the-world expedition commanded by his countryman, V. M. Golovnin, the picture is rich in carefully observed ethnographic detail and is the earliest-known image of a Native California shaman. *Courtesy Art Research Museum, St. Petersburg, Russia. Image courtesy Anchorage Museum of History and Art.*

their families for generations. As the following account of the Maidu Henry Shipes's dream will attest, people with shamanistic powers might not welcome the call:

> In this dream Henry Shipes realized that the shamans had discovered that he was possessed of great supernatural power, and that they were trying to kill him because he had repulsed their efforts to coerce him [to join them]. In his dreaming he prayed for good luck so that no shaman could force him to become one, and for good luck against witchcraft. After this a Maidu shaman from Genessee appeared in his dream. The shaman came to his bed and stood over him. He told Henry Shipes that he was going to die. Henry did not answer him, but he knew certainly that this man was an enemy. . . . When the shaman left the room, a white man with a long white beard reaching to his knees appeared in the corner of Henry Shipes's room. This man was Dr. Sun. Dr. Sun came across the room to Henry and lifted him from the bed. This to Henry

was a sign that he would become well. . . . Dr. Sun killed the shamans who were threatening Henry Shipes. The dream ended; Henry recovered from his illness, and went about his normal life.[25]

Such helpers could assist the shaman in curing or injuring others and in protecting themselves from attacks by other shamans.

In addition to being assisted by their dream helpers who spoke through them, shamans sometimes spoke in the voices of the intruding enemy spirits. In the Wintu case, an intruding spirit might speak another Indian language that an interpreter would translate for the patient and for others present at the curing ritual. Chiefs and shamans often worked together to reinforce each other's interests. Gayton noted that "In every tribe [among the Western Mono and Yokuts of the plains and foothills of the San Joaquin Valley] a powerful shaman was the close friend and associate of the chief." George Dick, who was of both Yokuts and Western Mono descent, told Gayton that "If a man, especially a rich one, did not join in a fandango [dance], the chief and his doctors would plan to make this man or some member of his family sick" by a magical "air-shot."[26] The shaman would then be called to cure the afflicted individual and divide with the chief the obligatory pay for his services. Fear of illness caused by shamans thus worked as a social sanction, in this case against tribelet members who did not contribute to the chief's social activities.

THE PERSON

Given the small territories and the close ties of kinship and marriage that connected tribelet members through succeeding numbers of generations, Native Californians knew each other and their physical landscapes intimately. In her effort to understand what may be described as the sense of self, or the person, among Wintu speakers of the northern Sacramento Valley, Dorothy Lee observed that individuals tended to identify themselves in the context of, rather than apart from, the group:

When speaking about Wintu culture, we cannot speak of the self *and* society, but rather of the self *in* society.[27]

A study of the grammatical expression of identity, relationship and otherness, shows that the Wintu conceive of the self not as strictly delimited or defined, but as a concentration, at most, which gradually fades and gives place to the other. Most of what is other for us, is for the Wintu completely or partially or upon occasion, identified with the self. For example, the Wintu do not use *and* when referring to individuals who are, or live or act together. Instead of analysing the *we* into: *John and I,* they say *John we,* using the John as a specification. Only when two individuals who are not already in relatedness are brought together, is the *and* used.[28]

When Lee asked Sadie Marsh, a Wintu woman, to speak of her life story, Marsh framed her account in terms of her relationships in a cross-generational community:

> When I asked Sadie Marsh for her autobiography, she told me a story about her first husband, based on hearsay. When I insisted on her own life history, she told me a story which she called, "my story." The first three quarters of this, approximately, are occupied with the lives of her grandfather, her uncle and her mother before her birth; finally, she reaches the point where she was "that which was in my mother's womb," and from then on she speaks of herself, also.[29]

Anthropologists Burt and Ethel Aginsky interviewed Tom Jimerson, a Pomo man who in 1935 was said to be 112 years old, and therefore lived during the periods of early Russian, as well as Mexican and American, colonization. He confirmed in a different way the point made by Lee about the strong identification of self with community:

> What is man? A man is nothing. Without his family he is of less importance than that bug crossing the trail, of less importance than spit or dung. At least they can be used to help poison a man. A man must be with his family to amount to anything with us. If he had nobody else to help him, the first trouble he got into he would be killed by his enemies because there would be no relatives to help him fight the poison of the other group. No woman would marry him because her family would not let her marry a man with no family. . . . Each person was nothing; but as a group, joined by blood, the individual knew that he would get the support of all his relatives if anything happened. He also knew that if he was a bad person the head man of his family would pay another tribe to kill him so that there would be no trouble.[30]

As one without a family was nothing, so one who left the community had in a sense died. A nineteenth-century Nisenan chief of Auburn known as Captain Tom conducted a funeral burning ritual for his son after he was arrested and taken away to prison for ten years. Captain Tom and his family "mourned for Dick as for one dead," then proceeded to gather together "all the things that had ever belonged to him, carried them out to the family burning-ground, erected a pyre, and placed them on it." When Dick's brother died a few years later, they sprinkled his ashes on Dick's funeral pyre that the brother's 'spirit' might carry the remains of Dick's burned possessions to wherever he had been conveyed.[31] Once the mourners cremated or buried the body, the spirit might remain in the area for a brief time then depart to a distant homeland for the dead. For the Coast Miwok this home was in the ocean beyond Point Reyes toward the west, "All [the dead] went there, good and bad." They were said to "go to be with Coyote where the sun goes down."[32] Although the dead might return in forms such as owls, coyotes, foxes, and whirlwinds, their relatives feared and generally did not welcome them. So great was the separation between the worlds of the living and dead that people would not even mention the names of the deceased. Father Juan Amoros wrote of the Ohlone at Mission San Carlos Borromeo in 1814:

> these natives consider it very disrespectful to talk about their deceased parents and relatives. Thus a boy whose parents have died when he was quite young has no one to tell him the names of his father, grandfather or kinsfolk. In the course of a quarrel for greater vituperation they exclaim: "Your father is dead," and the flame of their fury grows greater. So they have no means of remembering their ancestors. When someone dies his clothing and belongings are burned.[33]

Similarly, "If some one in a group of merry talkers . . . inadvertantly mentions the name," wrote Powers of the Wintu, "there falls upon all an awful silence. . . . shuddering and heart-sickening terror . . . at the utterance of that fearful word."[34]

Details regarding the behavior, final journey, and destinations of the dead vary greatly in detail from one region to another. C. Hart Merriam recorded an Eastern Sierra Miwok account of the soul's movements and transformations:

> When a person dies, *Oo'leus* the heart-spirit remains in the dead body for four days. During these four days everyone is quiet and the children are not allowed to run about or make a noise. On the morning of the fourth day the people sprinkle ashes on the ground over the buried basket of burnt bones—or over the grave if the corpse were buried instead of burned. On that day the heart spirit leaves the body in the invisible form of *Hinnan Soos* the Wind Spirit, or *Soo-les'-ko* the Ghost, and proceeds westward. That night it may come back in *Soo-koo'-me* the Owl, or in some other animal; so look out.
>
> Some Ghosts are good, others bad. At last they all go to the ocean and cross over on a long pole to the Roundhouse of the dead, where they remain.[35]

THE NATURAL WORLD

Native Californians knew the sounds and habits of neighboring wildlife and understood animals to participate in the social life of humans, the dead, and numerous other personages known particularly through myth. When stalking deer, for example, hunters throughout California knew how to imitate the appearance and movements of their prey and a variety of ways to circumvent the deer's ability to smell humans. Mayfield's early account of Choynumne Yokuts portrays one widespread stalking technique:

> When I was quite young the Indians used to kill many deer by stalking and shooting them with the bow and arrow. For this sort of hunting they prepared the horns and hide of the deer and placed it over them. The head of the deer was hollowed out and fitted over the head of the hunter. The skin covered the back of the hunter. A short stick

was carried in the right hand, and was used, when the hunter bent forward, to imitate the forelegs of a deer. The bow and arrows were carried in the left hand. They would imitate a deer feeding and rubbing his horns on the brush and many other actions of the deer until they approached quite close to the game. Sometimes the hunter would work an hour to get just ten feet closer to the deer.[36]

Across North America, including all of California, native people believed themselves to be capable of communicating with animals through speech, thought, and dreams. Shamans, as we have seen, could speak the language of their dream helpers and of hostile spirits whom they confronted in curing ceremonies. Others, too, had animal spirit helpers, as well as the ability to communicate with various living creatures. Maria Copa, a Coast Miwok, recalled that "My grandmother used to say that when you saw a snake, it would talk. . . . She would say to it, 'Go on, don't bother me.'"[37] Roxie Peconom, a Maidu woman born near Susanville in the mid-nineteenth century, would talk with a particular kind of bird (killdeer) each morning to start the day. The killdeer would tell her how old and unattractive she was, and she would praise its singing and beauty.[38]

The Sierra and Coast Miwok, Mono, and some Yokuts groups classified people according to their relationships to animal species. The Central Sierra Miwok of Tuolumne County, for example, were divided into two groups based on descent through the father. One was known as the "water" side and the other was known as the "land" or "dry" side. All persons belonged to one or the other following from the side of their father. Those whose fathers belonged to the "water" side were "bullfrog people," and those born into the "land" side were "bluejay people." This binary classification embraced all of nature, including people, animals, and places. For reasons derived from events in their creation mythology, coyote, deer, antelope, beaver, otter, quail, dove, goose, crane, minnow, clouds, rain, and other entities belonged to the "water" side, while tree squirrel, dog, mountain lion, raccoon, raven, flicker, sky, and clear weather, among others, belonged to the "land" side. The grandfather or another near relative named the child shortly after birth with a permanent name that had an implied or actual reference to the creatures or other phenomena that belonged to the child's side. Although the rule was not always followed, people tended to select mates from the side of their mother and would not marry someone from the father's side. By this comprehensive system that included marriage, descent, and certain ritual responsibilities, the Sierra Miwok related themselves to their biological and physical surroundings.[39]

The Miwok also used this binary classification as a way to map space. The Southern Sierra Miwok of Yosemite Valley, for example, referred to all villages and camps north of the Merced River as the "land side" (and also the "grizzly bear side"), and all villages and camps to the south as the "water side" (and also the "coyote side").[40]

In addition to being the source of most food and other material resources, the tribelet territory was alive in a sense through stories told by adults to children. Particular trees, bodies of water, rock formations and other natural features had histories that connected them to the activities of preceding generations of tribelet ancestors and to an even earlier period of non-human occupancy. Frank Latta, a self-defined ethnographer and folklorist who worked extensively with the Yokuts of the San Joaquin Valley, recorded one such account from a Wukchumne husband and wife (I'-chow and Wah-nom'-kot) who were born and raised near Lemon Cove in eastern Tulare County. This legend explains the origin of certain local rock formations including one rock that resembles and once was a giant conical burden basket of the type used by Yokuts women for gathering acorns:

> Long before the *Wuk-chum'-nees* came to *Ti-up'-in-ish*, the old-time bird and animal people lived at the old beginning village of *Sho-no'-yoo* near Lemon Cove. Each year they used to go to *Too-chee'-oo*, which the white people call Squaw Valley, and to *Tah'-low*, now Dunlap Valley. They used an old trail from Woodlake North the same way that the Badger Road leads to General Grant Park.
>
> One time, so long ago that we do not know when, those old-time people named a place near Stokes Mountain. . . . They called it *Ahng'-ush-in*, place of the Acorn Carrying Basket.
>
> Both the old-time people and the *Wuk-chum'-nees* all wanted to be buried at the old village where they were born. Even if they died fifty miles away their people would carry them home to bury them.
>
> Once a man from *Tah'-low*, now Dunlap, died at *Sho-no'-yoo* near Lemon Cove. His people started to carry him to *Tah'-low*. They were scattered along the trail in a line. . . .
>
> Two people were carrying the dead person. One was at his feet and the other at his head. When they came to an Oak tree close to where General Grant Park Road is now, the dead person came alive again. He rose up. All of the people were frightened and turned to stone. The man who had died turned to stone, too.
>
> You can still see the line of rocks where the people were walking along the trail. Our people, the *Wuk-chum'-nees*, have always said that those rocks are the people who were going back to *Tah'-low* with the dead person. Near the North end of the rocks is a saddle-shaped rock that my people told me was the dead man who had risen up.
>
> One of the party was a young girl. She was ahead of the rest and was carrying *Ahng'-ush*, the cone-shaped Acorn Basket. The basket turned to stone too. A large *Ahng'-ush*-shaped rock stands just West of the road about two hundred yards North of the other rocks. Our people told us that this rock was the basket carried by that old-time girl. Because of this rock, the place has always been called *Ahng'-ush-in*.[41]

Isabel Kelly recorded a similar legend of stones that had once been old-time "people" related by Maria Copa, the Coast Miwok woman with intimate knowledge of Marin County.[42]

Leona Morales, a Maidu of Susanville in the Honey Lake Valley area of Lassen County, learned an extensive creation story from her mother, Roxie Peconom, who was born nearby. As the "Maker" (K'odojapem) proceeded in his original journey over the Sierra to the Honey Lake Valley, he paused on the crest of a hill overlooking the Susan River and said, "I'm going to let some nice water out of this mountain, come down the canyon." He drove his stick deep into the earth, and water came rushing out. The springs that he thereby created for humans were used by local Maidu until the city capped them for public use.[43] Through such legends and myths, Native Californians recognized rock formations, mountains, springs, rivers, soil colors, and other natural features as the signs of their predecessors' activities, inscribed in and imparting ancestral meanings to their physical landscapes.

MYTH

Old people, usually men, told the myths, tales, and legends to audiences assembled at night by firelight, almost always during the winter months. As was the case with language, social organization, and material culture, the several culture areas of California differed in some basic respects in their ideas about the creation of the physical world and the arrival of humans with their distinctive cultures. In northwest California, for example, the myths begin with the physical world already present but inhabited by a human-like immortal race that prepared the earth for humans, then disappeared when humans arrived. In central California, creation myths emphasize "the making of the world . . . embodied in a myth postulating an original world of primeval water, in which an already-existing creator (usually an eagle or another raptorial bird) solves the problem of earth-making by the familiar earth-diver method."[44] A Rumsen Ohlone myth begins with a great flood and three "persons," humming-bird, eagle, and coyote, whose actions initiate the beginnings of human culture:

> When this world was finished, the eagle, the humming-bird, and Coyote were standing on the top of Pico Blanco. When the water rose to their feet, the eagle, carrying the humming-bird and Coyote, flew to the Sierra de Gabilan. There they stood until the water went down. Then the eagle sent Coyote down the mountain to see if the world were dry. Coyote came back and said: "The whole world is dry." The eagle said to him: "Go and look in the river. See what there is there." Coyote came back and said: "There is a beautiful girl." The eagle said: "She will be your wife in order that people may be raised again." He gave Coyote a digging implement of abalone shell and a digging stick. Coyote asked: "How will my children be raised?" The eagle would not say. He wanted to see if Coyote was wise enough to know.[45]

Coyote, an important and widespread figure in California mythology, appears as a trickster, fool, and hero in various regional contexts. One of the finest accounts of

Native Californian Coyote stories and of Coyote's role in the events of creation is William Shipley's *The Maidu Indian Myths and Stories of Hanc'ibyjim*. In this book, Shipley retranslated the Maidu texts recorded at the turn of the century by Roland Dixon from Tom Young, a half Maidu and half Atsugewi man who was then living at Genesee in Plumas County. At the beginning of Tom Young's creation story, Earthmaker and Coyote are floating on an earth completely covered with water, looking for any sign of land where they and others might live. At last they saw "something like a bird's nest," and Earthmaker said, "It would be good if it were a little bigger. . . . I wonder how I might stretch it apart a little." Then Earthmaker stretched it "to where the day breaks. . . . [then] to the south. . . . [then] to the place where the sun goes down. . . . [then] to the North Country. . . . [and finally] to the rim of the world." Coyote and Meadowlark admired what Earthmaker had done and suggested various improvements. Coyote then challenged Earthmaker for advantage, with Coyote getting "the best of Earthmaker" and making him very angry. Earthmaker then "went away from there. . . . because all his work was done."[46]

The long and ongoing contest between Earthmaker and Coyote was not one that can be reduced to good overcoming evil, however. Earthmaker, although creative and benevolent, was often incapable of outwitting or defeating his adversary, while Coyote often mourned his victories, as when he overruled Earthmaker by introducing death into the world and then regretted it when his own son died. Earthmaker and Coyote, although opponents and differing in their respective wisdom and moral weight, are not altogether polarized. Coyote is clever, selfish, self-destructive, and comical, while Earthmaker is more group- than self-oriented and therefore heroic, but also incapable of defending himself at times. It is not difficult to read into their conflicts a morality tale in which Earthmaker, the architect of a benevolent parental order, struggles constantly with Coyote to subdue his selfish desires and ambitions with no expectation that either side will fully carry the day.

PERCEPTIONS OF FOREIGNERS

The first known written account about foreigners by a Native Californian is that by Pablo Tac, a Luiseño neophyte born at Mission San Luis Rey in 1822. During a visit to Rome, where he died in 1837, Tac wrote a record of Indian life at that mission in which he included a tradition of what was probably the arrival of the missionary expedition in 1772:

> When the missionary arrived in our country with a small troop, our captain and also the others were astonished, seeing them from afar, but they did not run away or seize arms to kill them, but having sat down, they watched them. But when they drew near, then the captain got up (for he was seated with the others) and met them. They halted,

A drawing made at Monterey in 1791 by Tomás de Suría, an artist with the Malaspina expedition, *The Indian Manner of Combat* depicts native warriors defending themselves against a Spanish dragoon armed with a lance and a bull-hide shield. The thatched hut and native costumes are typical of those of Rumsen and other Costanoan peoples. Although California Indians often fled in fear when they first encountered Europeans, they also were capable of vigorously defending themselves. *Courtesy Museo Naval, Madrid. Photograph courtesy Iris Engstrand.*

and the missionary then began to speak, the captain saying perhaps in his language. . . . "What is it that you seek here? Get out of our country!" But they did not understand him, and they answered him in Spanish, and the captain began with signs, and the Fernandino, understanding him, gave him gifts and in this manner made him his friend.[47]

Beginning with the initial visits of Cabrillo, Francis Drake, Junípero Serra, and Gaspar de Portolá, California Indians responded to foreigners in a variety of ways, often with fear. In some cases, as with the Cabrillo expedition, southern coastal Native Californians communicated through sign language that they already knew of people who looked and were armed like them who were moving through the interior. A Salinan woman named Agueda told the Franciscans at the founding of Mission San Antonio that people dressed like them had flown over their country at an earlier time:

According to what those friars told me, there was among those Indians a woman named Agueda, so ancient that in appearance she seemed to be about a hundred years old. She came, asking the fathers to baptize her. When they inquired of her why she wanted to become a Christian, she answered that when she was young she heard her parents tell of a man coming to their lands who was dressed in the same habit the missionaries wore. He did not walk through the land, but flew. He told them the same things the missionaries were now preaching.[48]

In several known cases Native Californians interpreted Europeans and other foreigners within the categories of their indigenous mythology. Robert Heizer, for example, speculated that the responses of Coast Miwok people to Drake's presence in 1579 suggest that they "looked upon the English as the dead returned" from their home at sea.[49] Hugo Reid, an early settler near Mission San Gabriel who was married to a Gabrielino woman, wrote that when Indians in that area first saw the Spanish, they "were sadly afraid. . . . Thinking them gods, the women ran to the brush, and hid themselves, while the men put out the fires in their huts."[50] When the Kashaya Pomo first saw a sailing ship on their horizon they thought it was a giant bird that portended the end of the world. Essie Parrish, a Kashaya Pomo healer and prophetess recounted this story as recently as 1958:

In the old days, before the white people came up here, there was a boat sailing on the ocean from the south. Because before that they had never seen a boat, they said, "Our world must be coming to an end. Couldn't we do something? This big bird floating on the ocean is from somewhere, probably from up high. Let us plan a feast. Let us have a dance." They followed its course with their eyes to see what it would do. Having done so, they promised Our Father [a feast] saying that destruction was upon them.[51]

In 1906, the anthropologist Samuel Barret asked several Wintu, including two shamans who lived in the western foothills of the Sacramento Valley, what they thought of the recent earthquake that had devastated San Francisco. Interestingly, one shaman saw it as a sign that the world was about to be leveled "like the Wintun abode of the dead." The other saw it as a continuation of the stretching process, also present in the Maidu creation story, that made the world large enough for all the people who would live on it:

The world was originally much smaller than at present. As the Indian population in times past increased, the earth was rent and stretched by Coyote Old Man, the southern Wintun culture-hero, in order to make room for the newcomers. . . . the disturbances were the forerunners of another stretching of the earth, this time in order to make room for the ever-increasing white population. He was of the opinion, however, that immediately all the Indians are dead, which will be very soon, according to him, this great catastrophe will totally destroy all things on earth and render it like the Wintun abode of the dead.[52]

A Wintun woman, Kate Luckie, expressed to Cora Du Bois how she understood the physical world to feel as a consequence of having been taken over by a people who did not understand it or treat it well. Her statement conveys how appalled California hunter-gatherers were by the massive environmental upheavals caused by hunting, mining, logging, and agriculture in the American period and how closely and responsibly California hunter-gatherers identified with the animals, plants, and physical terrains of their tribelet worlds. The references to the coming of water predict a return of the flood that began the world and that also will end it:

When the Indians all die, then God will let the water come down from the north. Everyone will drown. That is because the white people never cared for land or deer or bear. When we Indians kill meat, we eat it all up. When we dig roots, we make little holes. When we build houses, we make little holes. When we burn grass for grasshoppers [for food], we don't ruin things. We shake down acorns and pine nuts. We don't chop down the trees. We only use dead wood. But the white people plow up the ground, pull up the trees, kill everything. The tree says, "Don't. I am sore. Don't hurt me." But they chop it down and cut it up. The spirit of the land hates them. They blast out trees and stir it up to its depths. They saw up the trees. That hurts them. . . . They blast rocks and scatter them on the earth. The rock says, "Don't! You are hurting me." But the white people pay no attention. When the Indians use rocks, they take little round ones for their cooking. The white people dig deep long tunnels. . . . eventually the water will come.[53]

This chapter began with the observation that scholars infer their understanding of California peoples in the pre-colonial past from post-colonial testimonies, from "downstream" accounts written after the Spanish, Mexican, Russian, and American expansions had overrun their lives. Despite the enormous consequences of their physical and social displacement in the eighteenth and nineteenth centuries, many communities survived to some degree, consulting their past as they navigated the present. From the first sightings of Europeans until this time near the end of the twentieth century, Native California peoples have continued to think about new and unprecedented historical experiences in ways that are informed by indigenous ideas. Myths, dreams, family memories, legends associated with places, and ideas about illness, health, and the afterlife guide them still in roundhouse gatherings and in the non-Indian world where they now find their way. Some expect that new dreamers yet to be born will seek and find spirit helpers for healing and for direction in the centuries ahead.

NOTES

1. The most authoritative overviews of the California culture area include A. L. Kroeber, *Handbook of the Indians of California* (Washington: Smithsonian Institution, Bureau of American Ethology, 1925); *Handbook of North American Indians: Volume 8, California*, ed. Robert F. Heizer, (Washington: Smithsonian Institution, 1978); Robert F. Heizer and Albert Elsasser, *The Natural World of the California Indians* (Berkeley: University of California Press, 1980); the chapters by Michael J. Moratto ("The California Culture Area"), Richard A. Gould ("The Indians of Northwest California"), Clinton M. Blount and Dorothea J. Theodoratus ("Central California Indians"), Lowell John Bean ("Indians of Southern California"), and Robert L. Bettinger ("Native Life in Desert California: The Great Basin and Its Aboriginal Inhabitants") in *Masterkey* 59 special edition, *People of California*, nos. 2 and 3 (Summer/Fall 1985): 4–11, 12–21, 22–31, 32–41, 42–50; Lowell J. Bean, "Indians of California: Diverse and Complex Peoples," *California History* LXXI (Fall 1992): 302–23; and Lowell J. Bean and Sylvia Brakke Vane, "The California Culture Area," in Daniel L. Boxberger, ed., *Native Americans: An Ethnohistorical Approach* (Dubuque: Kendall/Hunt Publishing Company, 1990), 265–300. Two basic source books include R. F. Heizer and M. A. Whipple, eds., *The California Indians: A Source Book* (Berkeley: University of California Press, 2nd ed., 1971), and Lowell John Bean and Thomas C. Blackburn, eds., *Native Californians: A Theoretical Retrospective* (Menlo Park: Ballena Press, 1976).

I am grateful to Kent Lightfoot and Ottis Parrish for reading and commenting helpfully on the original draft of this essay. I appreciate their suggestions and am responsible for any inaccuracies and misunderstandings that may be found herein.

2. Hubert Howe Bancroft, *The Works of Hubert Howe Bancroft, Volume 1: The Native Races; Volume 1, Wild Tribes* (San Francisco: A. L. Bancroft & Company, 1883), 325.

3. Alfred L. Kroeber, "The Nature of Land-Holding Groups in Aboriginal California," in Robert F. Heizer, ed., *Aboriginal California: Three Studies in Culture History* (Berkeley: University of California Press, 1963), 120.

4. Kent G. Lightfoot, "Long-Term Development in Complex Hunter-Gatherer Societies: Recent Perspectives from the Pacific Coast of North America," *Journal of Archaeological Research* I (1993): 185.

5. For additional sources on the emergence and nature of social complexity, see Jeanne E. Arnold, "Complex Hunter-Gatherer-Fishers of Prehistoric California: Chiefs, Specialists, and Maritime Adaptations of the Channel Islands," *American Antiquity* 57 (1992): 60–84, and "Organizational Transformations: Power and Labor among Complex Hunter-Gatherers and Other Intermediate Societies," in *Emergent Complexity: The Evolution of Intermediate Societies*, ed. Jeanne E. Arnold (International Monographs in Prehistory Archaeological Series 9, 1996), 59–73; J. M. Beaton, "Extensification and Intensification in Central California Prehistory," *Antiquity* 65 (1991): 946–52; Madonna L. Moss and Jon M. Erlandson, "Reflections on North American Pacific Coast Prehistory," *Journal of World Prehistory* 9 (1995): 1–45. The best up-to-date source on environmental adaptations is *Before the Wilderness: Environmental Management by Native Californians*, ed. Thomas C. Blackburn and M. Kat Anderson (Menlo Park: Ballena Press, 1993). For recent sources on religion, world-view, and myth, see Lowell John Bean, ed., *California Indian Shamanism* (Menlo Park: Ballena Press, 1992); *December's Child: A Book of Chumash Oral Narratives, Collected by J. P. Harrington*, ed. Thomas

C. Blackburn (Berkeley: University of California Press, 1975); Michael Kearney, *World View* (Novato: Chandler & Sharp Publishers, 1984), 147–69; and William Shipley, *The Maidu Indian Myths and Stories of Hanc'ibyjim* (Berkeley: Heyday Books, 1991). Three works that address gender and particularly women include Albert L. Hurtado, *Indian Survival on the California Frontier* (New Haven: Yale University Press, 1988); Victoria Brady, Sarah Crome, and Lyn Reese, "Resist! Survival Tactics of Indian Women," *California History* LXIII (Spring 1984): 140–51; and Victoria D. Patterson, "Evolving Gender Roles in Pomo Society," in *Women and Power in Native North America,* ed. Laura F. Klein and Lillian A. Ackerman (Norman: University of Oklahoma Press, 1995), 126–45. For new research on health and illness, see Phillip L. Walker and Travis Hudson, *Chumash Healing: Changing Health and Medical Practices in an American Indian Society* (Banning: Malki Museum Press, 1993); Phillip L. Walker and John R. Johnson, "Effects of Contact on the Chumash Indians," in *Disease and Demography in the Americas,* ed. John W. Verano and Douglas H. Ubelaker (Washington: Smithsonian Institution Press, 1992), 127–39; and Jon M. Erlandson and Kevin Bartoy, "Cabrillo, the Chumash, and Old World Diseases," *Journal of California and Great Basin Anthropology* 17 (1995): 153–73. Three new books on the impact of missions on Native Californians include Douglas Monroy, *Thrown among Strangers: The Making of Mexican Culture in Frontier California* (Berkeley: University of California Press, 1990), Robert H. Jackson and Edward Castillo, *Indians, Franciscans, and Spanish Colonization: The Impact of the Mission System on California Indians* (Albuquerque: University of New Mexico Press, 1995), and Randall Milliken, *A Time of Little Choice: The Disintegration of Tribal Culture in the San Francisco Bay Area, 1769–1810* (Menlo Park: Ballena Press, 1995). For new research on the Pomo-Russian interaction at Fort Ross colony, see Kent G. Lightfoot, T. A. Wake, and A. M. Schiff, *The Archaeology and Ethnohistory of Fort Ross, California, Volume 1: Introduction* (Berkeley: Contributions to the University of California Archaeological Research Facility 49, 1991). Given the importance of acorn processing to California hunter-gatherers, an important literature has grown on this subject. Five basic sources include C. Hart Merriam, "The Acorn, A Possibly Neglected Source of Food," *National Geographic* 34 (August 1918): 129–37; E. W. Gifford, "California Balanophagy," in *Essays in Anthropology Presented to A. L. Kroeber in Celebration of His Sixtieth Birthday, June 11, 1936* (Berkeley: University of California Press, 1936), 87–98; Bev Ortiz, *It Will Live Forever: Traditional Yosemite Indian Acorn Preparation* (Berkeley: Heyday Books, 1991); Helen McCarthy, "Managing Oaks and the Acorn Crop," in Blackburn and Anderson, *Before the Wilderness,* 213–28; Glen Martin, "Keepers of the Oaks," *Discover* (August 1996): 44–50.

6. Alfred L. Kroeber, "Culture Element Distributions, III: Area and Climax," *University of California Publications in American Archaeology and Ethnology* 37 (1936): 101–16.

7. For a review of pottery use in California, with substantial bibliographies, see the chapters by Joanne M. Mack ("Siskiyou Utility Ware: Hunter-Gatherer Pottery, It's Not Just For Cooking"), Jerald J. Johnson ("Cosumnes Brownware: A Pottery Type Centered on the Lower Cosumnes and Adjacent Sacramento Rivers in Central California"), Thomas L. Jackson ("Prehistoric Ceramics of the Southwestern Sierra Nevada, California"), William J. Wallace ("Another Look at Yokuts Pottery-Making"), and Suzanne Griset ("Historic Transformations of Tizon Brown Ware in Southern California") in *Hunter-Gatherer Pottery From The Far West,* ed. Joanne M. Mack, in *Nevada State Museum Anthropological Papers* 23 (1990): 123–30, 145–58, 159–70, 171–78, 179–200.

8. Jeanne E. Arnold, "Organizational Transformations: Power and Labor among Complex

Hunter-Gatherers and Other Intermediate Societies," in Arnold, *Emergent Complexity,* 66–68.

9. Lowell J. Bean and Harry W. Lawton, "Some Explanations for the Rise of Cultural Complexity in Native California With Comments on Proto-Agriculture and Agriculture," in Blackburn and Anderson, *Before the Wilderness,* 35.

10. California Great Basin groups such as the Northern Paiute, Washo, Owens Valley Paiute, Western Shoshone, Kawaiisu, and Southern Paiute are covered with extensive bibliographies in *Handbook of North American Indians,* Volume 11: *Great Basin,* ed. Warren L. D'Azevedo (Washington: Smithsonian Institution, 1986). See also Francis A. Riddell, "Honey Lake Paiute Ethnography," in *Nevada State Museum Occasional Papers 3,* ed. Donald R. Tuohy (1978): 1–116.

11. Two basic sources on language classification, with references pointing to the history of research on California Indian languages, include William F. Shipley, "Native Languages of California," in Heizer, *Handbook of North American Indians:* Volume 8, 80–90, and Leanne Hinton, *Flutes of Fire: Essays on California Indian Languages* (Berkeley: Heyday Books, 1994).

12. For sources on California tribelets, see A. L. Kroeber, "The Nature of Land-Holding Groups in Aboriginal California," in Heizer, ed., *Aboriginal California,* 81–120; Peter H. Kunkel, "The Pomo Kin-Group and the Political Unit in Aboriginal California," *Journal of California Anthropology* 1 (1974): 7–18; Lowell John Bean, "Social Organization," in Heizer, *Handbook of North American Indians,* Volume 8, 673–82; Sally McLendon and Robert L. Oswalt, "Pomo: Introduction," in Heizer, *Handbook of North American Indians,* Volume 8, 274–88; and Milliken, *A Time of Little Choice,* 21–24.

13. A. H. Gayton, "Yokuts-Mono Chiefs and Shamans," *University of California Publications in American Archaeology and Ethnology* 24 (1930): 372.

14. Robert F. Heizer, "Natural Forces and World View," in Heizer, *Handbook of North American Indians,* Volume 8, 649.

15. Roland B. Dixon, "The Northern Maidu," *Bulletin of the American Museum of Natural History* 17 (1905): 225.

16. Stephen Powers, "Tribes of California," Department of the Interior. U.S. Geographical and Geological Survey of the Rocky Mountain Region, *Contributions to North American Ethnology* 3 (1877): 109–10 [reprinted by University of California Press, 1976].

17. F. F. Latta *San Joaquin Primeval: Uncle Jeff's Story, A Tale of a San Joaquin Valley Pioneer and His Life With the Yokuts Indians* (Tulare: Tulare Times, 1929), 29, 31. For a new edition, edited by Malcolm Margolin, see Thomas Jefferson Mayfield, *Indian Summer: Traditional Life Among the Choinumne Indians of California's San Joaquin Valley* (Berkeley: Heyday Books and California Historical Society, 1993).

18. Henry R. Wagner, *Juan Rodríguez Cabrillo: Discoverer of the Coast of California* (San Francisco: California Historical Society, 1941), 51.

19. Sally McLendon and Robert L. Oswalt, "Pomo: Introduction," in Heizer, *Handbook of North American Indians,* Volume 8, 276.

20. L. J. Bean, "Social Organization," in Heizer, *Handbook of North American Indians,* Volume 8, 675–76.

21. A. H. Gayton, "Estudillo Among the Yokuts: 1819," in *Essays in Anthropology Presented to A. L. Kroeber in Celebration of His Sixtieth Birthday, June 11, 1936* (Berkeley: University of California Press, 1936), 75–76.

22. Gayton, "Yokuts-Mono Chiefs and Shamans," 390. For some early comparisons see

Maynard Geiger, "Questionnaire of the Spanish Government in 1812 Concerning the Native Culture of the California Mission Indians," *The Americas: A Quarterly Review of Inter-American Cultural History* V (April 1949): 488, and Geiger, "Reply of Mission San Carlos Borromeo to the Questionnaire of the Spanish Government in 1812 Concerning the Native Culture of the California Mission Indians," *The Americas: A Quarterly Review of Inter-American Cultural History* VI (April 1950): 479.

23. Dixon, "The Northern Maidu," *Bulletin of the American Museum of Natural History,* 267.

24. Ibid., 274.

25. Arden R. King, "The Dream Biography of a Mountain Maidu," *Character and Personality* 11 (March 1943): 230–31.

26. Gayton, "Yokuts-Mono Chiefs and Shamans," *University of California Publications in American Archaeology and Ethnology,* 399.

27. Dorothy Lee, *Freedom and Culture* (Englewood Cliffs, NJ: Prentice-Hall, 1959), 132.

28. Ibid., 134.

29. Ibid., 140.

30. Burt W. and Ethel G. Aginsky, *Deep Valley* (New York: Stein and Day Publishers, 1967), 18–19.

31. Stephen Powers, "The Northern California Indians: A Reprinting of 19 Articles on California Indians Originally Published 1872–1877," in *Contributions of the University of California Archaeological Research Facility* 25, ed. Robert F. Heizer (May 1975): 111–12.

32. "Interviews With Tom Smith and Maria Copa: Isabel Kelly's Ethnographic Notes on the Coast Miwok Indians of Marin and Southern Sonoma Counties California," ed. Mary E. T. Collier and Sylvia Barker Thalman, *MAPOM Occasional Papers* 6 (1991): 451.

33. Maynard Geiger and Clement W. Meighan, *As the Padres Saw Them: California Indian Life and Customs as Reported by the Franciscan Missionaries, 1813–1815* (Santa Barbara: Santa Barbara Mission Archive Library, 1976), 59.

34. Powers, "The Northern California Indians: A Reprinting of 19 Articles on California Indians Originally Published 1872–1877," 135–36.

35. C. Hart Merriam, *The Dawn of the World: Myths and Weird Tales Told by the Mewan Indians of California* (Cleveland: The Arthur H. Clark Company, 1910), 218; reprinted with an Introduction by Lowell J. Bean as *The Dawn of the World: Myths and Tales of the Miwok Indians of California* (Lincoln and London: University of Nebraska Press, 1993).

36. Latta, *San Joaquin Primeval,* 40–41.

37. Collier and Thalman, "Interviews With Tom Smith and Maria Copa: Isabel Kelly's Ethnographic Notes on the Coast Miwok Indians of Marin and Southern Sonoma Counties, California," *MAPOM Occasional Papers,* 495.

38. Ron Morales, personal communication, William Simmons fieldnotes, September 2, 1996.

39. Edward Winslow Gifford, "Miwok Moieties," *University of California Publications in American Archaeology and Ethnology* 12 (June 24, 1916): 139–94.

40. C. Hart Merriam, "Indian Village and Camp Sites in Yosemite Valley," *Sierra Club Bulletin* 10 (1917): 202–204.

41. F. F. Latta, *California Indian Folklore* (Shafter, Calif: F. F. Latta, 1936), 67–68.

42. Collier and Thalman, eds., "Interviews With Tom Smith and Maria Copa," 450.

43. Leona Morales, "Maker Story" (1956), tape recording in the possession of Ron Morales.

44. A. H. Gayton, "Areal Affiliations of California Folktales," *American Anthropologist* 37 (October–December 1935): 588 .

45. A. L. Kroeber, "Indian Myths of South Central California," *University of California Publications in American Archaeology and Ethnology* 4 (May 1907): 199.

46. Shipley, *The Maidu Indian Myths and Stories of Hanc'ibyjim*, 20, 62, 63.

47. Minna and Gordon Hewes, eds., "Indian Life and Customs at Mission San Luis Rey," *The Americas: A Quarterly Review of Inter-American Cultural History* IX (July 1952):8.

48. Maynard J. Geiger, trans., *Palou's Life of Fray Junípero Serra* (Washington: Academy of Franciscan History, 1955 [1787]), 112.

49. Robert F. Heizer, *Elizabethan California* (Ramona: Ballena Press, 1974), 75.

50. *The Indians of Los Angeles County: Hugo Reid's Letters of 1852*, ed. Robert F. Heizer, (Los Angeles: Southwest Museum Papers 21, 1968), 69.

51. Robert L. Oswalt, "Kashaya Texts," *University of California Publications in Linguistics* 36 (1974): 247.

52. S. A. Barrett, "Indian Opinions of the Earthquake of April, 1906," *Journal of American Folklore* XIX (1906): 324.

53. Cora Du Bois, "Wintu Ethnography," *University of California Publications in American Archaeology and Ethnology* 36 (1935): 75–76.

4

Seekers of the "Northern Mystery"

European Exploration of California and the Pacific

Iris H. W. Engstrand

HISTORIOGRAPHY

The history of exploration into the Pacific during the sixteenth century is open for continued investigation. Because the early documentation for this subject is approaching five centuries in age and is often difficult to decipher, few researchers have undertaken the task. The Columbus Quincentenary observances brought about significant gains in the details of the Columbian exchange, but these investigations were mainly concentrated in the Atlantic and Caribbean worlds. Although the first European forays into the Pacific took place with Magellan's epic voyage between 1519 and 1522, a similar concentration of scholarly effort in that area has yet to be realized. No one, for example, has yet updated Henry Raup Wagner's *Spanish Voyages to the Northwest Coast of America in the Sixteenth Century,* written in 1929. Recently, a major effort to unravel the story of Juan Rodríguez Cabrillo's life and travels was made by Harry Kelsey (1986), and a number of scholars have worked on the mysteries of Francis Drake's sojourn into the Pacific. W. Michael Mathes has edited a number of primary documents in his *Californiana* series, published in Madrid (1965–1987), but little has been done on the important Manila galleon trade, with the standard work remaining William Lytle Schurz's study of 1939.

Eighteenth-century exploration of the Pacific Coast, on the other hand, has recently received considerable attention from historians in Spain and elsewhere. There is ample documentation concerning these later voyages of explorers such as Juan Pérez, Alejandro Malaspina, and Juan Francisco de la Bodega y Quadra, which were motivated less by dreams of wealth and discovery than by considerations of defensive expansion, reconnaissance, and scientific investigation. The Spaniards involved dealt with Indians mostly on the simple terms of acquaintance, gift exchange, and acquisition of knowledge. The journals kept by expedition members were carefully written, straightforward accounts of first-hand observations that mainly described

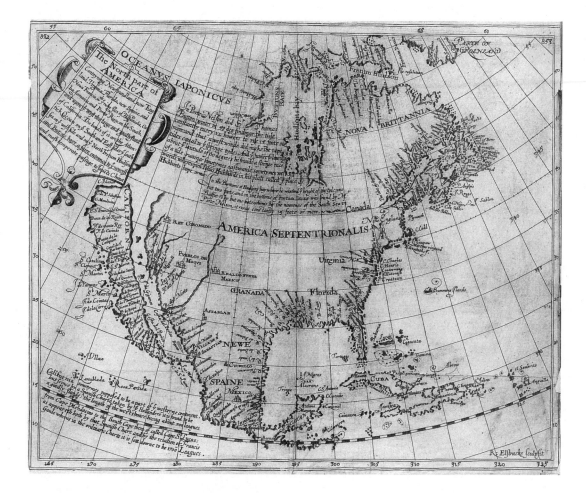

One of the earliest maps to depict California, Henry Briggs's *The North Part of America* was published in London in 1625. "California," proclaims the legend in the lower left, "sometymes supposed to be a part of ye westerne continent, but scince by a Spanish Charte taken by ye Hollanders it is found to be a goodly ilande." Described as an island in a Spanish romance of 1510, *Las sergas de Esplandián,* more than twenty years before Europeans first sighted the desolate lower peninsula, the two Californias—Baja and Alta—were not generally believed to be part of the mainland until the discoveries of Father Eusebio Kino in the late seventeenth and early eighteenth centuries settled the matter. From *Hakluytus Posthumus or Purchas His Pilgrimes* (London, 1625). *Courtesy Bancroft Library.*

rather than speculated about Indian life, customs, or religion. The expeditions devoted to scientific inquiry paid particular attention to geographic features, fauna and
flora, native vocabularies, and items of trade as representative of natural products
rather than as things to be coveted. The fur trade, particularly interesting to the English, Americans, and Russians, commanded less attention among Spaniards. Although many new works have been published both in English and Spanish on the
eighteenth-century voyages, abundant documentation awaits an editor or translator.
The Malaspina expedition alone, which has spawned numerous works in Spain since
its bicentennial years (1989–1994), still has open avenues of research.[1]

Recent authors have speculated about perceptions of "the other" and about the
philosophical differences between Spaniards and their New World counterparts.
Still others have contributed their expertise to evaluating descriptions, identifying
plants and animals with modern nomenclature, and comparing navigational charts
to present-day coastal features and indentations. Unlike the establishment of missions, or the exploitation of Indians, the subject of exploration into the North Pacific
is relatively noncontroversial. It lends itself, nevertheless, to discussions over environmental concerns, the changing landscape, and present Indian concerns. Future research could uncover distribution patterns of fauna and flora during the pre-contact
period, "disappeared" landing sites of early voyages, and perhaps identify other foreign visitors to California.

FIRST VOYAGES INTO THE PACIFIC

With the subjugation of the Aztec empire completed between 1519 and 1521,
Hernán Cortés and his fellow conquerors turned their thoughts toward further exploration.[2] The gold, silver, and jewels of Tenochtitlán naturally led the Spaniards to
believe that other areas of Indian wealth must lie to the south and north of the
Mexican capital. By 1522, Cortés had reached the Pacific in the region of Michoacán,
west of the capital city, and founded the port city of Zacatula. He ordered construction of four ships for northward exploration, but a lack of supplies and skilled
labor slowed progress. Essential European items such as ironwork and rigging had
to be transported slowly overland from Veracruz. Nevertheless, four ships were completed by 1527, just in time to comply with a royal order sending three of them to the
Moluccas to strengthen Spanish claims in the East Indies.

DISCOVERY OF BAJA CALIFORNIA

Cortés, hoping to find another city of wealth comparable to Tenochtitlán, as well as
the long-sought Strait of Anián somewhere in the north Pacific, authorized Diego

Hurtado de Mendoza as commander of two new ships that sailed from Zacatula in 1532 to pursue these objectives. The expedition ended in mutiny, however, so Cortés outfitted a second Pacific venture under his distant cousin Diego de Becerra, a haughty and disagreeable man who was put to death by his crew. Fortún Jiménez, first pilot and leader of the mutiny, took over command of the ship and, sometime in late 1533 or early 1534, reached what he thought was an island, but was actually the peninsula of today's Baja California. Jiménez anchored in a bay, which he named La Paz, and the Spaniards went ashore. A sudden attack by Indians brought the death of Jiménez and twenty of his men; the rest escaped to the Mexican port of Jalisco. The survivors reported that the natives of their newly discovered island were primitive savages but had collected an abundance of pearls.³ Pearls alone gave Cortés sufficient incentive to plan his own expedition. He was joined by a rush of volunteers who knew the captain's reputation for finding wealth.

Three vessels under the command of Cortés reached the Bay of La Paz on May 3, 1535. Naming the bay Santa Cruz, Cortés founded Baja California's first nonnative settlement on the dry, rocky coast. Native hostility and a lack of food made it necessary for two ships to return to the mainland for supplies—one of these was wrecked in the Gulf of California, then called the Red Sea of Cortés. On a second attempt to obtain supplies, the ship that Cortés himself commanded made it back across the treacherous, stormy waters to La Paz; in the meantime, twenty-three of his men died of starvation on Baja California's inhospitable shore. Cortés took the one remaining vessel and returned to Mexico to get further relief. Finally, toward the end of 1536, prospects of success seemed so remote that Cortés sent ships to pick up the surviving colonists. Thus ended the first in a long succession of failed attempts to settle California.⁴

ULLOA SEARCHES FOR THE "NORTHERN MYSTERY"

In 1539, Cortés issued instructions to the final expedition that, under his direction, would seek to pierce the mysteries of the north. Three vessels commanded by Francisco de Ulloa sailed from the port of Acapulco in July of that year; one, the tiny *Santo Tomás,* was wrecked in the stormy waters of the Gulf of California before reaching La Paz. Ulloa's fleet, reduced to the 120-ton *Santa Agueda* and its flagship, the *Trinidad,* a 35- to 40-ton vessel not more than 40 feet long, left La Paz and headed across the choppy Sea of Cortés to the mainland shore. Ulloa cruised northward to the port of Guaymas, and farther on expected to find a passage around the "island" of California. Instead, violent tides caused by the Colorado River descending into the sea at the head of the narrow gulf drove Ulloa southward, but he was the first Spaniard to learn that Baja California was not an island.

In 1533 the conqueror of the Aztec empire, Hernán Cortés, organized the expedition that discovered Baja California for Spain. Three years later, he himself led a colonizing expedition to the peninsula, hoping to reap the wealth of the land's fabled pearl beds. *Courtesy California Historical Society/ Title Insurance and Trust Photo Collection, University of Southern California.*

Ulloa took possession of the land he found "for the Marques [Cortés] in the name of the Emperor [Carlos V], our master, King of Castile" and then sailed along the eastern shore of the peninsula until again reaching La Paz. Ulloa tried to round the southern tip of Baja California at Cape San Lucas, but for eight days violent winds and tempestuous rains kept his ships beating up and down the Gulf coast. The two vessels finally rounded the cape by the end of January 1540, and then sailed up the western shore as far north as the Isla de Cedros (Island of Cedars), so named because "on the tops of the mountains therein, there grows a stand of these Cedars being very tall, as the nature of them is to be."[5] After three months, Ulloa sent the larger *Santa Agueda* home to Acapulco and, before returning, continued his explorations northward in the *Trinidad* to perhaps Point San Antonio, just south of latitude thirty degrees.[6]

Ulloa's expeditions, the last with which Cortés had any official connection, had faced severe storms to explore both the eastern and western coasts of the peninsula. His revelation that Baja California was a peninsula aroused little attention, however, and the "island" of California persisted on maps as late as the mid-1750s.[7] Ulloa's discovery of an island of cedars compensated little for the failure to find the expected cities of gold. Disappointment was great, and Cortés, angered that the new viceroy, Antonio de Mendoza, had effectively curbed his authority, sailed for Spain in 1540 to regain the king's favor.[8] Years of effort gave him little satisfaction, and finally, in 1547, death claimed the unhappy Cortés, first of the Spanish explorers to open the way to California.

JUAN RODRÍGUEZ CABRILLO: SOLDIER OF THE CONQUEST

Viceroy Mendoza, disillusioned by the meager results of overland expeditions by Francisco Vásquez de Coronado and Hernando deSoto into the interior of the continent, resolutely turned to the sea with yet another plan to find the elusive Strait of Anián, or Northwest Passage, which according to legend connected the Atlantic and Pacific oceans. Pedro de Alvarado, governor and *adelantado* of Guatemala, had appeared at the port of Acapulco in 1540 with a fleet of thirteen vessels, offering his services to the Crown for Pacific exploration. At his right hand stood Juan Rodríguez Cabrillo, navigator, horseman, captain of crossbowmen, and eventual discoverer of Alta California, second-in-command of Alvarado's fleet.[9]

Certain details of the background and life of Rodríguez Cabrillo prior to his arrival in California have come to light in recent years, but his exact age and place of birth are still unknown. Often described as "a Portuguese navigator sailing under the flag of Spain," new information about his early life, although inconclusive, points to his being Spanish. Rodríguez Cabrillo's original journal of exploration has not been found, but documents in the *Archivo General de Indias* in Seville and in the *Archivo General de Centro América* in Guatemala give an account of his service to Spain, his family and their property in Guatemala, and his activities in California.[10]

Cabrillo first engaged in farming and mining in Guatemala on the estates granted to him by Alvarado. In 1536 he directed construction of a fleet of ships capable of exploring the most dangerous and remote areas of the Pacific. Thirteen ships were finally completed by 1540, although one, the two hundred-ton galleon *San Salvador*, was built by Cabrillo at his own expense. When the vessels were ready to sail, Governor Alvarado asked his master shipwright to join the expedition in his own *San Salvador* as admiral of the entire fleet. Cabrillo agreed, and the ships reached the western Mexican port of Navidad, near Colima, on Christmas Day, 1540.[11]

Viceroy Mendoza and Alvarado entered into a partnership for Pacific exploration. Prior to their departure, however, Alvarado was killed in an Indian uprising known as the Mixton War. Mendoza took possession of Alvarado's fleet and, showing high regard for Cabrillo, commissioned him to sail his own ship, the smaller square-rigged vessel *La Victoria*, and a launch, probably a brigantine called *San Miguel*, northward along the Pacific Coast in search of the Strait of Anián.[12] The remaining vessels were dispatched to the Philippines under command of Ruy López de Villalobos.

CABRILLO OFFICIALLY LANDS IN CALIFORNIA

Cabrillo's expedition, with three vessels of Alvarado's fleet, set sail from the port of Navidad on June 27, 1542, to explore the remote, unchartered areas of the north

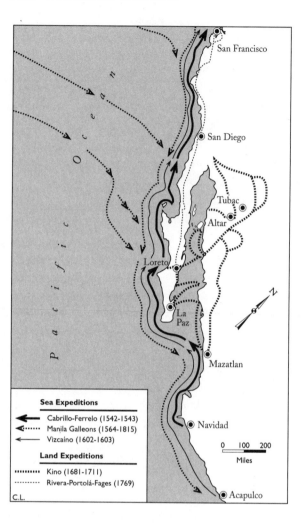

Spanish sea and land expeditions to California.

Pacific. They cruised northward along the west coast of Mexico, crossed the Sea of Cortés, and proceeded up the Pacific side of what Cabrillo knew as the California peninsula. His ships entered the Bay of Ensenada, Baja California, on September 17, 1542. The expedition remained there five days and then continued on, facing headwinds and adverse currents that limited daily progress to just fifteen to twenty miles. Within three days they sighted the three Coronado Islands, which Cabrillo called Las Islas Desiertas and mistakenly charted at 34 degrees latitude, about 2 degrees, or 140 miles, too far north. From these waters the Spanish seamen noticed the smoke of coastal Indian fires and, as they approached the mainland, saw a promising green valley backed by high mountains. On September 28, 1542, Cabrillo headed the *San Salvador* and *La Victoria* into San Diego Bay, dropped anchor on the lee side of Point Loma, and formally claimed Alta (Upper) California—as distinguished from Baja

(Lower) California. The Spaniards stepped ashore and were greeted by Indians who "gave signs of great fear" and indicated by signs that men, similarly bearded and clothed, were traveling in the interior. Cabrillo described the natives as well built and clothed in animal skins.[13] The admiral bestowed the name of San Miguel Arcangel on his newly discovered "sheltered and very good port," but in 1602 it was renamed by Sebastián Vizcaíno, who chose to honor San Diego de Alcalá (St. Didacus) instead.

Three Indians timidly approached Cabrillo's ship, communicating by signs that they knew of other similarly dressed white men, carrying crossbows and swords, traveling far inland. Cabrillo understood from their gestures that these strangers (probably a detachment from Coronado's expedition) wielded lances from horseback and had killed many Indians. For this reason the California natives were afraid, but the Spaniards gave them presents to calm their fears. When Indians wounded three seamen on a night fishing party near the shore, Cabrillo ordered his crew not to fire on them but to win their confidence. No further incidents of hostility occurred in this area, which the Indians called Guacamal.[14]

Sailing north from San Diego after six days' rest, the expedition sighted the Channel Islands of San Clemente and Santa Catalina, which they named San Salvador and La Victoria after their ships. Off Catalina the Spaniards searched the shoreline for signs of life. They anchored at one of the coves and the expedition's journal reported:

> They went ashore with the boat to see if there were people; and when the boat came near, a great number of Indians emerged from the bushes and grass, shouting, dancing and making signs that they should land. As they saw that the women were fleeing, from the boats they made signs that they should not be afraid. Immediately they were reassured, and laid their bows and arrows on the ground and launched in the water a good canoe which held eight or ten Indians, and came to the ships. They gave them beads and other articles, with which they were pleased, and then they returned. Afterward the Spaniards went ashore, and they, the Indian women, and all felt very secure.[15]

The *San Salvador* and *La Victoria* headed toward the mainland, and Cabrillo sighted the bay of San Pedro (naming it "Bay of Smokes"). They continued a course along the coast and visited an Indian fishing village, which Cabrillo called Pueblo de Canoas. Heavy winds from the northwest near Point Conception forced the ships to find shelter in a small port (Cuyler's Harbor) of San Miguel Island. On this island, which they named Isla de la Posesión, misfortune marred their enviable exploring record. While going ashore, Cabrillo fell and apparently broke his arm on the rocky beach.[16] Ignoring his wound, Cabrillo ordered his men to continue their mapping and coastal explorations. By mid-November, despite winter storms and adverse winds, they reached an area near San Francisco Bay. Here they again turned southward and set their course for the safety of San Miguel Island. By the end of December gangrene had severely complicated Cabrillo's injuries, finally causing his death on January 3, 1543. The crew buried their leader on the barren, windswept island of La Posesión and renamed it Isla de Juan Rodríguez. Shifting winds and sands have covered all traces of the grave.

Cabrillo's final words reflected the determination of the early Spanish explorers. He instructed his chief pilot, Bartolomé Ferrer (or Ferrelo, as he is sometimes known), not to give up their projected reconnaisance of the northern coast. The ships again sailed into the open sea and made their way northward against heavy gales. Finally driven dangerously near the shore at a point somewhere near the present-day California-Oregon border, they prayed for protection and were saved by a sudden change of wind. The expedition's journal describes few recognizable landmarks, making their exact course difficult to follow (their estimated latitude of forty-four degrees was again probably two degrees too high), but the document leaves no doubt that they were charting waters unknown to Europeans.[17]

Cabrillo's crew, weakened from exposure and scurvy, responded gratefully to Ferrer's order that the *San Salvador* and *La Victoria* return home. Praying to the Virgin of Guadalupe for a safe voyage, they reached the port of Navidad on April 14, 1543, bringing the sad news of Cabrillo's death and their discouraging discoveries. Mendoza closely guarded the charts of the explorations, and Cabrillo's own journal, kept a secret, has not yet been found.

THE MANILA GALLEON TRADE

Philip II, King of Spain from 1556 to 1598, inherited the Spanish empire at its most extensive, but he was also left with its most serious problems. While viceroys overseas strengthened Spain's hold in the Indies, the home country lagged behind the rest of Europe in developing new industries. The constant financial drain on the country caused by foreign enterprises, and heightened by frequent English raids on the Spanish treasure fleet, made new sources of income vital. Cabrillo's failure to find the Northwest Passage, and Spain's need for more trade, brought renewed efforts to conquer the Philippines. Discovered by Magellan in 1521, the islands nominally belonged to Portugal according to the Papal Donation of 1493.[18] Ruy López de Villalobos had nevertheless taken possession of the Philippines for Spain in 1542, but, unable to overcome native hostility, he was eventually captured by the Portuguese.[19] None of the explorers had even found a successful return route to New Spain. Vessels sailing eastward from the islands were quickly becalmed; the only certain way was around Africa to the Atlantic. Clearly a return route would have to be found. Therefore, Philip II ordered New Spain's Viceroy Luis de Velasco (1551–1564) to outfit an expedition for Pacific conquest.

The crucial navigational problems of the Philippine route were assigned to Andrés de Urdaneta, an Augustinian priest. The fleet reached the islands in February
1565, and about four hundred ground troops under Miguel López de Legazpi began
their conquest on Cebu. Urdaneta, after studying the winds and currents, took three
vessels and headed northward to the Japanese currents. He plotted a great circle
route reaching the Pacific Coast of North America at about Cape Mendocino.
When the vessels sighted California, they turned southward and sailed for Acapulco.
Urdaneta received credit for discovering a feasible, although long and difficult, trade
route that opened the way for Spain's famed Manila galleons.[20] In the meantime,
Legazpi's troops occupied Cebu, overcame native and Portuguese resistance, and
eventually took over Luzon. López de Legazpi, given authority by Viceroy Velasco,
founded the town of Manila in 1571.

A regular trade route was opened between Manila and Spain via Mexico, across
which one or two galleons passed annually. The ships, usually not larger than five
hundred tons, carried a crew of about 115 men; they were outfitted at royal expense
and commanded by an officer of the king. Profits were high, but miserable conditions on board caused heavy losses from death and desertion. The inadequate water
supply often turned brackish, and even the vermin-invested food ran out before
shore was reached. Essential provisions were sacrificed for trade goods—silks, velvet,
gold and silver brocades, jewelry, perfumes, exotic preserves of orange and peach,
cedar chests, fine thread, ornaments of all kinds, and the highly-prized pepper and
other spices for the preservation and palatability of meat.[21]

Prices for these Asian commodities were so high, bringing as much as $25,000
profit to the captain on a single trip, that Spanish seamen, given permission to carry
a small share of goods, endured incredible hardships. Many, used to the hot Philippine
climate, died from the severe cold of the northern latitudes; others, weakened by exposure to wind and rain, were swept overboard by huge waves that threatened to sub-
merge the shaky craft. But the worst danger was disease. Scurvy and beri-beri resulted
from the lack of fresh provisions. The cause of these illnesses—lack of necessary
vitamins—was not realized for nearly two centuries.[22] The number of deaths often
reached 50 percent, and few persons, if any, reached Acapulco without suffering some
ravages from these diseases. For this reason the California coast was looked to as a
stopping place where the weak and dying galleon crews could obtain relief. Colonial
officials suggested that California be explored further to find a suitable natural harbor
where a port could be established. These plans, however, were slow in developing.

DRAKE'S VISIT TO CALIFORNIA

For 150 years Spain had enjoyed almost uncontested occupation of the Pacific
Ocean, but in 1578 Francis Drake, a daring English pirate later knighted for his cir-

cumnavigation of the globe, shattered Spanish confidence. Under the clever, energetic, and devoutly Protestant Queen Elizabeth I, England represented a thorny challenge to Philip II's Catholic empire. Drake's expedition, with five ships, sailed from Plymouth harbor in November 1577, originally planning to explore the coast of South America from Río de la Plata around to the frontier of Spanish settlement on the Chilean coast and then to return by the same route. Drake later claimed Queen Elizabeth's special charge was "to annoy the King of Spain in his Indies."[23]

Drake's flagship, the *Pelican,* successfully weathered sixteen treacherous days in the stormy Strait of Magellan, emerging alone into the Pacific.[24] Drake renamed his ship the *Golden Hind* and began a series of raids along the Chilean and Peruvian coasts, capturing unsuspecting Spanish vessels with ease. Finally, the eighty-foot *Golden Hind,* more heavily laden with treasure and provisions than a Manila galleon, sought shelter on the northern Pacific Coast. The English reached the California shore somewhere in the vicinity of San Francisco Bay on June 17, 1579. Because Drake's original journal has disappeared and his chaplain's diary was called unreliable by Drake himself, considerable mystery surrounds the precise location of the English visit.[25] Drake apparently called the country *Nova Albion* (New England) because of "the white bancks and cliffes," which bore a striking resemblance to England's "Seven Sisters of Sussex" on the English Channel coast.[26]

Drake took possession of the country for England, recording his claim on a plate of brass, inlaid with a sixpence by his blacksmith, and nailed to "a great and firm poste." The inscription read in part: "June 17, 1579, by the Grace of God and in the name of Her Majesty Queen Elizabeth of England . . . I take possession of this Kingdome . . . now named by me and to be known unto all men as Nova Albion. Francis Drake."[27] The Indians with whom Drake seems to have come into friendly and frequent contact were in recent times identified as Coast Miwok, inhabitants of the Drake's Bay region, by the anthropologist Robert Heizer of the University of California, Berkeley.[28] Nevertheless, the uncertainties of Drake's landfall lend credence to arguments advanced for Bodega Bay, Tomales Bay, a cove inside San Francisco Bay, Trinidad Head, or one of the Channel Islands in California. Whale Cove and Coos Bay, Oregon, have also been considered as candidates for the English campsite. This controversy does not, however, obscure Drake's ability. Contemporary accounts agree that he was an exceptional navigator, and his supporters believe that he ranks as one of the greatest of all English seamen. Drake's claim to California, or "Nova Albion," came to represent little more than a token gesture to honor Queen Elizabeth, but the presence of English ships posed a new threat to Spain's Pacific dominions. Knowing the difficulty of returning through the Strait of Magellan and aided by captured Spanish charts, Drake sailed the *Golden Hind* around the world, arriving at Plymouth "safely with joyfull minds and thankfull hearts to God" in the summer of 1580.[29]

Coast Miwok Indians greet the English sea dog Francis Drake in an illustration published in 1599, twenty years after the event, by the Flemish engraver Théodore de Bry. The earliest known image of California, this copper-plate engraving helped shape European conceptions of the distant Spanish possession. In the left foreground a local chief and his attendants, preceded by a native carrying "the Septer or royall mace," approach Drake prior to a ceremony in which a crown of feathers was placed on the head of the legendary navigator. In preparing his drawings of American Indians, de Bry, like other artists of that day, relied on classical sculpture in shaping his subjects' physiques and facial features. *Courtesy Bancroft Library.*

CAVENDISH, UNAMUNO, AND CERMEÑO

A second English interloper ravaged the Pacific Coast in 1586–1587. Thomas Cavendish, a native of Suffolk, assumed a pirate's role in a series of destructive raids, robbing, looting and burning Spanish ships, and amassing considerable treasure. His greatest prize was the capture of the great *Santa Ana,* a Manila galleon said to have been carrying more than $1 million in gold, to say nothing of its regular cargo of silks, perfumes, jewelry, and other valuable commodities. Cavendish first sighted the galleon off Cape San Lucas, where its pilot, Sebastián Rodríguez Cermeño, set a final course for the run to Acapulco and home. The slow-moving *Santa Ana* fell easy prey and was captured by Cavendish's two ships, the *Desire* and the *Content*, whose crews systematically looted the galleon, put the people ashore (with provisions), and set fire to the "Great St. Ann." Cavendish headed into the Pacific and continued his voyage around the world, returning to England as a swashbuckling hero. The Spaniards rescued the *Santa Ana's* burning hulk, repaired the hull, and eventually reached Acapulco.[30]

As Cavendish was plying the waters off Baja California, Pedro de Unamuno, another Manila galleon pilot, was searching the Pacific for two legendary islands called Rica de Oro and Rica de Plata—sometimes offered as evidence that Spaniards had discovered the Hawaiian Islands. After a fruitless effort, Unamuno sailed along the coast of California in late October 1587, anchoring in Morro Bay to the north of Santa Barbara. Unamuno's visit provided his crew with "an unlimited quantity of fish of different kinds" and trees suitable for masts and firewood. Unfortunately, unfriendly Indians, who killed two and wounded several Spaniards, cut Unamuno's visit short.[31]

The threat of English piracy gave New Spain's long-delayed plans to occupy California an added thrust. Cermeño, pilot of the tragic *Santa Ana*, was given command of the galleon *San Agustín* and instructed to look for possible California ports on his way back to Mexico from Manila. Cermeño anchored in present-day Drake's Bay (which he named the Port of San Francisco) early in November 1595. Fearful of taking the clumsy galleon too close to the rocky coast, he ordered his crew to assemble a large open sailing launch he had brought on board for detailed exploration. Cermeño, constantly apprehensive about the *San Agustín's* rich cargo, watched a fierce storm wreck his ship on the last day of November. The Spanish seamen completed and provisioned the open launch, christened the *San Buenaventura*, and Cermeño, with all seventy passengers and crew, headed southward. Over constant protest, the captain continued surveying and mapping, noting particularly the entrance to Monterey Bay. When the launch reached Cedros Island, malnutrition, scurvy, and exhaustion finally forced him to stop work. Thankful for reaching the safety of Acapulco, Cermeño recounted his epic tale of hunger, misery, and discouragement, but untouched officials, prejudiced by conflicting stories, reprimanded him for losing the *San Agustín*, while owners of the lost cargo threatened to sue for damages. The result was a royal order that Manila galleons no longer be used for exploration and survey.[32]

SEBASTIÁN VIZCAÍNO, 1602

The voyages of Drake and Cavendish, as well as the formation of the British East India Company in 1600, created further conflict for Spanish merchants in Asia. In the wake of the English came the Dutch, whose ships passed through the Strait of

Magellan at the end of the sixteenth century. With a view toward Spanish needs for protection and supplies on the Pacific Coast, Gaspar de Zúñiga, Conde de Monterey, Viceroy of New Spain (1595–1603), approved a new California expedition under Sebastián Vizcaíno, an experienced participant in the galleon trade, but not a professional mariner. Vizcaíno, an ambitious and capable Basque merchant established in Acapulco, had survived the capture of the *Santa Ana* (having organized the group that put out the flames on the burning galleon) and later headed an attempt to colonize Baja California. Believing that pearls, gold, and silver must exist somewhere in California, Vizcaíno finally convinced the viceroy to give him another chance at colonization. The Conde de Monterey recommended Vizcaíno's new expedition for royal approval primarily to establish pearl fishing and to shed new light on the defense and security of the Manila galleons.[33]

Royal instructions from the viceroy set Vizcaíno's objective specifically as "the discovery and demarkation of the ports, bays, and inlets which exist from Cape San Lucas, situated at 22 degrees 15 minutes, to Cape Mendocino, at 42 degrees." Because some earlier expeditions, notably those by Unamuno and Cermeño, had been endangered by altercations with Indians, Vizcaíno was warned "not to allow anyone to go inland in search of Indians, nor even find out if Indians were there, since the intent and principal purposes (of coastal charting and soundings) did not require it."[34] He was to follow Cabrillo's route and not change any of the place names already given.

Vizcaíno sailed from Acapulco on May 5, 1602, with the *San Diego, Santo Tomás,* and *Tres Reyes* (a small auxiliary). On board were a cosmographer, three Carmelite priests, and a company of nearly two hundred men carefully selected for their nautical experience. The ships took four months to reach Alta California, while Vizcaíno, claiming difficulty in recognizing localities, permanently renamed all of Cabrillo's landmarks except Magdalena Bay. Upon approaching Cabrillo's Islas Desiertas, Vizcaíno called them San Martín, but the name suggested by the Carmelite Father Antonio de la Ascención—Los Cuatro Coronados—won out. Vizcaíno entered Cabrillo's Bay of San Miguel on November 10, 1602, noting its good anchorage and abundant natural resources. "On the 12th of said month, which was the day of the glorious San Diego, almost everyone went ashore; they built a hut, said mass (and) celebrated the feast of San Diego."[35] About one hundred Indians with bows and arrows appeared on a nearby hill, but did nothing when the Spanish, with offerings of presents, assured them of friendship. At the crest of Point Loma, Father Ascención recorded the discovery of "another good port" (Mission Bay) and made a quick survey of the region. The priest thought the land fertile, the variety of fish most numerous, and the existence of gold assured by some sparkling gold pyrites he found. After ten days' rest, the Spaniards set sail from their naturally protected port, which Vizcaíno called San Diego de Alcalá.

The expedition continued northward, fighting high winds and seas virtually all the time, stopping briefly at Catalina Island, and then passing through the Santa Barbara Channel. On December 16, 1602, they anchored in the bay whose name they gave to honor their viceregal patron, the Count of Monterey. Vizcaíno's unqualified praise of Monterey Bay as the "best port that could be desired" and "sheltered from all winds" resulted in its later selection as Spain's first capital of California. Unfortunately, the infrequency of these ideal weather conditions made the port unrecognizable by California's first overland explorers, led by Gaspar de Portolá in 1769.[36]

Although one ship returned to Mexico with the grievously sick crew members on board, the remainder of the expedition explored farther northward despite fierce storms and the crew's failing health. Departing from Monterey on January 3, 1603, they reached Drake's Bay in two days (naming the headland *La Punta de los Santos Reyes,* or Point Reyes); a week later they sighted Cape Mendocino. Here, Vizcaíno decided to head back to Acapulco. The ships could not stop at any place along the coast since none of the men, all ravaged by scurvy, had the strength to pull up an anchor once dropped. Vizcaíno entered Acapulco on March 21, 1603, with his glowing reports about Monterey, and was able to impress the viceroy with his discovery. Monterey's successor, however, the Count of Montesclaros (1603–1607), distrusted Vizcaíno, ridiculed the idea of establishing a California port, and discouraged further exploration. The problem of protecting the galleon was solved instead by improvements in ship design and construction that added space for carrying needed provisions. Stopping along California's rugged and unfamiliar coast within so few days of reaching port in Mexico seemed an unnecessary risk to the cargo. As a result, no further sea expeditions sailed to Upper California for more than 165 years. Although several pearl-seeking expeditions explored the Gulf of California, advancement northward from Mexico was left to the slow but steady progress of overland parties.

NAVAL EXPLORATION DURING THE LATE EIGHTEENTH CENTURY: JUAN PÉREZ

After the initial settlement of Alta California in 1769 under the leadership of Governor Gaspar de Portolá and Franciscan Father President Junípero Serra, the defensive policies of Viceroy Antonio de Bucareli of New Spain were governed by California's strategic value as a buffer colony against foreign aggression.[37] Rumors of an English voyage to the North Pole and the threat of Russian activities in the Pacific Northwest led Bucareli to plan renewed naval exploration north of California. He wrote: "I deem it well that any establishment of the Russians on this continent or of any other foreign power ought to be guarded against . . . to avoid the consequences that would follow from having neighbors other than the Indians."[38]

The Presidio of Monterrey, an engraving that appeared in George Vancouver's *Voyage of Discovery* (London, 1798), was derived from a drawing made by John Sykes, a master's mate on the English explorer's epic expedition, which first visited the California capital in late 1792. Established in 1770, the presidio was one of four military fortifications constructed between San Diego and San Francisco to defend the province from foreign aggression and to guard neighboring missions from Indian depredations. *Courtesy California Historical Society, FN-30520.*

The viceroy's lengthy instructions to Ensign Juan Pérez of December 24, 1773, primarily designed for regulating all future explorations from San Blas to the Northwest, clearly set forth Spain's policy governing activities in the Pacific during this period.[39] The instructions stressed topics such as keeping accurate and complete logs, methods for approaching the coasts, regulations for friendly conduct among the native inhabitants, procedures for taking possession, and instructions for handling foreign contact. The thirty-two articles also covered a multitude of detail about supplies, medicines, discipline, and minor surveys along the coast. The expedition was not to turn back until the ship had reached sixty degrees north.[40]

Pérez sailed the newly constructed 225-ton frigate *Santiago* from San Blas on January 25, 1774. Aboard were eighty-six crewmen, Father Junípero Serra returning from a visit to Mexico to his missionary post at Monterey, Father Pablo Mugartegui, and a small company of settlers heading for California. After a brief stop at Monterey, Pérez, with Fathers Juan Crespí and Tomás de la Peña as chaplains and diarists, continued his voyage into unknown waters north of the Queen Charlotte Islands at approximately 55 degrees north latitude.[41] Dense fog and contrary currents prevented their making a landfall, however, and Pérez, plagued by constant sickness and worried about the lack of fresh water, turned back short of his instructed goal of 60 degrees. He sailed the *Santiago* along the coast of Vancouver Island and on August 9, 1775, anchored in a harbor that he named San Lorenzo. It later became known as Nootka Sound. Twenty-one canoes containing nearly 150 amazed Indians approached the *Santiago*. A Spanish diarist reported:

> The view of this ship at first filled the natives with terror . . . and they were seized with fright from the moment they saw the giant "machine" on the horizon, which little by little approached their coasts. They believed that Qua-utz [the Creator] was coming to make a second visit, and were fearful that it was to punish their misdeeds.[42]

Pérez did not land at Nootka but exchanged some gifts with the Indians.[43] He then set his course for Monterey, arriving with his by then scurvy-ridden crew on August 27. Father Serra was keenly disappointed that the expedition had failed to achieve its objective of 60 degrees, and criticized Pérez, still in poor health, for refusing to stay in California and help establish a settlement in San Francisco. The veteran mariner returned to San Blas early in November and almost immediately began to prepare for further exploration.[44] Bucareli advised his superiors in Madrid that no contact with Russian traders had been made and that a second expedition, scheduled to depart in the spring, would further investigate and take possession of northern lands.[45]

HEZETA, AYALA, AND BODEGA, 1775

As a follow-up expedition, three vessels left San Blas in March 1775 and headed into the Pacific. The *Santiago*, commanded by Bruno de Hezeta, a native of Bilbao, and the thirty-six-foot schooner *Sonora*, as consort under Juan Manuel de Ayala, sailed under similar instructions as those given to Pérez. They were to attempt a landfall at 60 degrees north latitude. The familiar San Blas supply ship *San Carlos*, under Manuel Manrique, was to make a thorough reconnaissance of San Francisco Bay for its proposed occupation. Unfortunately, shortly after the ships set sail, Manrique suffered a mental breakdown. Hezeta ordered his return to San Blas and transferred command of the *San Carlos* to Ayala. This event elevated the Peruvian-born Ensign Juan Francisco de la Bodega y Quadra to captain of the tiny *Sonora*.

The *Santiago*, with Juan Pérez as chief pilot, and Bodega's *Sonora* sailed directly to the North Pacific without stopping at Monterey. On June 9, 1775, the two Spanish vessels anchored in Trinidad Bay, in northern California, and took possession of the harbor in the name of King Carlos III. Within a few days, Hezeta entered the mouth of a river and recorded his discovery as the Entrada de Hezeta.[46] Continuing northward, the crewmen of the *Sonora* landed on the coast of present-day Washington state and were ambushed by some three hundred Indians. Seven men—half of the *Sonora's* crew—were killed while Bodega stood powerless to avenge his loss. Hezeta, the senior commander of the enterprise, gave up some men from his own *Santiago* to replenish the *Sonora* and suggested they return home.

Bodega and his second officer, Francisco Mourelle, from Galicia in northern Spain, daringly planned to continue the voyage, despite the reluctance of Hezeta. During a foggy night they allowed their vessel to drift away from the *Santiago* until it was out of sight and could set sail. Bodega and his men struggled north against prevailing winds in an effort to reach the sixtieth parallel. The *Sonora* hove to less than two degrees short of the aspired goal.[47] Bodega strengthened Spain's claim to the territory by taking possession at Puerto de los Remedios (57 degrees 20 minutes north) and Puerto de Bucareli (55 degrees 18 minutes north).

On the basis of their discoveries, as delineated on the charts completed by Bodega and Mourelle, Spain established a solid foundation for her claim of sovereignty over the Pacific Coast from Monterey to the Gulf of Alaska. On the return trip, his crew and himself stricken with scurvy, Bodega managed to survey one final port—the one he would leave as a namesake, *Puerto de Capitan de la Bodega,* or present-day Bodega Bay.[48] The *Sonora* anchored alongside its flagship *Santiago* in Monterey harbor, October 7, 1775. Bodega's epic exploration in a thirty-six-foot schooner gives ample testimony to the courage of these early navigators. Upon returning to Mexico, Bodega and Mourelle dispelled Bucareli's fears about the presence of Russian traders in the north.

The San Blas supply ship *San Carlos,* also lying at anchor in Monterey, had just returned from its forty-four-day survey of San Francisco Bay. Captain Ayala had sailed to the entrance of the bay on August 4, 1775, but strong currents and tides prevented his passing through the narrow entry (today's Golden Gate) until the next day. Finally successful, the *San Carlos* became the first European ship to enter California's largest natural port. Ayala anchored off present-day San Francisco's North Beach and, with a small launch, explored every part of the bay. Ayala's exploration set the stage for occupation of San Francisco and the foundation of its presidio and mission in early fall 1776.[49]

SCIENTIFIC EXPLORATION

Spain's desire to expand the frontiers of knowledge paralleled the nation's interest in controlling and settling new territory. Carlos III, following the lead of his Bourbon predecessors, actively sponsored the intellectual renovation of his realm. To encourage scientific studies, and to compete with British and French endeavors, Carlos promoted half a dozen major expeditions during the last quarter of the eighteenth century. After the king's death in 1788, Spain's royal government began its decline, but capable viceroys and other colonial officials nevertheless carried out projected scientific efforts, as well as other reform measures. Unfortunately, the exploring expeditions received little support or encouragement from Carlos IV (1788–1808) to assemble and edit the results of the investigations when they returned to the Iberian Peninsula. Many competent studies were denied publication. If Spain seemed to contribute little, therefore, to nineteenth-century science, it was not for lack of ideas and worthwhile experiments, but because events at home defeated their ambitious undertakings. The activities of these scientists have only recently become the subject of extensive investigation both in Spain and in the Americas.[50]

Factors influencing the flurry of scientific activity during the late eighteenth century were rooted in the changing climate of European thought. The concept of naturalism—the assumption that the whole universe of mind and matter was guided and controlled by natural law—caused men of the Enlightenment to reassess the resources of their own countries. Scientists throughout Europe catalogued minerals, classified fauna, and flora according to the system of Swedish botanist Carolus Linnaeus, surveyed natural products, recorded native customs, and rewrote standard natural histories. Intellectual interests shifted gradually from supernatural beliefs to a natural science based on investigation and demonstration. Scientific studies commanded the attention of scholars and the patronage of kings.[51]

CAPTAIN JAMES COOK

The object of Captain James Cook's third voyage around the world in 1776, in addition to gathering scientific data, was to discover for England the famed Northwest Passage—still the preoccupation of European mariners. In the course of his exploration, Cook discovered the islands that he named for the Earl of Sandwich—present-day Hawaii—and in 1778 visited the Pacific Northwest coast. Anchoring his two ships, the *Resolution* and the *Discovery*, at Nootka Sound in what Cook called Friendly Cove, his party recorded local observations for nearly a month. Eventually heading north into Alaskan waters, Cook again found himself blocked by a barrier of ice. The ships returned to the Sandwich Islands, where Cook was killed by natives at Kealakakua Bay in a trivial skirmish over a stolen boat.[52]

VOYAGE OF LA PÉROUSE, 1786

The French launched an around-the-world expedition under the command of Jean François de Galaup, Count of La Pérouse, that sailed from Brest on August 1, 1785.

Reception of Count de La Pérouse at Mission Carmel depicts Franciscans greeting the first foreign visitors to California. Made in 1791 by José Cardero, an artist with the Spanish exploring expedition commanded by Alejandro Malaspina, it is one of three copies of the long-lost original, which was drawn on the spot in 1786 by Gaspard Duché de Vancy, a skilled draftsman with the famed French voyager. Entering the mission courtyard, where the neophytes were assembled in close formation, they were received, wrote La Pérouse, "like the lords of manors when they first take possession of their estates." *Courtesy Museo Naval, Madrid. Photograph courtesy Robin Inglis.*

Its published objectives were to increase geographic knowledge and explore for the Northwest Passage; not stated were the commercial and political motives of trade and possible colonization of the Pacific area. Under special scrutiny were the Russian and Spanish ports on the North American coast. Following Cook's route, the enterprise visited Hawaii, spent a month along Alaskan shores in the summer of 1786, and then sailed directly for Monterey—paying the first official French visit to California.[53]

During the ten days La Pérouse remained in the province, his expedition gathered sufficient information to prepare comprehensive reports on California's geography, resources, political and military government, mission system, Indian population, and economic possibilities. Judging from the area of Monterey, La Pérouse thought California to be "inexpressibly fertile," abounding in fish and game, and its lack of flowing water compensated by the dampness of the air. He concluded, however, that any progress made by the Indians under authoritarian Spain would be slow.

Schooled in the philosophy of the encyclopedists and a firm believer in the equal rights of man, La Pérouse commented that even though the missionaries were perfectly fulfilling the paternalistic objective of their institution, and as individuals were gentle, humane, and charitable, he "wished that to the principles of Christianity a body of laws might have been joined which, little by little, would have made into citizens men whose condition hardly differs from that of the Negroes of those households in our colonies."[54] La Pérouse believed that his "novel plan" had difficulties, agreeing that the Indians had few modern ideas, would run away if not treated as children, were unaffected by reasoning, and responded only to a system of punishment and rewards. He still asked, however, that "with extreme patience" might it not be possible to make known to the Indians "the advantages of a society founded on the rights of man and to establish the right of property among them" so they would be persuaded to cultivate their fields "or engage in some other kind of labor?"[55] La Pérouse was not alone in his quest for that answer; the Spanish asked themselves the same question many times. The failure to find an answer during the mission period produced the unfortunate aftermath of secularization, when Indians were dispossessed of much of their land.

The French expedition sailed from Monterey August 24, 1786, to Macao, the Philippines, and then northward to the Sea of Japan. From a Russian port at Kamchatka, La Pérouse dispatched his daily journals and some of the scientific papers overland to Paris. Additional documents were also forwarded after the group visited the East Indies and Botany Bay. Known to have headed southward, the expedition mysteriously disappeared. La Pérouse's journals and other papers of the voyage, shipped to Paris from Hawaii, were published in Paris in 1791, and several searches were made for the missing expedition. Not until more than thirty-five years had passed was the wreckage of the French ships found north of the New Hebrides.

VOYAGE OF MALASPINA

The around-the-world expedition of Alejandro Malaspina, one of the most ambitious of the eighteenth-century scientific undertakings organized in Spain during the 1780s, is little known in California today. After stopping in South America and Mexico, an elite group of Spanish intellectuals paid an official visit to Alta California in 1791. Malaspina, a Spanish naval officer of Italian birth, had circumnavigated the earth in 1786–1788 as captain of *La Astrea*. He and a fellow officer, José Bustamante y Guerra, submitted a plan to the Spanish minister of marine, Antonio Valdés, for a scientific and political voyage that would follow in the wake of Cook and La Pérouse and "study the survival of Man in different climates, in extensive journeys, and among some almost incredible tasks and risks," and would represent "the most significant contribution that navigation has made."[56]

Two corvettes built especially for the project, the *Descubierta* and *Atrevida*, set sail from the port of Cádiz in July 1789, arriving in Montevideo the following September. Sailing around Cape Horn, the ships cruised along the coasts of Chile, Peru, Ecuador, Panama, and Nicaragua, stopping in major ports to make investigations of the surrounding territory. While in Acapulco in May 1791, Malaspina received a royal order to search for the Strait of Anián, or Northwest Passage. To make best use of his available time, Malaspina decided to leave a number of officers and scientists in Mexico for further study. He then sailed with the rest of his party in search of the elusive passage and to visit the Pacific Northwest and California.

Following a stay on the Alaskan coast, the Malaspina expedition stopped at Nootka Sound, where they set up an astronomical observatory, sketched local scenes, gathered fauna and flora, and exchanged various gifts with the natives. Malaspina and Maquinna, chief of the Nootka (Mowachaht) Indians, established a bond of friendship. After a two-week stay, during which time they learned much about local customs, the party then headed for Monterey in August 1791.[57] By this time, Governor Fages had relinquished his California command and returned to Mexico. The new provincial head, José Antonio Roméu, had not yet reached California, so Malaspina was greeted by the generous and amiable Lieutenant José Darío Argüello, acting commandant of the Monterey presidio. The expedition also brought to California its first American visitor, John Green from Boston, who had become seriously ill at Nootka and died in Monterey on the afternoon of September 13. He was buried after funeral services were conducted by Father Francisco de Paula Anino, chaplain of the *Atrevida*.

Upon hearing news of the expedition's arrival, California's Franciscan Father President Fermín Francisco de Lasuén returned from his work at the new mission establishment of Santa Cruz, founded just north of Monterey on August 28, 1791, to receive Malaspina and his scientists at Mission San Carlos. One of the Malaspina diarists reported that from the moment Lasuén arrived on the scene,

> . . . so great was his activity for our collections of natural history, so prolific and detailed his information and reflections on the prosperity of these missions, and finally so affable, natural and religiously abundant was his hospitality at any hour . . . that he would be poorly described in any other way than that of perpetual recognition and appreciation.[58]

During the expedition's fifteen-day visit to Monterey, naturalist Tadeo Haënke directed studies of local birds, quadrupeds, sea animals, and fish. He also prepared a comprehensive survey of plant life and listed the uses for California trees. Credited with the first scientific description of the redwood, Haënke is named as its botanical discoverer.[59] In the field of mineralogy, the talented Bohemian analyzed the soil of the Monterey coast beginning with the sands along the shore and continuing in-

A California thrasher was one of the birds drawn by José Cardero and described by the naturalist Tadeo Haënke during Alejandro Malaspina's sojourn at Monterey in 1791. It was hoped that the discoveries and achievements of Malaspina's scientific staff, which were encyclopedic in range, would enhance Spain's reputation as a major European power. *Courtesy Museo Naval, Madrid. Photograph courtesy Iris Engstrand.*

land for a considerable distance. Artists José Cardero and Tomás Suría contributed colorful illustrations of both a scientific and general nature.

The expedition left Monterey with exchanges of compliments and sad farewells. Returning first to Acapulco to pick up the rest of the group, the *Descubierta* and *Atrevida* directed their courses westward, visiting Guam, the Philippines, New Zealand, New South Wales, and the Fiji Islands. Recrossing the Pacific, the two vessels sailed for the port of Cádiz by way of South America. The expedition returned to Spain after sixty-two months of travel and exploration. It was praised for its success; but Malaspina's fame was short-lived. His inopportune involvement with Queen María Luisa of Parma, wife of Carlos IV, and his unpopular liberal views regarding the Americas resulted in his imprisonment in Spain and eventual exile to his home country. Malaspina's death in Pontremoli in 1810 effectively terminated the editing and publication of the expedition's documents. The expedition's material remained relatively unknown for a century.[60] According to the German naturalist

Baron Alexander von Humboldt, Malaspina was "more famous for his misfortunes than for his discoveries."[61]

BODEGA AND VANCOUVER

Juan Francisco de la Bodega y Quadra, veteran of two epic explorations to the North Pacific and commander of the Naval Department of San Blas, was commissioned in 1792 to represent Spain in a final effort to resolve the difficulties with England over territorial rights at Nootka Sound.[62] His "Expedition of the Limits to the North of California" was also the last major Spanish effort to make a full investigation of the northern area.[63] For this reason Viceroy Revillagigedo appointed Mexican-born José Mariano Moziño as botanist-naturalist of the expedition.[64] The scientist made some observations in California during a brief stop at Monterey, indicating his belief that the province had numerous advantages over the Nootka Sound area. Bodega, in his journal, commented that among the birds they saw, perhaps at Monterey, was a beautiful quail drawn by artist Atanasio Echeverría and "called by the naturalist *Tetrao de California.*"[65]

Two officers of the Malaspina expedition, Dionisio Alcalá Galiano and Cayetano Valdés, commanding the schooners *Sutil* and *Mexicana,* also joined Bodega y Quadra in further exploration of the Northwest coast. Viceroy Revillagigedo had accepted Malaspina's offer to leave these two officers in Mexico to head a special expedition to the northern area. They were instructed to prepare navigational charts; investigate natural resources; describe animals, birds, and fish; discover valuable metals or precious stones; and note objects of scientific curiosity. The talented José Cardero was also left to serve as official artist and cartographer.[66]

The expedition spent several months on the Northwest coast and accompanied the two ships of Captain George Vancouver on his circumnavigation of Vancouver Island. Alcalá Galiano and Valdés returned to Monterey prior to Bodega's return. They remained in California's capital from September 22 to October 26, 1792, where they continued their survey. Their official journal, published in Madrid in 1802, gave a description of Monterey and the surrounding area, a detailed account of Indian life and customs, and a summary of mission progress. Also included were a set of excellent maps and a series of illustrations by artist Cardero.[67]

Commissioned by the English to negotiate with the Spaniards at Nootka, Vancouver had been a member of Cook's second and third expeditions and an active explorer in the West Indies; he reached the Northwest coast in June 1792. With his ships the *Discovery* and *Chatham,* he entered the Strait of Juan de Fuca and circumnavigated the island that later would bear his name. Vancouver met Bodega y Quadra at Nootka in August, and after two conferences, the two commissioners agreed to refer settlement of the controversy back to their respective governments.

During these negotiations, Bodega suggested they sail to Monterey rather than suffer through a rigorous winter on the island they had christened Vancouver and Quadra.[68]

JOSÉ LONGINOS MARTÍNEZ

In the meantime, another Spanish scientist, naturalist José Longinos Martínez, member of the Royal Scientific Expedition to New Spain, had reached Monterey in early September 1792. He arrived in California's capital after a long, overland journey from Cape San Lucas at the tip of Baja California, during which he recorded details about fauna and flora, Indian life and customs, geographical conditions, and the progress of Spanish settlement.[69] Longinos was particularly impressed with the Chumash Indians of the Santa Barbara channel and described them in great detail. He thought their basketwork represented the "utmost delicacy" and their pots and pans, which were handed down from "father to son to grandson," were of a kind of soapstone that never wore out or became unserviceable. Their bows and arrows were "different from those of the other nations, excelling them in workmanship, beauty, and effectiveness." Longinos also listed natural products suitable for commercial exploitation and gave particular attention to medicinal plants.[70] After two months of study, Longinos sailed for Mexico from Monterey with Francisco de Eliza on the royal frigate *Concepción* and reached San Blas on November 22, 1792.

VANCOUVER IN CALIFORNIA

Earlier that month, on November 14, 1792, Vancouver sailed the *Discovery* into San Francisco Bay and was well received by Presidio Commander Ensign Hermengildo Sal. After an examination of the military fort and a visit to missions San Francisco and Santa Clara, Vancouver traveled south to be greeted by Bodega y Quadra at Monterey. The two officers proceeded to Mission San Carlos to pay their respects to the father-president.[71] Since Governor Romeú had arrived in poor health and remained confined until his death in April 1792, Father President Lasuén had been hosting official guests. He welcomed the Englishman with his usual gentle manner, warmth, and hospitality. Sailing southward along the California coast early in 1793, Vancouver honored the memory of his friendship with the cordial father-president by bestowing the names Point Fermín and Point Lasuén upon the extremities of San Pedro Bay. The British captain's departure for Hawaii was later delayed at San Diego by unfavorable winds, but Vancouver "did not regret the detention, as it afforded [them] the pleasure of a visit from our very highly esteemed . . . father-president of the missionaries."[72]

Vancouver's attitude toward California's progress was that Spanish efforts in es-

tablishing at least minimal settlements had "cleared the way for the ambitious en-
terprizers of those maritime powers, who in the avidity of commercial pursuits, may
seek to be benefitted by the advantages which the fertile soil of New Albion [Cali-
fornia] seems calculated to afford." The missionaries, by their "indefatigable labour,"
had trained a certain portion of the natives in useful occupations; and the potential
commerce of the province with China, India, Japan, and other places "under a judicious and well-regulated establishment," would some future day make California the
"object of serious and important consideration" to that nation deciding to challenge
Spain's sovereignty.[73]

Vancouver, whose prophesy was later viewed with suspicion by Spanish officials,
made a final visit to Monterey in November 1794. Settlement of the Nootka Sound
controversy had been made in Madrid, and British relations with California's newly
appointed governor, Diego de Borica, were cordial. The expedition departed from
the province amid amicable farewells. Vancouver completed his survey of the Pacific
Coast and reached England in September 1795. His careful notes of fortifications
and settlements, and his detailed commentary about life in California gave the
British a comprehensive view of Spanish progress. Local officials remembered Vancouver's visit to California with ambivalent feelings. José Joaquin de Arrillaga, always
suspicious of Vancouver's motives, recognized California's weak defenses and issued
new orders to strengthen the presidios when he became governor in 1802.

THE END OF AN ERA

Despite difficult conditions on the Iberian Peninsula at the beginning of the nineteenth century, future prospects for California were bright. Self-sustaining at last, the
distant province had profited under able leadership. While Spaniards at home struggled under the problems of Carlos IV, and though international controversies shook
the European world, California showed steady progress in pueblo development,
agriculture, manufacturing, and commerce. Foreign access to the Pacific had caused
officials of New Spain concern for the welfare of California, but local residents
would soon turn foreign contact into a profitable trade. A measure of cooperation
between church and state had permitted internal gains in terms of economic development and religious conversion, but illness still took its yearly toll of mission
Indians.

Spain's zealous efforts in the quest for knowledge during the late eighteenth century did not, unfortunately, result in fame for Spanish scientists or in utilization of
the newly discovered information. The nation's extensive collections of data, unlike
the journals of Captain Cook or the Count of La Pérouse, were made available to
few contemporaries in the academic world. The circumstances that greeted returning members of Spain's scientific expeditions—the lack of support by Carlos IV

and the French invasion of 1808—caused much of their valuable material to become disorganized, lost, given away, or sold to foreign collectors. These disheartening occurrences were followed by an even greater tragedy for the Spanish government—the imminent loss of its colonial empire. The same spirit of inquiry initially responsible for European scientific interest and enlightenment, subsequently awakened ideas about natural rights that would provoke revolution. These ideas presaged the outbreak of wars for independence in Spanish America, and Spain's opportunities for scientific study in California and other overseas areas were left to a new generation.

NOTES

1. Recent works on Malaspina include a seven-volume series called *La Expedición Malaspina (1789–1794)*, published by the Ministerio de Defensa-Museo Naval-Lunwerg Editores (1990–1996) and titled separately as Ricardo Cerezo Martínez, *Circunstancia Histórica del Viaje* (Tomo I); Cerezo Martínez, ed., *Diario General del Viaje* (Tomo II); Felix Muñoz Garmendia, *Diarios y Trabajos Botánicos de Luis Neé* (Tomo III); Victoria Ibañez Montoya, *Trabajos científicos y correspondencia de Tadeo Haenke* (Tomo IV); Juan Pimentel Igea, *Antropología y Noticias Etnográficas* (Tomo V); Luis Rafael Martínez-Cañavete Ballesteros, *Trabajos Astronómicos, geodésicos, e hidrográficos* (Tomo VI); Juan Pimentel Igea, *Descripciones y reflexiones políticas* (Tomo VII); others are Blanca Saíz, *Bibliografía sobre Alejandro Malaspina* (Madrid: Ediciones El Museo Universal, 1993); José de la Sota Rius, *Tras las Huellas de Malaspina* (Madrid: Lunwerg Editores, 1994); María Dolores Higueras, ed., *Catálogo crítico de los documentos de la Expedición Malaspina (1789–1794) del Museo Naval*, 3 vols. (Madrid: Museo Naval, 1985–1994); and Mercedes Palau Baquero and Antonio Orozco Acuaviva, eds., *Malaspina '92: Jornadas Internacionales* (Cádiz: Real Academia Hispanoamericana, 1994).

2. The first circumnavigation of the globe, headed by Ferdinand Magellan, a Portuguese sailing for Spain, was also completed during this period. After Magellan's death in the Philippines, a Spaniard, Juan Sebastián del Cano, brought the remaining ship into port.

3. Bernal Díaz Castillo, *Historia Verdadera de la conquista de la Nueva España* (Madrid, 1632), reprinted 3 vols. (México, D.F.: Pedro Robredo, 1939, and Editorial Porrúa, S. A., 1960).

4. See Maurice G. Holmes, *From New Spain to California by Sea, 1519–1668* (Glendale: Arthur H. Clark Co., 1963); Henry Raup Wagner, *Spanish Voyages to the Northwest Coast of America in the Sixteenth Century* (San Francisco: California Historical Society, 1929), 304–306; W. Michael Mathes, *The Conquistador in California: 1535: The Voyage of Fernando Cortés to Baja California in Chronicles and Documents* (Los Angeles: Dawson's Book Shop, 1973).

5. Holmes, *From New Spain to California by Sea*, 83.

6. Wagner, *Spanish Voyages*, 45; Lesley Byrd Simpson, ed. and trans., *Cortes: The Life of the Conqueror by His Secretary: Francisco López de Gomara* (Berkeley: University of California Press, 1964), 403; Doris Beale Polk, *The Island of California* (Spokane: Arthur H. Clark Co., 1991), 155.

7. This knowledge, however, was lost time and again. In the early 1700s the Jesuit Father Eusebio Kino temporarily laid to rest the popular perception that California was an island by

overland exploration at the head of the gulf. Nevertheless, the myth persisted until Ferdinand VI, in a royal decree of 1747, proclaimed: "California is not an island." See Polk, *The Island of California*, 326.

8. Mexico's conqueror argued his claims before the royal court, but his lawsuits dragged on before an unsympathetic officialdom.

9. Harry Kelsey, *Juan Rodríguez Cabrillo* (San Marino, Calif.: Huntington Library, 1986), is a definitive treatment of Cabrillo's life during the conquest of Mexico and his role in the California expedition.

10. The single early reference to Cabrillo as being of Portuguese descent comes from Antonio Herrera y Tordesillas, *Historia General de los hechos de los Castellanos en las Islas y Tierra Firme del Mar Oceano*, 4 vols. (Madrid: Imprenta Real, 1601–1615; also printed in 17 vols., Madrid: Real Academia de la Historia, 1936–1957). His name in Portuguese would be João Rodrigues Cabrilho, but he always signed himself Juan Rodríguez in the Spanish way. Cabrillo, or Cabrilho, is unknown as a surname in Portugal, although there are several Portuguese villages called Cabril, from which the name might have been derived, and that claim Juan Cabrillo as their own. Cabrillo as a surname, however, is found throughout Spain. See Kelsey, *Juan Rodríguez Cabrillo*, chapter 1, for convincing evidence of Rodríguez Cabrillo's Spanish nationality.

11. Holmes, *From New Spain to California*, 102.

12. Kelsey, *Cabrillo*, 105–107. The *San Miguel*, never very seaworthy, was left ashore on the California coast.

13. Herbert E. Bolton, ed., "A Summary Account of Juan Rodríguez Cabrillo's Voyage," *Spanish Exploration in the Southwest, 1542–1706* (New York: Charles Scribner's Sons, 1916), 23. The "bearded and clothed men" were no doubt Spaniards from the Coronado expedition of 1540–1541. Kelsey, *Cabrillo*, 144, reports that Guacamal was the name the Indians gave to the Spaniards.

14. Ibid., 24.

15. Ibid., 25.

16. Kelsey, *Cabrillo*, 158. Cabrillo, upon learning that his men were in need of help in a battle with the Indians, gathered a relief party and rowed ashore. "As he began to jump out of the boat," wrote Francisco de Vargas, "one foot struck a rocky ledge, and he splintered a shinbone." Later, in 1560, Cabrillo's son said that his father had a broken leg, while another narrative (that of Urdaneta) reports that he broke his arm close to the shoulder. Wherever the site of the injury, gangrene set in and became the cause of his death.

17. Ibid., 160.

18. Following the return of Columbus from "the Indies" in 1492, Pope Alexander VI, for the purpose of conversion of natives, divided the newly discovered lands between Spain and Portugal.

19. Amancio Landín Carrasco, et al., *Descubrimientos Españoles en el Mar de Sur* (Madrid: Editorial Naval, 1992), vol. II, chapter VII.

20. Henry R. Wagner, "Urdaneta and the Return Route from the Philippine Islands," *Pacific Historical Review* 13 (1944): 313–16; Charles E. Nowell, "Arellano vs. Urdaneta," *Pacific Historical Review* 31 (May 1962): 112.

21. See William Lytle Schurz, *The Manila Galleon* (New York: E. P. Dutton, 1939).

22. Captain James Cook's use of fresh lime juice during the 1770s is given credit as the first effective remedy against scurvy.

23. K. R. Andrews, "The Aims of Drake's Expedition," *American Historical Review* 73 (February 1968): 724–41; Henry R. Wagner, *Sir Francis Drake's Voyage Around the World: Its Aims and Achievements* (San Francisco: California Historical Society, 1926).

24. The other four ships had all turned back to England.

25. Harry Kelsey, "Did Francis Drake Really Visit California?" *Western Historical Quarterly* 21 (November 1990): 445–62; Norman J. H. Thrower, *Sir Francis Drake and the Famous Voyage, 1577–1580: Essays Commemorating the Quadricentennial of Drake's Circumnavigation of the Earth* (Berkeley: University of California Press, 1984); W. L. Hanna, *Lost Harbor: The Controversy over Drake's Anchorage* (Berkeley: University of California Press, 1979).

26. Adolph S. Oko, "Francis Drake and Nova Albion," *California Historical Quarterly* 43 (June 1964): 137.

27. Since no archeological remains of Drake's visit have been uncovered anywhere in the area, the alleged discovery of Drake's "Plate of Brass" at Drake's Bay in 1933, and its discovery or rediscovery in 1936 near Corte Madera Creek inside San Francisco Bay, have done little more than add a note of additional confusion. Following internal and external analysis, a metallurgical study, and identification of the writing as Elizabethan in style and spelling, the plate was duly authenticated shortly after it was found. After considerable speculation that the plate was fake, additional tests were made during the 1970s and 1980s. With new evidence that contradicted earlier findings, few persons remain who believe the artifact is genuine.

28. See Robert F. Heizer, *Francis Drake and the California Indians* (Berkeley: University of California Press, 1947). Harry Kelsey, in "Did Drake Really Visit California?" believes that the evidence is inconclusive regarding the identity of the Indians.

29. See W. S. W. Vaux, ed., *The World Encompassed by Sir Francis Drake, Being His Next Voyage . . . Collated with an Unpublished Manuscript of Francis Fletcher, Chaplain to the Expedition* (London: The Hakluyt Society, 1589; reprinted 1854).

30. Schurz, *The Manila Galleon*, 307–309.

31. Unamuno replaced another Manila galleon pilot, Francisco de Gali, who was given charge of exploring the California coast upon his return from Manila in 1584. Since Gali offered no new information, he was ordered by Viceroy Pedro Moya de Contreras to try again. Gali's sudden death gave Unamuno his opportunity. See H. R. Wagner, "The Voyage of Unamuno to California in 1587," *California Historical Society Quarterly* 2 (1923–24): 140–60; and "Relación del viaje y navegación que hizo el capitán Pedro de Unamuno," in W. Michael Mathes, ed., *Californiana* I, (Madrid: José Porrúa Turanzas, 1965), 18–37.

32. Robert F. Heizer, "Archeological Evidence of Sebastián Rodríguez Cermenho's California Visit," *California Historical Society Quarterly* 20 (December 1941): 315–28; see also "La Relación de lo sucedido en el viaje que yo el capitán Sebastián Rodríguez Cermenho hice en lo tocante al descubrimiento del cabo Mendocino," in W. Michael Mathes, ed., *Californiana* I, 163–76; and Henry R. Wagner, "The Voyage to California of Sebastián Rodrigues Cermenho in 1595," *California Historical Society Quarterly* 3 (April 1924): 3–24.

33. W. Michael Mathes, *Vizcaíno and Spanish Expansion in the Pacific Ocean: 1580–1630* (San Francisco: California Historical Society, 1968).

34. El virrey conde de Monterrey a Vizcaíno, 18 de marzo de 1602, Archivo General de Indias, Audiencia de Guadalajara, leg. 133 and in Manuel Ballesteros Gaibrois, ed., *Bibliotheca Indiana: Viajes y Viajeros por Norteamerica* (Madrid: Aguilar, 1958), 65. Also in Mathes, ed., *Californiana* I, 353–64.

35. Fray Antonio de la Ascensión, "Relación breve en que se da noticia del descubrimiento que se hizo en la Nueva España en la Mar del Sur, México, 12 de octubre de 1620," in Ballesteros Gaibrois, ed., *Bibliotheca Indiana, 77*. See also Herbert E. Bolton, ed., "Diary of Antonio de la Ascensión," *Spanish Exploration in the Southwest: 1542–1706,* and W. Michael Mathes, "Early California Propaganda: The Works of Fray Antonio de la Ascensión," *California Historical Quarterly* 50 (June 1971): 195–205.

36. See Frederick J. Teggert and Adolph van Hemert-Engert, *The Narrative of the Portolá Expedition 1769–1770* (Berkeley: University of California Press, 1910); and Peter Browning, ed., *The Discovery of San Francisco Bay: The Portolá Expedition of 1769–1770* (Lafayette, Calif: Great West Books, 1992).

37. Bucareli, Viceroy from 1769 to 1779, showed concern for religious matters and Indian welfare, but he also valued civilian settlement.

38. Charles E. Chapman, *History of California: The Spanish Period* (Boston: Macmillan Co., 1921), 272.

39. Michael Thurman, *The Naval Department of San Blas; New Spain's Bastion for Alta California and Nootka, 1767–1798* (Glendale: Arthur H. Clark Co., 1967), 126.

40. Manuel P. Servin, "Instructions of Viceroy Bucareli to Ensign Juan Perez," *California Historical Society Quarterly* 40 (September 1961): 238.

41. See Herbert K. Beals, ed. and trans., *Juan Pérez on the Northwest Coast: Six Documents of his Expedition in 1774* (Portland: Oregon Historical Society Press, 1989). It was later established that Pérez reached 54 degrees 40 minutes north latitude. Spain's claim to this northern boundary was taken over by the United States as a result of the Adams-Onís Treaty of 1819. See also the Diary of Juan Crespí in Donald C. Cutter and George Butler Griffin, eds. and trans., *The California Coast: A Bilingual Edition of Documents from the Sutro Collection* (Norman: University of Oklahoma Press, 1969).

42. José Mariano Moziño, in Iris H. Wilson Engstrand, ed. and trans., *Noticias de Nutka: An Account of Nootka Sound in 1792* (Seattle: University of Washington Press, 1970, rev. ed. 1991), 14.

43. For artifacts collected by the Spaniards, see Paz Cabello, "Materiales etnográficos de la Costa Noroeste recogidos en el siglo XVIII por viajeros españoles," in José Luis Peset, ed., *Culturas de la Costa Noroestede América* (Madrid: Turner Libros, 1989), 61–80.

44. James Caster, "The Last Days of Juan Pérez, the Mallorcan Mariner," *Journal of the West* 2 (June 1963): 19; see also Beals, ed. and trans., *Juan Pérez on the Northwest Coast.*

45. Thurman, *San Blas,* 139.

46. The American Robert Gray rediscovered the inlet and the river beyond in 1788, bestowing on it the name Columbia.

47. Donald Cutter, "California: Training Ground for Spanish Naval Heroes," *California Historical Society Quarterly* 40 (June 1961): 110.

48. Thurman, *San Blas,* 161.

49. See Theodore E. Treutlein, *San Francisco Bay: Discovery and Colonization, 1769–1776* (San Francisco: California Historical Society, 1968), chap I, 26. The presidio was founded as a result of the Anza overland expedition from Sonora in 1775, which brought the settlement's necessary soldiers and colonists to California. The presidio site was chosen by Lt. José Joaquín Moraga of Anza's company, and construction began on July 26, 1776. The founding ceremony took place on September 17, and Moraga, with fathers Francisco Palóu and Pedro

Cambón, selected a site on the Río Dolores for Mission San Francisco de Asís, which was dedicated on October 9, 1776.

50. See for example Donald C. Cutter, *Malaspina in California* (San Francisco: John Howell Books, 1961), and *California in 1792: A Spanish Naval Visit* (Norman: University of Oklahoma Press, 1990); Iris H. Wilson Engstrand, *Spanish Scientists in the New World: The Eighteenth Century Expeditions* (Seattle: University of Washington Press, 1981), and Engstrand, ed. and trans., *Noticias de Nutka*; María Pilar de San Pío, *Expediciones Españolas del Siglo XVIII* (Madrid: Editorial Mapfre, 1992); Antonio Lafuente and José Sala Catalá, eds., *Ciencia colonial en América* (Madrid: Alianza Editorial, 1992); Belén Sánchez, ed., *La Real Expedición Botánica a Nueva España* (Madrid: Real Jardín Botánico, 1987); María Dolores Higueras, ed., *La Botánica en la Expedición Malaspina* (Madrid: Turner Libros, 1989); Fermín del Pino Díaz, ed., *Ciencia y Contexto Histórico Nacional en las Expediciones Ilustradas a América* (Madrid: Consejo Superior de Investigaciones Científicas, 1988); and Andrés Galera Gómez, *La Ilustración Española y el Conocimiento del Nuevo Mundo* (Madrid: Consejo Superior de Investigaciones Científicas, 1988). See also footnote 1.

51. See Engstrand, *Spanish Scientists in the New World*, 3–12.

52. James Cook and James King, *A Voyage to the Pacific Ocean Undertaken by the Command of His Majesty, for Making Discoveries in the Northern Hemisphere in the Years 1776, 1777, 1778, 1779 and 1780*, 3 vols. and atlas (London: G. Nicol and G. Catell, 1784). John Ledyard of Connecticut, who sailed with Cook on the *Resolution*, compiled a narrative of the Englishman's last expedition that appeared in 1783. Cook's official record of the voyage, completed by Captain James King, was published in London in 1784. Among the cultural and scientific data were accounts of how Cook's men traded trinkets to the Nootkan Indians for fur pelts, items that they later sold in China for $100 apiece. The news excited American, British, and French interest in the possibilities of a Northwest fur trade and provided a strong motive for further exploration. The Russians by this time were actively trading in the Aleutian Islands. See James K. Mumford, ed., *John Ledyard's Journal of Captain Cook's Last Voyage* (Corvallis: Oregon State University Press, 1963).

53. Charles N. Rudkin, trans. and ed., *The First French Expedition to California: Lapérouse in 1786* (Los Angeles: Dawson's Book Shop, 1959), 62. Governor Pedro Fages, and especially his wife, Doña Eulalia, were pleased to entertain the count and his party and gave the French such a generous show of hospitality that La Pérouse was overwhelmed. Instructed by the Crown to treat the members of the expedition as if they were countrymen, Fages refused payment for provisions and supplies. In describing their welcome by Father Fermín Francisco de Lasuén, the count wrote: "We were received like lords of the parish making their first entry into their estates."

54. Ibid., 53.

55. Ibid., 56.

56. Engstrand, *Spanish Scientists in the New World*, 45.

57. Donald C. Cutter, *Malaspina in California*, 28.

58. Ibid., 31.

59. Willis L. Jepson, *The Silva of California* (Berkeley: University of California Press, 1910), 138.

60. A one-volume summary of the expedition was published in Madrid in 1885 by Pedro de Novo y Colson entitled *Viaje político-científico alrededor del mundo por las corbetas* Descu-

bierta y Atrevida *al mando de los Capitanes de Navio D. Alejandro Malaspina y D. José de Bustamante y Guerra desde 1789 a 1794* (Madrid: Imprenta de la Viuda e Hijos de Abienzo, 1885).

61. Quoted in Cutter, *Malaspina in California*, 36.

62. The British challenge to Spain's sovereignty north of the Strait of Juan de Fuca began in 1789. An agreement reached between Madrid and London—the Nootka Convention of 1790—effectively ended Spanish occupation of the area in 1795.

63. Viaje a la Costa N. O. de la America Septentrional por Juan Francisco de la Bodega y Quadra . . . en el año 1792. MS, Archivo del Ministerio de Asuntos Exteriores, Madrid.

64. Moziño, trained as a theologian, physician, and botanist, joined the Royal Scientific Expedition to New Spain in 1789 and was a part of botanical surveys throughout the area north of Mexico City. Because funding was short for the Spanish group, Viceroy Conde de Revillagigedo of New Spain appointed Moziño to accompany Bodega y Quadra to the Pacific Northwest.

65. Viaje de Bodega y Quadra 1792, Ministerio de Asuntos Exteriores, Madrid.

66. Cardero, a native of Ecija in southern Spain and former cabin-boy with the Malaspina expedition, had developed his ability throughout the journey, beginning with rough sketches off the coast of South America. By 1792, his skills were equal to or in some cases superior to the official artists.

67. Dionisio Alcalá Galiano and Cayetano Valdés, *Relación del viaje hecho por las goletas "Sutil" y "Mexicana" en el año 1792 para reconocer al estrecho de Fuca* (Madrid: Imprenta Real, 1802; reprinted Madrid, 1958); see also Cutter, *California in 1792: A Spanish Naval Visit;* and John Kendrick, trans., *The Voyage of Sutil and Mexicana, 1792: The Last Spanish Exploration of the Northwest Coast of America* (Spokane: Arthur H. Clark Company, 1996).

68. See Cook, *Floodtide of Empire*, 384.

69. See Engstrand, *Spanish Scientists in the New World*, 129–42. Longinos, a Spaniard who worked with José Mariano Moziño in the royal expedition in Mexico, had been at odds with the director, Dr. Martín de Sessé, and most of the other scientists. Viceroy Revillagigedo sent Longinos to California in 1791 via ship from San Blas as a means of avoiding ill feelings among members of the expedition.

70. The original Longinos journal is located in the Huntington Library, San Marino, California. It has been edited and translated by Lesley Byrd Simpson as *Journal of José Longinos Martínez, Notes and Observations of the Naturalist of the Botanical Expedition in Old and New California and the South Coast* (San Francisco: John Howell Books, 1961). A recent Spanish edition is by Salvador Bernabéu Albert, *Diario de las expediciones de José Longinos* (Madrid: Doce Calles, 1994).

71. Margaret Eyer Wilbur, ed., *Vancouver in California: The Original Account of George Vancouver* (Los Angeles: Dawson's Book Shop, 1954). After his visit to San Francisco, Vancouver wrote unsympathetically: "Instead of finding a country tolerably well inhabited and far advanced in cultivation, if we except its natural pastures, the flocks of sheep, and herds of cattle, there is not any object to indicate the most remote connection with any European, or other civilized nation. This sketch will be sufficient, without further comment, to convey some idea of the inactive spirit of the people, and the unprotected state of the establishment of this port, which I should conceive ought to be a principal object of the Spanish crown."

72. Chapman, *History of California*, 379; George Vancouver, *A Voyage of Discovery to the*

North Pacific Ocean and Round the World (London: C. J. and J. Robinson; J. Edwards, 1798), III, 1093. Off San Pedro on November 24, 1793, the captain noted in his journal that he had "been given to understand that a very advantageous settlement is established on a fertile spot somewhere in this neighborhood . . . at the distance of some miles from the coast called Pueblo de los Angeles; 'the country town of the Angels,' formed in the year 1781. This establishment was looked for in all directions, but nothing was perceived that indicated either habitations or inhabitants." In Vancouver, *Voyage of Discovery,* III, 1104.

    73. Wilbur, *Vancouver in California,* 233.

5

Land, Labor, and Production

The Colonial Economy of Spanish and Mexican California

Steven W. Hackel

As the sesquicentennial of California's admission to the Union approaches, California can boast of one of the most productive economies the world has ever seen: the Golden State annually produces more goods and services than all but a handful of the world's nations. But during the Spanish colonial period (1769–1821) and the Mexican national period (1822–1846), contemporaries lamented the lack of economic growth in Alta California. In 1796, the Franciscan missionary José Señán dismissed the region's settlers as lazy and unproductive, claiming that they preferred playing cards to plowing fields. Señán attributed most of their idleness to Spanish policies: the inflated cost of goods imported from central Mexico and the low market price of the settlers' agricultural products deprived settlers of incentive to produce beyond a basic subsistence level.[1] During the Mexican period, when the new government relaxed restrictions on free trade, foreign trade and domestic production increased, yet to Mexicans and Californios alike, California remained a land of untapped economic potential.

Assertions that Spain and Mexico had failed to develop California's economic riches increased after the Gold Rush and subsequently became enshrined in historical interpretations of California. After James Marshall made his discovery of gold at John Sutter's mill in 1848, it seemed to contemporary observers that California, for the first time, was all bustle and boom. The foreign-born population of the region grew dramatically, as did the economic infrastructure necessary to meet its needs. California's ascendance to the center of world commerce was so sudden that many observers concluded that there had been little or no economic development in California before the Gold Rush. One keen observer of capitalism, Friedrich Engels, believed that California's growth was unprecedented for, as he told Karl Marx in 1852, large new markets had been created "out of nothing."[2]

When the American amateur artist William R. Hutton drew *San Luis Rey Mission* in 1848, it had long ago entered into decline. At the height of its prosperity, however, San Luis Rey was one of the largest and most populous Indian missions in both Americas, part of the chain of Franciscan missions that dominated the colonial economy of California until their secularization in the 1830s at the order of Governor José Figueroa. In 1831 such was the success of San Luis Rey that Father Antonio Peyri could report that its herds of cattle and sheep each numbered over twenty-five thousand. *Courtesy Huntington Library.*

    While contemporaries were right to marvel at the rapid expansion of the California economy during and after the Gold Rush, they underestimated the economy of California during the Spanish and Mexican periods. Before 1848, as recent scholarship has shown, Indians, Franciscans, soldiers, settlers, and traders engaged in modes of exchange and production that reflected local and national strategies of economic development. Furthermore, the development during the Spanish and Mexican periods of intensive agriculture, cattle ranching, artisan crafts, and foreign commerce transformed the landscape of California and its native peoples and introduced forms of labor and production that continued into the American period. Thus, economic activity in Spanish and Mexican California, although limited in scale compared to the boom after 1848, contributed to much of the economic growth in the Golden State during and after the Gold Rush.

SPANISH IMPERIAL ECONOMIC PHILOSOPHIES

Spanish settlement in Alta California, unlike in many other areas of New Spain, was not motivated by a belief that the region and its peoples held great economic potential. Rather, Spain moved into Alta California in 1769 to protect the silver mines of northwestern New Spain from a feared Russian or English advance. To that end, from present-day San Diego to San Francisco, Spain created a coastal chain of twenty Franciscan missions, four military presidios, and three civilian settlements.

Spanish imperial ministers adhered to an economic doctrine known today as mercantilism. In contrast to capitalism, which relies on the state to develop a national economy hospitable for private business, mercantilism depended on the economy of the mother country to promote the growth of the nation-state.[3] Colonies would produce goods and raw materials for the mother country and purchase the finished goods it manufactured. Royal monopolies, exclusive contracts, import and export duties, and restricted access to colonial ports protected fledgling industries at home and in the colonies and ensured that the colonial economy worked to the advantage of the mother country, not a rival nation state. These mercantilist beliefs and practices greatly influenced the development of the economy of Spanish California. But during the late eighteenth century, the Spanish Crown became increasingly preoccupied with reducing the expense of its overseas empire. Therefore, the economic development of Alta California and the relationships among its missions, presidios, and pueblos also bore the imprint of officials who sought to ensure that the colonists could feed, clothe, and protect themselves with a minimum of royal support.

SUPPLY SHIPS AND ECONOMIC REGULATIONS

In Alta California, as elsewhere in the Spanish borderlands, the state formed the foundation for the colonial economy.[4] The state provided the soldiers with purchasing power in the form of salaries, and it supplied the annual shipments of goods they purchased and consumed. At first, each Franciscan missionary (usually two per mission) received an annual stipend of 350 pesos.[5] Newly established missions were granted an additional 1,000 pesos for agricultural implements, church ornaments, and other goods necessary for the mission.[6] These payments came from the state-controlled "Pious Fund," which had originally been established to support the Jesuit missions of Baja California.

During the first years of Spanish settlement in Alta California, soldiers, settlers, and padres depended on supplies imported from Mexico. José de Gálvez, *visitador general* (inspector general) of New Spain and architect of the Spanish occupation of Alta California, realized that Alta California would have to be supplied by sea, and he ordered the creation of a naval post at San Blas on the west coast of Mexico, in the present state of Nayarit, solely for that purpose.[7] Shipments of goods to Alta California were well documented. For example, when the packet boat *San Antonio* set sail for Monterey in 1771, it carried ten additional Franciscans and a wide array of provisions for the missions and presidios: agricultural tools, cooking implements, and most important, basic foodstuffs such as biscuits, ham, sugar, corn, flour, rice, beans, wheat, wine, and brandy. Even chickens and pigs made the journey.[8] Much to the despair of soldiers and missionaries, these supply shipments proved unreliable. Frequently, colonists, waited in vain for the ships to appear on the horizon, or else they found that their provisions had spoiled before they could be unloaded. When the ships arrived later than expected, missionaries and soldiers cut their rations to a minimum and relied on the food reserves of local Indians.

To address these and other problems, Fray Junípero Serra, father-president of the Alta California missions, traveled to Mexico City in 1773, where he appealed directly to the viceroy. Serra's petitions led to the promulgation of the *Echeveste Reglamento,* named after its author, Juan José Echeveste, the official in charge of forwarding supplies to Alta California. This new regulation increased the padres' and soldiers' annual salaries, set a standard markup for products imported into the region, and streamlined the purchase and shipment of provisions to Alta California.[9] Under the new regulation, the annual stipend of each mission rose to 800 pesos. Double rations for five years were allocated to padres in charge of establishing new missions. And soldiers' salaries, which were paid in kind, not coin, increased to 365 pesos a year. The Crown, however, took back this increase through a surcharge on all the "goods, clothings, and provisions" with which soldiers were paid.[10] Echeveste allowed prices for imported goods sold at the presidio to fluctuate according to their levels in Mexico.[11] Thus, forces in distant markets initially determined the purchasing power of soldiers and padres in Alta California. Overall, apart from authorizing a few sailors from San Blas to remain in the California missions as laborers, the *Echeveste Reglamento* did little to foster the colony's self-sufficiency or reduce the Crown's annual expenditures in Alta California.

In 1781, a new economic regulation, written by Governor Felipe de Neve (1775–1782), reorganized the finances of California and shaped the economy of the province until the advent of the Mexican period. One of the most serious problems Neve confronted in Alta California was the soldiers' poor morale, a condition he attributed partly to their low pay and the inflated prices they were charged for goods. Neve, therefore, gave his soldiers the equivalent of a raise. Although he reduced their salaries, he greatly increased their purchasing power by eliminating the surcharge on goods. Furthermore, soldiers were to receive one-fourth of their pay in coin.[12]

Drawn in 1791 by the Spanish expeditionary artist José Cardero, *Soldado de Monterey* depicts Gabriel Moraga, a young soldier at the Monterey presidio who served in the military for nearly thirty years, ultimately rising to the rank of lieutenant. Initially dependent on supply ships from Mexico, the presidios increasingly came to rely on the missions for food-stuffs and manufactured goods. Credits obtained in return by the Franciscans allowed them to import a range of important items, enriching the local economy. *Courtesy Museo Naval, Madrid. Photograph courtesy Iris Engstrand.*

MISSION ECONOMIC GROWTH

During the years when Spanish officials were articulating the structure of the economy of California, the missions, which would soon dominate the colonial economy, emerged as productive agricultural enterprises. In 1774, although dry soil impeded agriculture at Mission San Diego, seeds sown at missions San Carlos, San Gabriel, San Luis Obispo, and San Antonio all yielded abundant harvests, giving the colony its first taste of self-sufficiency. In 1775, these missions produced 1,029 *fanegas* of wheat and 974 *fanegas* of corn.[13] Missions Santa Clara, San Francisco, and San Juan Capistrano, all of which were founded in 1776 and 1777, quickly reaped abundant yields, and by 1778, the missions harvested enough agricultural foodstuffs to satisfy their own needs.[14] Although annual production at the individual missions fluctuated, the exchange of surpluses between missions alleviated local shortfalls; manufactured goods, however, were still imported from Mexico. By 1805, nineteen missions cultivated crops, and their collective harvests of wheat, corn, barley, and beans totaled almost sixty thousand *fanegas*, nearly a thirty-fold increase in aggregate mission productivity during three decades. An increase in Indian laborers and more careful selection of fields combined with the padres' realization that wheat, their preferred crop, had a much lower yield than corn, contributed to the expansion of mission agricultural productivity.[15]

Mission livestock also increased quickly, as the small herds of cattle herded overland from Baja California and Sonora in 1769 and the early 1770s multiplied.[16] In 1773, the five missions had 204 head of cattle; by 1775, they counted 427 head. By 1805, mission livestock holdings were so enormous that they had become a nuisance to Spaniards and Indians alike: the missions and their ranchos counted over 130,000 sheep, 95,000 cattle, 21,000 horses, 1,000 mules, 800 pigs, and 120 goats.[17] Missionaries controlled the best grazing lands, which they guarded from encroachment by Spanish settlers. Fewer than thirty active and retired soldiers successfully petitioned the governor for land on which to graze their own herds. These private ranchos, although enormous, never rivaled the missions' productivity, and grantees received only usufruct rights, not permanent title to the land.[18]

In California, the presidios rapidly became dependent on the missions for food and basic manufactured goods. At first, the missions sold only food to the presidios, but after the 1790s, once Indians had learned new crafts and trades, the missions became veritable general stores. The soap soldiers used to clean themselves, the shoes and boots they pulled on in the morning, the saddles they rode in, the candles they read by, the beds and blankets they slept in, even the coffins they were buried in— these goods and others were produced and sold by the missions. The military's dependence on the missions became nearly complete after 1810, when civil war in Mexico undercut Spain's ability to provision Alta California.

This dependence, however, was not one-sided, and mission-presidio exchange was equally important to the survival and growth of the missions. In return for goods sold to the presidios, the missions received a credit, which they redeemed in Mexico City through their purchasing agent. Through sales to the presidios, a mission could amass a credit worth double or triple the eight hundred peso annual stipend allocated to its missionaries, thereby enabling it to purchase goods it could not manufacture, such as prayer books, trade beads, woolen blankets, fine cloth, paper products, cooking spices, and wine, chocolate, and rice.[19]

THE PUEBLOS

To reduce the military's dependence on the missions and supply ships, Spain established civilian communities, or pueblos, in San José (1777), Los Angeles (1781), and the Villa de Branciforte (1797), near present-day Santa Cruz, in the hope that their inhabitants would produce enough food to feed the region's soldiers. The pueblos' economies have received less attention than those of the missions, but there is little doubt that during the Spanish period, the economies of the civilian communities were directed nearly exclusively toward providing the military with agricultural foodstuffs. San José produced large surpluses of grain within several years of its establishment.[20] According to Governor Neve, in 1781, the presidios of Monterey and San Francisco "were completely fed by the town of San José whose harvest exceeded 1,300 *fanegas* of grain."[21] During the remainder of the eighteenth century, San José harvested surplus quantities of beans, wheat, and especially corn. Production at San José fell after 1796, perhaps as a result of the establishment, twenty miles north, of Mission San José, which gained control of the Indian laborers who had done most of the community's agriculture work.

While statistics for agricultural production in Los Angeles are scarce, it is clear that the pueblo sporadically produced impressive amounts of corn. Agricultural production in Los Angeles, however, also stagnated after 1800.[22] The Villa de Branciforte, about which less is known, was the least productive of the three towns.[23] Although the pueblos were able to sustain themselves and the presidios during only a few years, their surpluses constituted an important supplement to the grain the presidios purchased directly from the missions. After 1790, in part because of the pueblos' productivity, supply ships no longer needed to carry flour, corn, or beans—the most important staples—from San Blas to Alta California.[24]

Critics of Spanish economic policy—including Governor Diego de Borica (1794–1800)—argued that economic development of the towns in Alta California would never reach its potential until the *pobladores* were allowed to market their grain beyond the presidios. In February 1801, the *Junta Superior de Real Hacienda* agreed and approved Borica's plan to allow the *pobladores* to sell their surplus grain to the San Blas supply ships. This experiment proved an immediate success. In 1801, San

José supplied the ships *Princesa* and *Concepción* with 1,830 *arrobas* of flour.[25] Apparently, the town's horse-powered mill turned day and night to fill the order. In July 1801, Los Angeles *vecinos* also offered to supply wheat to San Blas. The pueblos' opportunities for trade expanded further in 1806, when they began direct trade with the supply ships.[26] After 1810, however, civil war interrupted the San Blas-Alta California shipments, ending this developing market for the pueblos' surplus.

Throughout the colonial period the *pobladores* pursued agricultural occupations almost exclusively. The Crown's insistence that the *pobladores* produce agricultural foodstuffs and the ease with which the settlers and soldiers could purchase low-price household necessities from the missions stunted urban production of consumer goods and artisan crafts. In Los Angeles, for example, all of the eleven male heads of households in 1781 were identified as farmers; four of these, however, practiced additional trades: one was a blacksmith, two were cobblers, and a fourth was a tailor. In 1816, although the town's population was by then several hundred strong, of the eighty-seven males whose occupations were listed in a census, only three—a scribe, a cobbler, and a potter—practiced non-agricultural professions.[27] Thus, even as the town's population expanded, its artisan sector stagnated.

PRICE REGULATION AND CROWN-SPONSORED ECONOMIC INITIATIVES

In Spanish California few aspects of the colonial economy were more tightly controlled than prices. José de Echeveste and Felipe de Neve both set prices for goods imported into the region. And after the missions and pueblos produced surplus agricultural products, the governors also set maximum prices for goods produced and exchanged within Alta California. In 1781, Neve established maximum prices for sixty-one commodities produced by the missions.[28] Overall, during most of the colonial period, the governors reduced prices in California as mission production increased, and as these prices fell, the missions' forced subsidization of the military increased. Low prices reduced the potential income of the missions, but their effect on mission production awaits future study. Shifts in price, however, could encourage the padres to sell more of the missions' reserves. In 1786 and 1787, when a food shortage gripped California, Governor Pedro Fages (1782–1791) raised the price of corn, chickpeas, barley, chickens, and hens to encourage the padres to sell the soldiers some of the missions' surplus.[29]

Fages's willingness to adjust prices to reflect current levels of production shaped the price schedule he issued in 1788. Animals raised in abundance at the missions and purchased regularly by the soldiers—bulls, cows, oxen, hogs, and sheep—and products produced from them—jerked beef, tallow, and hides—dropped in price. Corn, wheat, and flour prices were unchanged, the price of beans fell, and the cost of chickens and barley rose. For the most part, these early price schedules remained for the duration of the Spanish period with only slight modification. In 1799, Governor Diego de Borica raised the price of wheat and reduced the prices of horses, mares, and colts,[30] and in 1802 Governor José Joaquín de Arrillaga (1800–1814) made only a few changes.[31]

In addition to fixing prices and supporting the development of the missions, presidios, and pueblos, the Crown sponsored three distinct initiatives to speed the economic development of the region. The first two—the promotion of sea otter hunting and the introduction of hemp cultivation—emerged primarily out of the Crown's need for fur pelts and durable cordage to support mining and shipping industries outside Alta California. The third, the transplantation into the region of skilled artisans, however, was designed to expand the range of goods manufactured in Alta California and thereby lessen the province's dependence on imported goods.

As early as the mid-1770s, Spaniards in California had acquired sea otter pelts from coastal Indians.[32] In the mid-1780s, however, two factors rendered sea otter pelts especially valuable to Spanish officials. Their warm and luxurious fur was prized in China, where a prime pelt could fetch a considerable sum. More important, though, in Canton, furs could be traded for mercury, a metal that was in short supply in New Spain, although it figured prominently in the Crown's plans to maximize silver production there. In 1784, Vicente Vasadre y Vega requested royal authority to establish and oversee just such a trade, adding that his plan would prevent the Russians and English from expanding their otter hunting into Spain's waters. The Crown responded enthusiastically, and by 1786 Vasadre was in California overseeing the collection of pelts.[33]

Despite its initial commercial success, bureaucratic obstacles soon thwarted this promising enterprise. Franciscans and soldiers competed with one another for the pelts Indians hunted; Spanish officials felt that Vasadre had paid too much for the skins; and the goods the Franciscans had been promised in return were slow to arrive. In themselves none of these problems could have doomed Vasadre's plan, but the powerful Philippine Company, which had been granted certain monopoly rights to trade with China, obstructed Vasadre's efforts in Canton. In December 1788, Vasadre abandoned the Far East, and in 1790 the Crown terminated Spanish California's first export industry. After 1790, padres and soldiers occasionally shipped pelts to San Blas; most skins, however, were either purchased or gathered by Anglo-American traders or Russian hunters, who ventured more frequently into California's waters after the mid-1790s.[34]

A year after the Crown withdrew its support for the export of otter pelts from California, Franciscans began to cultivate a second and briefly more successful export commodity, hemp.[35] Hemp cultivation figured prominently in Spain's attempt to revitalize its colonial economy. Production of hemp in Spain fell short of domestic needs, and the fiber was essential for the cordage and rigging materials required by New Spain's navy. To spur production, the Crown in 1777 despatched hemp-raising experts to several of its American colonies, and Alta California was selected as one province in which hemp cultivation would be especially promoted.[36]

As early as 1791, a few of the northern missions had planted small quantities of hemp, but they had neither the time nor the expertise to produce large amounts.[37] Hemp production took a more serious turn after 1795, when special instructions were sent from Mexico on how to cultivate the crop. In December Governor Borica ordered the settlers at San José to begin cultivation and authorized them to hire Indians from the surrounding region to help.[38] The following fall, Indians and settlers harvested 560 pounds of hemp.[39] Production at San José and the northern missions, however, never really took off, even though the Crown in 1801 or 1802 transferred to Monterey Joaquín Sánchez, a marine sergeant stationed in San Blas who was experienced at raising hemp.[40] An accidental fire consumed most of the 1804 harvest, and the next year fog and bad weather reduced the yield to 150 pounds.[41]

Hemp cultivation increased dramatically after the harvest of 1805, when Sánchez, having wisely concluded that he had taught the settlers of San José more than they were willing to learn, focused his efforts in the Los Angeles region.[42] The following year, exports exceeded 1,800 pounds. Production further accelerated in 1807, when the governor increased the government's purchase price from three pesos four *reales* to four pesos per *arroba*. The results of Sánchez's relocation to the south and the government's increase in price became clear in 1810: the province produced a whopping 220,000 pounds of hemp, a total that alone probably exceeded the previous two decades' production.[43] The Crown and colonists had finally found an export staple that could be abundantly produced in Alta California; but within a year, commercial production of hemp in Alta California was finished, an early victim in Mexico's struggle for independence. After 1810 there were too few Spanish supply ships to transfer hemp to San Blas, and in February of 1811, Governor Arrillaga told Sánchez to restrict hemp cultivation to the needs of the province.[44]

At the same time that the missions began to cultivate hemp, the Crown transported a group of artisans to Alta California to teach Indians specific trades. Royal officials hoped that these men, through their work with the mission Indians, could eventually increase the range and number of goods produced in the region. Between 1791 and 1795, about twenty skilled artisans worked in Alta California on four- or five-year contracts.[45] Most came from Mexico City or Guadalajara. Among those sent to California were men skilled in stone and brick masonry, carpentry, pottery, tanning, shoemaking, and blacksmithing. A few, namely two tailors and a lathe worker, brought skills that were of little or no value to the missions.[46]

Even though their numbers were few and their stays brief, Mexican artisans left their mark on Alta California. In the mid-1790s, Indians working under their tute-

Constructed between 1810 and 1812 by the mason Claudio López under the supervision of Father José María Zalvidea of Mission San Gabriel, El Molino Viejo was the first water-powered gristmill in California. Since 1965 it has been the southern California headquarters of the California Historical Society. *Courtesy California Historical Society, FN-30501.*

lage completed the church at Mission San Carlos Borromeo, the reconstruction of the Monterey presidio, and large-scale projects elsewhere, such as water-powered flour mills at Missions San Gabriel and Santa Cruz.[47] More importantly, the artisans proved to be valuable teachers. At Mission San Carlos, eight Indians learned carpentry, two mastered blacksmithing, and another eleven, stone masonry and bricklaying.[48] According to Fray Fermín Lasuén, Antonio Domínguez Henríquez successfully taught textile arts throughout Alta California.[49] Thus, long after most Mexican artisans left California, Indians at the missions and the presidios practiced European-style building and manufacturing techniques.

INDIAN LABOR IN THE MISSIONS, PRESIDIOS, AND PUEBLOS OF SPANISH CALIFORNIA

Spain's exploitation of the riches of the Americas depended primarily on Indian labor, and demography and historical precedent left little possibility for Alta California to prove exceptional. Therefore, nearly everything grown or manufactured in the missions, presidios, and pueblos resulted from the labor of Indians. Few Spaniards or Mexicans emigrated to California; those who did employed Indians to do their manual labor. In Alta California, despite the rapid decline in the native population, the population of the *gente de razón* never approached that of the Indians. In the coastal portion of Alta California that Spain controlled, scholars estimate that Indians outnumbered the soldiers and settlers 59,700 to 150 in 1770; 57,000 to 480 in 1780; 43,600 to 1,060 in 1790; 35,850 to 1,800 in 1800; 25,900 to 2,300 in 1810; and 21,750 to 3,400 in 1820.[50] Although *encomienda, repartimiento,* and slavery—the most infamous of Spanish labor systems—had been abolished by 1769, when Alta California was founded, the Franciscans', soldiers', and settlers' treatment of Indian laborers has been the subject of heated controversy ever since the colonial period. Today, Native Americans, church historians, and academic scholars continue to debate whether or not the Spaniards' labor systems amounted to slavery, genocide, or salvation for California Indians.[51]

For the Franciscans, Indian labor amounted to more than the production of food and material goods: it was a morally enriching disciplinary activity that figured prominently in the Indians' conversion from savagery to civilization. To the padres, Indians lived as wild animals, at the whim of nature, without comfort or recourse to work. Franciscans, therefore, saw the transformation of savage Indians into industrious Christians as a wrenching process that was quite literally "unnatural" for the Indians. The recitation and memorization of the catechism and *doctrina* may have prepared the Indians' souls for salvation, but it was the missions' regimented daily work schedule that provided the structure and discipline the padres believed the Indians lacked. In the missions, therefore, the daily schedules of work and prayer dovetailed. In the morning, a bell or an Indian *alcalde* summoned the community to prayer. An hour later, the able-bodied would begin working and continue until around 11:00 A.M. After a meal and a short break, labor would resume. According to the padres, work concluded an hour or so before sunset, in time for communal prayers; soldiers asserted that Indians worked until sunset.[52] Indians worked at the missions five to eight hours a day, five or six days a week.[53] Indians did not work for the missions on Sundays or religious holidays, which numbered as many as ninety-two days in the calendar of Catholic worship.[54] Some of the work around the mission was piecework. Women, for example, could be required to grind a specific amount of grain per day; men could be held responsible for the manufacture of a certain number of adobe bricks. Indians were not paid a daily wage for working in the missions; rather, they were provided with food, housing, religious instruction, and an occasional change of clothing.

All able-bodied Indians, regardless of age, performed some sort of task. The type of work, however, depended on the season, the level of economic development of the mission, and the age, gender, and skills of the individual. Just as with language and religious instruction, the Franciscans placed their greatest hopes for Indian economic advancement in children, who they believed could be taught "with ease and without violence to grow accustomed to work."[55] Children, therefore, were assigned simple chores, such as ensuring that weeds and birds did not damage vegetable gardens. Privileged young men and boys worked directly for the Franciscans as pages, acolytes, and sacristans. And a select group of men held the supervisory positions of *alcalde* and *regidor*. Most men were trained in trades, such as masonry, carpentry, or leather working, or performed basic manual labor around the mission or in the fields. By contrast, women worked in domestic activities: sewing, washing, culling wheat, and grinding *piñole*.[56] Not all of the jobs in the missions were segregated by sex, however. At Mission Santa Cruz, for example, in 1825, forty men and forty-six women labored in the mission's textile workshops.[57]

After the mid-1790s, when artisans began to teach specific trades at the missions, skilled Indians made up an increasingly large percentage of the mission labor force. By 1825, for example, 31 percent of the 277 laborers at Mission Santa Cruz worked on textile looms, and another 10 percent were listed as artisans or apprentices: carpenters (7), shoemakers (4), masons (4), gunsmiths (3), soapmakers (3), and blacksmiths (2).[58] During the 1820s, the military frequently called on mission masons, bricklayers, and carpenters to maintain and reconstruct the presidios.[59] For a few Indians, the acquisition of such specialized skills provided liberation from the missions. In December 1822, José Chaquiles, a cobbler, petitioned for emancipation from Mission Soledad, claiming that he had the skills to support himself. A month later he was making shoes in San José.[60]

For the economic productivity of the mission, perhaps the most important aspect of Indian labor was its flexibility. When it came time to sow the fields or harvest the crops, bricklayers put down their tools, weaving workshops closed, and all of the mission's able-bodied laborers took to the fields. Shearing sheep, branding livestock, and other indispensable seasonal work, such as producing lime and salt, preparing the tannery, and making tiles so that the mission would have a reserve of roofing material for the soaking winter rains—all of these required a concentration of workers in one industry for a limited amount of time. During these periods of communal work, gendered notions of labor were displaced by the immediate needs of the mission community.

Most scholars have concluded that the average workload in the missions was not so onerous as to have damaged the Indians' physical health. But the coercive measures that Franciscans employed to enforce their labor regime proved both psychologically and physically damaging to the neophytes. Franciscans or Indian *alcaldes* frequently took roll at the missions to make sure that laborers were not shirking their duties. Indians who avoided work were first scolded. Then, if they did not mend their ways, they were whipped or imprisoned. Consequently, many Indians fled the missions. At the request of the Franciscans, soldiers attempted to force runaways back to the missions, an effort that succeeded haphazardly and only served to perpetuate the cycle of coercion and violence. As Sherburne F. Cook suggested in the early 1940s and Robert H. Jackson and Edward Castillo have recently argued, the psychological effects of the Spaniards' coercive measures probably contributed to the high levels of illness and mortality in the missions.[61]

Illness—real and pretended—and absenteeism greatly reduced the labor force at the missions. "The healthy [Indians] are clever at offering as a pretext chronic ailments," Lasuén lamented, "and they know that they are generally believed, and that even in cases of doubt the missionary dispenses them from work."[62] Large-scale exoduses occasionally decimated a mission's workforce, but more common, especially in the later years of the mission period, was slow attrition. For example, in December 1825 nearly a quarter of the adult population at Mission Santa Cruz was unable to work because of flight or some form of illness.[63] In the summer, when the Franciscans allowed Indians a few weeks leave from the missions to visit their unbaptized relatives or ancestral villages, the percentage of available workers frequently dropped to half the adult population.[64]

In addition to linking high rates of mortality and desertion to the missions' coercive labor regime, scholars have argued that Indian laborers suffered incapacitating psychological disorientation when they tried to reconcile Spanish tools, technologies, and schedules with their own worldviews.[65] This approach calls attention to the difficult transitions that the mission workplace demanded of Indians, but it hobbles the scholarship on labor in the missions by depicting Indian people as static, immutably bound to a wild landscape and a savage mentality. By arguing that Indians could not make the difficult transition to the modes of labor and forms of technology that the missions brought to Alta California, scholars—like the Franciscans—have largely disregarded or misunderstood the Indians who did adjust to mission labor. Ironically, in much of this scholarship, Indians are ascribed the power to reject the Franciscans' labor regime but denied the ability to incorporate aspects of it selectively into their own lives.

Had Indians not proven so adept with European technologies, Alta California would have remained a colony dependent on imported grains, where Franciscans, soldiers, settlers, and Indians lived and prayed in thatched huts. Perhaps as a way of assuaging psychological trauma and maintaining continuity, Indians blended old and new economic activities in their work at the missions and in their villages. Despite their attempt to fill the Indians' days with a novel routine of work and prayer, the Franciscan regime never completely displaced indigenous economic activities or manufacturing processes. Rather, mission Indians continued to gather roots, acorns, and grasses, and hunt fowl, game, and fish even as they worked in the missions' fields and workshops, thereby interweaving Indian and Spanish technologies, work rhythms, and productive processes.

Outside the missions, the presidios constituted a second important site of labor in colonial California. Recent archaeological work even suggests that the presidios, in part because of their reliance on Indian labor, became significant areas of acculturation between Indians and soldiers during the colonial period.[66] In Alta California, soldiers were few and averse to manual labor. Each of the four presidios usually had between forty-five and sixty men assigned to it. But only a small fraction of these soldiers was at the presidio at any given time. When available soldiers were forced to work on the construction of the presidios, they griped that the work was too hard and the pay too low; one soldier even complained that "slaves could not have been treated worse."[67]

Faced with grumbling soldiers and crumbling presidios, the Spanish military leaders quickly turned to local Indians as a source of labor. Indian labor at the presidios took at least five different forms, yet scholars have focused on only two of these forms: convict labor and mission contract labor. Convict labor involved Indians—baptized and unbaptized—arrested for a crime and sentenced to presidial labor. The military did not pay convict laborers a daily stipend; it merely provided sustenance. Convict labor at the presidios was so common that Father Lasuén complained that the soldiers' "greedy desire to obtain free labor" led them to arrest Indians for crimes the Franciscans could have punished.[68]

Even as they condemned the military's use of Indian convicts, the Franciscans readily supplied the military with contract laborers, who performed a host of tasks at the presidios, from cooking the soldiers' meals to rebuilding the presidio's walls. The presidios paid the mission—not the Indian laborers—one and one-half *reales* a day for each unskilled laborer and slightly more for carpenters or masons.[69] As contemporary accounts and mission records make clear, the export of mission laborers to the presidios was extensive. For example, in the years 1787, 1797, 1808, and 1817, the Monterey presidio was charged for 544, 741, 2,880, and 484 days of Indian labor.[70] In spite of of their conviction that the soldiers' behavior would undermine the missions' religious teachings, Franciscans willingly supplied the presidios with a steady supply of Indian laborers. For in doing so, the padres added hundreds or even thousands of pesos to the mission's accounts in a given year.

Historians still need to learn more about the quantity and nature of convict and mission contract labor at the presidios, but the near-exclusive focus on these forms of labor has diverted attention from the considerable number of unbaptized (gentile) Indians who came to work at the presidios on a pre-arranged basis.[71] The initial construction and maintenance of the presidios, when not undertaken by grumbling soldiers, was carried out by gentile contract laborers. For example, from April 1790 to September 1796 groups of Indians from the Santa Clara Valley worked one-month

Soldiers and Indians busy themselves outside the Monterey presidio in a pen-and-ink drawing executed in 1791 by José Cardero, an artist with the Spanish exploring expedition commanded by Alejandro Malaspina. When Cardero visited the capital of California, work on the new presidio buildings, which had begun the previous year, was well advanced. Like most other undertakings that contributed to the growth and development of the province, the Hispanic building program relied heavily on Indian labor. *Courtesy Museo Naval, Madrid. Photograph courtesy Iris Engstrand.*

shifts rebuilding the Monterey presidio.[72] For one month's work, the military paid an unbaptized laborer one blanket, valued at between five and nine *reales;* by comparison, the military paid the mission thirty-six *reales* a month for each mission laborer. Thus, in June 1790, Governor Fages was justified when he boasted to his superiors that his employment of gentile Indians had saved "the major expense of paying the daily wages of the Indians from the missions."[73] Unbaptized Indians, most likely, agreed to work for the military to obtain European goods without becoming entangled in the Franciscans' confining web. Labor at the presidio also guaranteed a daily ration of food, which was a powerful incentive during the mid-1790s, when drought stunted the region's wild seeds and killed many of its grazing animals.

Beyond the various forms of convict and contract labor, informal labor by baptized and unbaptized Indians formed a fourth form of Indian labor at the presidios. Unbaptized Indians frequently performed small tasks at the presidios, in return for food and trade goods. The Franciscans allowed mission Indians who had completed their assigned tasks to work at a presidio, and many mission Indians worked at the presidios in what little free time they had. On mission holidays, Sundays, and during the summer when the Franciscans let the Indians leave the mission for a few weeks, some men and women went to the presidios to cook food, wash clothes, mill grain, and carry wood.[74]

This informal labor at the presidios was not limited to the few brief periods when padres gave Indians leave from the missions; many baptized Indians worked for soldiers on the sly, out of sight of the Franciscans. Thus, covert informal labor comprised a fifth and final form of Indian labor at the presidios. Covert informal labor at the presidios is poorly documented because by necessity Indians and soldiers hid most of it from the Franciscans, who kept the best written records on colonial California. With a small piece of leather or a handful of corn, soldiers often paid Indians to gather wood, grind corn, and wash clothes. This labor was so common that the soldiers, in paying the Indians for their work, often exhausted their weekly rations a few days after they received them.[75] Men with special skills—shoemakers, tanners, and deer-skin workers—frequently slipped away to the presidios.[76] Women, too, would occasionally leave the missions to sell wood or wash the soldiers' clothes. Thus, despite the Franciscans' opposition, mission Indians worked at the presidios covertly to supplement their diets, to obtain trade goods, and to maintain independence from the Franciscans.

In addition to the missions and the presidios, the two principal pueblos of Alta California—San José and Los Angeles—constituted a third center of labor during the colonial period. The majority of settlers, most of whom were retired soldiers, eschewed manual labor and hired local Indians to perform virtually all their tasks. In San José, settlers quickly became dependent on Indian laborers. As early as 1782, the military issued strict guidelines for the employment of local unbaptized Indians, prohibiting "the familiar intercourse which has been observed to occur between the households of the settlers and the pagan men and women." Requests for Indian laborers were to be channeled through a ranking military officer, who would contact a local Indian headman. Indians were to be paid for work done; coercion would not be tolerated in their recruitment. Tellingly, Indian women, who were frequently employed to mill grain or perform other domestic tasks, were not allowed to enter into the *pobladores'* homes, as had been the practice, because such "familiarity" had led to "grievances against both populations."[77]

In the early 1780s, the settlers of Los Angeles developed a similar dependence on Indian laborers.[78] But as many Franciscans and soldiers had discovered during the first years of the missions and presidios, much to their frustration, local Indians would only work for the Spaniards when doing so did not conflict with their own subsistence economy. In April 1784, Lieutenant José Francisco de Ortega must have felt that he alone cared about the pueblo's corn and wheat. With great concern, he reported to the governor that the settlers were "few and useless," and the Indians, who had tilled the land and planted the crop, had offered to help with the harvest, but only after they had finished their own seasonal gathering.[79] That fall, after completing their own harvest, the Gabrielinos reaped from the *pobladores'* fields over 1,800 *fanegas* of corn, 340 *fanegas* of kidney beans, and 9 *fanegas* each of wheat, lentils, and garbanzos.[80]

Within less than a decade of the establishment of Los Angeles, the expansion of the *pobladores'* and *vecinos'* fields and the steady increase in their livestock must have imperiled the Gabrielino economy and made full-time work for the settlers imperative. Thus, in January of 1787, Governor Fages modified for Los Angeles the guidelines issued for San José regulating the recruitment and employment of gentile laborers.[81] Here, too, the governor sought to end the "pernicious familiarity" that resulted from the presence of so many Indian laborers: Indians were not to live in town or enter the settlers' homes, and they were to sleep under the watch of the sentry if they spent the night. Under these restrictive regulations, Indians worked in the settlers' fields, where they earned a third to a half of the crops they harvested.[82] Gabrielinos also toiled in Los Angeles as vaqueros, cooks, muleteers, water carriers, and domestic servants. By the mid-1790s, the presence of so many Indian laborers had led to considerable acculturation between the Indian and Spanish communities. Many Indian laborers spoke Spanish and dressed like their employers, "clad in shoes, with sombreros and blankets."[83] Moreover, many settlers spoke the Indians' language; some even married Indian women.[84]

Only the Franciscans objected to the working relationships between Indians and settlers. The padres knew that the settlers offered the same material incentives the missions used to attract Indians: food, clothing, and beads. But in the missions, Franciscan oversight proved oppressive, housing was crowded, and disease ran rampant, whereas in the pueblos *pobladores* cared little about changing the Indians' religion or sexuality and required laborers to return to their own *rancherías* at the end of the day. The inability of the missions to compete with the attractions of the pueblos led Lasuén to conclude that the towns and their inhabitants were "an immense hindrance to the conversion of the pagans, for they give them bad example, they scandalize them, and they actually persuade them not to become Christians, lest they themselves suffer the loss of free labor."[85] More frustrating to the Franciscans than the loss of these potential converts was the disaffection of those who had previously professed their allegiance to the mission. Baptized Indians also sought work and refuge in the pueblos, even though Governor Fages prescribed ten lashes for neophytes who were repeatedly found in town without permission from the missionaries.

THE COLLAPSE OF ROYAL SUPPORT

During the final decade of Spanish California, revolutionary movements in Spain and Mexico ruptured virtually all state support for California's missions and presidios, rendering Alta California's ties to central Mexico increasingly tenuous. Neither padre nor soldier could count on an annual salary or the goods bought with them, and, as noted above, promising industries, such as the export of hemp and grain, collapsed. The colonial project survived mainly through the productivity of the missions, which continued to feed and clothe the padres and Indians while providing soldiers and *pobladores* with food, basic commodities, and manufactured goods. Father-president Mariano Payeras estimated that after 1810 the missions provided five hundred thousand pesos in assistance to the presidios and the pueblos.[86] The extraction of so much surplus labor and production exacted an enormous toll on the neophytes. "These poor people," lamented Payeras, "will be the most unfortunate and wretched in the world, if they alone, many only recently baptized and civilized, have to support so many troops for so long a time."[87]

Between 1810 and 1821, only one official supply ship arrived from San Blas; however, a minimum of twenty Spanish merchant ships called in Alta California, and this maritime trade helped to buoy up the local economy.[88] Most of the legal trade was carried on between missionaries and Lima traders, who largely took over the function of the San Blas supply ships. The Limeños purchased tallow—a fat rendered from slaughtered cattle—from the Franciscans and in return conveyed goods from Mexico bought specifically for the missions. The presidios also participated in this trade, although only through the assistance of the missions, which provided the cash and tallow that presidial commanders used to purchase goods from visiting ships.

Clandestine trade with Anglo-American, British, and Russian traders also helped padres and soldiers obtain imported necessities. Governors José Joaquín de Arrillaga and Pablo Vicente de Solá (1815–1822) publicly condemned this illegal trade, but in private, they orchestrated it.[89] José Dario Argüello (acting governor 1814–1815) probably spoke for most soldiers, settlers, and padres in Alta California, when, in regard to this contraband trade, he observed wryly: "Necessity makes licit what is not licit by law."[90] While the governors and Franciscans applauded their ingenuity in trading with foreign nationals, the isolation of Alta California from the economies of Spain and central Mexico steadily increased. And although this illicit trade met many of the immediate needs of the province, it fostered a dependence in the region on foreign markets that most Californios would soon regret.

THE MEXICAN PERIOD

The overthrow of Spanish rule in New Spain ushered in a brief period of hope that Alta California's economy would expand and become fully integrated into the national economy.[91] In the mid-1820s the new Mexican government set up a commission, the Junta de Fomento de Californias, and charged it to devise plans for the defense and economic development of California. The junta's bold plans to transfer the San Blas shipworks to Monterey and establish alongside it a monopolistic trading house, the Asian-Mexican Company, however, bore no fruit. As Governor Juan Bautista Alvarado lamented, the program "died without being born."[92]

In fact, to the disappointment of the residents of California, independent Mexico did little to integrate California into the national economy or support the soldiers stationed in the region. And by most accounts, during the decade after Mexican independence, the economic well-being of the region's colonists, soldiers, and Indians further deteriorated. Don José María Herrera, the deputy commissioner of finances whom Mexico sent to Monterey in 1825, was nearly powerless to ensure the effective fiscal administration of Alta California. Soldiers, unpaid for years, refused to serve until paid or simply abandoned the disintegrating presidios.[93] A spectacular, yet unsuccessful, mutiny occurred in Monterey in 1829, when soldiers seized the presidio and railed against the central government for sending them a governor who ignored their privations.[94] The revolt did little to improve the conditions of the rebels; it did, however, prove something of a temporary setback for deputy commissioner Herrera. In May 1830, having been accused by Governor José María de Echeandía of playing a central role in the uprising, Herrera found himself imprisoned on the American ship *Volunteer* and bound for Mexico.[95]

While California politicos complained that the central government neglected their basic needs, the new economic policies pursued by the governors alienated both soldiers and settlers alike. Although Mexico dispensed with Spain's restrictive mercantile policies and opened California to foreign trade, import and export taxes remained high, and after 1826 Monterey was the sole official port of entry.[96] The inadequacy of Mexican coastal patrols and customs officials, however, left most Californians to practice the free trade they preached.[97] A host of forced contributions, fee assessments, and taxes on everything from otter pelts to cattle brands whittled away at the *pobladores'* and soldiers' incomes. Finally, with the important exception of the Híjar-Padrés colony, which brought numerous artisans and teachers to California, the only colonists the Mexican Republic sent to California were foundlings and convicts. In large measure, because of these economic policies, many Californios came to view the central government in Mexico and its representatives in Alta California with skepticism or outright hostility.[98]

Despite the provincials' own frustrations with the local economy, the Mexican period stands out as an era of great and rapid economic transformation. Most importantly, with the opening up of California to international trade immediately after Mexican independence, California's reliance on foreign markets for the sale of its surplus goods accelerated dramatically. A host of foreign companies quickly vied for access to the region's developing hide-and-tallow industry. In June of 1822, months before the Spanish flag was officially lowered in Monterey, the English trading concern of McCulloch, Hartnell and Company negotiated a three-year monopoly on

Monterey, the capital of Alta California, as portrayed in the autumn of 1827 by William Smyth, a young admiralty mate and amateur artist on a British exploring expedition commanded by Frederick Beechey. Though the presidio and a dozen or so adobes scattered about the surrounding plain composed the entire town, it was nonetheless the official center of this distant Mexican province, the seat of the custom house and the single official port of entry. *Courtesy Bancroft Library.*

the purchase of the province's surplus hides and tallow.[99] Both the father-president and the governor could hardly contain their optimism about the expansion of the hide-and-tallow trade. "The poverty of the Province will disappear," wrote Fray Mariano Payeras, " . . . and it will be even less necessary to order items from Mexico City."[100] To his secular counterpart, Governor Pablo Vicente de Solá, who had previously relied on *contrabandistas* to provision his troops, this legalized trade represented the opportunity for which the region had been waiting.[101]

Through the early 1830s, the missions increasingly dominated the production of hides and tallow in California; the extent to which the Franciscans reoriented the mission economy to supply foreign demand for hides and tallow, however, has sparked recent debate. Some scholars have suggested that the padres maximized production of livestock by diverting surplus labor away from other agricultural pursuits and measures that could have arrested the decline of the neophyte population.[102] One scholar has countered that the padres did not reduce the amount of grain sown and that poor climate conditions and soil exhaustion reduced mission agricultural productivity in the 1820s.[103] Each of these arguments suggests new directions for research, and taken collectively they demonstrate how differently historical geographers, archaeologists, and historians interpret economic change.

In addition to opening California to international trade, the Mexican government transferred control over the most important economic resources in the region—land, livestock, and laborers—from the missionaries to the settlers. The Colonization Act of 1824 and the Supplemental Regulations of 1828 created mechanisms through which private individuals—Mexican nationals and foreign immigrants—could for the first time obtain title to land in California.[104] The Supplemental Regulations, however, specified that mission lands, by far the most valuable and accessible, could not be colonized "at present." The Secularization Act of 1833 swept this qualification aside, transferring the temporal authority of the missionaries to secular priests and opening up prime mission lands for pasturage and settlement. Taken together, these laws ushered in the greatest transfer of land and resources in California since the Spaniards first set foot in the region. As a result, by 1840 the private rancho had replaced the mission as the dominant social and economic institution in California, and all but a handful of former mission Indians had been rendered landless.

The privatization of land holding in California occurred at a dizzying pace. During the entire Spanish period fewer than thirty soldiers had received usufruct rights to land; in the first decade of Mexican rule, fewer still gained title.[105] But after 1833, when the Secularization Act went into effect, Mexican governors approved some seven hundred petitions for land, most of which came after 1840.[106] By 1846, retired soldiers, *pobladores,* and recent immigrants from Mexico controlled virtually all the best land along the coast, the interior valleys near the sea, and the Napa and Sacramento valleys situated farther inland.[107] At least sixty-six women—mostly single or widowed—received grants after 1821.[108] While exact figures remain elusive, approximately one-third of all grants in the 1840s went to settlers with non-Spanish, mostly British or American, surnames.[109] Overall, some ten million acres of land, or 10 percent of the surface area of present-day California, had passed into private hands by the close of the Mexican period.[110]

Political influence, economic power, and enormous land holdings quickly became synonymous in Mexican California. In 1846, Thomas Larkin estimated that a group of forty-six men of substance ruled California.[111] Most grants issued during the Mexican period were for parcels of land between ten and twenty thousand acres, but some individuals or families, such as the Yorbas and the Castros, amassed tracts of several hundred thousand acres.[112] Most of this land became pasturage for the large herds required for the hide-and-tallow trade that boomed during the 1830s and early 1840s.

The nature and growth of the hide-and-tallow trade, especially after mission secularization, reinforced the growing dependence of California's economy on Anglo-American trading concerns. Precise figures of the volume of the trade do not exist, but in all likelihood, more than six million hides and seven thousand tons of tallow

Californio vaqueros lasso a steer in a painting by the Cuban artist Augusto Ferran that probably dates to the late 1840s. From late mission days through the era of the great ranchos, livestock raising was the most important industry in California. Cattle provided not only beef for local consumption but hides and tallow for international trade, which blossomed under Mexican rule, enriching large landowners and the American traders who dominated the commerce. *Courtesy Bancroft Library.*

were exported from California between 1826 and 1848.[113] Virtually all of this trade was orchestrated by New England-based merchant houses.[114] The demand for hides was greatest in the eastern United States, where manufacturers turned hides into shoes and other leather products. Traders from Boston purchased the California hides outright or, more commonly, bartered for them with a wide array of manufactured products, which they sold at three to four times their New England value. Shipped to Peru, tallow was made into soap and candles, and then sold to silver miners. Maritime traders encouraged rancheros or missionaries to go deep into debt, thereby tightening their monopoly on the trade.[115] Anglo-American merchants such as Thomas Larkin and Abel Stearns, who purchased hides and sold Boston goods from their stores in California, also controlled a portion of the trade. After a fall in the price of hides on the Boston market rendered the trade unprofitable, and the deterioration of relations between the United States and Mexico in the mid-1840s made Boston traders wary of sending their ships into California's waters, decisions in the eastern United States, not in central Mexico or in California, precipitated the collapse of the hide-and-tallow trade. When gold was discovered in 1848, the heyday of the trade had already passed, and most remaining hide droghers quickly abandoned their ships for the gold fields.[116]

The rise and fall of the hide-and-tallow trade owed much to Anglo-American entrepreneurs, but the production of these export goods depended first and foremost on the rancheros' access to the unemployed and landless Indians who had recently been emancipated from the missions.[117] On the ranchos, former mission Indians performed the same basic tasks that had allowed the Franciscans to dominate the production of hides and tallow until 1834: they herded and slaughtered cattle, preserved hides, and rendered tallow. While the smallest ranchos employed only a handful of Indians, the largest, like Bernardo Yorba's Rancho Cañada de Santa Ana, employed more than a hundred workers to raise and slaughter livestock and dozens more to attend to the rancho's domestic chores.[118] On these enormous ranchos, a gendered division of labor seems to have placed men in the fields and women in the adobes, where they sewed, washed, and cooked.[119] Indian ranch hands usually lived in clusters of makeshift dwellings, where they continued to practice many elements of their culture. As recent archaeological work suggests, even well into the American period, Indians at some of the ranchos continued to manufacture their own pottery from local clay.[120]

Indians who worked on the ranchos rarely received cash for their services. Most were caught up in a complicated system of reciprocal obligations that scholars have variously described as "peonage," "seigneurialism," or "paternalism."[121] In this system Indians worked for the ranchero for basic supplies and a daily ration of food, which they supplemented through their own vegetable gardens or any stray cattle they could pilfer from the rancho's herd. Some ranch hands, like their own employers, accepted goods in advance and then found themselves bound until they had repaid their debt.[122] While by no means the dominant labor institution on the ranchos, a few unscrupulous rancheros did enslave Indians who had been captured on punitive raids.[123] Most rancheros, however, combined aspects of these different labor arrangements to ensure the availability and compliance of Indian workers.[124] Few rancheros became rich from the profits they derived from the Indians' work, but most made enough money to acquire some of life's comforts and to purchase fine cloth, extravagant garments, and luxury goods in an effort to distinguish themselves from their laborers and define themselves as an elevated social class.[125]

Until quite recently, scholars believed that the ranchos, like the missions before

William R. Hutton's drawing of Los Angeles in 1847 shows the white-washed adobes and village church fronting on the plaza, the heart of the principal pueblo of southern California. Though essentially an agricultural town, Los Angeles was also a provincial center for artisans, craftsmen, and merchants, including the Massachusetts-born trader Abel Stearns, a naturalized Mexican citizen and reputedly the richest man in southern California. *Courtesy Huntington Library.*

them, had left little room for economic development in the pueblos. Since the late 1970s, however, historians have begun to recapture the complexity of economic growth and change in the pueblos, particularly in Los Angeles.[126] True to its Spanish design, Mexican Los Angeles remained agricultural. By 1836 Los Angeles could count roughly 170 farms, orchards, gardens, and vineyards, and wine and brandy produced in Los Angeles and its environs were being poured in homes and taverns as distant as Hawaii and New England.[127] While it seems clear that the missions remained the most important centers of artisan production in California until secularization, Los Angeles *pobladores* during the mid-1830s practiced thirty-one different occupations. The pueblos increasingly became centers for artisan work after mission secularization, and the Los Angeles community supported a growing merchant class and numerous artisans and craftsmen during the 1840s.[128] Urban merchants and artisans may even have found local rancheros to be active consumers of their goods, for recent work suggests that the ranchos were not nearly as self-sufficient as previously believed. Only the very largest of the ranchos, it seems, actually employed their own artisans.[129]

Although the economy of Los Angeles grew more complex and varied during the

Mexican period, one factor remained fixed: Indians constituted the mainstay of the manual labor force. After mission secularization, the population of Indian laborers in Los Angeles rose steadily, although clearly not to the height or at the rate scholars have asserted. In 1830, approximately 198 Indians lived in Los Angeles; the number who worked in the town, however, remains unclear.[130] Census lists taken later in the Mexican period provide important clues to the expansion of the Indian labor force in Los Angeles after secularization. The 1836 census enumerated 252 Indians in Los Angeles.[131] Scholars have taken this figure to represent the number of Indian laborers in the town, but it seems implausible that all toiled for the settlers.[132] When the infirm and children too young and adults too old to work are subtracted, a more reasonable figure of 225 laborers emerges.[133] Eight years later, approximately 377 Indians lived in the town of Los Angeles, far below the asserted figure of 650; of these, 339 were likely laborers.[134] Thus, the number of Indian residents and Indian laborers in Los Angeles increased in the years after secularization by roughly 50 percent, not 300 percent as scholars have suggested.[135]

These reduced figures and new work on the economy of Mexican Los Angeles suggest that scholars need to revisit the belief that Indian laborers "inundated" Los Angeles after secularization, where many "remained perpetually unemployed."[136] Furthermore, we need to reexamine the origins and magnitude of pathological behavior, such as drunkenness and homicide, that has been widely attributed to Indians in Mexican Los Angeles. These vices—and the repressive legislation that they prompted—have been described in the light of an underestimation of the strength of the Los Angeles economy, an overestimation of the number of Indians who lived in the town, and an unwitting tendency on the part of scholars to project the problems of contemporary urban Indians into the past. Only after scholars have mined the census reports, criminal records, account books, and personal correspondence pertaining to California's three principal towns—San José, Los Angeles, and Monterey—will a full picture emerge of Indian participation in Mexican California's urban economy.

CONCLUSION

In the decades after Mexican independence, the laws that fomented economic development in the ranchos and the pueblos, namely the opening up of California to international trade, the Colonization Act of 1824, the Supplemental Regulations of 1828, and the Secularization Act of 1833—all manifested unforeseen political transformations. Gradually, the laws of 1824 and 1828 facilitated a dramatic increase in the number of foreigners residing in California. In 1821, only 20 foreigners lived in Alta California, but their numbers increased to 120 in 1830 and 380 in 1840. By 1845, 680 of the region's 7,300 non-Indian residents were foreign immigrants. After 1845, the number of immigrants increased dramatically; some estimates place the number at 7,000 in 1846, fully one-half the non-Indian population.[137] Many of these new-comers, especially merchants, successfully married into the local elite and adopted much of Californio culture; most, however, never renounced their commercial ties to the United States.

Samuel Hastings, a shipmaster who plied California's waters in the early 1840s, testified to the political implications of these ties, predicting to Thomas Larkin that California eventually would go the way of Texas, and "American agents and American capital will be at the bottom of it."[138] Although Hastings could not fore-see the exact means through which the United States would acquire California, he recognized—as had Spanish mercantilists long before—that commercial interests could determine political allegiance. Upon the outbreak of the Mexican-American War in 1846, even before California had been seized by the United States, the eco-nomic ties between California and the United States—the most important of which dated to the hide-and-tallow trade—metamorphosed into political loyalty. Soon thereafter, these political and economic relationships hardened during the Gold Rush, hastening the admission in 1850 of California as the thirty-first state of the Union.

The men whose efforts and writings helped to promote California's statehood were often anti-Catholic, Hispanophobic, and quick, therefore, to dismiss the in-habitants and the economy of Mexican California as primitive and backwards. To Alfred Robinson, author of *Life in California* (1846), the Californios were "generally indolent, and addicted to many vices." Of their use of the land and the economy, Englishman Sir George Simpson scoffed: "Nature doing everything, man doing nothing."[139] Fortunately, the scholarship of recent decades has challenged these and other incorrect early assessments. Stereotypes of idling dons, dusty pueblos, and placid missions are giving way to a more subtle understanding of how economic re-lationships in Alta California were a blend of the initiatives of Spanish and Mexican secular officials and the priorities and skills of the regions' missionaries, soldiers, set-tlers, and most importantly, Indians.

As scholars continue to revise our understanding of the economy of Alta Cali-fornia, they need to continue examining the tensions between local needs and na-tional policies, the interrelatedness of social, cultural, and economic change, the full implications of Indian participation in the colonial economy, and the place of Alta California's economy within the Spanish colonial frontier. Historians should have ample opportunity and abundant cause for such inquiries. The current increase in scholarly and public interest in the colonial history of the Spanish Borderlands will, no doubt, spur new studies, while the charged nature of current economic ties be-tween Mexico and California renders them all the more timely.

NOTES

1. Fray José Señán to Viceroy Miguel de la Grúa Talamanca y Branciforte, May 14, 1796, in Lesley B. Simpson, ed., *The Letters of José Señán O.F.M.: Mission San Buenaventura, 1796–1823* (San Francisco: John Howell Books, 1962), 2.

2. Engels quoted in E. J. Hobsbawm, *The Age of Capital, 1848–1875* (London: Weidenfeld and Nicolson, 1975), 62.

3. John J. McCusker, "Mercantilism," in *The Encyclopedia of the North American Colonies* (New York: C. Scribner & Sons, 1993), 1:459–65.

4. Edwin A. Beilharz, *Felipe de Neve: First Governor of California* (San Francisco: California Historical Society, 1971), 34. Beilharz provides a concise discussion of the economy of California during the 1770s. See especially chapters 3 and 6.

5. Robert Archibald, *The Economic Aspects of the California Missions* (Washington, D.C.: Academy of American Franciscan History, 1978), 3. This is the most comprehensive study of the economy of Spanish California and the missions. For a discussion of the economy of Alta California in the context of the other provinces of northwestern New Spain, see Sergio Ortega Noriega, *Un ensayo de historia regional: el noroeste de México, 1530–1880* (Mexico: Universidad Nacional Autónoma de México, 1993). Most secondary sources cited in this article draw to varying degrees on the first three volumes of Hubert Howe Bancroft's monumental *History of California,* 7 vols. (San Francisco: History Company, 1884–1886). Especially useful are Bancroft's footnotes, which list numerous documents concerning the economy of Spanish California.

6. Archibald, *Economic Aspects,* 3–4.

7. Michael E. Thurman, *The Naval Department of San Blas: New Spain's Bastion for Alta California and Nootka, 1767 to 1798* (Glendale: Arthur H. Clark Company, 1967).

8. Junípero Serra, Memorandum, June 20, 1771, San Carlos de Monterey, in Antonine Tibesar, ed., *Writings of Junípero Serra,* 4 vols. (Washington D.C.: Academy of American Franciscan History, 1955–66), 1:226–35.

9. Serra's formal appeals are found in Serra, *Writings of Serra,* 1:295–329. The *Echeveste Reglamento,* dated May 19, 1773, can be found in Fray Francisco Palóu, *Historical Memoirs of New California,* trans. and ed. Herbert E. Bolton, 4 vols. (Berkeley: University of California Press, 1926), 58–77.

10. Ibid., 69.

11. Serra to Antonio María de Bucareli y Ursúa, Mexico City, March 13, 1773, *Writings of Serra,* 1:308–309.

12. Neve had written the new regulation by June 1779, but it was not formally approved by his superiors until October 1781. Under the new regulation, a soldier received 217.50 pesos, compared to 365 under the old schedule. Beilharz, *Felipe de Neve,* 86–92; see also, Archibald, *Economic Aspects,* 10. For a translation of the complete regulation, see *Regulations for governing the province of the Californias, approved by His Majesty by Royal order, dated October 24, 1781,* trans. John Everett Johnson (San Francisco: Grabhorn Press, 1929).

13. A *fanega* was equivalent to roughly 1.575 bushels. As a unit of weight, a *fanega* measured 101.5 lbs. of corn and 82.4 lbs. of wheat.

14. Archibald, *Economic Aspects,* 164; Ortega Noriega, *Un ensayo de historia regional,* 121.

15. Archibald, *Economic Aspects,* 163–64, and 167.

16. The most concise and informative discussion of cattle ranching in Spanish Califor-

nia and the only study to trace its Old World origins is Terry G. Jordan, *North American Cattle-Ranching Frontiers: Origins, Diffusion, and Differentiation* (Albuquerque: University of New Mexico Press, 1993), 159–69. Although dated and racist, Hubert Howe Bancroft's *California Pastoral, 1769–1848* (San Francisco: History Company, 1888) remains influential. Scholars frequently attribute the tremendous increase in livestock in Alta California to the region's "pristine" pasturage. See, for example, Jordan, *North American Cattle-Ranching Frontiers,* 159–61; L. T. Burcham, "Cattle and Range Forage in California: 1770–1880," *Agricultural History* 35 (July 1961): 140–49; and R. Louis Gentilcore, "Missions and Mission Lands of Alta California," *Annals of the Association of American Geographers* 51 (March 1961): 46–72. For Indian proto-agricultural practices and their considerable effects upon California's landscape, see Thomas C. Blackburn and Kat Anderson, eds. *Before the Wilderness: Environmental Management by Native Californians* (Menlo Park, Calif.: Ballena Press, 1993).

17. Archibald, *Economic Aspects,* 179–81.

18. David Hornbeck, "Land Tenure and Rancho Expansion in Alta California, 1784–1846," *Journal of Historical Geography* 4 (October 1978): 371–90, especially 374–76. The procedures governing land grants during the Spanish and Mexican periods and their origins in the legal heritage of Castile are the subject of Iris H. W. Engstrand, "California Ranchos: Their Hispanic Heritage," *Southern California Quarterly* 67 (March 1985): 281–90.

19. Steven W. Hackel, "Indian-Spanish Relations in Colonial California: Mission San Carlos Borromeo, 1770–1834" (Ph.D. diss., Cornell University, 1994), 269–75; Archibald, *Economic Aspects,* 74–114.

20. Daniel J. Garr, "A Frontier Agrarian Settlement: San José de Guadalupe, 1777–1850," *San José Studies* 2 (November 1976): 93–105, especially 94–97.

21. Felipe de Neve, September 1782, quoted in Beilharz, *Felipe de Neve,* 165.

22. Francis Florian Guest, "Municipal Institutions in Spanish California, 1789–1821" (Ph.D. diss., University of Southern California, 1961), 261–74; Antonio Ríos-Bustamante, "Los Angeles, Pueblo and Region, 1781–1850: Continuity and Adaptation on the North Mexican Periphery" (Ph.D. diss., University of California, Los Angeles, 1985), 108–20.

23. For the history of Branciforte, see Daniel J. Garr, "Villa de Branciforte: Innovation and Adaptation on the Frontier," *The Americas* 35 (July 1978): 95–109; Francis F. Guest, "The Foundation of the Villa de Branciforte," *California Historical Society Quarterly* 46 (December 1967): 307–35; and Guest, "Municipal Institutions," 130–92.

24. Guest, "Municipal Institutions," 247.

25. An *arroba* was usually 25 lbs. of corn, wheat, or flour.

26. Guest, "Municipal Institutions," 275, 289–91; Ríos-Bustamante, "Los Angeles," 112.

27. The non-Indian population of Los Angeles numbered approximately 650 in 1820; Ríos-Bustamante, "Los Angeles, Pueblo and Region," 182–91.

28. Sanford A. Mosk, "Price-Fixing in Spanish California," *California Historical Society Quarterly* 17 (1938): 118–22. Archibald in ch. 2 of *Economic Aspects* builds upon Mosk's discussion, adding greater depth to a complicated issue.

29. Mosk, "Price-Fixing," 120; Archibald, *Economic Aspects,* 17–18.

30. Borica adjusted the price of wheat because the standard measure of a *fanega* in Alta California held a *fanega* of corn and a *fanega* and a half of wheat. Governor Diego de Borica, June 26, 1799, Monterey, Archivo General de la Nación, Californias (hereinafter cited as AGN CA) 48:2:426; Lasuén, June 19, 1801, Mission San Carlos de Monterey, Archivo General de la Nación, Provincias Internas (hereinafter cited as AGN PI) 216: 76r and 76v.

31. Mosk, "Price-Fixing," 121. Arrillaga was interim governor until November 1804.

32. The most authoritative discussion of sea otter hunting in California is Adele Ogden, *The California Sea Otter Trade, 1784–1848* (Berkeley: University of California Press, 1941). See also Archibald, *Economic Aspects,* 116–18.

33. Ogden, *California Sea Otter Trade,* 6 and 15.

34. Ibid., 20–24

35. Sanford A. Mosk, "Subsidized Hemp Production in Spanish California," *Agricultural History* 13 (October 1939): 171–75; Archibald, *Economic Aspects,* 119–20.

36. Mosk, "Hemp Production in Spanish California," 171.

37. Fray Fermín Francisco de Lasuén to Father Guardian Tomás Pangua, December 16, 1793, Mission San Diego, *Writings of Fermín Francisco de Lasuén,* trans. and ed. Finbar Kenneally (Washington, D.C.: Academy of American Franciscan History, 1965), 2 vols. 1:328–29; Mosk, "Hemp Production in Spanish California," 172; Archibald, *Economic Aspects,* 118.

38. Governor Diego de Borica to *Comisionado* of San José, December 23, 1795, Monterey, *Archives of California,* Bancroft Library, University of California, Berkeley, 23:517.

39. Mosk, "Hemp Production in Spanish California," 172.

40. Ibid., 173; Archibald, *Economic Aspects,* 120.

41. Joaquín Sanchez to Arrillaga, August 30, 1805, San José, *Archives of California* 11:184; Mosk, "Hemp Production in Spanish California," 174.

42. Viceroy José de Iturrigaray to Governor of California [José Joaquín de Arrillaga], December 4, 1805, Mexico, *Archives of California* 12:74.

43. For the 1810 production total, see Mosk, "Hemp Production in Spanish California," 175.

44. Arrillaga to Sánchez, February 22, 1811, Monterey, *Archives of California* 26:12.

45. María del Carmen Velázquez, *Notas sobre sirvientes de las Californias y proyecto de obraje en Nuevo México* (Mexico City: El Colegio de Mexico, 1979), 41–45. Archibald, *Economic Aspects,* 146–52; Edith Buckland Webb, *Indian Life at the Old Missions* (Lincoln: University of Nebraska, 1982 reprint, orig. 1952), 122–48; Bancroft, *History of California,* 1:615–18.

46. Lasuén to Don José Joaquín de Arrillaga, Mission San Carlos, December 21, 1792, *Writings of Lasuén,* 1:263; Lasuén to Don Diego de Borica, Mission San Carlos, July 23, 1796, ibid., 1:389. Manuel Muñoz's trade, a *listonero* (lathe worker), has been incorrectly translated as a ribbon maker. See Bancroft, *History of California,* 1:615 n. 29, and *Writings of Lasuén,* 1:389. For information on artisans, see Mardith K. Schuetz-Miller, *Buildings and Builders in Historic California, 1769–1850* (Tucson: Southwestern Mission Research Center; Santa Barbara: Santa Barbara Trust for Historic Preservation; Presidio Research Publication, 1994).

47. Webb, *Indian Life,* 130; Bancroft, *History of California,* 1:618.

48. Borica to Branciforte, December 3, 1795, Monterey, AGN CA 49:1:265–67.

49. Lasuén to Don José Joaquín de Arrillaga, Mission San Carlos, December 21, 1792, *Writings of Lasuén,* 1:263–64.

50. Peter Gerhard, *The North Frontier of New Spain,* rev. ed. (Norman: University of Oklahoma Press, 1993), 309.

51. Robert Archibald, "Indian Labor at the California Missions[:] Slavery or Salvation?" *Journal of San Diego History* 24 (Spring 1978): 172–83. Differing assessments of the nature of Indian labor in the missions are juxtaposed in Rupert Costo and Jeannette Henry Costo, eds., *The Missions of California: A Legacy of Genocide* (San Francisco: Indian Historian Press, 1987).

52. For soldiers' descriptions of Indian labor in the missions during the mid-1790s, see Sherburne F. Cook, *The Conflict between the California Indian and White Civilization* (Berke-

ley: University of California Press, 1976), 91–94. See also the Franciscans responses, especially Missions San Miguel and San Antonio, to the 1812 questionnaire in Maynard Geiger, ed. and trans., *As the Padres Saw Them: California Indian Life and Customs as Reported by the Franciscan Missionaries, 1813–1815* (Santa Barbara: Santa Barbara Mission Archive Library, 1976), 82–83.

53. Lasuén, Mission San Carlos, June 19, 1801, AGN PI 216:69v; Lasuén, *Writings of Lasuén*, 2:207; Cook, *Conflict*, 94; Douglas Monroy, *Thrown among Strangers: The Making of Mexican Culture in Frontier California* (Berkeley: University of California Press, 1990), 65.

54. Maynard Geiger, *The Indians of Mission Santa Barbara in Paganism and Christianity* (Santa Barbara, 1982), 32; and Richard Steven Street, "'We Are Not Slaves': A History of California Farmworkers, 1769–1869—The Formative Years" (Ph.D. diss., University of Wisconsin, Madison, 1995), 165–66.

55. Lasuén, Mission San Carlos, June 19, 1801, AGN PI 216: 70v; Lasuén, *Writings of Lasuén*, 2:211.

56. Historians have yet to fully examine the implications of the differences between indigenous and Spanish gender divisions of labor in the missions of California. For a discussion of some of the work performed by Indian women in the missions, see Virginia Mayo Bouvier, "Women, Conquest, and the Production of History: Hispanic California, 1542–1840" (Ph.D. diss., University of California, Berkeley, 1995), 156–61.

57. Fray Luís Gil [y Taboada], December 31, 1825, Mission Santa Cruz, Documentos para la Historia de California, C-B 50 4:2:607–9, Bancroft Library.

58. Ibid.

59. Hackel, "Indian-Spanish Relations," 319–23. Governor Pablo Vicente de Solá to Fray Mariano Payeras, March 25, 1820, Alexander S. Taylor Collection, Doc. no. 1075, Henry E. Huntington Library, San Marino, California.

60. Paul Farnsworth, "The Economics of Acculturation in the California Missions: A Historical and Archaeological Study of Mission Nuestra Senora de la Soledad" (Ph.D. diss., University of California, Los Angeles, 1987), 303.

61. Cook, *Conflict*, 91–101; Robert H. Jackson and Edward Castillo, *Indians, Franciscans, and Spanish Colonization: The Impact of the Mission System on California Indians* (Albuquerque: University of New Mexico Press, 1995), 44; and Robert H. Jackson, *Indian Population Decline: The Missions of Northwestern New Spain, 1687–1840* (Albuquerque: University of New Mexico Press, 1994), 126, 165–66.

62. Lasuén, Mission San Carlos, June 19, 1801, AGN PI 216: 69v; Lasuén, *Writings of Lasuén*, 2:207.

63. Fray Luís Gil [y Taboada], December 31, 1825, Mission Santa Cruz, Documentos para la Historia de California, C-B 50 4:2:607–9.

64. Lasuén, Mission San Carlos, June 19, 1801, AGN PI 216: 69v; Lasuén, *Writings of Lasuén*, 2:207.

65. Cook, *Conflict*, 101; and Monroy, *Thrown among Strangers*, 52, 54, and 58.

66. Diane Everett Barbolla, "Alta California Troops: Acculturation and Material Wealth in a Presidio and Mission Context, 1769–1810" (Ph.D. diss., University of California, Riverside, 1992).

67. "Report of Corporal Periquez to Captain Callis," n.d., *Writings of Serra*, 1:402–6.

68. Lasuén to Don Jacabo Ugarte y Loyola, October 20, 1787, Mission San Carlos, *Writings of Lasuén*, 1:168.

69. Scholars have put forward different estimates of the value of mission contract labor.

In *Economic Aspects,* 103, Archibald discussed how Indian labor was valued at 1 1/2 *reales* a day. Cook argued that Indian labor after 1790 was "compulsory" and not compensated, *Conflict,* 1–194. Castillo argued that "The presidios, like the missions and most other buildings in colonial California, were built with the free native labor provided by the neophytes and prisoners," "The Impact of Euro-American Exploration and Settlement," in Robert F. Heizer, ed., *Handbook of North American Indians,* Vol. 8, *California* (Washington D.C.: Smithsonian Institution Press, 1978), 102.

70. Hackel, "Indian-Spanish Relations," 272–73. The number of "days" of Indian labor equals the total of pesos charged multiplied by eight (eight *reales* to a peso) and divided by 1 and 1/2 (the daily wage).

71. Hackel, "Indian Labor in Colonial California: A Reappraisal of the Spanish Presidios" (Paper delivered at the 35th Annual Conference of the Western History Association, Denver, Colorado, October 1995).

72. Hackel, "Indian-Spanish Relations," 297–308; Randall Milliken, *A Time of Little Choice: The Disintegration of Tribal Culture in the San Francisco Bay Area, 1769–1810* (Menlo Park: Ballena Press, 1995), 104–107.

73. Pedro Fages to Jacobo Ugarte y Loyola, June 2, 1790, Monterey, AGN CA 46:31.

74. Lasuén, Mission San Carlos, June 19, 1801, AGN PI: 216: 71r; Lasuén, *Writings of Lasuén,* 2:212.

75. Señán to Lasuén, October 2[?], 1800, Mission San Buenaventura AGN PI 216:96.

76. Lasuén, Mission San Carlos, June 19, 1801, AGN PI: 216: 71v; Lasuén, *Writings of Lasuén,* 2:213.

77. José Joaquín Moraga to the Corporal of the Guard at the Pueblo of San José, San Francisco, December 1782, quoted in Randall T. Milliken, "An Ethnohistory of the Indian People of the San Francisco Bay Area from 1770 to 1810" (Ph.D. diss., University of California, Berkeley, 1991), 510. Governor Fages incorporated these regulations into the guidelines he issued for the *comisionado* of San José, Fages to [Ignacio] Vallejo, Instrucciones al director de San José, July 18, 1785, Monterey, *Archives of California* 22:338–41.

78. William Mason, "Indian-Mexican Cultural Exchange in the Los Angeles Area, 1781–1834," *Aztlán* 15 (Spring 1984): 123–44. See also George Harwood Phillips, "Indians in Los Angeles, 1781–1875: Economic Integration, Social Disintegration," *Pacific Historical Review* 49 (August 1980): 427–51.

79. Ortega to Fages, April 18, 1784, Pueblo de la Reyna de los Angeles, *Archives of California* 22:176–77.

80. Ríos-Bustamante, "Los Angeles, Pueblo and Region," 110.

81. Fages to Captain Vicente Feliz, San Gabriel, January 13, 1787, *Archives of California* 4:148–55, partially translated in William Marvin Mason, "Fages' Code of Conduct Toward Indians, 1787," *Journal of California Anthropology* 2 (Summer 1975): 90–100.

82. Response of the Franciscans of Mission San Gabriel, in Geiger, *As the Padres Saw Them,* 129.

83. Father Vicente de Santa María, 1795, quoted in Mason, "Indian-Mexican Cultural Exchange," 129.

84. Ibid., 131–33; Ríos-Bustamante, "Los Angeles, Pueblo and Region," 90–96.

85. Lasuén to Don Jacobo Ugarte y Loyola, October 20, 1787, Mission San Carlos, *Writings of Lasuén,* 1:168.

86. Fray Mariano Payeras to Reverend Father Guardian, June 18, 1821, Mission San An-

tonio de Padua, *Writings of Mariano Payeras*, trans. and ed. Donald Cutter (Santa Barbara: Bellerophon Books, 1995), 294, 299.

87. Ibid., 299.

88. Archibald, *Economic Aspects*, 124.

89. Ibid., 133–38.

90. Quoted in David J. Weber, *The Mexican Frontier, 1821–1846* (New Haven: Yale University Press, 1982), 125.

91. The best synthetic overview of the economy of Mexican California remains Weber, *Mexican Frontier*, especially, 122–57. The relevant sections of the bibliographic essay at the end of the volume provide an indispensable guide to the literature on the economy of Mexican California. For an exhaustive and encyclopedic account of the economy of Mexican California, surpassed in detail only by Bancroft's *History of California*, see Jessie Davies Francis, "An Economic and Social History of Mexican California, 1822–1846: Volume I, Chiefly Economic" (Ph.D. diss., University of California, Berkeley, 1935; New York: Arno Press, 1976).

92. Quoted in Francis, "Economic and Social History," 51. For more on the Junta, see ibid., 23–51; Bancroft, *History of California*, 3:2–6; and C. Alan Hutchinson, *Frontier Settlement in Mexican California: The Híjar-Padrés Colony, and Its Origins, 1769–1835* (New Haven: Yale University Press, 1969), 115–21.

93. Francis, "Economic and Social History of Mexican California," 344–48 and 364–68; Weber, *Mexican Frontier*, 112.

94. Bancroft, *History of California*, 3:67–86.

95. Ibid., 85. Echeandía was in control of southern California in 1832–1833.

96. Weber, *Mexican Frontier*, 151.

97. Francis, "Economic and Social History," 265–89. In 1826, Mexico had only five vessels to patrol ten thousand miles of coastline; Weber, *Mexican Frontier*, 149.

98. Weber, *Mexican Frontier*, 156–57 and 255–60.

99. Bancroft states that the Spanish flag came down in Monterey in late September or early October; *History of California*, 2:458. For more on these negotiations and the final agreement, see Adele Ogden, "Hides and Tallow: McCulloch, Hartnell and Company, 1822–1828," *California Historical Society Quarterly* 6 (September 1927): 255–56; and Bancroft, *History of California*, 2:475–77.

100. Fray Mariano Payeras to Reverend Father Guardian José Gasol, Mission La Soledad, June 26, 1822, *Writings of Payeras*, 322.

101. Ogden, "Hides and Tallow," 255.

102. David Hornbeck, "Economic Growth and Change at the Missions of Alta California, 1769–1846," in David Hurst Thomas, ed., *Columbian Consequences, Volume 1: Archaeological and Historical Perspectives on the Spanish Borderlands West* (Smithsonian Institution Press: Washington and London, 1989), 423–33, especially 426–29. See also Julia G. Costello, "Variability among the Alta California Missions: The Economics of Agricultural Production," in *Columbian Consequences*, 435–49. Monroy notes a similar shift in the outlook of the Franciscans, although he suggests that as early as 1810 the padres became more concerned with "buying and selling than with souls"; *Thrown among Strangers*, 69.

103. Robert H. Jackson, "The Changing Economic Structure of the Alta California Missions—A Reinterpretation," *Pacific Historical Review* 61 (August 1992): 387–415.

104. Weber, *Mexican Frontier*, 162, 180–81; Hutchinson, *Frontier Settlement*, 112–13, 137.

For a brief summary of the provisions of this legislation, see Bancroft, *History of California,* 2:515–16, n. 8; ibid., 3:34, n. 7; and Hornbeck, "Land Tenure and Rancho Expansion," 378.

105. From 1784 to 1834 the governors confirmed some fifty-one land grants; Paul W. Gates, *California Ranchos and Farms, 1846–1862* (Madison: The State Historical Society of Wisconsin, 1967), 3.

106. Robert Glass Cleland, *The Cattle on a Thousand Hills: Southern California, 1850–1870,* 2d ed. (San Marino: Huntington Library, 1964), 23; Weber, *Mexican Frontier,* 196; Francis, "Economic and Social History," 478–83.

107. Hornbeck, "Land Tenure and Rancho Expansion," 383–88.

108. Lisbeth Haas, *Conquests and Historical Identities in California, 1769–1936* (Berkeley: University of California Press, 1995), 83.

109. Hornbeck, "Land Tenure and Rancho Expansion," 388; Weber, *Mexican Frontier,* 205–6 and 350 n. 89. These ranches were on average slightly larger than those granted to Mexicans. Most non-Hispanic immigrants came late to California and had to settle for less desirable land farther inland; Hornbeck, "Land Tenure and Rancho Expansion," 388.

110. Hornbeck, "Land Tenure and Rancho Expansion," 388; Jordan, *North American Cattle-Ranching Frontiers,* 166.

111. Leonard Pitt, *The Decline of the Californios: A Social History of the Spanish-Speaking Californians, 1846–1890* (Berkeley: University of California Press, 1966), 10.

112. Hornbeck, "Land Tenure and Rancho Expansion," 385; Gates, *California Ranchos,* 7–9.

113. Francis, "Economic and Social History," 532; Weber, *Mexican Frontier,* 138–39.

114. Francis, "Economic and Social History," 525–26; Weber, *Mexican Frontier,* 138–39. The most important of these firms, Bryant, Sturgis, and Company, which exported some 500,000 hides from California between 1822 and 1842, is the focus of Adele Ogden, "Boston Hide Droghers Along California Shores," *California Historical Society Quarterly* 8 (December 1929): 289–305.

115. Odgen, "Boston Hide Droghers," 302; Francis, "Economic and Social History," 524.

116. Ogden, "Boston Hide Droghers," 299–300.

117. Only a handful of Indians received land after secularization, despite the laws that specified otherwise. For descriptions of some who did, see Monroy, *Thrown among Strangers,* 125; Haas, *Conquests and Historical Identities,* 53–56.

118. Tomás Almaguer, *Racial Fault Lines: The Historical Origins of White Supremacy in California* (Berkeley: University of California Press, 1994), 48–51. Scholars have consistently borrowed Sherburne Cook's estimate that 4,000 Indians worked on ranchos during the Mexican period, but this figure seems too low; Cook, *Conflict,* 304.

119. Almaguer, *Racial Fault Lines,* 49. See also the first-hand description of rancho life, "Life of a Rancher by Don José del Carmen Lugo," *Historical Society of Southern California Quarterly* 32 (September 1950): 185–236.

120. Roberta S. Greenwood, "The California Ranchero: Fact and Fancy," in *Columbian Consequences,* 451–65.

121. Cook and others have described the ranchos as a peonage system, *Conflict,* 51; Weber, *Mexican Frontier,* 211. Monroy concludes that the ranchos were "seigneurial"; *Thrown among Strangers,* 100–102 and 150. Almaguer sees the Indian-rancho ties as constituting "paternalism"; *Racial Fault Lines,* 50. Despite these subtle differences, all see the ranchos as based upon an exploitation and degradation of Indian labor. Even though most scholars do

not categorize labor relations on the ranchos as constituting slavery, recent scholarship on Indian–ranchero relations owes much to the historiography on slave plantations, especially the work of Eugene D. Genovese. See, for example, Almaguer, *Racial Fault Lines*, 49, and Monroy, *Thrown among Strangers*, 100.

122. Weber, *Mexican Frontier*, 211.

123. Francis, "Economic and Social History," 505–509.

124. The best documented example of the variability of labor relations on the ranchos occurred on the periphery of Mexican California, in John A. Sutter's inland rancho, New Helvetia. See Albert L. Hurtado, *Indian Survival on the California Frontier* (New Haven: Yale University Press, 1988), especially 55–71. For a comparative study of the variability of labor relations on ranchos, see Ricardo D. Salvatore, "Modes of Labor Control in Cattle-Ranching Economies: California, Southern Brazil, and Argentina, 1820–1860," *Journal of Economic History* 55 (June 1991): 441–51.

125. Monroy, *Thrown among Strangers*, 136–38.

126. Recent interpretations draw heavily from Howard J. Nelson, "The Two Pueblos of Los Angeles: Agricultural Village and Embryo Town," *Southern California Quarterly* 59 (Spring 1977): 1–10. Two dissertations extend and add greater complexity to Nelson's thesis: Antonio Ríos-Bustamante, "Los Angeles, Pueblo and Region," and Michael J. González, "Searching for the Feathered Serpent: Exploring the Origins of Mexican Culture in Los Angeles, 1830–1850" (Ph.D. diss., University of California, Berkeley, 1993). Unfortunately, there are no studies of economic growth during the Mexican period of San José, Monterey, or the sizable presidial communities. For a brief description of the agricultural character of San José in the Mexican period, consult Garr, " A Frontier Agrarian Settlement: San José de Guadalupe."

127. Ríos-Bustamante, "Los Angeles, Pueblo and Region," 195 –96. For a discussion of the beginnings of the Los Angeles wine industry, see Iris Ann Wilson, "Early Southern California Viniculture, 1830–1865," *Southern California Quarterly* 39 (September 1957): 242–50. For wine production at the missions, see Webb, *Indian Life*, 84–99 and 217–30.

128. Nelson, "The Two Pueblos," 5–6; Ríos-Bustamante, "Los Angeles, Pueblo and Region," 192–94. González argues that the diversification of the economy of Los Angeles was in no small part due to the arrival of a large group of Mexican colonists in 1835; "Searching for the Feathered Serpent," 47, 53–59.

129. Nelson, "The Two Pueblos," 8.

130. Mason, "Indian-Mexican Cultural Exchange," 138–39.

131. J. Gregg Layne, ed., "The 1836 Census of Los Angeles," *Historical Society of Southern California Quarterly* 18 (September–December 1936): 159–163.

132. Mason asserts that all 252 were laborers; "Indian-Mexican Cultural Exchange," 139. Phillips gives the incorrect figure of 255; "Indians in Los Angeles," 436.

133. This total does not include children age six and younger or adults eighty years and older.

134. Census of 1844, 603–626, Los Angeles City Archives. Phillips put forward the figure of 650 Indians in Los Angeles; "Indians in Los Angeles," 436. Phillips however, mistakenly included in this count 273 Indians who actually worked and lived on the ranchos in the vicinity of Los Angeles.

135. Phillips asserts that the "total number of Indian residents tripled"; "Indians in Los Angeles," 436. See also Monroy, *Thrown among Strangers*, 128.

136. Phillips, "Indians in Los Angeles," 436; Monroy, *Thrown among Strangers,* 128.

137. Figures are from Donald Cutter and Iris Engstrand, *Quest for Empire: Spanish Settlement in the Southwest* (Golden, Colorado: Fulcrum Publishing, 1996), 301; and Weber, *Mexican Frontier,* 206. Cutter and Engstrand put forward the population estimates for 1846. On immigration to California during the Mexican period, see Weber, *Mexican Frontier,* 179–206.

138. Hasting to Larkin, November 9, 1845, quoted in Ogden, "Boston Hide Droghers," 300, n. 74.

139. Robinson and Simpson, quoted in Pitt, *Decline of the Californios,* 15–16. For an exploration of the negative stereotypes Anglo-Americans used to describe the Californios, see James Rawls, *Indians of California: The Changing Image* (Norman: University of Oklahoma Press, 1984), especially 60–65.

6

"The Child of the Wilderness Weeps for the Father of Our Country"

The Indian and the Politics of Church and State in Provincial California

Michael J. González

From the Spanish era (1769–1821) into the Mexican period (1822–1846), Franciscan missionaries vied with provincial governors and their subordinates to rule Indians. The Spanish Crown, and later independent Mexico, expected each group to help convert the Native Californians into tax-paying Catholics, but the rivals debated who would supervise the transformation. The clamor attracted many participants. Priests from other orders, foreign visitors, American emigres, and military men—indeed military men often doubled as governors—likewise wondered what kind of regimen to impose on the Indians. These outsiders, however, rarely contributed new ideas and left the conflict to the devices of the Franciscans and provincial executives.

At one remove, California's dispute resembles the church-state conflicts that convulsed Latin America and Europe into the nineteenth century. In Mexico, France, and Spain, the members of each institution argued that only one side cared for the people while the other threatened religious fanaticism or anarchy. California's contest follows similar logic. From the beginning of settlement, the Franciscans insisted that the province and its native inhabitants prospered from the clergy's guidance. The priests filled mission lands with cattle or orchards. Amid the plenty appeared Indians, who, by yielding to the lure of gifts, or even to the occasional display of force, abandoned their pagan ways and accepted instruction in the Catholic religion. Initially, the civil administrators had few means to challenge the priests' economic and spiritual influence. Undaunted, the governors and some settlers protested that the mission routine stifled initiative and left the neophytes (Indian converts) helpless before their Franciscan tutors. The critics, many envious of Franciscan lands

Fray Antonio Peyrí, one of the gray-robed Franciscans who participated in the spiritual conquest of California, as depicted in a contemporary nineteenth-century lithograph. The Spanish-born Peyrí, who arrived in 1798, spent over thirty years at San Luis Rey, building the mission from a rude brush chapel to a magnificent adobe compound surrounded by rich agricultural lands and huge herds of cattle and sheep. Based on a portrait made in Mexico City in the mid-1830s, the lithograph was praised by old Californians as a true likeness of the able and energetic friar. From Alexander Forbes, *California* (London, 1839). *Courtesy California Historical Society, FN-30513.*

and Indian subjects, argued that a better existence awaited the natives if they dwelled in farming settlements alongside *gente de razón* (Mexican and Spanish settlers).[1] The conflict ended in 1834, when the provincial government secularized the missions and planned to distribute church property to converts. Bereft of their estates, the Franciscans soon lost power, and those who did not return to Mexico remained in California to minister their Indian and *gente de razón* congregations. The governors and their constituents, meanwhile, heady from the sight of land freed from church control, forgot concerns for the neophytes' welfare and divided up territory intended for Indians.[2] By the American invasion in 1846, *gente de razón* in and out of government had fattened themselves on the land's wealth, with a few citizens enjoying prosperity beyond any standard reached by the priests.

Yet, the province's disputes differed from troubles in other parts of the globe. Elsewhere, the poor and destitute, individuals whose status paralleled that of the Indians, had little sway over the religious and civil leadership. If the downtrodden participated in conflicts, it was to fight for, or suffer from, crusades that mostly served their betters. California's Indians, though never articulating arguments that could impress Franciscans and governors, wielded influence unusual for a subjugated people. Of course, it is hard to measure how the native Californians perceived their grasp on the clerical or civil imagination. Some court testimonies or written remembrances convey the Indians' ideas, but because Spanish, Mexican, and Anglo-

American amanuenses recorded these thoughts, the indigenous voice often passed through hostile or indifferent transcribers.[3] To complicate matters, the Indians did not comprise one group. Instead, they belonged to an ethnically diverse people whose tribelets, languages, and customs possessed great variety.[4]

Though muted or lacking a single mind, the Indians participated in church-state controversies. In a province where they numbered the large majority, the Indian presence initiated a dialogue words could not deliver. The Native Californians, at once servants, warriors, or prospective citizens, declared by virtue of their multitudinous tasks that they, and not priests and civil officials, could dictate the province's fate. In response, the authorities pursued policies, sometimes with compassion, other times with malice, that addressed the Indians' circumstances. As we will see, whoever could master the Indians, or in other cases win their cooperation, settled the question of who ran California best, Franciscans or governors.

HISTORIOGRAPHY

Contradictions menace neat theories, however. Scholars such as Sherburne Cook note that priests and governors needed each other to survive in a remote province, and no subject, even Indians, stopped one rival from helping the other.[5] Franciscans administered the sacraments to their civil counterparts and occasionally supplied them with food. For their part, governors ordered troops to hunt down fugitive neophytes or help priests convert Indians.[6] To be sure, most times the topic of Indians provided for little harmony, but, if provincial business did not involve Native Californians, the prospects for cooperation improved. Money matters, for instance, often angered clerics and administrators before circumstance cooled tempers and granted the wisdom that one group needed the other to prosper. Historian Hubert H. Bancroft illustrated how financial questions initially sparked resentment. He reported that at the beginning of colonization priests resented commands to help impoverished *gente de razón*. In the 1780s, governors Felipe de Neve, and later Pedro Fages, annoyed the clergy when they set low prices for the goods settlers bought from mission warehouses.[7] Rosaura Sánchez explains that bad feelings accumulated in later years when Franciscans bowed to the governors' request to lend money and they begrudged pueblo officials and settlers some loans. She notes that by the 1830s the priests had lent nearly seven hundred thousand pesos to their civil counterparts.[8] To the friars' chagrin, the loan recipients proved to be unreliable risks when their businesses sputtered or they refused to repay their debt. The *gente de razón*, meanwhile, imagined that the priests presided over swelling treasuries and did not deserve quick compensation. Even after secularization, when priests fell into poverty and cried out for help, few settlers believed that the friars needed money. Historian David Weber explained that the Reverend Diego García, the first bishop of California, lamented that the *gente de razón* donated so little to the church that he lacked cash to build his residence or a seminary.[9]

Other sources imply, however, that both sides learned to share their wealth. Woodrow Hansen shows that through the early nineteenth century the clergy relied on civil officials to collect mandatory tithes from settlers. The friars returned the favor and let administrators take a 5 percent cut of the proceeds.[10] When Mexico City made tithing voluntary in 1833, national leaders asked citizens to heed their conscience when the collection plate passed on Sunday.[11] While many people in this poor country could not afford charity, in places like Los Angeles, the *ayuntamiento* (city council) records show that residents often reached into their purses to help the church. To celebrate Mexican independence with a Mass, the *ayuntamiento* asked citizens in 1837 to donate money so that a priest could perform the ceremony.[12] There is no record that locals responded, but apparently such appeals worked other times. A year later, the council announced that the parish priest needed funds for a Mass "to honor the *Virgin del Refugio*," and it circulated a list of thirty-four men who gave pesos and *reales*.[13]

Like conflicts over money, legal and political arguments obscured any hint of concord between the two sides. Indeed, so many disagreements crowd the record it is no surprise that historians emphasize religious and civil discord. In some instances, Franciscan arrogance embittered their civil rivals. Manuel Servín explains that throughout the late eighteenth century provincial executives ordered the priests to organize elections in which the Indian converts elected their own *alcaldes*.[14] The missionaries ignored the command and appointed trusted neophytes to office. Other times, if the Franciscans failed to thwart civil authorities they sought help from Mexico City. After Comandante Pedro Fages (California did not receive its first governors until 1777) questioned the wisdom of sending troops to defend the future mission at San Buenaventura, an irate Father Junípero Serra convinced the viceroy to replace Fages with Fernando Rivera y Moncada.[15]

The new official, however, challenged the Franciscans, demonstrating that the provincial administrators could share the blame for church-state rancor. Soon after assuming office, Rivera y Moncada violated sanctuary and burst into Mission San Diego hunting for wanted Indians.[16] Serra excommunicated the comandante to restore church dignity, but it is doubtful the priests could intimidate their rivals. Daniel Garr notes that when civil officials founded settlements at San José and Villa Branciforte they ignored Franciscans who complained that the settlements sat dangerously close to the missions.[17]

Despite all these disputes, documents from Los Angeles show that the two sides often asked the other to help fulfill political or legal responsibilities. Sometimes provincial executives took the oath of office in the city and invited priests to bless the ceremony.[18] When Carlos Carrillo assumed the governor's seat in 1837, he cut short his inauguration so "his excellency, together with the *ayuntamiento* and the people, could attend a solemn *Te Deum* Mass."[19] On other occasions, city leaders welcomed the friars' attempts to regulate the public's morality. The same year that Carrillo took office, Father Narcíso Durán discovered that Manuel Arzaga, a retired army officer, lived with a woman who was not his wife. After the priest complained to the *alcalde,* city officials sent the woman to live at Mission San Gabriel and banished Arzaga to San Diego.[20]

Education, though, featured the best displays of cooperation. Municipal records and other sources from Los Angeles reveal that after lay teachers resigned to pursue other interests, priests accepted city council offers to work in the classroom. Military men sometimes tried instructing, but apparently most parents and civic leaders preferred clerics over officers or enlisted men.[21] When in 1836 the teaching position fell vacant (during the Mexican period, only one teacher, sometimes two, worked in Los Angeles), the *ayuntamiento* prevailed upon Father Alejo Bachelot, an experienced teacher in the Sandwich Islands, to take the job.[22] Three years later, the school once more lacked a teacher, and the city council asked the local curate to teach "forty to forty-five boys in the rectory."[23] The clerics' frequent turns in the classroom gave some priests the confidence to judge the city council's approach to education. After the American conquest, a Mexican priest urged the *ayuntamiento* to build a college and pull students away from "these examples of stupidity and immorality who congregated in Los Angeles' streets."[24] If lay teachers presided in the classroom, the religious presence remained in the primers children used for reading and writing. One primer warned children "that the fear of God is the beginning of wisdom."[25] Another cautioned youth to heed the law "because God sees all roads to iniquity."[26] The residents appreciated clerics who taught, and when priests departed for other assignments, disappointment spread. After Father Bachelot received orders from the bishop to return to the Sandwich Islands, the *ayuntamiento* and members of the populace appealed the decision. No new directives arrived, and Bachelot sailed out of San Pedro Bay with sad citizens in his wake.[27]

INDIAN POLICY

Compromise, however, usually vanished when the friars and civil officials regarded Indians. Such interest in the natives suggests that each side only wished to control the cheap labor they represented. Certainly, a glance at California's demography and the disciplines each side used to motivate native workers supports this contention. At the height of the mission period in 1830, the neophytes and gentile Indians totaled 98,000 souls and outnumbered the priests, soldiers, and settlers nearly ten to one.[28] The multitude invited priests and settlers to consider how Indian workers could exploit California's resources. For the Franciscans, neophyte laborers made the missions self-sufficient, and, as we will see, they also produced various items for trade. If converts lost interest in work, the priests revived enthusiasm by whipping neophytes who stole livestock or tried escaping into the interior.[29]

The civil authorities and their *gente de razón* constituents proved to be more demanding masters. Initially, the settlers rented Indian laborers from the missions and convinced gentiles to mind crops and cattle in exchange for coins or alcohol. By the 1830s, when neophytes gained their freedom from the secularized missions, the *gente de razón* grew bolder in dragooning native workers. In Los Angeles, municipal leaders ordered the night constable to arrest Indian drunks and make them work off their sentences fixing roads and public buildings.[30] After the American conquest in 1847, the city council instructed the "watchmen of the week" to collect Indian vagrants and assign them to "a master they will serve."[31] Around the same time, a judge noted that ex-neophytes often loitered at Mission San Gabriel. He promised to sweep up the loafers and "compel [them] to work hard."[32]

The exploitation of Indians, while horrific, does not contradict the clerics' and civil officials' claims that they were the Native Californians' protectors. Indeed, it can be said that many Indians who suffered whipping, forced labor, or other outrages faced punishment for displaying rebellious streaks.[33] For those who accepted their subservience, they flattered the pretensions of priests and civil administrators who played the parental sage to the Indian's obliging and willing child.[34] This arrangement suggests that authority figures wished their native wards to forever languish in an immature state. Others, however, found no delight in infantalized vassals and welcomed the chance to shepherd their Indian "children" to adulthood. But whatever the guise friars and governors imagined for their native subjects, it made little difference what the Indians wanted or needed. Only their patrons knew how to provide for the Indians' happiness.

The Franciscan fathers certainly relished their parental obligations. At the beginning of the mission era, Father Junípero Serra claimed that the "the spiritual fathers," the priests, "should be able to punish their sons, the Indians, with blows."[35] Later, Father Fermín Lasuén said that the priest, "like any good father . . . of a civilized nation . . . should forbid his children to go out with bad companions."[36] During the Chumash rebellion in 1824, Padre Ripoll of Santa Barbara saw troops muster to punish the rebels and rushed out to stop them. The priest threw himself at the commander's feet and begged, "My God, don't kill my children."[37]

The civil authorities likewise favored parental images. After Governor Felipe de Neve heard in 1780 that soldiers harassed neophytes, he ordered the offending troopers whipped and invited Indians to witness the punishment.[38] Years later, when Juan Bautista Alvarado penned José Figueroa's eulogy to honor the governor who secularized the missions, he celebrated the dead man as "the Father of our country," whose passing caused the Indian, "the child of the wilderness," to mourn.[39] Sometime later in 1841, Santiago Argüello, the prefect of southern California, looked out his office window in Los Angeles and saw a local resident "beat an Indian with the flat of his sword." Argüello ordered a criminal investigation to bring the man up on charges.[40]

To be sure, talk of hapless Indians basking in parental love would have soothed anyone troubled by the natives' suffering. But the talk of nurturing Native Californians was not always cant. In the American South, a place whose form of servitude might resemble the treatment accorded Indians, apologists spoke of slaves reclining in the bosom of the master's family. The rhetoric rang hollow, however, for it is difficult to imagine slave owners pleading with executioners to spare rebellious chattel, much less calling an assembly to watch brutal overseers receive the lash.[41]

In California, parental imagery usually prompted more sincere conduct, as priests and governors wanted their native subjects to mature in a world fashioned by religious or secular hands. The Franciscans wished to fill California with Indian converts who practiced Christian virtue in a world maddened by political and scientific revolution. Meanwhile, some civil authorities wanted to test liberal ideas in the province. Associating mission life with the excesses of the ancien régime, they proposed to free the neophytes from Franciscan control and award them portions of church property. Neither group succeeded, but measuring the triumph and failure of either side is not our intent. Instead, it is important to see how the men of church and state used the Native Californians to fulfill their designs for the province. And when the Indians reacted slowly to the schemes sketched by their saviors, priests and governors feared the defeat of their ambitions and blamed the natives for failures whose real authors sat in the missions or in the provincial capital.

CHURCH

Let us first examine Franciscan thinking. The Franciscan arrival in California coincided with the Enlightenment and the Age of Revolution, and the missionaries, fearful of the era's assaults on Catholic dogma, needed Indians to convert California into a redoubt impervious to change. During the period's excitement, the divine right of kings and church authority crumbled, revealing the idea of the individual, the new cult to which European and American savants directed their oblations.[42] The lineaments of the individual first appeared during the scientific revolution of the seventeenth century, when Newton published *De Principia*, his masterpiece on the theory of gravity. Newton theorized that natural laws governed the cosmos, and any educated observer could understand nature's workings by studying the forces that regulated the movement of the heavens. More radical minds extended Newton's logic and postulated that, if one person could understand how the universe functioned, then perhaps there was no reason to believe that God controlled nature.

In 1827, when the British amateur artist William Smyth made the watercolor drawing of San Carlos Borromeo from which this lithograph was derived, the mission was near the height of its prosperity. Founded more than half a century earlier by Junípero Serra, it was the seat of Franciscan authority in Alta California, the headquarters of Father-President Serra and his successor, Fermín Francisco de Lasuén. From Alexander Forbes, *California* (London, 1839). *Courtesy California Historical Society/Title Insurance and Trust Photo Collection, University of Southern California.*

And if divine authority lost its majesty, then other institutions, from the aristocracy to the papacy, likewise would lose their mystique. Newton's reasoning culminated in the belief that the only valid experience was that of the individual who had the intelligence to govern himself without the intervention of monarchs or priests.[43]

By the late eighteenth century, the time when Franciscans began building California's missions, political documents such as the United States Constitution or the French Declaration of the Rights of Man crowned the individual, or the ideal of what an individual should be, with inalienable rights. No longer subject to the whims of church or state authorities, the individual now loomed as a viable being who responded to incentives other than the fear the powerful had once used to exert their will. Private property, whether it took the shape of a farm or business, rewarded the individual with profit if he worked hard. Initiative, ambition, indeed cupidity, the very attributes that the ancient régime decreed as evil, now emerged not as sins, but as sacrosanct principles that only needed the seasoning of education or morality to control.[44]

To the Franciscans the individual was anathema.[45] Ambition and self-interest, attributes that shined forth from the individual's character, were but glosses for the more fiendish appetites of greed, lust, and gluttony. For the priests, covetous habits followed the logic of the eighteenth century, when revolution and scientific skepticism seemed the handiwork of people consumed by self-interest. To escape these depredations, the Franciscans rejected modern thought and possibly found solace in the teachings of Erasmus, a sixteenth-century Dutch theologian who wanted to purge pomp from Catholic belief and return to the simple practices of the Apostolic Age.[46] Erasmus, and those who later followed him, celebrated the "primitive church," the first Christian communities that renounced wealth or ambition and prayed to restore the purity of Eden.[47] While the connection between Erastian thought and the Franciscans requires more elaboration, the ideas of Serra and his brother priests suggest that the Dutchman's teachings had acquired great currency in the New World.

Erastian ideas worked their way into Mexico in the eighteenth century and prompted a clerical debate over whether Catholicism had lost its spirit. Needless to say, few critics dared question church dogma unless they cherished a trip before the Inquisition.[48] Nevertheless, Erastianism inspired brave churchmen to complain that incense, elaborate vestments, and holy relics deadened the upper classes and manipulated the Indians' ignorance. Francisco Antonio de Lorenzana, archbishop of Mexico, feared in 1766 that religious processions and the veneration of sacred objects led the people, especially the Indians, away from piety. Lorenzana's friend and bishop of Puebla, Francisco Fabián y Fuero, added soon after that "religious spectacles," grand pageants staged on holy days, persuaded destitute Indians to donate money so the church could throw up "fabulous temples."[49] God, the bishops believed, required reverence, and, in Mexican cities and towns, ostentation and ritual superseded faith.[50] Though many Mexicans seemed committed to religious pomp, in the mid-eighteenth century the natives of precolonial California stood free of excess and tantalized clerics to believe that they could learn more sincere forms of Christianity.

When the Franciscans first entered the province, Erastianism and images of Eden intertwined. The priests observed Indians living off the land's plenty, and rather than hoard the bounty nature granted them, the natives shared with the visitors. At last! The conduct of the first Christians and the innocence of paradise materialized in the form of California Indians who practiced the pieties Mexican believers had lost. Images of Eden abound in the priests' letters. After the Franciscans established the first mission at San Diego and set out to scout California's interior in 1769, they arrived in the midst of summer, when the sun pounds California's greenery into brown scrub. Junípero Serra, who admitted in his first letters that the Spaniards arrived in July, "the driest part of the year," did not let the arid expanses intrude on his sightings of Eden. He noted that around San Diego, "Land is plentiful and good. . . . Besides there are so many vines grown by nature and without help, that all it would

The Last Judgment, a huge allegorical canvas over nine feet in height, long hung in the church of Mission Santa Barbara. In their apostolic labors on the California frontier, the Franciscans relied on paintings and prints to instruct and discipline native converts. With its powerful imagery, especially the depiction of souls suffering in purgatory and hell, *The Last Judgment* was doubtless particularly effective. The French explorer la Pérouse, who saw a similar canvas at Mission Carmel, declared that "such a representation was never more useful in any country." *Courtesy Santa Barbara Mission Archive-Library.*

require [is little work] to cultivate." He exulted that "there are roses of Castile [here] and trees in abundance." Generous Indians walked amongst the blooms. "On many occasions," reported Serra, "we were regaled by the *gentiles* and they gave us food."[51]

At the same time Serra penned his letters, Fray Juan Crespi, then attached to the Portolá expedition seeking Monterey Bay, observed the same wonders flowering in the August heat farther north. When the party reached what is now Los Angeles, he saw a "large vineyard of wild grapes and an infinity of rosebushes in full bloom." The land teemed with happy Indians who, to today's eyes seem to have been eager to wave the strangers on to other places. To Crespi, however, they wanted to share the land's plenty with the visitors. At one place in the present-day San Fernando Valley, "friendly and docile Indians came to see us, bringing presents of sage and seeds." When Crespi and the expedition left the Los Angeles basin, more delegations appeared and bestowed "gifts of raisins, seeds, and honeycomb, very sweet and filling."[52]

The Indians, already inclined to perform Christian habits, only required the ministrations of the priests to complete their evolution into baptized believers. The natives' generous and sincere conduct, which so impressed the first Franciscans, would now, after conversion, become the template for the return of the primitive church. To be fair, the Franciscans grew less enchanted with their charges and later claimed that Indian innocence only disguised the influence of the "Evil One."[53] But initially, the plan to lure native converts into a mission indulged the priestly wish to banish individual selfishness and re-experience the sense of community enjoyed by ancient Christians.[54]

While few accounts describe the missions' daily activities, the spare portraits illustrate the communal ideal favored by the priests. At dawn, the priests rang a bell to summon the neophytes from mission dormitories or quarters just beyond the compound's walls; all gathered in or just outside the church for morning prayers, then received their chores before retiring to eat breakfast. At noon, the bell sounded again to call the community, and unless absorbed in tasks far from the mission, all stopped their chores to pray the Angelus before sitting down to lunch. When finished, they returned to work until the bell tolled at sunset to end the workday. One more prayer or Mass again turned the neophytes' thoughts heavenward, and the assembly prepared for dinner.[55]

During the day, the neophytes performed tasks that ensured the community's survival or produced goods that would bring cash to the mission treasury. At the outset of the mission era, most neophytes worked to make the mission self-sufficient. Inside the mission, women wove shirts, pants, blouses, and other items for Indian apparel. Nearby in surrounding fields, the men cultivated rows of wheat, corn, or fruit trees for the mission mess. Further out, other men watched cattle and sheep that would eventually meet the butcher's ax and soon bubble in cauldrons of *pozole* (stew).[56]

In later years, the priests directed neophytes to make products for trade. By the beginning of the nineteenth century, the priests sold mission food or clothes to the inhabitants of nearby settlements and presidios (forts). The missionaries also smuggled hides and tallow to Yankee ships that docked off the coast and awaited carts piled high with illicit products. All these activities did not enrich individual neophyte workers or accrue to the personal accounts of the Franciscans. Instead, all money from neophyte enterprise went into the mission's fund, and the priests determined how the money would best benefit the community.[57]

The chance to restore the primitive church may account for the priests' desires to separate the neophytes from the *gente de razón*. Throughout the mission period, priests forbade neophytes from consorting with the soldiers and settlers who lived in nearby presidios or pueblos. The missionaries complained that the *gente de razón* schooled the Indians in bad habits. But to the Franciscans' dismay, Indian corruption went beyond the pleasures of gambling or the bottle. The priests worried that Indian women often suffered the unwanted advances of *gente de razón* men. Sometimes the attackers only wished to steal a kiss or apply a furtive hand across the breasts, but often they forced themselves on the women and raped them. Even after the *gente de razón* assailant had scampered off, his ravages continued. Many times, the soldiers and settlers infected Indian women with venereal disease, which they spread to their lovers, husbands, and children.[58]

Apparently, the neophytes' contact with the *gente de razón* left them physical wrecks. A survey of the missions in 1813 asked the rector of each mission to describe neophyte misconduct. Some priests lamented that the Indians continued to practice sorcery, but others reported that the neophytes practiced evils that reflected *gente de razón* corruption. Venereal disease, an ailment that first festered in California's presidios and towns, now infected mission inhabitants. At San Gabriel the rector pitied children "permeated to the very marrow with venereal disease [which is] the only heritage their parents give them."[59] Drinking and gambling, another set of afflictions spawned amongst the *gente de razón*, also assaulted neophyte virtue. According to the priest at San Fernando Mission, "drunkenness" loomed as one of the neophytes' most notorious vices.[60] Up north at Mission San Antonio, the pastor mourned that "games of chance . . . absorbed" the Indians.[61]

These moral concerns, while sincere, revealed deeper, more hidden worries. By complaining about the pestilence unleashed on the indigenous population, the priests expressed another fear that the settlers infected Indians with notions of individualism and private property.[62] From the first expeditions that settled California in the late 1700s to the Híjar-Padrés expedition of the nineteenth century, the few settlers who made the trip received grants of land and seed so they could make the province productive.[63] Priests cringed at the thought of settlers using the bequests to turn a profit and disrupt the Franciscan sense of community. Therefore, when the Franciscans lamented that the *gente de razón* exposed the Indians to pestilence, one of the contagions no doubt was self-interest. Although few settlers could cite, much less read, the philosophical tracts extolling enlightened thought, their receipt of land and association with governors hostile to the church suggested that they had indeed embraced individualism. When the Franciscans complained to the first governors that the *gente de razón* threatened the neophytes, these appeals usually mentioned little about physical ailments and dwelled on the dangers of settler independence. At the outset of the mission era, for example, Serra worried that "pueblos without priests" threatened the neophytes.[64] The head of Santa Clara Mission complained in 1780 that law or religion seemed wasted on the *gente de razón*, a sad prospect that would cause "much annoyance . . . to our poor, converted Christians."[65] Years later, Father José Señan, father-president of the missions in the early nineteenth century,

An imaginary rendering of Junípero Serra appeared as the frontispiece to Francisco Palóu's biography of his old friend, published three years after the famed Franciscan's death in 1784. Although the artist depicted *gente de razón* and gentiles alike venerating Serra, and though later generations of Californians honored him as a founder of the Golden State, controversy now swirls about him, as scholars debate the larger issue of the mission experience. From Francisco Palóu, *Relación histórica de la vida . . . del venerable padre fray Junípero Serra* (Mexico, 1787). *Courtesy California Historical Society, FN-30517.*

wrote to the governor that if *gente de razón* continued to receive land grants, "they would have no king to rule them nor Pope to excommunicate them."[66]

STATE

Missionary complaints, however, failed to impress religious or civil superiors in Mexico, who favored new ideas about converting Indians.[67] The work of David Brading and C. Alan Hutchinson suggests that by the late eighteenth century, the Franciscan practice of herding Indians into a mission drew fewer and fewer advocates in Mexico City, or at the provincial capital of Monterey.[68] In Mexico, many priests and civil administrators admired enlightened thought, but lamented that the Mexican Indians' poverty belied any claim that the Franciscans could carry reason or progress to the northern colony.[69] The leaders of church and state argued that Mexico would sit in the world's first rank only when the status of the native populace improved. By the wars of Mexican independence from Spain, the various measures promoted by the Indians' champions fired rebel hearts and evolved into Mexican liberalism. Admittedly, the new leaders promising change focused on the Mexican interior, but their activities created the environment that inspired the secularization of California's frontier missions. But before we see how the Native Californians fared under secular rule, it is best to understand why intellectual developments in Mexico would worry or impress provincial priests and governors.

Throughout the eighteenth century many members of Mexico's upper echelons

lavished attention on the Indians.[70] Some Mexican *criollos* (people of European ancestry, born in America) tired of the prestige attached to the Old World and embraced the Indian, not the Spaniard, as their hero. The native they imagined, however, little resembled the ignorant, degraded mass crowding the countryside or
streets. Rather, they invoked the Aztec warrior who had once defied the Spaniard
and possessed qualities the *criollos* wanted to see in themselves. The exiled Jesuit
Francisco Clavijero claimed in 1781 that the Aztecs' triumphs eclipsed the glories of
Greece and Rome.[71] At the beginning of the Mexican fight for independence, the
clamor for Aztec idols increased. Fray Servando Teresa de Mier, a Dominican exiled
to London, urged his compatriots to summon the shade of Cuauhtémoc and restore
the tranquility that prevailed in Mexico before the conquest.[72] Around the same
time, Carlos María Bustamante, one of the rebellion's ideologues, exhorted the in-
surgents "to re-establish the Mexican [i.e., Aztec] empire."[73]

The Aztec revival coincided with plans to improve the lives of the current Indian
populace. Observers had long commiserated that Mexico abounded in poor, destitute Indians whose privation could lead to revolt.[74] The condition of native Mexicans varied from region to region, but a few generalities can describe their existence
under colonial rule.[75] In rural areas, Indians scratched out a living from communal
plots (*ejidos*), while their brethren in cities performed menial tasks. From such humble circumstances sprang an intrepid few who entered the priesthood or gained
wealth as merchants. The ability of so few to prosper testified not to Indian sloth but
to the suffocating force of a caste system that condemned the Mexican natives to in-
feriority. Under colonial law and custom, Indians could not bear arms, sit in the
viceregal government, or occupy church office higher than curate. As caste shackled
the Indians, the supposed purity of Spanish and *criollo* blood allowed Mexico's
whites every legal advantage.[76]

Many critics, most of them Spaniards or *criollos* who recognized how their privilege
pained the Indians, deliberated how to correct the colony's economic and political in-
justice. While every wrong, from poor schools to excessive Indian taxation, earned
criticism, most commentators traced Mexico's troubles to the "collective," the group,
racial, or social identity that subsumed the Indians to the fate their caste assigned
them.[77] In the late 1700s, pamphleteers fired off proposals to extend political and economic equality to the native Mexicans, but the viceroy considered few reforms. When
the colony gained independence in 1821, however, the triumphant rebels revived measures from years before and unveiled Mexican liberalism. The 1824 Constitution, for
example, abolished racial categories and offered full citizenship rights to all Mexican
males. Many liberals argued, however, that the Indians would remain legal and social
outcasts until they had a chance to escape their squalor.

To help the impoverished natives, José Luis Mora, Vicente Gómez Farias, and
other liberals planned to break up church estates and distribute territory to the male

heads of Indian households. They insisted that land ownership would help the recipient slough off inertia. As the freeholder swung a hoe or rake, he would cultivate good character alongside the fruits and vegetables sprouting on his property. The liberals presumed that when the Indian peasant received his grant, he would understand that merit, rather than caste, fixed one's place in society. Each individual would rise or fall according to how well he worked his property. If one labored hard, profit would come; yet if one loafed, poverty, destitution, or worse, would be the proper reward.

The liberals welcomed the discipline promised by a work ethic, but they also desired the riches diligent Indians would grant Mexico. In time, the Indians would produce food for market and learn the joys of making a profit. The money they earned would fill pockets and invite them to purchase other items. Eventually, argued Mora and friends, Indian farmers would help drive the Mexican economy by producing and consuming the goods the nation needed to find prosperity.

In California, many settlers shared the liberal conviction that the Indian wanted to be a yeoman farmer. The *gente de razón* erred, however, when they assumed that the distribution of land would transform Indians into happy cultivators eager to wring money from their plots. In fairness, the mistake seemed inevitable, since the Californios were trying to imitate their liberal contemporaries in Mexico. Sometimes, the provincials echoed the liberal refrains that had sounded first in Mexico's salons and coffeehouses. The *gente de razón*, for example, invoked the Aztec past to claim kinship with ancient Mexicans. In 1827, the California *diputación*, the body of citizens elected by the municipalities to advise the governor, proposed to rename California "Montezuma." The members also suggested a new coat of arms for California, in which an Indian with a plume, a bow, and a quiver would stand inside an oval bordered by an olive branch and an oak.[78] Neither idea came to pass, but the Indian romance continued. Governor José Figueroa told the *diputación* three years later that in "California you will recognize the country of our ancestors. You will see the original homes where the Aztecs lived before they moved onto Tenochtitlán and founded the empire of Montezuma."[79] Other times, prominent Californios did not drape themselves in Aztec regalia, but they sympathized with their Indian neighbors.[80] Mariano Vallejo and Pío Pico, among many distinguished locals, lamented the neophytes' servitude under Franciscan "fanaticism" and said that California's natives had a right to be free.[81]

These outpourings of sentiment implied that, at least in the abstract, a significant number of Californio leaders and settlers considered the Indians their equals. While some *gente de razón* wanted to embrace the Indians as brothers, by the early nineteenth century, warfare, horse-stealing, and other outrages turned most provincials against the Native Californians. Indeed, if we may digress, other evidence suggests that hostility toward the Indians may explain the Californio penchant for staging bloodless coups. For some *gente de razón*, affording Indians the privilege to tote firearms was a measure of equality that would have made California politics more tumultuous. Throughout the Mexican period, the residents of Monterey, Los Angeles, and occasionally San Diego, debated which settlement should seat California's governor. The site chosen by the provincial executive earned the rank of "capital" and received the customs house, a treasure that pleased dishonest locals who eyed the duties paid by passing ships. The men who reigned as governor either came from competing settlements or they held rank in the Mexican army. Peace, however, rarely graced the tenure of any governor. A volatile populace greeted the head of the province, and if one part of the public used force to topple the provincial executive, another group arrived to defend the embattled leader. At least five times between 1832 and 1846, rival parties mustered troops to ensure that their favorites donned the governor's sash.[82]

Nevertheless, no matter how impassioned the struggle for provincial power, the bickering *gente de razón* never staged epic battles in which one side slaughtered the other. Most times, the opposing forces met on a battlefield and slew an unlucky few before the force with the most men called on its enemy to surrender. These peculiar war tactics have elicited wry comments from historians, who often compare the confrontations to scenes from comic opera.[83] The battles certainly involved blustering, but the *gente de razón* avoided violent contests because the carnage would decimate the military and leave thinned ranks to defend settlements from restive Indians. Historians H. H. Bancroft and, later, George Harwood Phillips, report that by 1835, native marauders rustled horses from ranchos throughout the province and sometimes carried settlers into slavery.[84] More alarmingly for southern California, the residents of Los Angeles and San Diego often trembled at reports that raiders threatened to march on the settlements.

The Californio strategy to limit political violence and prepare for Indian attacks probably emerged in 1832, when José María Echeandía battled Agustín Zamorano for the governor's seat. Claiming California from Los Angeles to the Mexican border, Echeandía pondered how to combat troops Zamorano led down from Monterey. Apparently, few *gente de razón* flocked to his standard, and to increase his meager force, Echeandía promised freedom to the mission Indians in his jurisdiction if they fought for his side. Chaos erupted. If Zephyrin Engelhardt and Gerald Geary are accurate, the Indians rushed out of the missions, shouting "Soy libre"—I am free. They showed little interest in Echeandía's cause and devoted themselves to drinking, fighting, and gambling. The sight of unruly Indians no doubt worried the *gente de razón* that the mob would swoop down on settlements and ranchos. A chagrined Echeandía rescinded his emancipation decree and ordered the neophytes home to the missions.[85] Echeandía's experiment with Indian auxiliaries taught the lesson that Californios should not enlist native allies for political fights. In subsequent battles for the governor's seat, the disputants refused to arm Indians and risk the outbursts that had so alarmed Echeandía.[86]

To return to the discussion of brotherhood, the contradiction of honoring, even while fearing, the Indians is a puzzle easily reconciled. Before secularization, many observers noted that the church commanded the province's best lands, and the *gente de razón*, deprived of wealth, access to prosperity, and political influence, seemed as helpless as the Indians.[87] And, as suggested by the declarations of respect for Aztecs or neophytes, liberal minds could claim the natives as equals because all groups witnessed Franciscan might. When prominent Californios called for the break up of mission territory, many wanted the Indians to receive portions of church land. Yet, because the provincials endured the Franciscan yoke along with their native compatriots, a few *gente de razón* demanded part of the mission estates. If the poorest and most abject Indians could receive parcels, then the Californios, the natives' supposed brethren, certainly deserved their share.

Secularization had long intrigued California's administrators as the best way to satisfy the needs of their *gente de razón* and Indian constituents. At least four different provincial executives issued orders to seize mission land.[88] Felipe De Neve issued the first order in 1777. The priests protested and succeeded in overturning the command. Pedro de Solá issued another order in 1821, but the Franciscans once more prevailed. A decade later, José María Echeandía made one more attempt to secularize the missions, only to fail like his predecessors. José Figueroa finally succeeded in 1834, and decreed that administrators would supervise the missions' secularization over a three-year period.

Despite the differences that altered one plan from the other, they all shared the idea of distributing land and other items to emancipated neophytes. Like reformers in independent Mexico, provincial executives believed that farming plots would free individuals from the mission collective and encourage them to think for themselves rather than submit to priests. The secularization plans involved the distribution of church land to adult males. (In some cases Indians who did not feel comfortable leaving the mission could stay; but instead of obeying a priest they looked to a civil overseer.) The land parcels measured 200 square *varas* (a vara roughly measured more than a yard) and came with grants of seed, tools, and sometimes a passel of farm animals, such as mares, cattle, and sheep.[89] To discourage *gente de razón* from wheedling land titles away from the Indians, each plan forbade the native proprietors from leasing, selling, or renting their plots.[90]

The Indians did not thrive under secularization, and many eventually lost their property despite legal protections. When land fell free from church control, those Californios who once sympathized with the Indians now had little cause to remember any bond with their native counterparts. Even if a few *gente de razón* sincerely supported justice for the Indians, by the late 1830s the prospect of developing church territory obscured all other emotions. Affection withered for the ex-neophyte, and where some Californios once hailed the natives as fellow citizens before seculariza-

In company with his headmen, the Luiseño leader Pedro Pablo (center) attends a tribal affairs meeting with U.S. government officials in 1885 at San Antonio de Pala, the *asistencia* of Mission San Luis Rey. The descendants of neophytes displaced through secularization, Pablo and his people, like other California Indians, did not achieve significant legal protection of their rights until 1891, with the passage of the Act for the Relief of the Mission Indians. *Courtesy California Historical Society/Title Insurance and Trust Photo Collection, University of Southern California.*

tion, after 1834 they only saw laborers who could be controlled to reap the land's riches.

The native demise may seem self-inflicted, but the circumstances always betrayed the subtle or explicit work of the *gente de razón*. Although Indians had learned how to farm or tend cattle in the missions, they apparently acquired little preparation in how to offer their goods for trade or conduct business with merchants. Once free, some natives fell into arrears, and sold their property to *gente de razón* creditors. Californio guile also ruined the freed natives. By enticing the Indians with alcohol or drawing them into gambling debts, enterprising *gente de razón* soon relieved the ex-neophytes of their land titles.[91] By the beginning of the 1840s, many Indian grantees had lost their stakes and now worked for *gente de razón* landowners who prescribed routines harsher than any toil at the missions. As we saw earlier, if Indians landed in jail, judges in many Californio communities condemned the convicts to work off their sentences in labor gangs.[92] For those who avoided prison, hunger and their de-sire for alcohol made them easy game for clever landowners. Farmers and rancheros throughout California offered impoverished ex-neophytes food and alcohol if they agreed to work.[93] In one case, the offer went unfulfilled; Tiburcio Tapia of San Bernadino refused to compensate his Indian workers and drove them off his prop-erty when they finished their task.[94]

The *gente de razón*'s activities may invite charges of hypocrisy and fraud. Cer-tainly the Californios, who had cited liberal doctrine to promote Indian emancipa-tion, benefited greatly from secularization. Mariano Vallejo claimed the land around Mission San Francisco Solano, north of San Francisco Bay, and hired ex-neophytes to work on his estate. In southern California, his contemporary, Pío Pico, helped himself to territory that once belonged to Mission San Luis Rey, and he retained the resident Indians as employees.

The Californios hardly merit a defense for taking advantage of the Indians. Yet the *gente de razón*, although cruel and insensitive, had little incentive to respect the Na-tive Californians after secularization. Their standard of liberal conduct allowed them the luxury to excuse any abuse they heaped on Indians. In one sense, liberalism as-sumed progress. In a world free from the influences of church, caste, or any other im-pediment, all individuals had a chance to rise according to their own talents. Also, as reformers had argued in Mexico, in a liberal society the individual regulated his own behavior. Therefore, when the ex-neophytes reputedly squandered their liberty on a round of cards or drinks, they faced the contempt of many *gente de razón* who could claim that by rejecting the progress the Indians deserved to sink into misery.

Matters grow complicated, however, as liberal ideas intersected with the ac-knowledgment that the people ruining the Indians were none other than *gente de razón*. In many cases, the men who sat on city government, as was the case in Los Angeles, owned the establishments where Indians bought alcohol.[95] The local lead-ers also doubled as farmers and grew the grapes they distilled into the Indians' fa-vorite intoxicating beverage, *aguardiente*.[96] The reports of Indian "orgies," spectacles that included a few *gente de razón*, frequently agitated city council meetings.[97] It did not behoove city leaders to say that their own number and their constituents, some of whom claimed to be liberals, prevented the advance of Indians. Liberals would then stand accused of illiberal conduct. To resolve the paradox and justify the disci-pline of the Indians, city leaders re-interpreted liberalism not to mean political or economic progress, but improvements in health and hygiene. In communities like Los Angeles, local leaders transposed political and economic concerns onto the body and said the Indian deserved discipline because he was unclean.[98] City leaders also complained about Indians fighting or gambling, but a review of the city coun-cil minutes from Los Angeles shows that many lamentations about indigenous be-havior centered on dirty bodies. In the late 1840s, two citizens complained at an *ayuntamiento* meeting that "the aborigines become intoxicated [and spread] venereal disease."[99] During another session, the council worried that disease would float off the bodies of drunks and ordered the arrest of any inebriate who failed "to bathe regularly." Because most complaints about public intoxication often concerned Indians, it is not a stretch to imagine that the infected drunks were Native Californians.[100] Around the same time, the council heard complaints that Indians bathed in the *zanjas,* the city's irrigation canals. Concerned that they could infect society, the *ayuntamiento* ordered the Indians to perform their ablutions elsewhere.[101] Soon after, more *gente de razón* worried about pestilence wafting off Indian bodies. The *alcalde* ordered Indians to stand in the back of church during Mass because they were a "filthy and dirty people."[102]

THE END

Reports of unclean Indians overlooked the fact that in arid communities like Los Angeles, all inhabitants, from established merchant to humble field hand, had little water to wash off the landscape's dust. Nevertheless, emphasizing the Indian's filth accorded neatly with the *gente de razón*'s proclivity to see the native Californian any way they wished. If provincial authorities could imagine grimy Indians, they could conjure up natives who would embody the visions of their religious and civil patrons. In the late eighteenth and early nineteenth centuries, the priests wanted Indians to forsake their traditional ways and make the missions a prosperous, pious community. During the same time, provincial administrators hoped the Indians would learn self-interest and find success as farmers and craftsmen. Yet, Franciscan and civil dreams for the Indians did not materialize. Instead, the only role each side allowed the native was the work detail. Throughout the Spanish and Mexican periods, the Indians labored in mission fields, tended *gente de razón* properties, or performed various chores in provincial settlements. Occasionally, some Indians unhappy with their lot rebelled, while others found solace in alcohol. Whatever the form of native misconduct, the provincial powers found one more pretext to condemn the natives, and what they really debated was who had the authority to impose discipline. Sometimes disputes over money, land, and political power started arguments, but the Indian, always the Indian, caused the most enduring conflict between religious and civil leaders. Without the native Californians, any history of provincial politics is incomplete, and their story requires more research still.

NOTES

1. Ramón Gutiérrez says the term *gente de razón,* meaning literally "people of reason," is confusing and vague. He explains that "there is a great deal of confusion among contempo-

rary scholars over precisely what this label meant and to whom it applied." See *When Jesus Came the Corn Mothers Went Away* (Stanford: Stanford University Press, 1991), 195.

2. Hubert Howe Bancroft, *The History of California*, 7 vols. (San Francisco: The History Company, 1888), 3:346–47.

3. Rosaura Sánchez speaks of the difficulty of recovering the Indian's voice. See *Telling Identities, Californio Testimonios* (Minneapolis: University of Minnesota Press, 1995).

4. A good introduction to the life and ways of the native Californians is Robert Heizer and M. A. Whipple, eds., *The California Indians: A Source Book* (Berkeley: University of California Press, 1951).

5. Sherburne Cook, "The Indian Versus the Spanish Mission," in *The Conflict between the California Indian and White Civilization* (Berkeley: University of California Press, 1976), 76–84.

6. Douglas Monroy, *Thrown among Strangers* (Berkeley: University of California Press, 1990), 80. For another good study of church-state strategies to convert the Indian, see Lisbeth Haas, *Conquests and Historical Identities in California* (Berkeley: University of California Press, 1995).

7. Bancroft, *History*, 2:406, 517–18.

8. Sánchez, *Telling Identities*, 90. David Weber, in *The Mexican Frontier, 1821–1846* (Albuquerque: University of New Mexico Press, 1982), 400, says that the figure is closer to 500,000 pesos.

9. See Weber, *The Mexican Frontier*, 72–76.

10. Woodrow Hansen, *The Search for Authority in California* (Oakland: Biobooks, 1960), 2–3.

11. Weber, *The Mexican Frontier*, 75–76.

12. Los Angeles City Archives, v. 2, September 12, 1837, 197. There are several sets of the *ayuntamiento* records. The Spanish originals, called the Los Angeles City Archives, sit in the city clerk's office in Los Angeles. They are accompanied by English translations. Spanish transcriptions of the originals, called the Los Angeles Ayuntamiento Archives, sit at U.C. Berkeley's Bancroft Library. I use all three versions, and each set will be identified. Unless stated otherwise, the Spanish versions of the *ayuntamiento* records are used.

13. Ibid., v. 3, September 1, 1838, 309–10, trans. Before 1850, a peso equaled one American dollar. A *real* was worth at least twelve cents. See Michael P. Costeloe, *The Central Republic in Mexico, 1835–1846: Hombres de Bien in the Age of Santa Ana* (Cambridge, England: Cambridge University Press, 1993), 18.

14. Manuel Servín, "The Secularization of the California Missions," *Southern California Quarterly* 47:4 (1965): 136–38.

15. Monroy, *Thrown among Strangers*, 42–43.

16. Ibid.

17. Daniel Garr, "Church-State Boundary Disputes," in Dora Crouch, Daniel Garr, Axel Mundingo, *Spanish City Planning* (Cambridge, Mass: MIT Press, 1987), 248–49.

18. Los Angeles became the capital of California in 1835 and earned the rank of city. Within a year, Mexico City once more made Monterey the capital, but it allowed Los Angeles to retain the designation of city. Daniel Garr, "Los Angeles and the Challenge of Growth," *Southern California Quarterly* 61 (Summer 1979): 147–55. A casual reading of the Ayuntamiento Archives shows that, after 1835, citizens continued to call Los Angeles a city.

19. Los Angeles City Archives, v. 3, October 6, 1837, 179, city clerk's office of Los Angeles.

20. Bancroft, *History*, 3: 638.

21. Mariano Vallejo, a prominent ranchero in northern California, said that soldiers assigned to the classroom sometimes beat their charges. Vallejo, "Historia de California," 5 vols., Earl Hewitt, trans., 4:135, Bancroft Library. The page numbers in the translation are inconsistent and unreliable.

22. Bancroft, *History*, 3:638.

23. Narciso Botello, "Anales de Sur," ms., 178–79, Bancroft Library.

24. Los Angeles Ayuntamiento Archives, May 6, 1850, v. 5, 303, Bancroft Library.

25. Del Valle Collection, Seaver Center for Western History, Natural History Museum for Los Angeles Country. Grammar book in Spanish with six pages, and each page with a different style of writing, p. 1, Box 13, Item #679.

26. Antonio Coronel Collection, Seaver Center for Western History Natural History, Museum for Los Angeles County. Grammar book in Spanish, n.p., Item #714.

27. Bancroft, *History*, 3:317–18. Also see Los Angeles City Archives, v. 4, April 12 (?), 1837, p. 296, city clerk's office. Bachelot died en route to the Sandwich Islands.

28. Population estimates come from two sources. For the *gente de razón* see Leonard Pitt, *Decline of the Californios* (Berkeley: University of California Press, 1971), 4–5. By 1830, the *gente de razón* totaled more than ten thousand people. The figures for the Indians are more exact. See Sherburne Cook, "The Indian Versus the Spanish Mission," 4, table 1.

29. For more on mission discipline see Cook, "The Indian versus the Spanish Mission," 91–134.

30. Pio Pico, *Historical Narrative*, trans., Arthur Botello, edited by Martin Cole and Henry Welcome (Glendale, Calif.: Arthur H. Clark, 1973), 89; also see William Wilcox Robinson, *The Indians of Los Angeles: The Story of a Liquidation of a People* (Los Angeles: Glen Dawson Press, 1952); for a more current interpretation of the servitude endured by the Indians, see Tomás Almaguer, *Racial Fault Lines in California: The Historical Origins of White Supremacy in California* (Berkeley: University of California Press, 1994), 45–51.

31. Los Angeles Ayuntamiento Archives, July 3, 1847, p. 440, Bancroft Library.

32. Ibid, n.d., v. 3, 1847, p. 139.

33. My argument fails to consider the problem of Mexican Californians' impressing Indian children. By the end of the 1830s, the residents of Los Angeles regularly met Ute war parties at Tehachapi Pass and exchanged guns and horses for Paiute children. See Gerald Smith and Clifford Walker, *The Indian Slave Trade Along the Mojave Trail* (San Bernadino: San Bernadino County Museum, 1965). As late as 1857, Vicente Gómez, a resident of southern California, claimed that slave traders "brought children . . . from Baja California . . . with the object of selling them in Los Angeles"; Gomez, "Lo Que Sabe Sobre Cosas de California," ms., v.3, 759, Bancroft Library.

34. See Erik Erikson, *Childhood and Society* (New York: W. W. Norton and Company, 1964), 275–358 for more on child development and the formation of society.

35. Quotation in James Sandos, "Junípero Serra's Canonization and the Historical Record," *American Historical Review* 93:5 (1988): 1254.

36. Quotation in Dora Crouch, Daniel Garr, and Axel Mundingo, *Spanish City Planning in North America*, 240.

37. Quotation in Angustias de la Ord, *Occurrences in Hispanic California*, trans. Francis Price and William Ellison (Washington D.C.: American Academy of Franciscan History, 1956), 7.

38. Edwin Beilharz, *Felipe de Neve: First Governor of California* (San Francisco, 1971), 9–10.

39. José Figueroa, *Manifesto to the Mexican Republic,* trans. C. Alan Hutchinson (Berkeley: University of California Press, 1978), 96.

40. Archives of the Prefecture, v. 1, June 4, 1841, 370, part B, in English, city clerk's office of Los Angeles. There is no indication if the attacker ever faced trial.

41. A good overview of paternalism in the antebellum South can be found in George Frederickson, *Black Image in the White Mind* (New York: Harper Torchbooks, 1972), and Kenneth S. Greenberg, *Honor and Slavery* (Princeton: Princeton University Press, 1996).

42. For excellent reviews of enlightened thought's impact on philosophy, art, and religion in Europe and North and South America, see Hugh Honour, *Neo-Classicism* (London: Penguin Books, 1968), and George Kubler, *Mexican Architecture in the Sixteenth Century,* 2 vols., (New Haven: Yale University Press, 1948); also see his *The Shape of Time: Remarks on the History of Things* (New Haven: Yale University Press, 1970).

43. D. A. Brading has written extensively and wonderfully on the Enlightenment's impact on Mexican society. See *The First America: The Spanish Monarchy, Creole Patriots, and the Liberal State, 1492–1867* (Cambridge, England: Cambridge University Press, 1991), especially, 561–602. Also see *Prophecy and Myth in Mexican History* (Cambridge, England: Cambridge University Press, 1980) and *The Origins of Mexican Nationalism* (Cambridge, England: Cambridge University Press, 1985).

44. For more on instilling a sense of civic duty in Latin America, consult Brading, *Origins of Mexican Nationalism;* also see Charles Hale, *Mexican Liberalism in the Age of Mora, 1821–1853* (New Haven: Yale University Press, 1968); Jaime Rodriguez, ed., *The Evolution of the Mexican Political System* (Wilmington, Delaware: SR Books, 1984); and Jean Franco, *Plotting Women: Gender and Representation in Mexico* (New York: Columbian University Press, 1989). The political tract prepared by José Luis Mora, *Catecismo politico de la federacion mexicana* (Mexico, 1831), Nettie Lee Benson Rare Book Collection, University of Texas at Austin, is an example of how Mexican liberals wanted to transform the nation.

45. For more insights about those who attacked, and supported, the Enlightenment, see Isaiah Berlin, *The Crooked Timber of Humanity* (New York: Alfred Knopf, 1991).

46. See Arthur Quinn, *Broken Shore* (Inverness, Calif.: Redwood Press, 1981), 34–35, for the best intellectual study of the Franciscans in California. For other studies on the Franciscan mentality, see John Leddy Phelan, *The Millennial Kingdom of the Franciscans in the New World* (Berkeley: University of California Press, 1970); Jacques LaFaye, *From Quetzalcóatl to Guadalupe* (Chicago:University of Chicago Press, 1974), and Antonine Tibesar, O.F.M., ed., *The Writings of Junípero Serra,* 2 vols. (Washington D.C.: Academy of American Franciscan History, 1955), 1:xxiii–xxx.

47. All information on the Erastian and primitive church comes from Brading, *The First America,* 492–513.

48. For more on the Inquisition in Mexico, see Fernando Cervantes, *The Devil in the New World* (New Haven: Yale University Press, 1994).

49. For Lorenzana and Fabian y Fuero quotations, see Brading, *The First America,* 495–97.

50. Ibid, 490–97.

51. Junípero Serra to Father Francisco Palou, July 3, 1769, in Tibesar, *Writings of Junípero Serra,* 1:144–45. For ideas on Eden in America, see Silvio Zavala, *Sir Thomas More in New Spain* (Mexico City: Colegio de Mexico, 1955).

52. *Fray Juan Crespi, Missionary Explorer on the Pacific Coast, 1769–1774,* Herbert Bolton, ed. (Berkeley: University of Californian Press, 1927), 146–55.

53. For more on the charge of Satanic influence in Indian communities, see Governor José María Echeandía's report on neophytes charged with sorcery, in Cook, "The Indian versus the California Mission," 149; also see Father Gerónimo Boscana, *Chinigchinich,* in Alfred Robinson, *Life in California* (Pasadena: Grabhorn Press, 1950).

54. An eloquent defense of the mission system can be found in Francis Guest, O.F.M., "Cultural Perspectives on California Mission Life," *Southern California Quarterly* 65(1983).

55. Description of the Indians' activities from Cook, *The Conflict between the California Indian and White Civilization,* 97–99. For more perspectives on mission life, see *Columbian Consequences: Archaeological and Historical Perspectives on the Spanish Borderlands West,* 2 vols., ed., David Hurst Thomas (Washington D.C.: Smithsonian Institution Press, 1989).

56. Robert H. Jackson and Edward Castillo, *Indians, Franciscans, and Spanish Colonization: The Impact of the Mission System on California Indians* (Albuquerque: University, New Mexico Press 1995), 11–30.

57. Ibid. For a neo-Marxist view of the mission economy, see Daniel Fogel, *Junípero Serra, the Vatican, and Enslavement Theology* (San Francisco: ism Press, 1988), 41–81.

58. Examples come from Antonia Castañeda, "Sexual Violence in the Politics and Policies of Conquest," in *Building with Our Hands,* eds., Adela de la Torre and Beatríz Pesquera (Berkeley: University of California Press, 1992).

59. *As the Padres Saw Them,* Maynard Geiger, O.F.M., and Clement Meighan, eds., (Santa Barbara: Santa Barbara Mission Archive Library, 1976), 105.

60. Ibid.

61. Ibid., 105–106.

62. For ideas about the body as political symbol, see Caroline W. Bynum, *Fragmentation and Redemption* (New York: Zone Books, 1991), and Mary Douglas, *Natural Symbols* (New York: Pantheon Books, 1982).

63. For more on plans to settle the province see Crouch, et al., *Spanish City Planning,* esp. 5–61.

64. Serra complaint is in ibid., 240.

65. Ibid., 241.

66. Señan comment is in Servín's "The Secularization of the California Missions," 137.

67. For the sake of simplicity when we discuss the colonial period, we will refer to New Spain as Mexico.

68. See Brading, *Prophecy and Myth in Mexican History,* 37–44. Hutchinson, *Frontier Settlement in Mexican California,* 110–80. Michael Costeloe, *Church and State in Independent Mexico: A Study of the Patronage Debate, 1821–1857* (London: Royal Historical Society, 1978), provides a good review of the liberal critiques of the church.

69. Admittedly, it is difficult to piece together the social and personal world of Mexico's liberals. My ideas come from Costeloe, *The Central Republic in Mexico, 1836–1846.* Also see Hugh Hamill, *The Hidalgo Revolt* (Gainesville: University of Florida Press, 1968).

70. Brading, *The First America.* The status of the Indian in New Spain had concerned the colonial intelligentsia since the conquest. During some periods, the feeling was more intense than at other times.

71. Ibid., 450–53.

72. Brading, *Myth and Prophecy in the Mexican Nation,* 41.

73. Ibid., 42

74. For more on the fear of social upheavals and suspicions of the *léperos,* the lower classes of Mexico, see Torcuato S. Di Tella, "The Dangerous Classes in Early Nineteenth Century Mexico," *Journal of Latin American Studies* 5 (1973), and Donald Stevens, "Riot, Rebellion and Instability in Nineteenth-Century Mexico," *Five Centuries of Mexican History,* Virginia Guedea and Jaime Rodriguez, eds. (Mexico, 1992).

75. One study that examines the diversity of the Indian experience is John K. Chance, *Race and Class in Colonial Oaxaca* (Stanford: Stanford University Press, 1978).

76. All ideas on society in colonial Mexico come from Jaime Rodriguez, *Down From Colonialism* (Los Angeles: Chicano Studies Research Center, UCLA, 1983). Also see Rodriguez and Colin M. MacLachlan, *The Forging of the Cosmic Race: A Reinterpretation of Colonial Mexico* (Berkeley: University of California Press, 1980).

77. The best, and most entertaining, study on the dangers of the collective is Michael P. Rogin's *Ronald Reagan: The Movie, and Other Episodes in Political Demonology* (Berkeley: University of California Press, 1987); for the evolution of Mexican liberalism see D. A. Brading, *The First America,* 583–602.

78. See Bancroft, *History,* 3:38, for the campaign to change the province's name and seal.

79. Quotation in C. Alan Hutchinson, "The Secularization of California's Missions," *The Americas* 21 (1965): 248–49.

80. Pitt, *Decline of the Californios,* 2–3.

81. See, for example, Vallejo, "Historia de California," v. 3, n.p.. Vallejo opens the third volume by saying that the Californios battled against "superstition" and "tyranny," references to the priests' power.

82. Admittedly, the Californio penchant for coups or counter-coups may defy easy enumeration, as one battle overlapped with the other. For the best description of power struggles in California, see Bancroft, *History,* 2:3.

83. Pitt, *The Decline of the Californios,* 5. Pitt has written the best study of Mexican California to date. The only weakness of his excellent book is his first chapter, in which he discusses the political culture of Mexican California. Otherwise, his work endures and remains unparalleled.

84. Bancroft, *History,* 3:608–49; George Harwood Phillips, *Chiefs and Challengers: Indian Resistance and Cooperation in Southern California* (Berkeley: University of California Press, 1975). For more on the abduction of Californio captives, see Bancroft, *History,* 4:68, and Smith and Walker, *The Slave Trade Along the Mojave Trail,* 8–10.

85. The entire story of Echeandía's use of Indian allies is in Zephyrin Engelhardt, O.F.M., *The Missions and Missionaries of California,* 4 vols. (San Francisco: James Barry and Company, 1913), 3:416–17, and Gerald Geary, A.M., The *Secularization of the California Missions* (Washington D.C.: The Catholic University of America, 1934), 124–25.

86. The Californios and Mexican troopers, however, used Indian auxiliaries when they hunted runaway neophytes. Sherburne Cook, *Expeditions to the Interior of California, Central Valley,* 1820–1840 (Berkeley: University of California Press, 1961), 152–58.

87. Many Spanish and Mexican civil administrators, along with French naval officers and American trappers, commented on the missions' prosperity. One of the best and most vivid accounts is the diary left by Jedediah Smith, the American trader and trapper. See *The Southwest Expedition of Jedediah Smith: His Personal Account of the Journey to California, 1826–1827,* ed., George Brooks (Glendale: Arthur H. Clark Company, 1977), 96–105.

88. The best description of secularization remains Bancroft, *History*, vol. 3. Hutchinson's *Frontier Settlement in Mexican California* is the most thorough, modern study. For a good, abbreviated account, see Servín, "The Secularization of the California Missions: A Reappraisal," 133–40. All information on the plans to secularize the missions comes from Bancroft and Servín.

89. For example, see Figueroa's first secularization decree in 1833, a measure that did not take effect until a year later. Bancroft, *History*, 3:328, n. 50.

90. Ibid.

91. David Weber provides a good review of the Indians' troubles after secularization. See *The Mexican Frontier*, 60–64.

92. San Diego Ayuntamiento Archives, 2 vols., compiled by Benjamin Hayes, v. 1, p. 142, Bancroft Library.

93. Robert Heizer and Alan Almquist, *The Other Californians* (Berkeley: University of California Press, 1976), 48–50; for a more poetic view describing the "grimy bond" between landowner and Indian, see Monroy, *Thrown among Strangers*, 153–54.

94. Smith and Walker, *The Indian Slave Trade along the Mojave Trail*, 5–10.

95. Los Angeles City Archives, v. 3, "Fondo Municipal de 1836," pp. 75–83, city clerk's office of Los Angeles. See the entry for Manuel Requena, *alcalde* of Los Angeles in 1836. Requena applied for a liquor license. I am grateful to my colleague, Helen Lara-Cea, who informed me that the storekeepers and bar owners also served in municipal offices throughout Mexican California.

96. In many Mexican Californian communities, the residents grew grapes, citrus, and other fruit in surrounding fields. Grapes seemed to be the most profitable crop, as proprietors either sold the fruit to vintners or distilled it themselves. See the Los Angeles City Archives, v.3, "Fondo Municipal," for the years between 1830 and 1845 to see how many landowners and shopkeepers paid a license to market *aguardiente,* city clerk's office of Los Angeles.

97. Report of Rafael Gallardo of the Police Commission, Los Angeles City Archives, March 13, 1847, v.1, 361, city clerk's office of Los Angeles. For information on segregating *gente de razón* from Indians, see Los Angeles Ayuntamiento Archives, July 3, 1847, v. 5, 431–42, Bancroft Library.

98. See Jean Franco, *Plotting Women*, 95–97; also see Peter Stallybrass and Allon White, *The Politics and Poetics of Transgression* (Ithaca: Cornell University Press, 1986), 145–47.

99. Petition of Francisco Figueroa and Luis Vignes, Los Angeles City Archives, v. 1, February 19–21, May 2, 1846, trans., 412–17, city clerk's office of Los Angeles.

100. See Sherburne Cook, "Small Pox in Mexican California," *Bulletin of the History of Medicine* 7:2 (1939); also see Los Angeles Ayuntamiento Archives, v.3, n.d., 1844–1850, 7–11, Bancroft Library.

101. Information from William Wilcox Robinson's, "The Indians of Los Angeles," *The Historical Society of Southern California Quarterly* 20:4 (1938): 156–57.

102. Los Angeles Ayuntamiento Archives, v. 5, November 17, 1845, 271, Bancroft Library.

7

The Creation and Re-creation of Californio Society

Douglas Monroy

The Californios occupied center stage of California history for only a short while. They were a people who began utterly inauspiciously, forged themselves places on the landscape as owners of great landed estates, and created a singular identity for themselves out of their relationships to priests, Indians, lower-class immigrants, Americans, Mexico, and cows and horses. Then, simultaneously, they faded into physical obscurity in the political economy of California, and, after the Americans conquered their country and tides of gold rushes overwhelmed their number and their land, they participated in their mythical re-creation as gracious masters of a lost pastoral paradise. Their story portends much about the unfolding of California history, about the state's changing political concerns, and even about the contingencies and exigencies of human existence.

California society provides an excellent window into both how historical figures forge their own identities and how later generations re-conceive such historical characters based on their own concerns. This narrative interweaves both processes: how those who were the first upon the landscape to self-consciously formulate a sense of themselves as "Californians" actually did so, and then how the past 150 years have seen several re-creations that betray more about those who wrote the history than about the actual Californios.

Central to any understanding of these fabled people are their own accounts of themselves after they fell from influence, their lengthy *recuerdos* dictated in the 1870s. At once poignant and self-congratulating, aristocratic and pitiful, Californios detailed eloquently and self-consciously their own versions of their lives and times to collectors of autobiographies under the direction of Hubert Howe Bancroft, the true founder of studious California historiography. The testimonies, mostly in Spanish, form one of the centerpieces of the Bancroft Library at the University of California

Pío Pico, one of the most prominent Californios of his day, as portrayed by an unknown artist, probably in the early 1850s. The grandson of a soldier who in 1775 accompanied Juan Bautista de Anza to California, Pico twice served as governor of the Mexican province and acquired great wealth in immense landholdings. Like other rich rancheros whose storied hospitality and generosity helped give rise to romantic legends of Old California, Pico ultimately lost his estates and fortune under American rule, dying in near poverty in 1894 at the home of his daughter in Los Angeles. *Courtesy California State Library.*

at Berkeley, and are important sources for Bancroft's magisterial seven-volume *History of California.* Recently, literary critic Rosaura Sánchez has subjected many of the testimonials to rigorous textual analysis to reveal contemporary meaning. Those that are published are well worth reading, though one must always be aware of the narrators' agendas and the interviewers' biases and limited understanding of Spanish.[1]

People who have been subjects of imperial quests, like the Californios, are likely subjects of fantasies invented by their conquerors both before and after their defeat. In the years before the Mexican-American War (1846–1848), numerous Yankee and English traders and travelers, and several Europeans, published accounts of their sojourns in California that often disparaged the region's inhabitants. Richard Henry Dana's *Two Years before the Mast* was the most widely read and endures as the most typical view of those endowed with what has been so aptly named "the spirit of capitalism." In this Protestant New Englander's view, the Californios appeared "to be always on horseback" and "in their domestic relations are not better than in their public. The men are thriftless, proud, extravagant, and very much given to gaming; and the women have but little education, and a good deal of beauty, and their morality, of course is none the best." Another Yankee related how the Californios were "a proud indolent people doing nothing but ride after herds from place to place with no apparent object." "In the hands of an enterprising people," Dana concluded solidly within the spirit of Manifest Destiny, "what a country this might be!"[2]

Within a few decades after the American conquest, portrayals of the Californios underwent a different re-creation. Indeed it was Bancroft, wealthy from his San

Francisco–based business of publishing and selling books, who first sought to replace the skewed accounts of merchants, travelers, and priests with what he called "a complete, accurate, and impartial history of California." To this end he initiated a massive project of collecting testimonies and documents relating to California from archives throughout the Americas, and then writing collaboratively his remarkable history. Much bitterness ensued when his collaborators did not receive any credit (Henry L. Oak, for example, did most of the actual writing of the seven volumes), and only a positivist of the late nineteenth century like Bancroft could truly believe that the simple accumulation of facts in a long chronicle amounted to objective history. This entrepreneurial historian's assumptions about race and civilization radiate throughout the grand narrative. The Californios took shape only as a quaint people on the landscape, quite out of touch with modern civilization. Bancroft rather presumes his society's pervasive views about the intellectual and technological superiority of the Anglo-Saxon cultures of the North Atlantic. Obviously, Bancroft must be read within these contexts. But the old master included many alternative stories of events, along with facts that he deemed less important, in the footnotes. General readers and scholars alike should be aware that—its presumptions about "civilization," in which Hispanic and Native Californians seemingly did not take part, notwithstanding—this massive opus remains a masterful and engaging narrative, with remarkable footnotes that are often of great significance, of California's history from 1542 to 1890.[3]

Despite Anglo-Saxon bias, Bancroft, with the Californios' own narratives often as the sources, lapsed from positivism toward legend and celebrated the previously maligned traits of the Californios in his fanciful *California Pastoral* (1888). "And so they lived," he wrote, "opening their eyes in the morning when they saw the sun; they breathed the fresh air, and listened to the song of the birds; mounting their steeds they rode forth in the enjoyment of healthful exercise; they tended their flocks, held intercourse with each other, and ran up a fair credit in heaven."

By 1900, Anglo-Californians came to lament the passing of the Californios (and the missions), but to attribute that passing to their own shortcomings. During the last half of the nineteenth century, historical analyses of Spanish and Mexican California reflected Americans' optimism and faith in progress and technology and their negative judgement of peoples they deemed non-progressive. As early as 1846, Alfred Robinson's famous *Life in California* explained how "the early Californians, having lived a life of indolence without any aspiration beyond the requirement of the day, naturally fell behind their more energetic successors." The acclaimed works of Josiah Royce and Charles Nordhoff similarly sympathized with the Californios and savored their prosperous and genteel lifeways, while condescendingly criticizing their lack, in Nordhoff's words, "of the energy and ingenuity of civilized life." Civic, business, and antiquarian organizations, which such writers inspired and informed, began in the 1890s to extol Californio society with various "Fiesta Days" celebrations. Typically including floats depicting fanciful scenes of old California, local businessmen riding horses and dressed as caballeros and always presented as "Spanish," these gala rituals provided Americans an opportunity to romanticize the non-market social relations of the people whom they had summarily, often harshly, replaced on the landscape of California.[4]

These re-creations reveal dramatically how history is really more recent peoples' relationships with the past. Like all relationships, they change and grow over time. History is best appreciated not merely as the "facts," but rather as the meanings that people derive from the facts at different times and for different purposes. The first Americans who wrote about California did so while judging negatively those they considered generally inferior, and to vindicate their imperialist pursuits. Then, confined within their system of isolating market relationships, Anglo-American chroniclers made of the Californios that for which they so yearned: gracious gentlemen and ladies who acted solely out of considerations of honor, solicitousness, and faith towards one another and their subordinates.[5]

The now classic works of Carey McWilliams, *North from Mexico: The Spanish-Speaking People of the United States* (1948), and Leonard Pitt, *The Decline of the Californios: A Social History of the Spanish-Speaking Californians, 1846–1890* (1966), began a more modern and realistic re-evaluation of the Californios in the context of the Mexican American era, a time in the decades after World War II when many Mexican immigrants or their children sought to affirm a place for themselves as Americans. While neither ignored the Californios' own oppressive practices toward Indians and lower-class Mexicans, each of these authors portrayed the role that Mexican-origin people played in California history, the discrimination and exclusion that they had experienced, the clash of cultures that Manifest Destiny attempted to, but did not actually, justify, and the economic abuses upon which Anglo-California developed. Both referred to the "schizoid heritage" of Spanish-speaking people in twentieth-century California: they lived surrounded both by the romanticized history and place-names of their predecessors, who had been re-created as "Spanish," and at the same time by a social and economic system that branded them "Mexicans" and second-class Americans. These books sought to affirm the historical reality of "Spanish-speaking Californians" so that the political system could include the social reality of their presence in California and the Southwest.[6]

The 1990s has already seen the publication of three major books that treat the Californios extensively. In *Thrown among Strangers: The Making of Mexican Culture in Frontier California* (1990), I have attempted to place the Californios within the broader sweep of Indian, Spanish, Mexican, and American history with an emphasis on spirituality, desire, and production relations. Lisbeth Haas, in *Conquests and Historical Identities in California, 1769–1936* (1995), has insightfully interpreted the development of a Californio identity, which formed in the context of their own domination of the Indians, their subordination to the later-arriving Americans, and then, most impressively explored in her work, their efforts to maintain their social and cultural community in pockets of southern California well into the twentieth century. The aforementioned work of Rosaura Sánchez, *Telling Identities: The Californio Testimonios* (1995), explores Californio history "in terms of the discursive construction of collective identity" via the testimonials.[7] Insights from these more recent works, combined with useful information from primary sources and earlier histories, make possible a retelling of the Californio story.

LAND AND LIBERTY

The beginnings of the Californios were much less auspicious than any of the expansive re-creations would suggest. In 1784, Governor Pedro Fages, adversary of the mission strategy for the settlement of California, granted lands to veterans he had commanded as captain of the San Diego presidio. He explained to his superiors in Mexico

that the cattle are increasing in such manner, that it is necessary in the case of several owners to give them additional lands; they have asked me for some *sitios* which I have granted provisionally, namely to Juan José Domínguez who was a soldier in the presidio of San Diego and who at this moment has four herds of mares and about 200 head of cattle on the river below San Gabriel, to Manuel Nieto for a similar reason that of La Zanja on the highway from said mission . . . and to the sons of the widow Ignacio Carrillo that on the deep creek contiguous to the foregoing.

More than a response to the increase of the retired soldiers' herds, these provisional grants entitled these *inválidos* to use land as a reward for their service to the Crown. While Californios ultimately came to assume the permanence of these ambiguous concessions, they surely began the process by which many of them would be transformed into the grandees of the frontier California landscape. The mission remained the principal and most pivotal institution; fewer than twenty private land grants were awarded before the birth of the Mexican republic in 1821.[8]

About half of these were located within one hundred miles of the little pueblo of Los Angeles, a few near Monterey. All grants were imprecise in the actual terms of the boundaries and of the grantees' tenure; most included the phrase *mas o menos* (more or less) in the description of their confines. Before trade began to flourish with Yankee ships in the late 1820s and before the end of the missions (1834) freed up an Indian labor force, rancho life was quite rough. In one of the famous *recuerdos*, José del Carmen Lugo recalled the rustic beginnings of such grand domains as Rancho San Antonio, near Los Angeles, granted to his father, an ex-soldier from the Santa

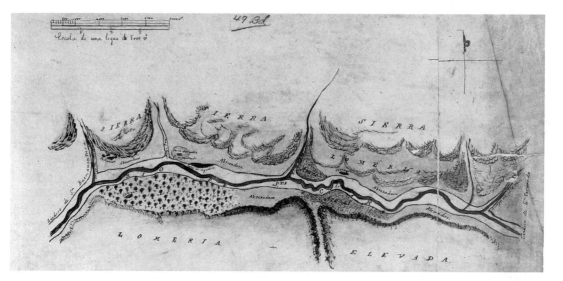

A *diseño,* or topographical map, of Rancho Sespe, which embraced six square leagues of land, *"un poco mas o menos,"* along the Santa Clara River, some thirty miles east of Mission San Buenaventura. Under Mexican law, a petition for land included a *diseño,* which showed boundaries and defining landscape features. In 1829 Cárlos Antonio Carrillo of Santa Barbara submitted his claim for Rancho Sespe, and five years later Governor José Figueroa officially confirmed the grant. *Courtesy Bancroft Library.*

Barbara Presidio: "The house on a little ranch was of rough timber roofed with tules. It rarely had more than two rooms." People slept on cots or "beds of cotton-wood or poplar, lined with leather." The presence of "sheets, blankets, coverlets, pillows, and so on" depended on "the resources of the owner." The number of ranchos doubled in the decade after Mexican independence, and they actually began to compete with the missions in production of trade goods, and even more intensely for the devotion of the Indians. As early as 1795 Fray Vicente Santa María noted how the Indians were "fond of the Pueblo of Los Angeles, of the rancho of Mariano Verdugo, of the rancho of Reyes, and of the [rancho of the] Zanja." Preferring the easier life of the rancho over the discipline of the missions, the Indians went about "clad in shoes, with sombreros and blankets, and serving as muleteers to the settlers and rancheros."[9]

It was not simply as laborers that the Indians served the Californios. As they emerged from their modest beginnings at the presidios, the largely mestizo and sometimes mulatto grantees came to refer to themselves as *gente de razón,* or "people of reason." This self-conception can only be understood in the context of its opposite, those *sin razón,* or "without reason." Originally, the Spanish Inquisition had created this concept—most certainly associated with childish inability to distinguish right from wrong as regards theology or deeds—to explain and release Indians from culpability for heretical actions. Positively defined in Mexican California, the phrase *gente de razón* came to refer to anyone who was Catholic, Spanish-speaking, and who renounced instinctual behavior in favor of service to work, community, and the Crown. Negatively, it came to contrast a resident of California with anyone who behaved like an "Indian," or how an Indian was imagined to be. The Californios' self-serving image of the Indian bore little resemblance to the complex spiritual and productive lifeways that the natives had developed over time, but derived from Spanish preconceptions about Indians in general, from the Indians' degradation in the missions, and from the behavior of those outside the missions who resisted, often with violence, further encroachments on their lands and livelihoods. This notion, not the actual qualities of the Indians and their cultures, formed the primary caste distinction in Alta California. The mulatto and mestizo Don Pío Pico, or the mestizo Governor José Figueroa, or one like Don Manuel Domínguez, who was so dark that he was banned from testifying in court after the American conquest, were all considered *de razón*. *Sin razón* were the Indians tyrannized in the missions, raiding in the wild, or alcoholic in the pueblo; the uncouth lower-class immigrants known as *cholos;* and the vulgar American trappers who wandered into California.

While the emergent Californios valued the efforts of the padres to make the neophytes *de razón,* they came to see only futility and fault in the mission compounds. Pressure mounted against the despotic missions, which were obviously failing to transform the Indians and which monopolized so much land. "It is just that twenty one mission establishments possess all the fertile lands of the peninsula," complained Mariano Vallejo, "and that more than a thousand families of *gente de razón* possess only that which has been benevolently given them by the missionaries." Peruvian-born *criollo* Juan Bandini summed up the dilemma:

> Indeed the system of these missions is the most appropriate to retard their [the Indians'] mental development, but to change it suddenly would cause serious disturbance in the territory. The missions extend their possessions in one continuous line although not needing the land for their crops and herds and in this way they have appropriated nearly all this territory, their object being to keep private parties from coming between the mission grants. This is a system which the *gente de razón* should reform.

Thus, the pressure of the *gente de razón* combined with the waxing and waning faith of Mexican elites in liberal ideology to secularize the missions. This process, which Governor Figueroa initiated in 1834, set the stage for the blossoming of Californio society. Now, with the missions converted into mere churches, stripped of their estates and control over the Indians, the most fertile lands and thousands of laborers were freed from what Figueroa called "monastic despotism."[10]

The administration of Governor Echeandía (1825–1831) had marked the introduction of liberalism in Alta California. "When he arrived in California in 1825," Angustias de la Guerra Ord commented, "he came speaking of the republican and liberal principles which filled the heads of Mexicans in those days." This actually inflexible and quirky man encouraged study groups in the north that excited several young men—most notably Mariano Vallejo, his nephew Juan Bautista Alvarado, and José Castro—about these ideas of liberty and equality. According to Alvarado, Eche-andía's encouragement of the ideas of the Enlightenment and of education for all fostered "the true principles of republicanism and liberty" among these young men, concepts that directly and profoundly challenged the reigning beliefs emanating from the missions.[11]

In the Californios' view, secularization, though, would not make of the Indians free and independent citizens, something for which the missions had not prepared them anyway. Seeing the natives as *sin razón* contradicted liberalism's concepts of liberty and equality, but was essential to ensure and to justify that the ex-mission Indians would remain in the lower caste and subservient. Thus it was that the Indians figured in such important and complicated ways in the Californios' lives: contrasting their lives with Indians would reassure Californios that they were *de razón;* the ill-fated Indian participation in the despotic missions proved the latter's utter failure; and quickly the Indians would become the actual producers on the great ranchos.

Mexico's adoption of the Colonization Act of 1824 and a supporting *reglamento* of 1828 intended to encourage immigration to the far northwestern department, but it was secularization of the missions that actually made the civil settlements, especially the rancho, the dominant economic and social institutions on the California landscape. In the thirteen years between secularization and the American possession, the Mexican governors of California made a stunning eight hundred land grants, mostly to Californios. It would appear that individuals simply applied to the governor for a grant, and in the context of Mexico's eagerness to fill the land with loyal citizens in light of the apparent designs of the United States and other nations on the prize of California, millions of acres were simply given away to earnest settlers. Actually, intense political intrigue had positioned only certain people to benefit from the largesse.

In the first place, the male children born to the original settlers and presidial soldiers, *hijos del país,* had successfully asserted control over the affairs of California. In the context of the new republic's regional disunity, economic distress, and political instability, Mexico became the errant mother, or as Alvarado put it, the "stepmother," of California. And, as in New Mexico, Mexico wanted to collect revenues from its province, but neither would, nor even could, send troops to fight Indians. Increasingly the *hijos del país* came to understand themselves as Californios, and more recent immigrants as *mexicanos* and *extranjeros.* California became their *patria,* and

Mexico a foreign place. This sentiment crystallized in the *Manifesto a la República Mejicana,* a series of documents that Governor Figueroa assembled and that were widely circulated in California after 1834. The *Manifesto* affirmed regional control over disposition of the ex-mission lands and California's territorial sovereignty—an interesting problem should, say, England or the United States attack California. This emerging consciousness provided the proto-nationalist climate in which the Californios stormed against governors Chico and Gutiérrez, both of whom had been sent from Mexico. Their reigns had much to do with arguments over liberalism and then federalism versus centralism, issues that raged all the more fiercely in Mexico. Particularly decisive, in late 1836, Juan Bautista Alvarado, an *hijo del país,* became governor of California.[12]

Inconsistent with some of the images of graciousness and indolence to which the introductory passages of this narrative introduced us, the *gente de razón* swarmed over the mission lands just as energetically as did the flies over the cowpies in the mission pastures. The governors of California appointed the hijos del país as commissioners and *mayordomos* of the ex-mission lands and of the Indians, to the great advantage of the Californios. "Of the administrators of the missions," stated De la Guerra Ord, "some were incapable, others without morality, and some, a very few, were men of good faith who did everything possible to conserve the properties." Mostly, the ex-mission lands became the property of *hijos del país,* who grabbed them with little or no attention to Indian rights to those lands, or attention to the Indians' *rancherías* (settlements) on or near the sprawling expanses. Liberalism, then, came to mean the right of the Californios to control private property.

The disposition of the lands of Mission San Juan Capistrano illuminates the process: José Sepúlveda received from his father—the government-appointed administrator of San Juan—a grant of mission lands in 1837, and then two more leagues in 1842. In that year, ranchos El Niguel and La Cañada de los Alisos went to in-laws of the Sepúlvedas (there were many Sepúlvedas among southern California rancheros; those of Rancho Palos Verdes are the most famous), and the year previous saw the granting of Rancho Trabuco to Santiago Argüello, after he too had been administrator of Mission San Juan Capistrano lands. Tomás and Bernardo Yorba were sons of former Sergeant Antonio Yorba, who in 1809 had received Rancho Santiago de Santa Ana, and who was one of the grandest rancheros. Tomás received the only grant from San Juan lands not made to family members of administrators. When Indians, or priests acting for them, contested the grants, civil authorities almost always ruled in favor of the *gente de razón.* When Bernardo petitioned in 1834 for a grant of Mission San Gabriel lands, for example, a priest from the old mission denounced his efforts to the Los Angeles town council, claiming (properly) that the land belonged legally to the mission Indians. The *ayuntamiento,* however, proclaimed the virtues of Bernardo's enterprise and validated his claim.[13]

LIFE ON THE RANCHOS

Stories of the ranchos have been told in various ways; likely there are few better illustrations of how history consists of our changing relationship with the past. Numerous books and articles have appeared listing the ranchos, their proprietors, and
their geneologies. Often relying extensively on the *recuerdos* and travelers' accounts,
such writings described in precise detail social and productive life on the ranchos. On
the other hand, little effort was devoted to interpretation of Californio society,
though the picture one gets certainly reflects the writers' pastoralist yearnings and
assumptions about civilization, the productive hardiness of different cultures, and
racial hierarchies.[14] The more recent works cited above have dramatically and fundamentally recast the study of the Californios. Each has attempted to derive *meaning* from the factual descriptions of land tenure, rituals such as fiestas and marriage
ceremonies, and relations with the Indians.

As more recent works demonstrate, several factors converged to beget a particular style of life on these fabled ranchos. The availability of land and Indians to work
on it, both resulting from the spoliation of the missions, along with trade with the
Yankee ships, a seigneurial mindset, and a fecund environment, all combined to
produce a particular society. The grasses that grew readily on the warm coastal landscape of California could feed many cows. Later in the century, one Anglo traveler
would see at San Gabriel "herds of cattle, lying down, as if oppressed by surplus
food." The routine slaughter of a few cows could feed amply everyone attached to a
rancho; but in these most majestic days of the ranchos, the cows' only exchange
value derived from their hides and tallow. We can only know approximately what
quantities were loaded on the American and English ships and exchanged for manufactured goods from the North Atlantic—perhaps a million and a quarter hides and
sixty million pounds of tallow between 1826 and 1848. Yet it should be easy to imagine the lifestyle that the trade for cows raised on the nearly half-million acres be-
longing to the De la Guerras in the Santa Barbara area, on the nearly quarter-
million acres of the several Yorba families, or even on the seventy thousand acres that
Joaquin Estrada occupied in Monterey County. The Lugo and Avila families probably grazed between forty thousand and twenty thousand head respectively, and in
the north the grandee of the Sonoma area, Mariano Vallejo, husbanded twenty-five
thousand cows, twenty-four thousand sheep, and two thousand horses on his nearly
three hundred thousand acres. The several dons of the Pico family claimed seven
hundred thousand acres.[15]

The dramatic size of some of these ranchos should not obscure the fact that most
Californios occupied modest-sized holdings. Then, too, many of them labored as
ranch foremen or as artisans in the pueblos. The hides that these Californios of the
middling sort either raised or with which they were often paid allowed them a

Vaqueros drive a herd of cattle past Mission San Gabriel in a drawing titled *Rodeo* by the artist Emanuel Wyttenbach. During California's pastoral era, cattle composed the source of wealth for the ruling class of rancheros, with the economic development of the province resting almost entirely on the hide-and-tallow trade. *Rodeo* was produced under the direction of William Heath Davis, who first came to California in the 1830s, and who late in the century commissioned a series of illustrations for his reminiscences, *Seventy-Five Years in California* (San Francisco, 1929). *Courtesy California State Library.*

lifestyle that received little remark from outsiders who called them "middle class" if they had land, or "greasers" if they did not.[16]

History, place, and culture, though, resolve what sort of society a particular group of people will create from their productive endeavors. The dons did not transform the bovine produce of the land into anything resembling "capital," that is, the sort of machinery, land, or money to reinvest that would generate more profit and wealth. Instead, they sought trade goods to facilitate a particular style of life. With the Yankee traders aboard ship or those who had set up mercantile shops in the towns, they bartered hides and tallow, typically for "the cheapest rebozos for the Indian women . . . (and) pieces of 'Indian cloth'" to clothe their laborers, and for such luxury goods as silk dresses, laces, necklaces, muslin pants, window glass, metal knives and forks, furniture, and even books for themselves. These served not merely for comfort, but also for show.[17]

The meanings evoked in the word "seigneurialism" best represent the society that evolved from those rough beginnings on those first ranchos. Affirmation of social standing, not the mere accumulation of goods and capital, motivated the Californios'

José Antonio de la Guerra, soldier,
ranchero, and long the illustrious patriarch
of Santa Barbara, as painted in 1850 by
the Italian-born artist Leonardo Barbieri.
De la Guerra, who proudly traced his
lineage to Spanish nobility, personified the
seigneurial tradition in Mexican California. Revered and respected, a lord of land,
labor, and cattle, he exercised wide authority while assuming responsibility for the
well-being not only of family and friends
but of the larger community as well.
Courtesy Santa Barbara Historical Society.

aspirations for land, production, and trade. Payment in kind and the relations of reciprocal obligation attached the poor—the landless—to both the wealthy and the
middling sort—the landed. Notions of honor bound wives to husbands and children
to parents. These values of hierarchical societies we connect with "feudalism," rather
than those of freely associating individuals we identify with modernity. Yet it is best
not to apply the name of this classical system of medieval Europe to mid-nine-
teenth-century California. This regional social and productive system certainly bears
remnants of feudalism, but many other factors also shaped Californio society. The
exigencies of the Spanish empire, the profound but ambiguous spiritual and sexual
inheritance from the missions, trade with the North Atlantic markets, and the curious and tempestuous bonds between ranchero and Indian laborer all recommend
the word *seigneurial*—implying the rule of a "big" man over family, laborers, and
land—instead of simply *feudal*.[18] People exist in relation to the spirit world, to their
families and enemies, to politics and ideologies, and to labor and their desires for
pleasure. Each of these became remarkable manifestations of the Californios'
seigneurialism.

The Californios were, above all else, *de razón.* José Antonio de la Guerra, actually
an ally of the missions, ex-commandant of the Santa Barbara Presidio, and then
grandee of the area and father of the previously cited Angustias, recited how "the
Holy Father . . . gave man reason in order to understand, appetite in order to love,
liberty in order to work with merit. . . . He gave faith to govern reason, charity in order to guide and balance his appetite, and grace in order to strengthen his liberty."

Vaqueros capture a grizzly bear in a spirited engraving taken from a drawing by the pioneer California artist Charles Nahl. Legendary horsemen, the Californios caught bears for sport, either dispatching the beast on the spot or later pitting it against a wild bull as part of holiday festivities. *Courtesy California Historical Society, FN-10706.*

These mellifluous words express the views of an elite, but the religious views of common Californios remain obscure. We do know, though, that people typically expressed their devotion through collective ritual that both government and social convention prescribed.

José del Carmen Lugo—son of one of the first soldier grantees, Antonio María Lugo, who in 1810 had received Rancho San Antonio, in present-day Los Angeles—told how "everyone was expected by the government to fulfill the obligations of the Church. Everyone except for the sick . . . had to attend mass on Sundays and other days of obligation." In Lugo's recollections everyone confessed, learned church doctrine, and received the sacraments. He recalled how for the wealthy "the praying of their devotions"—which he claimed began upon awakening at 3:00 A.M.—initiated a family's day, and the nightly praying of the rosary concluded it. A saint's day, for example, provided an occasion for the expression of faith, exuberant festivities, and community solidarity. Carlos Híjar recollected that in Santa Barbara, on the town's patron saint's day, preparation began well in advance. In the morning a solemn Mass would be celebrated, followed by the ringing of bells and the firing of cannon. In the afternoon would be a bull fight (actually people and a bull chasing one another around an arena), or a bull-and-bear fight. (This was one of the most curious and unique customs of the Californios—pitting a bull against a captured bear and cheering the grisly outcome.) Dancing and drinking brandy (at least for the men) lasted several more days.[19] The authority of the church remained strong in Mexican California, despite the wavering intrusion of liberalism. Their celebrations of faith glorified not only God but the Californios' communities, affections, and affectations.

Family life took place firmly within this seigneurial mentality. Ideally, respect and honor prevailed between the patriarch and the rest of his family. Customarily, women and children submitted to the will and judgment of men, but a father was reciprocally obligated to consider his charges' needs and wishes as he directed the family and production. José María Amador, recipient of a vast land grant in present-day Santa Clara and Alameda counties, described explicitly how he conceived of Californio men in the early rancho period, and implicitly the ideal type: "In the years before 1830, the men were of good habits with few exceptions—without prejudice there were cases of prostitution, drunkenness, games of chance, and abandonment of families—these things existed but scarcely." Women had protections. Bancroft relates that "wives were not to be abused. One García was sentenced for maltreating his wife, and one Higuera likewise for cutting off his wife's hair out of jealousy. A soldier who had ruined a girl, and refused to make her his wife, was confined in a fort in irons, and forced to pay her $50 out of his savings in the *fondo de retención*." These and many other instances indicate that such breaches of public decency happened regularly, and that the culture and civil authorities considered them sufficiently deviant to punish them, however erratically. Honorable men for the most part did not treat people who were *de razón* disrespectfully.[20]

Californio men guarded nothing more closely than their daughters' honor, which, by extension, meant their families' honor. Lugo described a scene at once arcadian and suspicion-filled: "The boys (slept) in the outside porches, exposed to the weather, and the girls in a locked room, of which the parents kept the key, if there was any key." Other *recuerdos* confirm this practice, which paralleled the surveillance of neophyte females at the missions. Richard Henry Dana, whose comments about Californio manners and morals must be approached with distrust, did note that while "the instances of infidelity are much less frequent than one would at first suppose . . . , the very men who would lay down their lives to avenge the dishonor of their own family, would risk the same lives to complete the dishonor of another." Apparently, the rituals of seduction and revenge prevailed much less among Californio *de razón* than they did in New Mexico, yet we see here the complex association of patriarchal authority, women's virtue, and family virtue among those who set the moral tone in California.[21]

Marriage took place firmly within the considerations of the family's fortunes. The *recuerdos* differ slightly on the thoroughness of parental prerogatives regarding marriage. Híjar claimed that "these arrangements took place only between the fathers of the children, and they tried hard to keep them from learning of their plans." It could be, though, that for some sons, if a fancy arose at Mass or a fiesta, they could make their preferences known. Nonetheless, the sources speak resolutely on "the respect and obedience of children towards their parents in those times," as De la Guerra Ord put it, "because paternal authority was unlimited and did not cease even after the children married or even when they had their own children." A Frenchman who traveled to California in 1827 even noted how "seldom does one see a child of either sex sitting at the table of his father who, more often, eats alone, served by his wife, sons and daughters." Such decorum undoubtedly restrained behavior, but did not necessarily preclude affection; fathers built toys and furniture for their infants, and relatives exchanged locks of their children's hair.[22]

Production on the ranchos, be they grand or middling, further reveals the centrality of gender considerations in understanding Californio society. "Riding on horseback and lounging lazily around is the gamut of their days," Juan Bandini told of the men in 1828, "and the women bear all the responsibility of the house." The men's *recuerdos* sung the praises of women for their labors: "A woman of the house," noted Lugo, was always in charge of milking cows (though it took several male servants to hold their feet and another to milk) "so that the milk would be clean and neat." "Women and the Indian servants under the direction of the former," he continued, "made *asaderas* [a sort of curds], cheese, butter, and a mixture prepared to be eaten with beans." To these tasks, Híjar added that they "busied themselves with their domestic duties, cut the wood necessary for the meal, sowed in their gardens the seeds indispensable to the household, using the hoe, pick, shovel etc., and went to the streams to wash under an arbor which they themselves made." An American traveler, Edwin Bryant, affirmed that "while the men are employed in attending to the herds of cattle and horses, and engaged in their other amusements, the women (I speak of the middle classes on the ranchos) superintend and perform most of the drudgery appertaining to housekeeping, and the cultivation of the gardens."[23]

Women, often Indians, did the healing. Eulalia Pérez, the Hispanicized Indian who guarded the virtue of the neophyte women at Mission San Gabriel, recalled "María Ignacia Amador . . . She knew how to cook, sew, read and write, and to take care of the sick—she was a good *curandera* [healer]." The climate and the abundance of the land meant that people did not get sick often but when they did they went largely to Indian practitioners who treated them with local herbs. The record indicates that treatments for infected arrow wounds were especially sought.[24]

The men rode horses. That this was a "cow and horse culture" refers to more than the primary trade goods and the means of herding them. Being *a caballo*, on a horse, meant that one was literally socially elevated, a *caballero*. Lugo affirmed that "no Indian who was not a vaquero was permitted to ride a horse," though this prohibition was unevenly enforced in such a far-flung, loosely governed province. Dons not only supervised the herds and their Indian tenders on horseback, but raced other caballeros. Horse racing, and betting lavishly and sometimes destructively on the outcome, provided the outstanding pastime for the men of California.[25]

Not only the horse, but the all-important matter of dress ceremoniously displayed the hierarchies of Californio society. The representative *chaleco,* or men's waistcoat, and the short-sleeved and voluminous gowns of the women, along with their gilt-laced pantaloons, sashes, and necklaces and earrings, were all purchased with hides sold to the Yankee clippers. In the *recuerdos,* Californios' descriptions of their clothes ring with pride, and lament for the lost days. In the later fanciful writings about "California pastoral," dress symbolized what was elegant and genteel.[26] In the rancho era it symbolized the aspiration of elite Californios—the affirmation of their status. Such was the goal of life and work on ranchos grand and middling: tallow and hides and subsistence foodstuffs brought a prosperity that one displayed on one's body; a home in which to guide, protect, and sequester one's wife and children; and horses and clothing to project clearly one's distinction both from the repugnant cholos, and especially from the dreaded , frustrating, and frightening Indians.

The famous fiestas that the dons sponsored rendered more than diversion. These highly ritualized occasions gathered all elements of Californio society into a public spectacle at which elites wore their finery, supplied abundant food and copious drink, and danced with elegance. In other words, they displayed their wealth and status to their Indian laborers, the common folk, and themselves. "All the town was invited to participate," marveled Alfred Robinson about a De la Guerra family (into which he would soon marry) wedding in Santa Barbara, "when old and young, rich and poor, lame and blind, black and white, joined in the feast." A Californio recalled how they would "kill a calf a day" to feed the guests," another how "they served there wine in abundance," and another relished wine and brandy "without limit." Lugo recalled with gusto quite an array of dances and about the etiquette of who would dance with whom: the elderly proceeded to the floor first, and young men and women never danced, according to Lugo, "without first having received permission" from their parents. The dances carried on with these formalities, and they did so often for several nights in a row, often for a week if a daughter's wedding provided the occasion. Certainly such decorum waned as the old folks retired for the evening, and as the wine consumption waxed.[27]

The fiesta simultaneously bound the society together via the dispensing of food and drink, especially to the poor, at the same time that it proclaimed the prevailing hierarchies and glorified the status of the big man giving it. Those who appropriated the bounty of the land shared some of it with those who produced so much of it. Caste distinctions prevailed when people danced, or drank, or courted, but everyone, at least in the first decade of the rancho era, mixed in the splendid amusement. It appears, though, that as California drew both more American merchants who quickly

The *sala,* or main room, of the De la Guerra adobe in Santa Barbara, sometime in the 1870s. Built a half-century earlier by Don José Antonio, whose portrait hangs to the far left over his concertina, the house suggests the comfort and provincial elegance enjoyed by one of the elite families of California society. It was here in 1836 that Richard Henry Dana attended the wedding feast of a De la Guerra daughter and "found nearly all the people of town—men, women, and children—collected and crowded together, leaving barely room for the dancers." *Courtesy Santa Barbara Historical Society.*

became prosperous, as well as more troublesome *cholos,* the fiestas of *la gente escojida* (the select) became increasingly exclusive.[28]

California society was a very personalist one, that is, people related to one another by means of an elaborate series of primary, personal relationships. This included the Californios' fabled and genuine hospitality. The *recuerdos* and the travelers' accounts all marvel at the eagerness with which "they literally vie with each other in devoting their time, their homes, and their means to the entertainment of a stranger," not to mention a friend, family member, or godparent. Upon the arrival of a guest, "the men would proceed to kill a calf to eat, a calf which they had run down and lassoed from the road, without noticing whether or not it was theirs. They only were careful that the beast was fat and not tame." This exchange of effects bound society members in yet more webs of reciprocity: "They all treated each other as cousins," noted Híjar (and this also explains how they could connive so easily to control all of the ex-mission lands); "they considered themselves as members of a single family." Even the poor received donations of beef; such generosity eased any social tensions that these tremendous disparities of wealth might have created.[29] The Californios' munificence also reveals how in this culture, the more a man gave away the more he increased his social stature, which was, after all, a principal aspiration of these ex-soldiers cum grandees.

This personalism also explains the passions of the Californios' legendary squabbles. It was not just that liberal ideas did not resonate so positively in the south, or that the *abajeños* (literally, "lowlanders") were jealous of the preponderance of political power that the less-populated north held, but rather that regional leaders understood one another to have violated family solidarity. Political differences were personal affronts. The numerous revolts of the Californios (most notably against Governor Micheltorena, whom Mexico sent in 1842 to re-establish authority) and violent schisms resulted in near civil war in 1845. Pío Pico had been appointed governor and the capital moved to Los Angeles, while his *arribeño* (literally, "highlander") enemies—military commander José Castro in Monterey and Mariano Vallejo from Sonoma—controlled the north.[30]

CALIFORNIOS AND INDIOS

While we behold many of the compelling manifestations of life in the rancho era in these descriptions, one of the bases of Californio society has only dimly emerged here: this was a society based on the work of others. These became halcyon days as recalled in the *recuerdos* and in the later histories because men who presumed entitlement to the service of women and especially people of color, mostly, chronicled them. By the waterholes and the corrals where the herds lingered, Indian laborers lived in their *rancherías* in *jacales* made of tules and sticks tied together and stuck in the mud, or else they lived in the *indiada*, or servants' quarters. Some of these natives had attached themselves to ranchos after the secularization of the missions, others had entered into service on the ranchos as their remnant indigenous societies crumbled under the Spanish onslaught, and some few others had even been captured in the wild and given over to the rancheros for what Híjar called "training." Life on the ranchos did not require the discipline characteristic of the missions; labor on the ranchos was hard, but not consistently demanding, and no one worked very diligently anyway. For their labors they received food, clothing, or perhaps a few hides, which they so often traded for drink. And this was central to the construction of Californio society: the continuing destruction of California Indian society. Those were, after all, Indian lands—which the missions had appropriated for the "Spiritual Conquest"—

upon which the cows and horses now grazed. Yet those very Indians did so much of the work, whether the tending and slaughter of cows; the building of palatial homes and digging of ditches (the *ayuntamiento* of Los Angeles prescribed labor on the public ditches for Indians convicted of drunkenness); or the washing, cooking, sweeping, and serving of pampered guests under the direction of the *doña*.[31]

California society relied on the Indians in other ways as well. Except for a few who remained in the dramatically diminished mission compounds, the Indians remained resolutely, in the Californio mind, *sin razón*. Missionization had usually only succeeded in destroying the intricately forged old ways, replacing them with, at best, a tenuous new sense of discipline. Secularization all too often left the Indians without much social organization, a situation that the *gente de razón* indulgently exploited. Drunkenness and vice most apparently manifested the shock of the European conquest, and visibly demonstrated to the *de razón* that the Indians remained unsalvageable. Recall here De la Guerra's felicitous words on the meaning of *de razón:* none of them would he have applied to Indians. Thus their irredeemable nature not only ordained their servitude, but qualified Indians to serve as caricatures of everything that the *de razón* thought they themselves were not. Ascendant Californios, often mestizo, were, in other words, *gente de razón* because they were not Indians.

That they grabbed so much land after secularization meant that Californios would continue to contest with Indians "in the wild" for those lands to which Indians still laid claim. Furthermore, with lands available for hunting and foraging always receding, these Indians reasonably and fittingly saw cows and horses grazing upon their lands as legitimate quarry for their subsistence. These factors produced a constant situation of raiding and revenge between Californios and the many Indians who still ranged free. This was one way in which the Californios forged a collective identity—they were a people whom hostile forces besieged and from whom their incapable stepmother, Mexico, could not provide rescue. Repeated brutal fights with the Indians necessarily discolor the peaceful, genteel pastoral imagery of Californio society.

Historical perspective facilitates an awareness of how the Indians' desperation derived from the consequences of coercive missionization, and how their violent actions resisted invasion and conquest. Californios understood the Indian raids as criminal acts and proof of *de razón* virtue for protecting civilization from, in Governor Alvarado's words, "*bárbaros infiéles* (barbarous infidels)." Not incidentally, horses proved an important object of the raids: the Indians were now *a caballo,* too. The governor received a letter in 1839 from Señor Argüello in Los Angeles exclaiming how "the number of Indians who have run away to take up criminal pursuits is so great that the entire southern district is paralyzed." The San Diego area experienced the Indians' desperate fury most spectacularly. Raiders, erstwhile occupants of the lands, plundered most ranchos there at one time or another in the late 1830s, and rancheros periodically evacuated to the town for safety. In 1837 Rancho Jamul, home to Doña Eustaquia de Pico (mother of Pío and Andrés) underwent the most sensational episode in Indian-Californio relations. Attackers assassinated Mayordomo Leyva and several defenders, and kidnapped Leyva's two daughters, who were never seen again. This widely related story of the time melodramatically trumpeted the threat Indians posed to the *gente de razón,* and especially to Californio society's most prized and guarded possessions, its women and girls.[32]

Disease killed far more Indians than swords or guns throughout California history, but this is not to say that many Indians did not meet death at the hands of raging caballeros. British voyager Sir George Simpson could not help noticing when he visited in 1841–42 how "the Indians of all tribes are, from day to day, rendered more audacious by impunity. Too indolent to be always on the alert, the Californians overlook the constant pilferings of cattle and horses, til they are aroused beyond the measure of even their patience, by some outrage of more than ordinary mark." At these moments, for which such incidents as that at Rancho Jamul had been contributing tinder, Californio *gente* took leave of their reason and exploded into violence against people they called, among other things, *bestias* (beasts). Typical of retaliations against Indian raids throughout the Americas, it was the peaceful natives who especially suffered the wrath of the righteous avengers. José del Carmen Lugo arranged an ambuscade in league with his allies, Temecula Indians under the leadership of Juan Antonio, near a pillaged Lugo family rancho near San Bernardino. He claimed that he ordered his men "to fire only at the fighters because they were the chiefs and came only in the middle of the main body." Still, "we made a great slaughter, and falling upon them from the rear killed many of them." "On reaching Aguanga we amused ourselves killing some three Indians who continued fighting," he related. "Perhaps a hundred Indians perished."[33]

Our stories of the Californios must conclude here, but not without a recommendation for further inquiry and reflection. At the beginning of this narrative I suggested that study of the Californios may have something to relate even about "human existence." Indeed Californio society poses questions about the overall purposes of life: Labor or leisure? Familial convivialty or personal choice? Reciprocal obligations or the individual prerogatives of liberalism? Racial hierarchy or biological and cultural mixing? These are all weighty matters about which the Californios press us to reflect. I urge my readers to do so in the Californio spirit of honor and grace. Recall, though, the complexity of this remarkable Californio society, in which people lived with considerable caste distinctions, and yet participated (however unequally) in such experiences as drought and earthquakes, the joyful fiestas and the brutalizing fights with the Indians, salubrious weather and scads of fleas, and vice and faith. "And so they lived," with apologies to Bancroft, "opening their eyes" to the

modern world, but entangled in the gratifying bonds of the old; they believed in reason and gentility, and practiced lust and passion; they bought goods in the world
market, the very one that would ruin their ranchos after the Americans came; they
guarded their families, and alternately treated hospitably and raged against "each
other, and ran up a fair (debit) in heaven."

NOTES

1. Hubert Howe Bancroft, *History of California*, 7 vols. (Santa Barbara: Wallace Hebberd,
1963, facsimile of 1884 edition); see the bibliography in Rosaura Sánchez, *Telling Identities:
The California testimonios* (Minneapolis, 1995), which also notes which narratives are published in English.

2. Richard Henry Dana, *Two Years before the Mast* [1840] (New York, 1963), 64, 135–36;
George Clyman is quoted in Leonard Pitt, *The Decline of the Californios: A Social History of
the Spanish-Speaking Californians, 1846–1890* (Berkeley: University of California Press, 1966),
16, and see his bibliography on pages 298–300 for a rich selection of the travelers' accounts;
for an analysis the Anglo-American view of Mexican California, see ibid., 13–21, and Douglas Monroy, *Thrown among Strangers: The Making of Mexican Culture in Frontier California*
(Berkeley: University of California Press, 1990), 165–77.

3. For a thorough review of Bancroft's life and work, see John Walton Caughey, *Herbert
Howe Bancroft: Historian of the West* (Berkeley: University of California Press, 1946), and for
a more contemporary critique, see Sánchez, *Telling Identities*, 16–25, in which this paragraph's quote from Bancroft about "impartial history" comes on page 20.

4. Hubert Howe Bancroft, *California Pastoral* (San Francisco: History Co., 1888), 360;
Alfred Robinson, *Life in California before the Conquest* [1846] (San Francisco: Thomas C.
Russell, 1925); Charles Nordhoff, *California for Health, Pleasure, and Residence* (New York:
Harper and Brothers, 1873), 160; Josiah Royce, *California from the Conquest in 1846 to the Sec-
ond Vigilance Committee in San Francisco: A Study of American Character* [1887] (New York: Al-
fred A. Knopf, 1948); Carey McWilliams, *Southern California: An Island on the Land* [1946]
(Santa Barbara: Peregrine, Smith, Inc., 1973), 77–83; Monroy, *Thrown among Strangers*,
258–63; and Christina Wiebus Mead, "Las Fiestas de Los Angeles: A Survey of the Yearly
Celebrations, 1894–1898," *Historical Society of Southern California Quarterly* 31 (March and
June 1949): 61–113.

5. See, for example, Irving Berdine Richman, *California under Spain and Mexico, 1535–1847*
(Boston: Houghton Miflin Company, 1911), and Nellie Van de Grift Sanchez, *Spanish Arcadia* (Los Angeles: Powell Publishing Co., 1929).

6. Carey McWilliams, *North from Mexico: The Spanish-Speaking People of the United States*
[1948] (Westport: Greenwood Publishing Group, Inc., 1990), 88–94; McWilliams, *Southern
California*, 21–69; and Pitt, *Decline of the Californios*.

7. Monroy, *Thrown among Strangers*, 99–232; Lisbeth Haas, *Conquests and Historical
Identities in California, 1769–1936* (Berkeley: University of California Press, 1995), 29–38,
45–88, 130–37; Sánchez, *Telling Identities*.

8. Robert Glass Cleland, *Cattle on a Thousand Hills: Southern California, 1850–80* [1941]
(San Marino: The Huntington Library, 1975), 7–17 (Fages's request is quoted on page 7);
Manuel Perez Nieto's "Petition for a Land Grant" is reprinted in John and LaRee Caughey,

eds., *Los Angeles: Biography of a City* (Berkeley: University of California Press, 1977), 71–73; Bancroft, *History of California*, I:609–11, 659–65; W. W. Robinson, "The Domínguez Rancho," *Historical Society of Southern California Quarterly* 35 (December 1953): 343; W. W. Robinson, *Ranchos Become Cities* (Pasadena: San Pascual Press, 1939), 11.

9. José del Carmen Lugo, "Life of a Rancher," G. W. Beattie, ed. and trans., *Southern California Quarterly* 32 (September 1950): 187, 216–17; Fray Santa Maria is quoted in John Caughey, "The Country Town of the Angels," in Caughey, *Los Angeles,* 76.

10. On the secularization of the missions, see the texts and endnotes (for an abundance of sources) in David J. Weber, *The Mexican Frontier, 1821–1846: The American Southwest under Mexico* (Albuquerque: University of New Mexico Press, 1982), 62–68; Monroy, *Thrown among Strangers,* 117–34; Bancroft, *History of California,* III:301–56; and Sánchez, *Telling Identities,* 121–39. Vallejo is quoted in Daniel Garr, "Planning, Politics and Plunder: The Missions and Indian Pueblos of Hispanic California," *Southern California Quarterly* 54 (Winter 1972): 297–98; Juan Bandini to Eustace Barron, December 8, 1828, Stearns Papers, Box 4, The Huntington Library; and Figueroa is quoted in Weber, *The Mexican Frontier,* 64.

11. Angustias de la Guerra Ord, *Occurrences in Hispanic California,* trans. and ed. from the Bancroft Library MS. by Francis Price and William H. Ellison (Washington D.C.: Academy of Franciscan History, 1956), 25; Sánchez, *Telling Identities,* 110–13, and Alvarado is quoted on page 111; Howard A. DeWitt, *California Civilization: An Interpretation* (Dubuque: Kendall Hunt Publishing Company, 1979), 57–59.

12. Sánchez, *Telling Identities,* 229–31, 237–45; Haas, *Conquests and Historical Identities,* 36–37; Bancroft, *History of California,* III:445–57; Weber, *The Mexican Frontier,* 255–60.

13. Ord, *Occurrences,* 49; Haas, *Conquests and Historical Identities,* 47–49; J. Gregg Layne, "The First Census of the Los Angeles District," *Southern California Quarterly* 18 (September–December 1936): 92–93, 96; Bancroft, *History of California,* III:633–44n, lists those who received grants between 1831 and 1840; Robert G. Cowan, *Ranchos of California: A List of Spanish Concessions, 1775–1822, and Mexican Grants, 1822–1846.* [1956] (San Bernardino: The Borgo Press, 1985), lists them all.

14. See, for example, W. W. Robinson, *Land in California* (Berkeley: University of California Press, 1948); Robinson, *Ranchos Become Cities;* Robinson, "The Domínguez Rancho"; Cowan, *Ranchos of California;* Bruce Conde, "Santa Ana of the Yorbas," *Southern California Quarterly* 21 (1939); Robert Cameron Gillingham, *The Rancho San Pedro: The Story of a Famous Rancho in Los Angeles County and of Its Owners, the Domínguez Family* (Los Angeles: Domínguez Estate Company, 1961), to cite only a very few.

15. S. M. Lee, *Glimpses of Mexico and California* (Boston: George H. Ellis, 1887), 71; José Arnaz, "Recuerdos," Bancroft Library MS. (1878), 17–18; Paul W. Gates, *California Ranchos and Farms, 1846–1862, Including the Letters of John Quincy Adams Warren* (Madison: The State Historical Society of Wisconsin, 1967), 4–9.

16. Tomás Almaguer, *Racial Fault Lines: The Historical Origins of White Supremacy in California* (Berkeley: University of California Press, 1994), 45–46; Haas, *Conquests and Historical Identities,* 52–53.

17. José Antonio Pico to Abel Stearns, February 28, 1836, Stearns Papers, Box 49, places the order for the rebozos and cloth; Sanchez, *Spanish Arcadia,*39; José del Carmen Lugo, "Vida de un Ranchero," Bancroft Library MS., 86–97.

18. For a fuller discussion of this concept of seigneurialism, see Monroy, *Thrown among Strangers,* 100–102, and on the legacy of the missions, 3–96.

19. "Prayers, religious verses . . . of José Antonio de la Guerra y Noriega," in Personal Papers file, De la Guerra papers, The Huntington Library; Lugo, "Vida de un Ranchero," 75–76, 84–85, 98; Híjar, *California in 1834: Recollections,* Bancroft Library MS. (1877), 9–12.

20. José María Amador, "Memorias sobre la Historia de California," Bancroft Library MS. (1877), 207–208; Bancroft, *California Pastoral,* 588, and see also 333–34, and *History of California,* II:575.

21. José del Carmen Lugo, "The Days of a Rancher in Spanish California," Nellie Van de Grift Sanchez, ed., *Touring Topics* 22 (April 1930): 22; Amador, "Memorias," 228; Dana, *Two Years before the Mast,* 135–36.

22. Híjar, "Recollections," 22; Arnaz, "Recuerdos," 24–25; Sanchez, *Spanish Arcadia,* 273; Ord, "Occurrences," 25; "Duhaut-Cilly's Account of California in the Year 1827," edited and translated by Charles Franklin Carter, *California Historical Society Quarterly* 7 (1929): 311; Gloria E. Miranda, "Hispano-Mexican Childrearing Practices in Pre-American Santa Barbara," *Southern California Quarterly* 63 (Spring 1983): 308–13.

23. Juan Bandini to Eustace Barron, December 8, 1828, Stearns Papers, Box 4; Lugo, "Vida de un Ranchero," 76–77; Híjar, "Recuerdos," 9; Edwin Bryant, *What I Saw in California; Being the Journal of a Tour in the Years 1846–1847* (New York: D. Appleton and Company, 1848), 448.

24. Eulalia Pérez, "Una Vieja y Sus Recuerdos," Bancroft MS. (1877), 6; José Bandini, *A Description of California in 1828* (Berkeley: Friends of the Bancroft Library, 1951), 9–19; Nellie Van de Grift Sanchez, *The Spanish Period* (Chicago: Lewis Publishing Co., 1926), 478–79.

25. Lugo, "Life of a Rancher," 27; Cleland, *Cattle on a Thousand Hills,* 87–90.

26. See, for example, the precision and relish with which Lugo describes dress in "Life of a Rancher," 219–22; Amador, "Memorias," 216; Bancroft, *California Pastoral,* 373–74.

27. Robinson, *Life in California,* 101, 171; Híjar, "Recollections," 23; Vicente P. Gómez, "Lo que Sabe sobre Cosas de California," Bancroft Library MS. (1876), 8; Amador, "Memorias," Lugo, "Vida de un Ranchero," 116–28, and Lugo, "Life of a Rancher," 233–36, for a translation.

28. Arnaz, "Recuerdos," 14–16.

29. Sir George Simpson, *Narrative of a Journey Round the World During the Years 1841 and 1842,* Vol. 1 (London: Henry Colburn, 1847), 387; Híjar, "Recollections," 21.

30. DeWitt, *California Civilization,* 66–67; and Bancroft, *History of California,* IV: 455–545

31. Híjar, "Recollections," 15–17, 35. Almost surprisingly, given her usual romanticization of the Californios, Nellie Van de Grift Sanchez, *The Spanish Period,* discusses briefly the role of Indian labor on pages 432–35.

32. Argüello is quoted in Robert F. Heizer and Alan F. Almquist, *The Other Californians: Prejudice and Discrimination under Spain, Mexico, and the United States to 1820* (Berkeley: University of California Press, 1971), 17–18; George H. Phillips, *Chiefs and Challengers: Indian Resistance and Cooperation in Southern California* (Berkeley: University of California Press, 1975), 47–59. On the Leyva episode see Juana Machado, "Los Tiempos Pasados de la Alta California," Bancroft Library MS. (1878), 11–15; Richard Griswold del Castillo, "Neither Activists Nor Victims: Mexican Women's Historical Discourse—The Case of San Diego, 1820–1850," *California History* 74 (Fall 1995): 236–37; and Sánchez, *Telling Identities,* 144–51, and on page 151 she quotes Alvarado.

33. Simpson, *Narrative,* 1:353; Phillips, *Chiefs and Challengers,* 48–51; Lugo, "Life of a Rancher," 209.

8

Between Crucifix and Lance

Indian-White Relations in California, 1769–1848

James A. Sandos

¡Basta ya! (Enough!) This "new" western history began to irritate Mariano Guadalupe Vallejo the more he read. Working in his study at *Lachryma Montis* (tear of the mountain), the two-story, Victorian "Boston House" located outside the plaza of Sonoma, which he had laid out, Vallejo, like a modern reviewer, read carefully the historical text before him, evaluating it in light of his own expertise. Unlike a modern reviewer, however, Mariano had played a prominent role in some of the past recounted in George Tinkham's *A History of Stockton* (1880), and Vallejo knew firsthand many of the people and incidents described.

As he read, Vallejo grew progressively frustrated at both Tinkham's inaccuracies and at the American's preference for recounting the deeds of Anglo "pioneers," those who in his words "made the wilderness blossom like the rose, and the desert bring forth the fruits of the earth"—as though Mariano and his compatriots had not done likewise. "[O]f their achievements [mainly American]," Tinkham continued in celebratory tones, "I now write that their works may be known and honored."[1] Vallejo, at least, would not allow this "new" western history to pass unchallenged. At issue was the political and cultural memory of the Spanish/Mexican colony of Alta California, into which Vallejo had been born, versus that of the rebaptized state of California within the American federal union, about which Tinkham wrote. Vallejo knew an older Spanish and Mexican history and tried to tell it.[2] Where Tinkham had written that "the Californians [Californios] then wore moccasins made of smoked elk and deer skins, prepared by the Indian squaws of the trappers," in the margin Vallejo wrote a single word, "mentira" (lie!).

If this distortion of the truth is true of the state's early historians, how can I, even farther removed from the events, write an account of Indian-white relations in California from the beginning of effective Spanish colonization in 1769, to the

A patriarchal Mariano Guadalupe Vallejo relaxes on the veranda of his Gothic-revival house in Sonoma, probably in 1884. The leading Californio of his day, Vallejo began his military career as a fifteen-year-old cadet at the Monterey presidio, and six years later, in 1829, he commanded one of the largest military campaigns ever mounted in the province, crushing the Indian revolt led by the former mission neophyte Estanislao. In the course of a long lifetime, Vallejo achieved not only military power, but acquired vast landholdings that employed hundreds of Indians and made him one of the richest and most influential men in Mexican California. *Courtesy California Historical Society, FN-30504.*

American conquest and subsequent onslaught of settlers/invaders from 1846 through 1850, without also writing a "lie"? One way to avoid that result is to recognize that our known stories of California's history are frequently no more than the most recent telling by the conquerors of their own great deeds, to recognize that recovering a more accurate view of the past demands that we see it as a palimpsest, with other stories written before the current ones erased by subsequent writers. We must also be alert to Indian voices from the past. Although California Indians had no written language, and written documents are the core of any historical record, there yet have come down to us Indian views of their experiences in the era being studied.

One of these is the only known example of a Native American's written history of the missionization of his people in California. Pablo Tac, an Indian born at Mission San Luis Rey and educated there in Spanish by the Franciscans, was sent to Europe to further his studies and to become a priest. He died before achieving his—or perhaps his religious mentor's—goal, but at about age thirteen, he wrote his account of the arrival of the Spanish among his people, whom the Europeans called Luiseños,[3] and of the missionary activities of the Franciscan priests known as Fernandinos.[4] Because his command of Spanish grammar was weak and because the priests undoubtedly made him write the account, it would be easy to dismiss Tac's document as childish and reflecting only Christian triumphalism. Such an approach, however, would blind us to the resistance to Spanish invasion that Tac smuggled into his version of events. For example, describing the first contact between a Fernandino and a chief of the *Quechnajuichom,* as Tac called his people in his native tongue, the Indian declared in his dialect, "What is it you seek here? Get out of our country!" Tac also concluded his narrative by describing an encounter between a Luiseño man and an armed Spanish soldier seeking to restore order after a ball game between Luiseños and Indians from Mission San Juan Capistrano had become unruly. The Luiseño challenged the Spaniard by saying, "Raise your saber and I will eat you." Both of these Indian statements, Tac tells us, were made in the original language of *Quechla,* his Indian territory, meaning that the Spanish could not understand them.[5] Thanks to Tac, however, we can.

Mindful of the way in which Native Americans often, even today, shift to Indian language to convey feelings that cannot be expressed in the dominant language shared by Indian and non-Indian groups, we can understand the powerful opposition to Spanish invasion Luiseños communicated both in precontact and late mission times.[6] Moreover, in recounting daily life at the mission, Tac inserted a trickster tale involving a mission Indian boy who enters the Fernandino's forbidden garden to eat figs, is discovered by the Indian gardener, and then transforms himself into a raven.[7] Whatever else may have happened to Tac in the course of his European-style education begun in California, continued in Mexico, and ended in Italy, where he wrote his history, Tac had not lost his Indian identity or his peoples' sense of outrage at Spanish occupation. A more accurate history of Indian-white relations, then, must include the stories and the messages behind the stories of people like Tac and Vallejo.

FRONTIER PROCESSES

By recognizing that California history is a palimpsest, by listening to the voices of Vallejo and Tac, among others, we can avoid Tinkham's narrowness. To avoid *una mentira* is more difficult because all of the considered events occurred in an ever-shifting cultural frontier, and we must think about frontiers in ways different from the received popular wisdom. Instead of regarding a frontier as an ever-moving line, it is more useful and accurate to think of a frontier as a series of simultaneous processes.

William Cronon, George Miles, and Jay Gitlin, distinguished historians of the space now called the American West and fully cognizant that many different peoples contended for power in that space, have proposed six simultaneous processes for analyzing frontiers in North America that move us beyond old paradigms. Those processes are species-shifting, boundary-setting, state-forming, land-taking, market-making, and self-shaping.[8] The simultaneity of these processes is particularly pertinent to our inquiry and helps to explain how, by focusing on only one aspect of the frontier, contrasting views of the past have been ignored.

Species-shifting the authors define as "the movement of alien organisms into ecosystems from which they were once absent . . . the nonhuman invaders that accompanied Old World migrants: strange crops, new weeds, tame animals, and—worst of all—lethal microorganisms."[9] In the California experience, Spanish colonists, soldiers, and priests introduced European horses, cattle, mules, sheep, and pigs, which ate Indian foods such as acorns and delicate indigenous grasses, and replaced them with coarser European varieties through seeds borne in animal hooves, fur, and excrement.[10] Because California Indians had no large domesticated animals, these new, tame beasts disrupted native proto-agriculture and hunting and gathering. Since the new grasses and weeds the animals dispersed proved less edible to Indians, native diet began to suffer as soon as the first Spaniards turned their horses and cattle loose to forage.[11]

Because Spaniards failed to recognize and honor Indian cultivation, they settled where they pleased without regard to native concerns. At San Diego, Padre Junípero Serra moved his first mission into a cultivated field between two Diegueño (Kumeyaay) villages, building over an Indian food source and overlapping onto indigenous human settlements as well. Initially, Indians resisted this encroachment by shooting arrows into cattle at night, killing the beasts when possible, otherwise disabling them, and infuriating the Spanish, who never seemed to appreciate the reason for Indian opposition.[12]

Even more tragic were the results of the introduction of Old World microorganisms. California natives, like other New World peoples, had been separated from the ancient disease pools in Europe, Africa, and Asia for so long that they had lost all immunity to their infections. Thus when Europeans entered the New World, in various stages of exploration and expansion, they unwittingly unleashed disease microbes into what demographers call "virgin soil," and the resulting wildfire-like spread of contagion, called "virgin soil epidemics," decimated American Indian populations by the millions in both North and South America.[13] In California, disease intensified human destruction in a nearly incalculable way because of the further ravages of syphilis. The Spanish introduced syphilis both directly, through sexual congress, and indirectly, through their earlier introduction of this venereal infection among the Baja California Indians, some of whom accompanied the Spanish in northern colonization. Death by syphilis is almost impossible to diagnose clinically,

Native Californians mingle with Hispanic colonists and explorers in the courtyard of Mission San Carlos, while in the background stands the Indian *ranchería*, or village, in a drawing made in 1791 by José Cardero, an artist with the Malaspina expedition. Europeans inadvertently introduced a variety of deadly diseases to the native population, which spread especially quickly in the missions, with their confined living quarters and generally unsanitary conditions. *Courtesy Museo Naval, Madrid. Photograph courtesy Iris Engstrand.*

and without the benefit of modern autopsy in colonial California, thousands of deaths from this early killer passed unrecorded, misattributed to some other cause.[14]

By the time of California's colonization, syphilis had long been endemic in Europe, but the Indians were vulnerable. Many of their cultural and medical activities—scarification for tattooing, and bleeding of the sick—also inadvertently contributed to disease spread. In the missions, uninfected children sleeping with infected parents could have contracted the disease while nursing or by touching the mission blanket or dress or pants infected by a bleeding host. Nearly all observations on the health of mission Indians remarked on the prevalence of venereal disease and lamented its effects.

But eighteenth- and nineteenth-century observers did not know how sinister syphilis, and its fellow-traveler, gonorrhea, could be, especially in causing stillbirths, birth defects, and infertility. In addition to painful bone inflammation, cranial palsies, and damage to liver, spleen, lungs, stomach, pancreas, and kidneys, eight out of nine children born with congenital syphilis would also have suffered from anemia, and six would have had jaundice; these last two conditions would have resulted in weakness, lassitude, and loss of appetite.[15] Thus, some of the alleged indolence of California Indians noted by Spanish and foreign observers probably had its root in newly introduced diseases.

In colonial California, many syphilitic mothers' pregnancies ended in miscarriage or spontaneous abortion.[16] Along with other colonial practices, such as taking many women from tribal villages into missions, pueblos, and ranchos, venereal disease contributed mightily to the family disorganization and population decline that devastated many coastal Indian groups. Venereal disease also, ironically, conflicted with Franciscan expectations for female Indian behavior. If a woman suffered a miscarriage or if she did not conceive, priests, upon learning of these conditions, prescribed a dire punishment. The woman, after being flogged and having her head shaved, would be forced to dress in sackcloth, cover herself with ashes, and carry a wooden image of a child or doll, painted red if abortion were suspected, as she went about her daily duties. At Sunday Mass she stood before the mission church to receive the taunts and jeers of churchgoers, including other Indians.[17] Such punishment, which could last months, was designed to make Indian women exercise a European-mandated control over their bodies that many of them lacked because of European-introduced illness.

This friction between Spanish priests and Indian women also raises another of the frontier processes we are considering, *boundary-setting*. Missionization created boundaries between baptized Indians, called neophytes, and the unbaptized, called gentiles, by which the Spanish meant pagans. When some Indians began living the new life of Christians, the concept of priest-defined sin, frequently accompanied by physical correction when detected, defined another boundary between those Indians who conformed their behavior to priestly expectations and those who did not.

In the theory of Spanish colonial enterprise, Indians were the raw material of another process as well, *state-forming*.[18] Indians were to become the labor force in a new Spanish world, created in Alta California, by being drawn voluntarily into the missions, where they would be converted to Christianity, baptized as neophytes into the new faith, and taught the rules of religion, language, and law.[19] After ten years of tutelage to make mission Indians into good Spanish subjects, they were to receive the mission lands held in trust for them by the padres and to form pueblos. This plan was designed to give Spain effective settlements on its northern frontier and to hold the territory against foreign encroachment. The prominence of mission and padre over presidio and soldier in Alta California, particularly in governing relations with Indians, went against recent Spanish frontier policy and stemmed from royal financial shortages. Paradoxically, according to borderlands historian David Weber, the missions in Alta California became "the dominant Spanish institution in an era when government officials sought to minimize their influence."[20]

For Spanish state-forming to succeed, Indians and colonists needed to know their boundaries and how to live according to the expectations of Crown and cross. Such transformation for Indians was particularly difficult, since it demanded radical cultural change even as another frontier process, *land-taking*, deprived them of their resource base. What Europeans called "'settlement' meant land taking, and land taking meant violence."[21] Personal ownership and control of land by individual Europeans differed sharply from Indian tribal approaches to land-use, and as Europeans, and later Americans, acquired more and more property, Indians lost access to their sources of survival. It is this difference in approaching the land—tribal, communal sharing bounded by river and creek drainages versus Spanish and Mexican grants of extensive acreage to individuals and subsequent American subdivision into personal plots—that caused most of the Indian-white conflict in early California. Neither Spanish colonizer nor American settler found "empty" land in California; each had to fight the Indians for it. In winning the initial struggle, Spain imprinted settlement patterns along the coast. Americans later displaced Mexican, Spanish, and Indian patterns.

When Indians met intruders in California, trade usually ensued, and *market-making* accompanied the other simultaneous frontier processes.[22] Even under Spanish conquest, Indians, both neophytes and unmissionized gentiles, traded labor, services, and products desired by the Spanish in return for beads, axes, cloth, and other material goods. Gentiles who worked building Spanish presidios or serving settler families continued their freedom from mission rule, but entered the market through direct trade. Those within the missions, or working in Spanish settlements under colonial control, were drawn indirectly into the world market through their largely uncompensated labor, as well as through occasional trading. In the region beyond Hispanic settlement, Indians traded goods such as salmon, animal skins, and horses, mules, and cattle, often stolen from Spanish settlements, for firearms, iron objects, beads, and other European material goods, and thus gentiles, too, gradually entered the world market far beyond California. Changing markets reflected changing Indian coping strategies for competing in those markets, a theme for later discussion.

Self-shaping, our final frontier process, refers to the way individuals refashioned themselves to meet new conditions.[23] An adventurer from Switzerland, John Sutter dramatically exemplifies the concept. Sutter arrived in Mexican California posing as a well-financed entrepreneur with impressive foreign references, most of them obtained by falsehood. No one then in California knew that he was a financial deadbeat, a deserter of wife and family, and a clever prevaricator.[24] Sutter became powerful, temporarily wealthy, and a major player in expanding the Mexican frontier. His many roles, some of which will be considered later in more detail, flamboyantly demonstrate one man's capacity to reshape himself many times over.

On a less visible scale, others in the Spanish-Indian frontier shaped themselves—

played roles—to suit their circumstances. The Spanish sovereigns' intentions toward the Indian were, as Herbert E. Bolton, the dean of borderlands historians, wrote, "to convert him, to civilize [sic] him, and to exploit him. . . . It was soon found that if the savage were to be converted, or disciplined, or exploited, he must be put under control."[25] Hence, Indians became neophytes and worked at priest-assigned tasks. Some Indians did so through genuine transformation, but others did so only reluctantly and temporarily. A thirty-five-year-old Christian Indian at Mission San Juan Capistrano (Juaneño), for example, dying of European disease, renounced his baptism and Christian religion on his deathbed. Padre Gerónimo Boscana asked the neophyte to confess his sins before meeting his god. "I will not," replied the Indian vehemently. "If I have been deceived whilst living," he continued, "I do not wish to die in the delusion!"[26] To Boscana, this was the action of an apostate.

Shape-shifting among Indians did not proceed in any simple or single direction. During the large Chumash uprising in 1824 in the Santa Barbara area missions, for example, an unnamed neophyte caught in a chapel surrounded by armed Spaniards firing upon it, spied a crucifix. Disregarding the Spanish-taught polite speech to be used by Indians in addressing their superiors, including the Christian god, this neophyte used the familiar *tú* form, and spoke to the god on the crucifix as an equal. "Now I will know if you are god almighty as the padre says. Carrying you completely hidden so that no one will see you, I am going alone to fight against all of the soldiers. If they don't kill me or shoot me, I will serve you well until I die."[27]

The armed Indian concealed the crucifix under his shirt, then fled the church. Once outside he emptied his quiver at the soldiers and returned, walking at a normal pace, to the chapel. Despite the shots fired at him he remained untouched. Afterward, he fulfilled his vow by working as sacristan at the mission until he died. This instance of Indian self-shaping occurred during one of the largest rebellions in California mission history, one in which Indians from missions La Purísima, Santa Inés, and Santa Barbara challenged Spanish and Franciscan authority; this personal incident within the collective episode raises the larger issue of Indian resistance to the missions.

MISSIONS AND RESISTANCE

In the last twenty years, scholars have amassed impressive detail about Indian resistance to the missions, yet such knowledge has not been accompanied by a corresponding increase in our conceptual understanding of it.[28] This anomaly seems caused by the tendency of recent mission critics to focus almost exclusively on the material exploitation of the Indian, at the expense of the christianization and civilization components of Bolton's triad.

Anthropologist James Scott, however, in studying colonized peoples, proposes to emphasize "the issues of dignity and autonomy, which have typically been seen as secondary to material exploitation."[29] In a situation of dominance by involuntary subordination, Scott argues, elites create a public record that usually serves as the official story of the relationship between rulers and subordinates. This public record encompasses three areas: an imposed division of labor; a specification of public rituals of hierarchy, deference, speech, punishment, and humiliation; and an ideological justification for inequalities flowing from the dominant group's religious beliefs and political world view. Spanish colonization and dominance over native peoples of Alta California demonstrates the validity of many of Scott's insights.

An uprising, such as the 1824 Chumash rebellion, was portrayed as aberrant in the official explanation of events in California because it challenged the notion of smooth Spanish control of the colony and its people. Since elites leave the written documents of their rule, and present the view of subordinates, if at all, within the dominant tale, the elite view is often mistaken for the totality of experience by others. From the elite perspective, only bloody, violent acts constitute resistance, and because such acts are portrayed as rare, they constitute the only real, but infrequent, opposition to foreign power.

Scott contends, to the contrary, that subordinate groups respond to the public record of elites by creating a hidden story of their own. However, since many subordinate groups lack a written language, and many are illiterate in the dominant tongue, and since their acts must be conducted in secrecy, it is difficult for the outside observer to detect the hidden story. Moreover, according to Scott, the creation of the hidden story is site-specific, meaning that in California one would need to study carefully the elite-written documents and histories of all twenty-one missions to reconstruct the many hidden native stories.

Nevertheless, Scott argues, the hidden story is present in the public transcript but in disguised form. The hidden story is frequently conveyed in rumors, folktales, trickster stories, wish-fulfillment, gambling, gossip, and a host of other indicators of opposition to domination that it is encumbent on us to recognize. Thus, from the hidden story, cryptically contained within the public record, we can see the wish-fulfilling language of the original Luiseños in Tac's history of their missionization and the transformation of the neophyte trickster who became a raven. In the Juaneño neophyte's renunciation of his baptism lies the hidden affirmation of Indian culture, which the priest who told the tale saw as Indian apostasy. And in the Chumash neophyte's disregarding foreign-imposed deferential speech, and the asymmetrical power relationship it entailed, we can see a deal-maker negotiating with the Christian god as an equal, rather than a divine act of intervention to help sustain the mission system.

That the hidden story of mission Indian resistance is long should not surprise us given the anomalous position of the Indian within that institution. Proselytized by

Indian neophytes at Mission Dolores wager on a game of chance in a lithograph based on a watercolor made in 1816 by the expeditionary artist Louis Choris. Widely popular among native men, gambling was invariably prohibited by the Franciscans, and the practice of the custom at the missions was both a source of entertainment and a form of everyday rebellion against Hispanic authority. From Louis Choris, *Voyage pittoresque autour du monde* (Paris, 1822). *Courtesy California Historical Society, FN-30509.*

missionaries offering gifts of beads, and later, food, with the threat of Spanish arms nearby, and beset by new diseases their shamans or doctors could not heal, California Indians faced a bewildering offering of European spiritual and material culture and were torn between trying to sustain existing Indian ways or joining the new. As Vallejo saw it, Spaniards offered Indians the crucifix or the lance, leaving them, in the words of an Indian leader, "no room to choose between Christ and death."[30]

"Most [Indian] individuals," anthropologist Randall Milliken wrote in an important study of the San Francisco Bay area missions with applicability to the entire system, "struggled with mixed feelings, hatred and respect, in a terrible, internally destructive attempt to cope with external change beyond their control. . . . Day in day out . . . ambivalent people struggled with a choice to join the mission. They could make the choice to reject the mission life ways a thousand days in a row, but they were allowed to make the choice to join a mission community only once."[31] When Indians voluntarily joined the missions, symbolized by baptism following eight or more days of religious instruction, they were not permitted to change their minds.[32]

Baptized Indians became legal wards, children subservient to their priests/fathers at the mission to which they were assigned. Mission Indians lost personal freedom and could travel about only with a pass signed by a priest. California historian and State Librarian Kevin Starr called it "churchly captivity."[33]

In the missions, Indians were subjected to a hierarchy and a subordination by gender previously unknown. "In the Mission of San Luis Rey de Francia," Tac wrote, "the Fernandino Father is like a King, having his pages, Alcaldes [Indian officials and overseers], Mayordomos [Spanish overseers], Musicians, [and] Soldiers."[34] *Alcaldes* had particular responsibility to get other Indians to work in every activity needed to sustain the mission, including farming, herding, gardening, adobe-making, carpentry, blacksmithing, tallow-making, hide-skinning and tanning, weaving, corn-grinding, and food preparation. *Alcaldes* were masters of the Spanish language and of the European sense of time, since, regulated by clock and sundial, the daily tasks were announced by the sound of the bell. The bell tolled for religious and secular purposes, but each toll reinforced for the Indians a time-consciousness and a sense of timely performance of duty unknown to them before colonization.

Priests taught Indians patriarchy and, in the process, lowered the status of Indian women within Indian culture. Such devaluation was further compounded by the shameful rape of Indian women by Spanish and Mexican soldiers and settlers. Angry Indian men were killed for their opposition to the rape of tribal women.[35] Partly to protect them from soldiers, priests in the missions had unmarried Indian women above the age of seven locked together at night in a room known as the *monjería* (nunnery) to preserve their chastity. Female separation from the extended family must have been emotionally painful. Confining them in a group, moreover, spread infectious disease, making them more vulnerable to microbes than men. All of these changes created tension and required personal adjustment, profoundly difficult for some, less so for others.

In the public record, priests equated baptism with conversion and viewed moral backsliding, along with the failure of many neophytes to learn Spanish, as indications of the innately limited moral and intellectual capacity of their charges.[36] To the Franciscans, baptism was supposed to symbolize the Indians' rejection of native religion, accompanied by the unconditional acceptance of Christianity. From the Indians' perspective, however, conversion was a process of some indeterminate length subsequent to, rather than signified by, baptism.[37] Over time, this process involved tension between nominal and effective conversion—if effective conversion occurred at all—and we can glimpse it through the priestly concern over sin.[38]

Viewed from the perspective of the hidden story, Indian "sin" constituted resistance. Sin affirmed Indian culture through reiteration of aboriginal social and sexual practices that the priests proscribed and for which observed sinners were physically punished. These corrections included flogging, being hobbled with irons, or

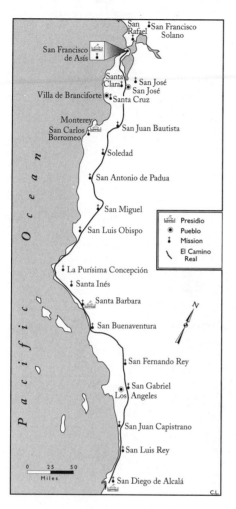

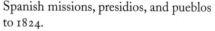

Spanish missions, presidios, and pueblos to 1824.

being placed in stocks. In their preoccupation with Indian sin, priests blinded themselves to something more fundamental and important: Indian resistance and the continuation of native culture within the mission compound.

Indians learned ways to camouflage their resistance. Franciscan dedication to the ritual of the Stations of the Cross prompted them to have Indians paint a fourteen-scene set at Mission San Fernando. Historian George Harwood Phillips, in a controversial study, has argued that the faces of Jesus' tormentors along the *via dolorosa*, while artistically crude, are the only ones with recognizable features, and they are Indian. Phillips thinks that these portrayed Indians are *alcaldes*, the Indian overseers.[39] If such protest is hidden in authorized graphic renderings, what might be present in clandestine drawings?

Art historian Norman Neuerburg contends that graffiti, unauthorized graphic works by Indians in the missions, which he calls "abusive," must have been "found in

The murals in the church of Mission San Miguel were executed about 1820 by the Spaniard Estevan Munrás, who was assisted in his labors by mission Indians. Subsequent to completing the painted decorations, which were intended to suggest an elegant and ornate ecclesiastical architecture, neophytes surreptitiously incised native designs into the walls, one of numerous forms of Indian resistance to a conquering culture. *Photograph by Anthony Kirk.*

most, if not all, of the missions." Neuerburg has found them at only five missions because the priests tended to whitewash them when they were discovered. Yet he has found these Indian-made symbols at the earliest level of whitewash, indicating that this form of resistance began at the earliest stages of church building.[40] "These abusive drawings are either painted or scratched," Neuerburg continued. "They are the equivalents, on mission walls, of [precolonial] pictographs and petroglyphs of which they are really a continuation." Although not all the symbols can be deciphered, at Mission San Juan Capistrano there appear to be at least two depictions of the Tobet, a human figure wearing a headdress and a skirt, the primary Juaneño god.[41] Did Juaneños continue to practice their religion in the Christian compound, and if so, when, if ever, did they stop?

At Mission San Miguel, Indian graffiti entered the church proper, where, according to Neuerburg, "the number of scratched designs is enormous. . . . Presumably, all the Indian ones were done while the Indians were seated on the floor, quite possibly during mass. Most are concentrated in the area of the choir loft itself, the area beneath it, and surprisingly, opposite the pulpit."[42] Even if, these inscriptions were no more than doodling, which seems doubtful, they suggest that the Indian churchgoer's attention was not always on the Christian ritual.

Emphasizing material exploitation of Indians means subtly accepting missionization on exclusively priestly terms, and uncritically accepting the public record. Certainly the missionaries wanted to accept as many Indians as they could feed, but such was not always the case.[43] When Indians chose to enter the missions in large numbers, as did the Miwok and Costanoan (Ohlone) of the San Francisco Bay area in 1794 and 1795 and the Chumash of the central coast in 1803 and 1804, for example, the priests were overwhelmed by what they took to be the success of their preaching and the will of their god.

The Indian population of Mission San Francisco increased by 75 percent from October 1794 to May 1795 (628 to 1,095), and at Mission Santa Clara in the same period it grew by 83 percent (852 to 1,558).[44] A decade later, 25 percent of all Chumash baptized in the mission era entered the compounds of Santa Barbara, Santa Inés, and La Purísima.[45] In each case Indians made a tactical decision about coping with the Spanish by entering their missions, and in each case they disoriented their colonizers, who could neither feed nor manage their numbers for some months or years to come.

Such disorienting behavior testifies to the complexity of Indian response to the missions. Once inside the compound, the sheer numbers ensured at least temporary cultural perpetuation.[46] To guarantee sufficient food, priests often had to give them frequent passes to leave the missions and to hunt and gather in the traditional manner. Simultaneously, however, the massing made Indians more susceptible to disease. At the simplest level, proximity to the Spanish permitted more Indians to observe and plot against the colonizers.

Even before such large-scale ingress, Indians conspired to overturn the missions. In 1785, in Gabrielino (Kumi·vit) territory, for example, the gentile female shaman and leader Toypurina, with assistance inside the mission from neophyte Nicolas José, led a pan-tribal movement against Mission San Gabriel designed to expel the Spanish. After scaling the walls and entering the quadrangle, Toypurina and her attacking party were surrounded and disarmed by Spanish soldiers already alerted to the plot. At her trial she allegedly denounced the Spanish and declared her purpose was to drive the foreigners from her land. Sentenced to banishment to Monterey, and threatened with death by her former allies, she accepted baptism and received the Christian name Regina Josefa. At Monterey she married a presidio soldier, bore him four children, and died ten years later of European-introduced disease.[47] Other large-scale rebellions by neophytes and nearby gentiles led to the murder of priests and annihilation of missions at San Diego in 1775 and along the Colorado River in 1781.[48]

Even beyond the famous, full-fledged uprisings, a strong current of Indian resistance ran through the entire mission period. In 1801, for instance, before the dramatic Chumash influx two years later and perhaps the cause of that influx, during the course of an epidemic of pneumonia and pleurisy, a female neophyte at Mission Santa Barbara had a dream. The Chumash god Chupu appeared to her with a warning: all gentiles must refuse baptism or they would die, and all neophytes must renounce their baptism and give offerings to Chupu, or they too would die. Neophytes were to wash their heads with a special water called "tears of the sun" to cancel the Christian holy water. Almost all neophytes, including *alcaldes,* came to visit her, bringing beads and seeds as offerings and undergoing the new ritual. The conspiracy extended to all Chumash settlements of the channel and mountains before the priests discovered it. How they suppressed the movement is unknown, but certainly the woman was made to recant publicly.[49] Nevertheless, this incident instilled suspicion and no little fear in Franciscan hearts. In both instances at San Gabriel and Santa Barbara, it appears that women leaders saw more clearly than others exactly what their gender would lose in the new social order of Spanish "civilization."

ALCALDES: RESISTANCE AND ACCOMMODATION

Women could not be *alcaldes* in the Franciscan missions, and this office became progressively more important as the missions persisted, grew, and became more complex communities. As suggested by Phillips's interpretation of the Stations of the Cross, the alcalde's position was anomalous, part Indian, part Spaniard, with a wide degree of power over subordinates that could be used or abused for personal advantage. Conventional thinking has been that priests generally chose the *alcaldes,* deliberately seeking to undermine traditional Indian village chiefs' authority by selecting new men who were approved by a vote among mission Indians. These newly elected officials were rank accommodationists who gave little thought to the people from whom they had come. *Alcaldes*, in this view, represented a sharp break from the tribal kinship groups of pre-contact days. Historian Steven Hackel, in his important study of alcaldes at Mission San Carlos Borromeo from 1770 to 1833, disputes the conventional view. He finds that the political accommodation at the mission depended not so much on personalities as on functions and that the duties of village chiefs resembled those of mission Indian officials. Both, for example, "performed police duties, were responsible for the economic stability of the Indian group, had proven military skills, and enjoyed similar advantages of office."[50]

A strong convergence, therefore, existed between precolonial Indian and Spanish office. Moreover, half of the mission Indian officials in the fifty years of study came from high-status Indian families, thus conserving some elements of traditional Indian leadership. Yet the remaining 50 percent of officials whose extended families could not be found in the mission registers leaves room for the type of individuals described in the conventional view. Indian officials, then, were probably of two types: those with traditional ties to the Indians they served based on kinship and prior status, and the new men. Both types could, and in some instances did, abuse their office, depending on Spanish or Indian perspective.

During the 1824 Chumash uprising, *alcaldes* played significant insurgent roles. Those Indians who occupied La Purísima for a month, reinforced by other neophyte fugitives and gentiles from the interior region called the *tulares* (reeds), sought an armed confrontation with the Spanish. Certainly the neophyte who struck a deal with the Christian god during the fight at La Purísima faced great odds with gritty determination. Spanish arms prevailed, however, reinforced with muskets clandestinely supplied by the Russians from their distant colony at Ross.[51] This proved the first instance in which competing imperial powers cooperated to vanquish native resistance in California, a resistance sustained and led by native mission officials.

Alcaldes from Santa Barbara took their followers to the tulares of the southern San Joaquin Valley, where all reverted to Indian cultural practices and made camp with the Yokuts. Only after pursuit by Spanish soldiers, accompanied by Franciscans as peacemakers, and following several violent skirmishes, did these *alcaldes* shift shape to accommodate a reality they could not change, and bring their people back.[52] Andrés Sagimomatsse had been the most prominent of the *alcaldes*, going from trusted aide of the Franciscans to Indian insurgent and back again, seeking to cope with the changing pressures of his position. The Chumash flight to the interior during the 1824 uprising both reflected and contributed to a process of neophyte fugitivism and cooperation with gentiles that began to intensify from the 1820s onward. The general purpose of such flight was not individual freedom per se but joint action, combining neophyte knowledge of the foreigners with gentile military force, to raid the

Spanish/Mexican settlements to seize livestock and supplies and to revenge themselves on the settlers.

Many factors were contributing to this process by the 1820s, most notably the spread among the Indians of a previously unknown common language (Spanish), the acquisition of horses by the natives, particularly the gentiles, and the enlargement of market opportunities provided by other outsiders among interior Indians. This coincided with political and military instability among the Spanish-speaking elites in California and was intensified by demands by leaders in Mexico that the Indians be emancipated from the missions. In short, Indians progressively used Spanish as their lingua franca for joint actions both in trading and raiding, while colonials, divided by struggles over political rule, presented a weakened common front against Indian depredation just as Indians began to be freed from the missions. A series of Mexican decisions in the 1820s would culminate in total neophyte emancipation through secularization of the missions from 1834 to 1836.[53] Beset by these multiple changes, mission Indian officials experienced a role crisis.

The most dramatic of the insurgent alcaldes, and perhaps the most tragic, proved to be Estanislao of Mission San José. Estanislao seems to have been born of high-status among the Lakisamni Yokuts of the northern San Joaquin Valley about 1800, and brought to the mission for baptism at an early age. He rose in the mission hierarchy, and Padre Narcíso Durán eventually made him an *alcalde*. With the release of selected married neophytes under the orders of Governor José María Echeandía in 1826, dissatisfaction among remaining Indians at Mission San José mushroomed. In the fall of 1828, Estanislao and many other neophytes, while on a pass to visit relatives in the interior, simply stayed. Estanislao sent a defiant warning to Padre Durán that the Indians were in rebellion, that "they have no fear of the soldiers because they, the soldiers, are few in number, are very young, and do not shoot well."[54] Other neophyte fugitives from missions San Juan Bautista and Santa Cruz, the latter led by *alcalde* Cipriano, joined Estanislao at his cluster of Lakisamni villages along a tributary of the San Joaquin River, and a pan-Indian movement of gentiles and neophytes of some magnitude now challenged Mexican authority.

Californios mounted two expeditions against Estanislao, and he defeated both. The rebellious villages lay in an extended, dense thicket, and, by using breastworks and trenches covered with vines and trees, Estanislao denied Europeans the advantage of their horses, muskets, and cannon. Through taunts and challenges to their *machismo*, Estanislao lured the soldiers into the thicket for hand-to-hand combat. Mexican dead were mutilated and their body parts paraded in defiance. As Estanislao's reputation among Indians grew, his followers increased to nearly one thousand ex-neophyte and gentile warriors. Since throughout California about 22,000 Indians remained in the missions, and the colonial population numbered only a few thousand, Estanislao's success and continued defiance aggravated white fear and demanded action.

In retaliation, in May 1829, the California government massed its meager northern military forces and sent them under twenty-two-year-old Lieutenant Mariano
G. Vallejo to attack Estanislao. After three days of relentless fighting, Vallejo won.
Estanislao, however, with many of his followers, disappeared. Despite atrocities
committed by his soldiers and Indian auxiliaries seeking revenge against their enemies, Vallejo returned a hero because he had accomplished what no one else had. But
Vallejo found new frustration when he learned that Estanislao secretly had returned
to Mission San José, and Padre Durán had secured the governor's pardon for him.
Upon his return, Estanislao refashioned himself once again, becoming a skilled
hunter of fugitive neophytes until smallpox killed him four years later.

Following his "victory" over Estanislao, Vallejo rose to greater prominence with
a land grant eventually comprising 66,000 acres, called the Rancho Petaluma, and
with a military post at Sonoma carrying an assignment to secure the northern frontier against both Indians and Russians. To help him succeed, the Mexican government also gave Vallejo the right to introduce colonists to his lands. Vallejo's most
important white ally proved to be George Yount, a widower and former trapper and
trader, who had grown up on the Indian frontier in southern Missouri. Yount early
earned a reputation as an exceptional marksman. Yount's childhood—as he recalled
it, living in "constant danger, with continual privations, the rifle always in my hand
as soon as I could hold it, and ever on the alert against scouting enemy"—prepared
him well for his role in California with Vallejo.[55] Vallejo laid out the plaza of
Sonoma, some forty miles north of San Francisco, in 1835. This followed on the
establishment of missions San Rafael (1819) on the Marin peninsula and San
Francisco Solano (1824) at Sonoma, all of which were designed to counter possible
southward movement of the Russians from their northern California coastal
outpost.

MEXICAN FRONTIER CONCERNS

By the time of Vallejo's northern venture, Russians were hunting sea otter as far
south as Monterey. In 1811, after months of negotiations with local Coast Indians to
secure their permission, the Russian-American Fur Company had established a
colony eighteen miles north of Bodega Bay and called it Rus, after an old name for
Russia (later translated as "Ross" by Americans).[56] The company pursued a twofold
purpose in California, hunting sea otter for their pelts for the international market
and producing food in this milder climate to supply its other hunting operations at
Kodiak and Sitka. Russians, their Aleut assistants, and the native Pomo felled trees
to build a large log stockade, and in the cleared land cultivated grain and cereals and
raised cattle. The population varied from two hundred to four hundred depending
on the otter-hunting season, which lasted from December through March. Russians

Inhabitant of Rumiantsev Bay, a watercolor executed in 1818 by the expeditionary
artist Mikhail Tikhanov, portrays a young Indian woman, probably Coast Miwok or
Kashaya Pomo, at the Russian settlement at Bodega Bay, some twenty-five miles south
of the colony at Ross. Unlike the Spanish and Mexicans, the Russians lived generally
in more amiable accord with the native peoples of California. The woman's handsome
decorative necklaces and ornamented basket suggest she had achieved high social
standing or had recently been given in marriage. *Courtesy Art Research Museum,
St. Petersburg, Russia. Photograph courtesy Anchorage Museum of History and Art.*

acted as officers, supervisors of hunting parties, mechanics, tanners, craftsmen, and farm and cattle overseers. Aleuts hunted and fished; local Indians worked as agricultural laborers, vaqueros, and servants.

Missionaries traded illegally with the Russians, who regularly brought goods down to San Francisco by boat along with Aleuts, their sea going *baidarkas* (kayaks), and Russian supervisors. While Russians and Aleuts occasionally defected when in Spanish/Mexican territory, it seemed to at least one observer that the natives fared better at Ross than did their missionized brethren to the south. According to Otto von Kotzebue, "the inhabitants of Ross live in the greatest concord with the Indians, who repair, in considerable numbers, to the fortress, and work as day labourers, for wages. At night they usually remain outside the palisades. They willingly give their daughters in marriage to Russians and Aleutians; and from these unions ties of relationship have arisen which strengthen the good understanding between them."[57]

Russians thus brought the local Indians into a local market, and through it native agricultural labor contributed to the international fur trade. At Ross, Indians spent their money on materials provided by the company; and Indians responded to the sound of a bell to report for work details. Religious proselytizing at Ross, however, was low key, and Indians who wanted baptism had to ask. Spanish and Mexican settlers worried that Russian treatment of Indians at Ross set a potentially dangerous example for mission Indians.

Meanwhile, to counteract the Russian threat to the Mexican colony, Vallejo and Yount, along with their own Miwok allies led by chiefs Solano and Jota, battled hostile Indians while following the Roman principle of divide and rule. Vallejo and Solano campaigned vigorously against the Indians below Ross, who were raiding the missions and ranchos around Sonoma. But Vallejo also continued to trade with the Russians.[58]

In late 1837, Vallejo sent a detachment of men to Ross to purchase cloth and leather goods for his troops at Sonoma. In addition to these products, they also brought back smallpox. Indian California had remained unaffected by this disease until 1828, when it arrived through San Francisco Bay and ravaged some communities south of the bay and spread slightly inland. In contrast, the epidemic of 1837–1839 spread quickly throughout the valleys of Sonoma, the Russian River, Petaluma, Santa Rosa, and Sacramento as far north as the slopes of Mount Shasta. Vallejo knew enough about medicine to move the Mission San Francisco Solano Indian population to a distant spot for quarantine, but nonetheless they "died daily like bugs."[59] Smallpox devastated the Indian population, killing perhaps 60 percent of the gentiles in the north of Vallejo's territory but, incredibly, never reaching the south. The disease reduced the company of Vallejo's personal Indian guard by half.[60]

Such decimation in areas of recent or established Hispanic settlement, caused by species-shifting, was paralleled by another virgin soil epidemic among the Indians of the *tulares* of the San Joaquin Valley in the early 1830s, this one by malaria. Fur traders and trappers coming south from the Pacific Northwest undoubtedly brought the disease with them into the great Central Valley in 1833, and mosquitoes spread it among the Indians. J. J. Warner, with the Ewing Young expedition of 1832–1833, observed dense Indian settlements in the interior upon his entrance in 1832. "The banks of the Sacramento River," he wrote, "in its whole course through the valley, were studded with Indian villages," many containing fifty to one hundred dwellings. "On our return, late in the summer of 1833," Warner continued, "we found the valleys depopulated."[61] In another reminiscence, Warner detailed his observations, noting that, as the dead became too numerous to bury, the survivors burned the corpses until, losing strength even for this, the barely living fled their villages singly or in small clusters to die in the open near a spring or beneath a tree. "Around the naked villages," wrote Warner, "graves and the ashes of funeral pyres, the skeletons and swollen bodies told a tale of death such as no written record had ever revealed."[62] Demographer Sherburne F. Cook later estimated that this epidemic killed at least twenty thousand Indians.[63]

Destruction of interior Indians by disease did not mean permanent weakening of Indian resistance to colonization, however, because secularization of the coastal missions accelerated mission Indian flight to the great valley. Former *alcaldes* and neophytes combined with survivors among the gentiles to intensify raiding of mission and rancho settlements in the 1830s, particularly for livestock. The horse had radically transformed Indian life, especially among the gentiles, because the horse changed everything. Sedentary life eroded as native peoples became mobile. Newfound mobility encouraged encroachment on previously unavailable food sources, either among neighboring tribes or colonials, and thus warfare escalated. And, as the market for saddle-broken horses for the New Mexican trade increased, so did Indian assaults on Californio herds. Toward the decade's end, Mexican officials in California began to take action to expand the frontier, to check Indian depredations, and to monitor more closely and curtail if possible the increasing intrusion of foreigners.

CALIFORNIA CAUDILLOS

By the 1830s and 1840s, powerful men operated on the interior edge of Spanish/ Mexican settlement in California, men who expanded that frontier at the expense of Indians living there. These men primarily exploited Indian labor to produce goods and render services for themselves that stimulated the simple domestic economy and, over time, brought Indians and themselves into the more complex European market economy. Regardless of their original nationality, such men functioned in a Spanish/Mexican culture to carve out personal fiefdoms in the wilderness. Their independent enterprises, no matter how much they might wish to appear as self-

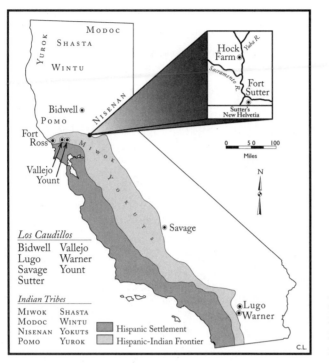

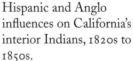

Hispanic and Anglo influences on California's interior Indians, 1820s to 1850s.

sufficient, nevertheless were linked to the larger society by economic, military, and political ties. For some, the ties also included family.

Geographically, these men acted as individual vanguards in an arc running from present-day Sonoma to Sacramento, down the great valley named for the San Joaquin River, and from the Cajon Pass to northeastern San Diego County. From north to south, these men were: Mariano Guadalupe Vallejo, George C. Yount, John Bidwell, John August Sutter, James D. Savage, José del Carmen Lugo, and Jonathan Turnbull (J. J.) Warner. All knew and used the Spanish language, along with some Indian dialects from their areas of operation; all but one also spoke English. Employing the precept of divide and conquer, these men made alliances with one group of Indians to combat another. For their own part, Indians made those alliances to use the white man's power to augment their own in order to adjust to a rapidly changing world.

A group portrait of general traits, allowing for individual variations, would reveal men of some cunning and ruthlessness, cruelty in dealing with Indians, boldness in striking out into uncharted terrain, strong desire for personal wealth, and an uneven record of business success. They were also military powers and sexual conquistadores. In searching for an appropriate Spanish term for these warlords of California, *caudillo* (man-on-horseback) seems right. A *caudillo* is a man who seeks to dominate the space he occupies socially, sexually, politically, and economically; a leader who acts as though his word is law, his authority absolute, even if the reality of his situation belies his assumptions. In later Mexican California, with official institutions and power structures weakening, these *caudillos* proved critical in holding the frontier against Indian depredations from the interior and in extending Hispanic rule beyond the zone of effective occupation. Their role heretofore has been unappreciated because the later influx of American settlers accompanying the Gold Rush pulled some of the *caudillos* effectively into the new political orbit, drastically limited their old power, and provided several reversals of fortune.

One of these frontier lords, John Sutter, recently has been reconsidered by historians in the context of the larger history of the American West, thereby ignoring the Mexican character of much of his behavior and the Mexican context in which he operated.[64] Sutter achieved status and lands not because his initial deceitful representations had been believed, but because the California governor wanted someone to check Vallejo's power, and Sutter, a Swiss émigré and an outsider, seemed a likely choice. Moreover, Sutter chose to locate in 1839 near the confluence of the American and the Sacramento rivers, at a point accessible to navigation from San Francisco and by land through the great valley or over the Sierra Nevada. Vallejo knew the reasons for Sutter's governmental favors—a 44,000-acre land grant and civil military authority nearly equal to his own—resented them, and became even more outraged when Sutter acquired the Russian improvements at Ross to add to his operation at Sutter's Fort.[65]

At his fort, Sutter envisioned a "New Helvetia," his own empire, where, he was fond of declaiming, "I, Sutter, am the law."[66] Sutter favored acculturating Indians. He used the Russian bells to teach Nisenan, Miwok, and Yokuts the European calendar, sense of time, and work rhythms that Franciscans and Russians had taught coastal peoples. "The Indians I did not marry or bury," he wrote, "I was everything [to]: patriarch, priest, father & judge."[67] Sutter eliminated polygamy among the Indians who worked for him and lived on his vast holdings, and he taught them the precepts of patriarchy. In this way he followed the practices of Vallejo and Yount. On his own 22,000-acre Chico Rancheria, ninety miles north of New Helvetia, John Bidwell, Sutter's former employee, taught the same precepts to Maidu, Wintun, and Yana.[68] In the south, J. J. Warner made the same efforts among the Cupeño on his 48,000-acre ranch northeast of San Diego.[69] James Savage, on the other hand, found many Indian practices compatible, even desirable. As a boy in Illinois with a flare for learning languages and as one who "never refused a dare,"[70] Savage grew into a tall, handsome, vigorous young man and made his way to California in the mid-1840s. He served in the California Battalion during the Bear Flag Revolt and later worked with James W. Marshall in building Sutter's mill. In working for Sutter, he learned how to use Indian labor. Savage then drifted down into the great valley, learning

Sutter's Fort as depicted in a lithograph based on a drawing by the American naval officer and amateur artist Joseph Warren Revere, who arrived in California early in the Mexican-American War. Like other powerful frontier men in California, John Sutter maintained complex relations with the Indians he employed at his fortified feudal empire in the Sacramento Valley, protecting them as well as exploiting them. From Joseph Warren Revere, *A Tour of Duty in California* (New York, 1849). *Courtesy California Historical Society, FN-30530.*

Indian dialects as he went, impressing Indians with his physical prowess, and earning the nickname *El rey huero* (the blonde king), which he refashioned into *El rey tulareño* (king of the tulare Indians).[71]

In his new role Savage married at least five Indian women from different tribes and formed alliances with Indian leaders such as José Juárez of the Chowchilla Yokuts. Through these kinship networks and alliances, Savage, just like all the other *caudillos,* drew Indians to him as laborers, food-gatherers, and personal soldiers. He created trading posts on the Fresno and Mariposa rivers and encouraged Indians to bring him anything to exchange for clothing, food, and beads. In this trade he learned of and became the first to exploit the southern mining district of the California gold fields with Indian labor. Bidwell employed similar tactics in securing Indian labor to locate and extract mineral wealth for him in the central mining district. In contrast to Sutter, who failed to make anything lasting from the gold findings on his holdings, both Savage and Bidwell amassed significant wealth in gold from the labor of their Indians.

After 1846, the number of American settlers in the interior steadily increased, and Savage discovered through one of his wives that many of his former Indian friends, dismayed by this influx, were conspiring to expel whites. When in a series of depredations Indians burned his trading posts, Savage retaliated by raising a white company of soldiers, and, with some of his Indian allies, he punished those Indians who dared oppose him. The 1851 conflict, known as the Mariposa War, reestablished Savage's power. As an unintended consequence of hostilities, whites "discovered" Yosemite Valley, the allure of which meant the end of effective Indian occupation of it.

Savage's difficulties were mirrored by those of Lugo and Warner farther south. Those *caudillos* made alliances with Cahuilla and Cupeño chiefs, such as Antonio Garra and Manuelito, to curb horse and mule theft by other Indians. Such rustling fed an ever-growing trade with New Mexican rustlers and made life on the southern California frontier hazardous. But with the American takeover, former allies became adversaries, as white encroachment invariably meant Indian loss.[72]

As American emigrants to California increased in the 1840s, especially when the lure of gold overcame the natural apprehension that followed the Donner Party tragedy, wayfarers entered overland by crossing the Sierra, traversing Cajon Pass, or trekking from the Colorado River. Sojourners and settlers found respite and refreshment north at Sutter's Fort and south at Warner's Ranch. The emphasis placed by historians on Sutter's Fort as the gateway to California overlooks the fact that Santa Fe traders, with their large retinues, and many American emigrants routinely passed through Warner's Ranch, so that in the late Mexican and early American period tens of thousands had stopped there.[73]

In coping with the American takeover, the *caudillos* played important, albeit brief, roles in continuing to manage Indian labor. Based on their frontier knowledge and their paternalism, they sought to protect Indians from what they regarded as abusive treatment by Americans, while still maintaining, sometimes harshly, their own privileged access to Indian workers.

Vallejo and Bidwell, who secured their standing in American California in part by working in the new state legislature, took the most important actions on behalf of Indians, but their work had long-range, unanticipated negative consequences. The "Act for the Government and Protection of Indians," enacted in 1850 and later expanded, permitted three unpleasant means of labor control. Indians arrested for vagrancy or any other minor offense could be hired out for up to four months by any white man who could pay their bail. Whites could also obtain Indian children legally as servants, and Indian adults could be hired as indentured servants. Abuses under the law led to virtual Indian slavery. Not until the Civil War, and following the Emancipation Proclamation, was the California law repealed, since it countered Union policy.[74] The *caudillos'* ambiguous legacy thus left California Indians still subordinate in their native land.

A publicity photograph taken for the Los Angeles Chamber of Commerce in the early twentieth century testifies to the popular image of the California missions that evolved in the decades following publication, in 1884, of Helen Hunt Jackson's great novel, *Ramona*. A romantic conception of an imaginary Spanish aristocracy—of music, dance, and colorful costumes—supplanted the hard reality of mission life, a life of hardship and drudgery in which thousands of Indians fell victim to foreign diseases and died in virtual confinement. Ironically, the only American Indian evident in the tableau is a Great Plains warrior with a feathered headdress. *Courtesy California Historical Society/Title Insurance and Trust Photo Collection, University of Southern California.*

REMEMBERING THE PAST

For over a century, California's colonial past has been remembered largely through its missions. Helen Hunt Jackson, through her novel *Ramona* (1884), and Charles Fletcher Lummis, through his writings in the magazines *Land of Sunshine* and *Out West,* along with his promotion of mission restoration, helped to sell a romantic image of Spanish California that captured the popular imagination. Pageants, elaborately staged and costumed, became the rage in southern California early in the twentieth century, with John Steven McGroarty's "Mission Play" performed thousands of times adjacent to Mission San Gabriel, and "Ramona" performed as a pageant and reenacted even today at Hemet.[75]

Such portrayals of a glorious, arcadian past, one in which, according to Kevin Starr, "grateful Indians, happy as peasants in an Italian opera, knelt dutifully before the Franciscans to receive the baptism of a superior culture, while in the background the angelus tolled from a swallow-guarded campanile and a choir of friars intoned the Te Deum," have produced enduring, stereotypical images in popular consciousness.[76] Scholarship produced by Franciscans and their sympathizers, primarily geared since the 1930s to support a campaign to canonize California mission founder Junípero Serra, built upon these popular images.[77]

Such uncritical studies of missionaries belong to a tradition that David Weber has called "Christophilic Triumphalism."[78] It rests upon an assumption of European superiority, forgetting, as Weber points out, that "Franciscans did not succeed unless Indians cooperated, and Indians only cooperated when they believed that they had something to gain from the new religion and the material benefits that accompanied it, or too much to lose from resisting it."[79]

Christophilic Triumphalists have had their critics, however, and, beginning in the 1940s, psychologist and demographer Sherburne F. Cook initiated a sustained examination of the missions from an Indian perspective.[80] Cook focused on the reduction of Indian population caused by missionization and accompanying European diseases. Postulating the number of California Indians at contact as 310,000, Cook calculated a decline from 1770 to 1830 of about 21 percent, or 65,000 people. In the missions, the decline was far more precipitous. Cook estimated that approximately 72,000 Indians had been in the missionized zone in 1770, but only 18,000 remained in 1830, prior to secularization, meaning a decline of 75 percent. Although violence contributed, decline came primarily from the unintended introduction of disease.[81]

Both Indian and non-Indian scholars and activists have recently made the mission Indian death rate the center of a progressively more critical and one-sided version of mission history. In this telling, missionaries have become monsters, and nothing positive came from the Spanish experience. Some have even directly and wrongly accused the Franciscans of genocide, comparing Serra to Adolf Hitler and the missions to Nazi death camps, thereby confusing results with intent. I have called this school of writing "Christophilic Nihilism," since it is reminiscent of Christophilic Triumphalism, but in the opposite direction.[82]

Despite the contemporary polarization of much writing about the missions, it is now possible to detect the beginnings of a "new school" of historiography, one that, at least nominally, seeks to move beyond the old pro- and anti-mission dichotomy. These scholars seek to incorporate new social history, demography, cultural anthropology, ecological science, ethnohistory, and comparison to other colonial situations so that previously excluded Indian voices can be heard. In the process, these researchers have discovered new sources and innovative methods for analyzing them.[83]

In applying some of these new approaches in this chapter, I hope to demonstrate that a richer, more interesting, and more inclusive history of colonial California awaits.

NOTES

1. George H. Tinkham, *A History of Stockton* (San Francisco: W. M. Hunton, 1880), iv, with marginal comments by Mariano Guadalupe Vallejo on pp. 60 and 63, copy located at the Huntington Library, San Marino. A superior new biography of Vallejo, focusing on his middle years, is Alan Rosenus, *General M. G. Vallejo and the Advent of the Americans* (Albuquerque: University of New Mexico Press, 1995).

2. Mariano G. Vallejo, "Historical and Personal Memoirs Relating to Alta California," 5 vols., ms, given to Hubert Howe Bancroft, April 10, 1875, translated by Earl R. Hewitt, Bancroft Library, University of California, Berkeley.

3. I use the long-standing names for Indian groups, since most general readers are more familiar with them than with the more precise names anthropologists now employ. Where appropriate, however, I note newer names in parentheses.

4. Pablo Tac, "Studio garammaticali sulla lingua della California, ca. 1835," mss., Mezzofanti, Caps. III, I, Biblioteca Comunale dell' Archiginnasio, Bologna, Italy, Huntington Library. Minna and Gordon Hewes, eds., "Indian Life and Customs at Mission San Luis Rey: A Record of California Mission Life Written By Pablo Tac, An Indian Neophyte (Rome, ca. 1835)," *The Americas* 9 (July 1952): 87–106, is a generally fine and accessible English translation of a published Italian version. Where I differ from their translation, I cite the Italian title at the Huntington Library.

5. Hewes and Hewes, "Indian Life and Customs," 94, 106.

6. Keith Basso, *Portraits of "the Whiteman": Linguistic Play and Cultural Symbols Among the Western Apache* (Cambridge: Cambridge University Press, 1979), 8–12.

7. Tac, "Studio garammaticali," page following 862, in which Tac uses *"cuervo,"* and it is more accurate within Luiseño folklore to translate this as "raven" rather than as "crow."

8. William Cronon, George Miles, and Jay Gitlin, "Becoming West: Toward a New Meaning for Western History," in William Cronon, George Miles, and Jay Gitlin, eds., *Under an Open Sky: Rethinking America's Western Past* (New York: W. W. Norton, 1992), 3–27.

9. Ibid., 11.

10. Alfred W. Crosby, *Ecological Imperialism: The Biological Expansion of Europe* (New York: Cambridge University Press, 1988).

11. Thomas C. Blackburn and M. Kat Anderson, eds., *Before the Wilderness: Environmental Management by Native Californians* (Menlo Park, Calif.: Ballena Press, 1993), presents fifteen essays published over the twenty years prior to publication, which demonstrate that California Indians in many ways were the functional equivalent of what anthropologists call "food producers." I have used the older term "proto-agriculture," as it is more familiar to general readers.

12. Florence C. Shipek, "California Indian Reactions to the Franciscans," *The Americas* 41 (1985): 480–92.

13. Alfred W. Crosby, "Virgin Soil Epidemics as a Factor in the Aboriginal Depopulation in America," *The William and Mary Quarterly*, 3rd Series, 33 (April 1976): 289–99.

14. My discussion, unless otherwise noted, comes from James A. Sandos, "An Aphonic Cry: Syphilis and Gonorrhea Among the California Mission Indians," ms., part of a book in progress on the California missions.

15. David Ingall and Daniel Musher, "Syphilis," in Jack S. Remington and Jerome O. Klein, eds., *Infectious Diseases of the Fetus and Newborn Infant*, 2nd ed. (Philadelphia: W. B. Saunders, 1983), 335–74.

16. Ibid., 345, notes this as a potential contemporary outcome, but historically it would have been more common. Moreover, a mother also infected with gonorrhea, or with gonorrhea alone, would have a progressively greater likelihood of spontaneous abortion as the scarring of her fallopian tubes gradually obstructed them.

17. [Mariano] Guadalupe Vallejo, "Ranch and Mission Days in Alta California," *The Century Magazine* 41 (December 1890): 186; Hugo Reid, "New Era in Mission Affairs," in Robert Heizer, ed., *The Indians of Los Angeles County: Hugo Reid's Letters of 1852* (Los Angeles: Southwest Museum Papers, No. 21, 1968), 87; Edward D. Castillo, trans. and ed., "An Indian Account of the Decline and Collapse of Mexico's Hegemony Over the Missionized Indians of California," *American Indian Quarterly* 12 (Fall 1989): 397–98. Hugo Reid, a Scot married to a high-status Gabrielino woman, and Lorenzo Asisara, a former mission Santa Cruz neophyte, along with Vallejo, constituted a knowledgeable spectrum of observers.

18. Cronon, Miles, and Gitlin, "Becoming West," 16.

19. The notion, first advanced by Sherburne F. Cook, that the Spanish military forcibly rounded up gentiles and brought them to the missions to be baptized—the "forced-conversion" thesis—has been shown to be wrong, based on Cook's incorrect translation of the Spanish term *empressa*. See Francis F. Guest, "An Examination of the Thesis of S. F. Cook on the Forced Conversion of Indians in the California Missions," *Southern California Quarterly* 61 (1979): 1–77. Unfortunately, other scholars have continued to repeat Cook's error. See Ed D. Castillo, "The Native Response to the Colonization of Alta California," in *Columbian Consequences*, vol. 1, *Archaeological and Historical Perspectives on the Spanish Borderlands West*, David Hurst Thomas, ed. (Washington, D.C.: Smithsonian Institution Press, 1989), 379.

20. David J. Weber, *The Spanish Frontier in North America* (New Haven: Yale University Press, 1992), 264.

21. Cronon, Miles, and Gitlin, "Becoming West," 14–15.

22. Ibid., 12–13.

23. Ibid, 18.

24. Iris H. W. Engstrand, "John Sutter: A Biographical Examination," in Kenneth N. Owens, ed., *John Sutter and a Wider West* (Lincoln: University of Nebraska Press, 1994), 76–92.

25. Herbert E. Bolton, "The Mission as a Frontier Institution in the Spanish American Colonies," *American Historical Review* 12 (October 1917): 44–45.

26. Gerónimo Boscana, *Chinigchinich: Historical Account of the Belief, Usages, Customs and Extravagancies of the Indians of this Mission of San Juan Capistrano Called the Acagchemem Tribe*, Alfred Robinson, trans., John P. Harrinton, anno. (Banning: Malki Museum Press, 1978), 80.

27. Antonio María Osio, *The History of Alta California: A Memoir of Mexican California*, Rose Marie Beebe and Robert M. Senkewicz, trans., (Madison: University of Wisconsin

Press, 1996), 68. This is, in general, an excellently translated and superbly annotated edition of an important early California manuscript published now for the first time. My translation follows theirs, but with differences. The copy of the original version of Osio's account that I used, entitled "Cronica de los acontecimientos ocurridos en California desde 1815 hasta 1846," p. 78, copiado por Gulielmo B. Chase, 1876, and called the Doyle version, after John Doyle for whom it was made, is at the Huntington Library. Although the Doyle copy is corrupt in spots, this account is not and accurately reflects the *tú* rather than the *usted* usage first provided in the original.

28. No one has done more over the last two decades to bring forward data on Indian resistance than Edward D. Castillo, a descendant of missionized Indians (Cahuilla-Luiseño). See his: "The Impact of Euro-American Exploration and Settlement," in *Handbook of North American Indians*, Vol. 8, California (Washington, D.C.: Smithsonian Institution Press, 1978), 99–127, henceforth *HBNAI*, 8; *Native American Perspectives on the Hispanic Colonization of Alta California* (New York: Garland Publishing, 1991); "Neophyte Resistance and Accommodation in the Missions of California," in *The Spanish Missionary Heritage of the United States* (San Antonio: National Parks Service, 1993), 60–75. Additional works by Castillo are cited in other notes. George Harwood Phillips, *Indians and Intruders in Central California, 1769–1849* (Norman: University of Oklahoma Press, 1993), argues that Indians in the interior after 1810 engaged in "defensive resistance" to the Spanish and after 1830, initiated "active resistance." Phillips does not clearly define these concepts, nor does he apply them to mission Indians. See the review of Phillips's book by James A. Sandos in *American Indian Quarterly* 18 (Spring 1994): 266–67. Robert H. Jackson and Edward Castillo, *Indians, Franciscans, and Spanish Colonization: The Impact of the Mission System on California Indians* (Albuquerque: University of New Mexico Press, 1995), 73–86, try to distinguish among primary and secondary, passive and active, resistance, but, as they indicate on page 73 in discussing primary and secondary, "there was no clear discontinuity between the two forms of resistance." On the conceptual problems plaguing analysis of mission Indian resistance see James A. Sandos, "Neophyte Resistance in the Alta California Missions," in Timothy J. O'Keefe, ed., *Columbus, Confrontation, Christianity: The European-American Encounter Revisited* (Palo Alto: Forbes Mill Press, 1994), 170–78.

29. James C. Scott, *Domination and the Arts of Resistance: Hidden Transcripts* (New Haven: Yale University press, 1990), xi and passim.

30. Vallejo, "Historical and Personal Memoirs," I, 15.

31. Randall Milliken, "An Ethnohistory of the Indian People of the San Francisco Bay Area from 1770 to 1810" (Ph.D. diss., University of California, Berkeley, 1991), 2, 23. Milliken's dissertation has been published as *A Time of Little Choice: The Disintegration of Tribal Culture in the San Francisco Bay Area, 1769–1810* (Menlo Park: Ballena Press, 1995).

32. Hubert Howe Bancroft, *History of California* (San Francisco: The History Company, 1889), I, 590 ff.

33. Kevin Starr, *Inventing the Dream: California through the Progressive Era* (New York: Oxford University Press, 1985), 58.

34. Tac, "Studio garammaticali," 64–65.

35. Antonia I. Castañeda, "Sexual Violence in the Politics and Policies of Conquest: Amerindian Women and the Spanish Conquest of Alta California," in Adela de la Torre and Beatríz M. Pesquera, eds., *Building with Our Hands: New Directions in Chicana Studies* (Berkeley: University of California Press, 1993), 15–33.

36. Failure to learn a new language, or feigning such ignorance, is an old trick of resistance, one that caused Eric Hobsbawm to claim that "the refusal to understand is a form of class struggle." Quoted in Scott, *Domination and the Arts of Resistance,* 133, n. 46.

37. James A. Sandos, "Christianization Among the Chumash: An Ethnohistoric Approach," *American Indian Quarterly* 15 (Winter 1991): 65–89.

38. Sandos, "Neophyte Resistance," 173.

39. George Harwood Phillips, "Indian Paintings for Mission San Fernando: An Historical Interpretation," *Journal of California Anthropology* 3 (Summer 1976): 96–114. Ed Castillo, "The Other Side of the 'Christian Curtain': California Indians and the Missionaries," *The Californians* 10 (Sept/Oct 1992): 8–17, commented on the paintings, following Phillips, and drew a harsh letter from art historian Norman Neuerburg; see *The Californians* 11 (Sept/Oct 1993): 4, 50.

40. Norman Neuerberg, "Indians As Artists In California before and after Contact with the Europeans," in Román Piña Homs, ed., *Les Illes Balears i Amèrica* (Palma: Congrés Internacional d'Estudis Històrics, 1992), 43–60, quoted at 47. This is a "much revised version" of Georgia Lee and Norman Neuerburg, "The Alta California Indians as Artists before and after Contact," in *Columbian Consequences,* I, 467–80. See also Norman Neuerburg, "Indian Pictographs at Mission San Juan Capistrano," *The Masterkey* 56 (1982): 55–58.

41. Neuerburg, "Indians As Artists," 47. Boscana, *Chinigchinich,* facing 58.

42. Neuerburg, "Indians As Artists," 48.

43. Much of the fuel for the argument that Franciscans carefully balanced baptisms against food resources can be found in the work of anthropologists Gary Coombs and Fred Plog. See their "Chumash Baptism: An Ecological Perspective," in Lowell John Bean and Thomas F. King, eds., *?Antap: California Indian Political and Economic Organization* (Ramona, Calif.: Ballena Press, 1974), 137–53; and "The Conversion of the Chumash Indians: An Ecological Interpretation," *Human Ecology* 5 (1977): 309–28. The evidence does not support their thesis. See Sandos, "Christianization Among the Chumash," 68–70.

44. Milliken, "An Ethnohistory of the Indian People," 202–206.

45. Calculation derived from John R. Johnson, "Chumash Social Organization: An Ethnohistoric Perspective" (Ph.D. diss., University of California, Santa Barbara, 1988), 88.

46. An important topic, which space does not permit covering, is the examination of abortion and infanticide as acts of resistance.

47. Edward D. Castillo, "Gender Status Decline, Resistance, and Accommodation among Female Neophytes in the Missions of California: A San Gabriel Case Study," *American Indian Culture and Research Journal* 18 (1994): 67–93, especially 78–81.

48. Edwin A. Beilharz, *Felipe de Neve: First Governor of California* (San Francisco: California Historical Society, 1971), 70, 121–29.

49. Sandos, "Christianization Among the Chumash," 73–74; Robert F. Heizer, "A California Messianic Movement of 1801 Among the Chumash," *American Anthropologist* New Series 43 (1941): 128–29.

50. Steven Hackel, "Indian-Spanish Relations in Alta California: Mission San Carlos Borromeo, 1770–1833" (Ph.D. diss., Cornell University, 1994), 202 and passim.

51. *Colonial Russian America: Kyrill T. Khlebnikov's Reports, 1817–1832,* trans. and anno. by Basil Dmytryshyn and E. A. P. Crownhart-Vaughan (Portland: Oregon Historical Society, 1976), 130.

52. In addition to the fight the Chumash waged at La Purísima and the flight to the tu-

lares, other Chumash took Mission Santa Barbara's two ocean-going plank canoes (*tomols*) and fled to the Channel Islands. Yet others among those who fled initially to the tulares went farther inland into what is now Kern County in the area later called Walker Pass, where they fused Spanish and traditional ways to form a new culture. See James A. Sandos, "Levantamiento!: The 1824 Chumash Uprising Reconsidered," *Southern California Quarterly* 67 (Summer 1985): 109–33. See also Sandos, "Christianization Among the Chumash," 76–86.

53. Phillips, *Indians and Intruders,* 65–106, which also incorporates his earlier work on Indians and secularization; C. Alan Hutchinson, "The Mexican Government and the Missions of Upper California, 1821–1835," *The Americas* 21 (April 1965): 335–62; Manuel Servin, "The Secularization of the California Missions: A Reappraisal," *Southern California Quarterly* 47 (June 1965): 133–49.

54. My reconstruction of Estanislao's revolt is derived from: Sherburne F. Cook, "Expeditions to the Interior of California: Central Valley, 1820–1840," *Anthropological Records* 20 (1962): 168–80, 205–206; Osio, *The History of Alta California,* 89–94; Richard J. Orsi, "Estanislao's Rebellion, 1829," in Richard B. Rice, William A. Bullough, and Richard J. Orsi, *The Elusive Eden: A New History of California,* 2nd ed. (New York: Alfred A. Knopf, 1996), 53–68; Rosenus, *General M. G. Vallejo,* 11–12.

55. George C. Yount, "Memoirs," ms., Huntington Library; Rosenus, *General M. G. Vallejo,* 13–14.

56. Unless otherwise specified, my reconstruction of Fort Ross comes, inter alia, from: *Colonial Russian America,* 106–34; [no author given], "The Russian Colonies in California: A Russian Version," E. O. Essig, "The Russian Settlement at Ross," and Adele Ogden, "Russian Sea-Otter and Seal Hunting on the California Coast, 1803–1841," all from the *Quarterly of the California Historical Society* 12 (September 1933): 189–239; Robert A. Thompson, *The Russian Settlement in California Known as Fort Ross* (Santa Rosa: Sonoma Democrat Publishing Co., 1896), 1–34.

57. Otto von Kotzebue, *A New Voyage Round the World in the Years 1823, 1824, 1825, and 1826,* 2 vols. (London: Henry Colburn and Richard Bentley, 1830), II, 123–24.

58. Vallejo, "Historical and Personal Memoirs," I, 4–5, passim; Transcript of the Proceedings in Land Commission Case Number 243, George C. Yount, Claimant, vs. the United States, Defendant, for the Place Named "Caymus," Case 32nd in District Court, 1852, Huntington Library; hereinafter Proceedings of California Land Cases, followed by the district court case number.

59. Sherburne F. Cook, "Smallpox in Spanish and Mexican California, 1770–1845," *Bulletin of the History of Medicine* 12 (February 1939): 182, 184–87.

60. Ibid., 185, n. 45; Joseph Warren Revere, *A Tour of Duty in California Including a Description of the Gold Region and an Account of the Voyage around Cape Horn* (New York: CCS Francis and Co., 1849), 119, reports that Vallejo told him that half of the Indians living in the Sonoma Valley died in a single year from this epidemic.

61. Warner, quoted in Sherburne F. Cook, "The Epidemic of 1830–1833 in California and Oregon," *University of California Publications in American Archaeology and Ethnology* 3 (1955): 318.

62. J. J. Warner, "The Indian Pestilence in 1833," *Los Angeles Daily Star,* August 23, 1874, reprinted in the *Kern County Weekly Courier,* August 29, 1874, both newspapers in the California Section of the California State Library. Warner frequently used the initials J. J. after

Juan José, the names he adopted in becoming a Mexican citizen, replacing his christened names Jonathan Turnbull.

63. Cook, "The Epidemic of 1830–1833," 322. Throughout his essay, Cook assesses the data carefully and holds to conservative estimates. Phillips, *Indians and Intruders,* 94–95, 181 n. 4, thinks that Cook's figures are too high because the disease did not spread into the Tulare Valley.

64. Owens, ed., *John A. Sutter and a Wider West,* presents essays by historians Howard R. Lamar, Albert L. Hurtado, Iris H. W. Engstrand, Richard White, and Patricia Nelson Limerick.

65. Vallejo had hoped to acquire the Russian improvements (they could not sell the land, Russians argued, because they leased it from the Indians, ignoring the Spanish land claim altogether) by waiting for the asking price to drop. Sutter, however, did not wait and accepted the Russian terms.

66. Marguerite Eyer Wilbur, trans, ed., anno., *A Pioneer at Sutter's Fort, 1846–1850: The Adventures of Heinrich Lienhard* (Los Angeles: The Calafía Society, 1941), 77.

67. John A. Sutter, "Personal Reminiscences of General John Augustus Sutter," ms., 22, Bancroft Library.

68. Dorothy Hill, *The Indians of Chico Ranchería* (Sacramento: State of California Resources Agency, Department of Parks and Recreation, 1978), 1–7. See also Annie K. Bidwell, *Rancho Chico Indians,* Dorothy Hill, ed. (Chico: Bidwell Mansion Cooperating Association, 1980).

69. Lorrin L. Morrison, *Warner: The Man and the Ranch* (Los Angeles: Published by the Author, 1962), 20–22. Warner also bought four Indians from the Mojave as house servants.

70. "Princeton Woman Furnishes Much Historical Data on Life of James Savage," Princeton, Illinois, *Bureau County Record,* July 17, 1929, clipping in the file "Material Relating to James D. Savage," compiled by Lilbourne Winchell, Bancroft Library.

71. In addition to the Winchell file, I have drawn my picture of Savage from Annie R. Mitchell, *Jim Savage and the Tulareño Indians* (Los Angeles: Westernlore Press, 1957); Albert L. Hurtado, *Indian Survival on the California Frontier* (New Haven: Yale University Press, 1988), 112–42; and various newspaper clippings and fragments, especially about the Mariposa Indian War, from the John G. Marvin Scrapbook, Huntington Library. Mitchell, p. 34, gives the names of two of Savage's wives as Ho-mut and Ee-ki-no, but without tribal affiliation.

72. George Harwood Phillips, *Chiefs and Challengers: Indian Resistance and Cooperation in Southern California* (Berkeley: University of California Press, 1975), 47–165; "José del Carmen Lugo, Life of a Rancher," Helen Pruitt Beattie, trans., *Historical Society of Southern California Quarterly* 32 (September 1950): 185–236; Roy Elmer Whitehead, *Lugo: A Chronicle of Early California* (Redlands: San Bernardino County Museum Association, 1978), 130–376; George William Beattie, "San Bernardino Valley before the Americans Came," *Quarterly of the California Historical Society* 12 (June 1933): 11–124.

73. "Crumbs of '49," Journal of Benjamin Butler Harris, Part 1, Huntington Library; Morrison, *Warner: The Man and the Ranch,* 39, claims that over a thirty-year period "more than 200,000 people entered and left California through the valley [Warner's]."

74. Robert F. Heizer and Alan J. Almquist, *The Other Californians: Prejudice and Discrimination under Spain, Mexico, and the United States to 1920* (Berkeley: University of California Press, 1971), 39–58, 212–17, for text of act and amendments; Rosenus, *General M. G. Vallejo,* 211.

75. See the extended discussion in David Hurst Thomas, "Harvesting Ramona's Garden: Life in California's Mythical Mission Past," in *Columbian Consequences,* Vol. 3, *The Spanish Borderlands in Pan-American Perspective,* David Hurst Thomas, ed., (Washington, D.C.: Smithsonian Institution Press, 1991), 119–57.

76. Starr, *Inventing the Dream,* 58.

77. James A. Sandos, "Junípero Serra's Canonization and the Historical Record," *The American Historical Review* 93 (December 1988): 1253–69; and "Junípero Serra, Canonization, and the California Indian Controversy," *The Journal of Religious History* 15 (June 1989): 311–29, summarize both the literature and the process of sainthood through 1988.

78. David J. Weber, "Blood of Martyrs, Blood of Indians: Toward a More Balanced View of Spanish Missions in Seventeenth Century North America," in *Columbian Consequences,* vol. 2, *Archaeological and Historical Perspectives on the Spanish Borderlands East,* David Hurst Thomas, ed. (Washington, D.C.: Smithsonian Institution Press, 1990), 429–48, reprinted in O'Keefe, *Columbus, Confrontation, Christianity,* 128–50.

79. Weber, *The Spanish Frontier in North America,* 115.

80. Cook published a series of studies in the 1940s in the scholarly journal *Ibero Americana,* which were gathered together and reprinted after his death as Sherburne F. Cook, *The Conflict between the California Indian and White Civilization* (Berkeley: University of California Press, 1976).

81. Sherburne F. Cook, "Historical Demography," *HBNAI,* 8, pp. 91–98, is the culmination of much of his earlier work. Although he died in 1974, and volume 8 appeared in 1978, Cook's last-minute revisions continued to appear long after his death. Sherburne F. Cook and Cesare R. Marino, "Roman Catholic Missions in California and the Southwest," *HBNAI,* Vol. 4, *History of Indian-White Relations* (Washington, D.C.: Smithsonian Institution Press, 1988), 472–80, gives figures of 83,000 Indians baptized, with 17,000 remaining in the missions in 1832, meaning a decline of 79.5 percent. Hurtado, *Indian Survival on the California Frontier,* 1, follows Cook's earlier figures. Much contemporary Indian population work seeks to refine Cook's mission figures while ignoring the non-missionized Indians. See John R. Johnson, "Mission Registers as Anthropological Questionnaires: Understanding the Limitations of the Data," *American Indian Culture and Research Journal* 12 (1988): 9–30, which discusses those doing mission population research to 1988, and his "Chumash Social Organization"; Milliken, "An Ethnohistory of the Indian People," and *A Time of Little Choice;* Hackel, "Indian-Spanish Relations in Alta California"; Robert Jackson, *Indian Population Decline: The Missions of Northwestern New Spain, 1687–1840* (Albuquerque: University of New Mexico Press, 1994); Jackson and Castillo, *Indians, Franciscans, and Spanish Colonization.* For an extreme statement of the anti-mission school, see Rupert and Jeannette Henry Costo, eds., *The Missions of California: A Legacy of Genocide* (San Francisco: Indian Historian Press, 1987).

82. Sandos, "Neophyte Resistance in the Alta California Missions," 171–72, 178, n. 8.

83. See the works cited in this essay, and others, by (in alphabetical order): Rose Marie Beebe, Thomas Blackburn, Antonia Castañeda, Edward Castillo, Iris Engstrand, Steven Hackel, Albert Hurtado, Robert Jackson, John Johnson, Randall Milliken, Richard Orsi, George Phillips, Alan Rosenus, Robert Senkewicz, David Hurst Thomas, and David Weber. See also Lisbeth Haas, *Conquests and Historical Identities in California, 1769–1936* (Berkeley: University of California Press, 1995); and William McCawley, *The First Angelenos: The Gabrielino Indians of Los Angeles* (Banning, Calif.: Malki Museum Press/Ballena Press Cooperative Publication, 1996).

9

Engendering the History of Alta California, 1769–1848

Gender, Sexuality, and the Family

Antonia I. Castañeda

> The frontier is a liminal zone . . . its subjects, interstitial beings. . . . For more than two centuries the North was a society organized for warfare.
>
> Ana María Alonso[1]

From 1769, when the first *entrada* (incursion) of soldiers and priests arrived in California to extend Spanish colonial hegemony to the farthest reaches of the northern frontier, women and girls were the target of sexual violence and brutal attacks. In the San Gabriel region, for example, soldiers on horseback swooped into villages, chased, lassoed, raped, beat, and sometimes killed women.[2] As had occurred in successive incursions into new territory since the fifteenth century, sexual aggression against native women was among the first recorded acts of Spanish colonial domination in Alta California. This political violence effected on the bodies of women made colonial California a land of endemic warfare.

   This essay examines the gendered and sexualized construction of the colonial order and relations of power in Alta California from 1769 to 1848 as this land passed from Spanish to Mexican to Euro-American rule. Using gender and sexuality as categories of analysis, it explores how women articulated their power, subjectivity, and identity in the militarized colonial order reigning on this remote outpost. In this study, gender denotes the social construction of masculinity, as well as of femininity—and thus the social construction of distinctions between male and female. Gender is also a principal realm for the production of more general effects of power and meaning. Thus, gender is here interpreted as a relational dimension of colonialism and as one aspect of an imperial power matrix within which gender, sexuality, race, class, and culture operate. This matrix is brought to bear in recent studies on gender and colo-

A young Huchnom woman with the characteristic facial tattooing of her people. Although knowledge of pre-Hispanic Indian
gender and sexuality systems is slender, it is
generally thought that, despite male dominance in most spheres, a more open and
flexible relation existed between the sexes
than obtained in European society. Among
the Huchnom, whose lands lay along the
South Fork of the Eel River, it was the custom
for newly married couples to settle with the
bride's relations, one of several exceptions to
the otherwise patrilocal practice of California
Indians. From Stephen Powers, *Tribes of
California* (Washington, 1877). *Courtesy
California Historical Society, FN-30507.*

nialism on the northern frontiers of New Spain by historian Ramón Gutiérrez and
anthropologist Ana María Alonso, who examine the ideology of honor in order to
theorize and interpret constructions of masculinity and femininity within the power
relations of colonialism.[3]

This chapter examines how indigenous and mestiza women (Indo-mestiza and
Afro-mestiza) became subjects of colonial domination in California. It draws on
studies that view gender and sexuality as dimensions of subjectivity that are both an
"effect of power and a technology of rule," and that analyze colonial domination in
relation to the construction of subjectivities—meaning forms of personhood, power,
and social positioning. It also focuses on female agency, that is, the ways in which
women manipulated circumstances and used cultural, spiritual, religious, and legal
actions to resist patriarchal domination.[4]

Recent interdisciplinary works center women and other subordinated (subaltern)
groups as subjects of history and use gender and sexuality as categories of analysis to
examine broad historical processes. This scholarship seeks to find and analyze the
subalterns' voices, agency, and identities in the fissures and spaces, the interstices, the
hidden, masked meanings of events and documents.[5] Using gender and sexuality to
analyze resistance strategies within larger structures and processes, these studies explore women's power to reshape and refabricate their social identity—to fashion
their own response, their own experience, and their own histories.

GENDER, SEXUALITY, AND OPPOSING IDEOLOGIES

Little is known about native systems of gender and sexuality in California at the time of the Spanish invasion.[6] Nevertheless, it is clear that indigenous practices were antithetical to a patriarchal ideology in which gender hierarchy, male domination, and heterosexuality were the exclusive organizing principles of desire, sexuality, marriage, and the family. In the European order, until passage of the Bourbon Reforms in the late eighteenth century, Roman Catholic ideology and canon law, which conceptualized the body as base and vile, imposed a regime of sexual repression that tied sexuality to morality.[7] While canon law regulated marriage and the sociosexual life, of the physical body, civil law regulated the body politic and controlled family law, reinforcing inheritance and property rights and strengthening the patriarchal family. In this ideology, woman was conceptualized in opposition to, and as the possession of, man. Woman's reproductive capacity, as the vehicle for the production of legitimate heirs and the transference of private property, was defined as the single-most important source of her value. Spanish law defined women as sexual beings and delineated their sexual lives through the institution of indissoluble, monogamous marriage. And although canon law upheld the principle that marriage required the consent of both parties, that principle was not always adhered to.

Sexual intercourse, in theory, was confined to marriage, a sacrament intended for the procreation of children, for companionship, and for the containment of lust. Woman's sexuality had to be controlled through virginity before monogamous marriage and fidelity after in order to ensure legitimate transference of the patrimony. By regularizing inheritance of status and property, marriage institutionalized the legal exchange of women's bodies. The family, the sociopolitical organization within which these transactions occurred, reproduced the hierarchical, male-dominated social order. The Spanish cultural idiom of honor—the ideology of personal subordination to familial concerns—held the larger patriarchal edifice together at the fundamental unit of the family and family relationships.

Gender was a key dimension of honor, which defined the value accorded to both the individual person (personhood) and the family. Thus, ideal social conduct was defined by gender and differed according to appropriate male and female qualities and roles. Women's honor centered on their sexuality, and on their own and their family's control of it. Men's honor and ideal conduct centered on their conquest and domination of others, including women, as well as on protection, which included protecting the honor (sexual reputation) of females in the family. These gendered qualities of honor maintained the patrimony and perpetuated an honored image of the self and family across time. The result was extreme sexual oppression of women and a double standard of sexual behavior. Individuals possessed individual honor, and families possessed collective honor.

A page dated April 1781 from the San Carlos Borromeo "First Book of Matrimony," in which Fray Junípero Serra recorded marriages of neophytes, as well as of Spanish soldiers, performed in the mission church. The ceremony of Christian marriage, with its attendant imperatives of appropriate social and sexual relations between men and women, was part of the complex pattern of Hispanic life that the Franciscans imposed on the California Indians, thereby radically reshaping traditional native society. *Courtesy California Historical Society/Title Insurance and Trust Photo Collection, University of Southern California.*

Systems of gender and sexuality among indigenous peoples, in contrast, generally conceptualized females and males as complementary, not opposed, principles.[8] Woman was not a derivative of man, sexuality was not repressed, and both gender and sexual systems were relatively fluid. With variations, native systems included gender parallelism, matriarchal sociopolitical organization, and matrilineal forms of reckoning and descent. Within these diverse cultures, women's power and authority could derive from one or more elements: the culture's basic principle of individual autonomy that structured political relationships, including those between men and women; women's important productive or reproductive role in the economy; and the authority accorded women by their bearing and raising of children.[9] Further, women's power and authority were integral to, and also derived from, the tribe's core religious and spiritual beliefs, values, and traditions, which generally accorded women and men equivalent value, power, and range of practices.

As part of the natural world, sexuality, for many indigenous people, was related to the sacred and, as such, was central to their religious and cosmic order. Sexuality was celebrated by women and men in song, dance, and other ritual observances to awaken the earth's fertility and ensure that they were blessed with fecundity. Accepted practices extended to premarital sexual activity, polygamy, polyandry, homosexuality, transvestitism, same-sex marriage, and ritual sexual practices. Divorce was easily attainable, and, under particular conditions, abortion and infanticide were practiced.

Woman—the female principle—was a pivotal force in American cosmologies and worldviews. Woman, whether in the form of Grandmother, Thought Woman, or another female being, was at the center of the originating principle that brought the people into being and sustained them. On arriving in California in 1769, Europeans confronted the reality of Amerindian societies in which women not only controlled their own resources, sexuality, and reproductive processes, but also held religious, political, economic, and sometimes, military power.[10] The colonial church and state sought to eradicate native traditions that were centered on and controlled by women. In California, the Franciscan mission system was the principal vehicle for efforts to extirpate native systems of gender and sexuality and hence of women's resistance to them.

In the confessional, priests queried both women and men about their sexual lives and activities and meted out punishments. While prohibitions against fornication, adultery, masturbation, sodomy, incest, bestiality, and coitus interruptus applied to all, abortion and infanticide—violations of the Fifth Commandment, which condemned killing—applied specifically to women and were punished harshly.[11] Hugo Reid writes that the priests at Mission San Gabriel attributed all miscarriages to infanticide and that Gabrielino women were punished by "shaving the head, flogging for fifteen subsequent days, [wearing] iron on the feet for three months, and having to appear every Sunday in church, on the steps leading up the altar, with a hideous painted wooden child [a *monigote*] in her arms" representing the dead infant.[12]

The imperative to control and remake native sexuality, in particular to control women's procreation, was driven as much by material interest as by doctrinal issues. California needed a growing Hispanicized Indian population as both a source of labor and as a defense against foreign invasion, and thus missionaries sometimes took extraordinary measures to assure reproduction. Father Olbes at Mission Santa Cruz ordered an infertile couple to have sexual intercourse in his presence because he did not believe they could not have children. The couple refused, but Olbes forcibly inspected the man's penis to learn "whether or not it was in good order" and tried to inspect the woman's genitalia.[13] She refused, fought with him, and tried to bite him. Olbes ordered that she be tied by the hands, and given fifty lashes, shackled, and locked up in the *monjero* (women's dormitory). He then had a *monigote* made and commanded that she "treat the doll as though it were a child and carry it in the presence of everyone for nine days." While the woman was beaten and her sexuality demeaned, the husband, who had been intimate with another woman, was ridiculed and humiliated. A set of cow horns was tied to his head with leather thongs, thereby converting him into a cuckold, and he was herded to daily Mass in cow horns and fetters.

Franciscan priests also prohibited initiation ceremonies, dances, and songs in the mission system. They sought to destroy the ideological, moral, and ethical systems that defined native life. They demonized noncomplying women, especially those who resisted openly, as witches. Indeed, Ramón Gutiérrez argues that, in the northern borderlands of New Spain, "One can interpret the whole history of the persecution of Indian women as witches . . . as a struggle over [these] competing ways of defining the body and of regulating procreation as the church endeavored to constrain the expression of desire within boundaries that clerics defined proper and acceptable."[14]

NATIVE WOMEN, POWER, AND RESISTANCE

> No trayaba armas . . . vino para animarlos a que tubieran corazón para pelear. (She was unarmed . . . she came to animate their will to fight.)
> —Toypurina, "Ynterrogatorio de la india gentil" (1785)

Some indigenous women countered the everyday violence inflicted upon them with gender-centered strategies that authorized them to speak, to act, to lead, and to empower others. They fought the ideological power of the colonial church and state with powerful ideologies that vested women with power and authority over their own sexuality.

Toypurina, the medicine woman of the Japchavit *ranchería*, in the vicinity of Mission San Gabriel, used her power as a wise woman in an attempt to rid her people of the priests and soldiers. On October 25, 1785, Toypurina and three Gabrielino men led eight villages in an attack against the priests and soldiers of the mission. Toypurina, who had been about ten years old when the villages from the coast and the nearby mountains had attacked the mission some thirteen years earlier, used her influence as a medicine woman to recruit six of the eight villages that joined the 1785 battle.

At San Gabriel, the soldiers got wind of the attack and, lying in wait, captured Toypurina, her three companions, and twenty other warriors. Governor Pedro Fages convicted the four leaders and sentenced them to *prisión segura* in the missions. After a three-year imprisonment at San Gabriel, Toypurina was exiled north to Mission San Carlos Borromeo in 1788. The twenty warriors captured with her were sentenced to between twenty and twenty-five lashes plus time already served. This punishment was levied as much for following the leadership of a woman as for rebelling against Spanish domination. On sentencing them, Fages stated that their public whippings were "to serve as a warning to all," for he would "admonish them about their ingratitude, underscoring their perversity, and unmasking the deceit and tricks by which *they allowed themselves to be dominated by the aforesaid woman*" (emphasis added).[15]

Toypurina's power and influence derived from a non-Western religious-political ideological system of power in which women were central to the ritual and spiritual life of the tribe. Neither the source of Toypurina's religious-political power nor the threat she posed to the colonialist project in Alta California was lost on Fages, who, refusing to acknowledge her political power, constructed her instead as a sorceress. In his account, Fages sought to erase Toypurina's actual identity and to fabricate an identity consistent with colonialist gender values and ideologies.

Archival records show that native women continued to resist colonial domination with a range of actions and activities, including religious-political movements that vested power in a female deity and placed the health and well-being of the community in the hands of a female visionary.[16] In 1801, at the height of an epidemic ravaging the Chumash in the missions and the *rancherías,* a woman at Mission Santa Barbara launched a clandestine, large-scale revitalization movement. Drawing her authority from visions and revelations from Chupu, the Chumash earth goddess, this neophyte woman—who remains unnamed in the documents—called for a return to the worship of Chupu, who told her that "The pagan Indians were to die if they were baptized and that the same fate would befall the Christian Indians who would not give alms to [her] and who refused to wash their heads with a certain water."[17] Her revelation "spread immediately through all the houses of the mission. Almost all the neophytes, the *alcaldes* included, went to the house of the visionary to present beads and seeds and to go through the rite of renouncing Christianity."

Precisely because historical documents portray both Toypurina and the Chumash visionary of 1801 as "witches and sorceresses," we need to understand witchcraft within gendered relations of power in the Spanish/European world in general and

within gendered relations of power and subordination under conditions of colonialism in particular. Ostensibly, all women in colonial Mexico and Latin America,
like their counterparts throughout the Christian world, were suspected of being
witches on the basis of gender, but women of colonized groups were suspect on
multiple grounds.[18] Indian women, African-origin women, and racially mixed
women—whether Indo-mestiza or Afro-mestiza—were suspect by virtue of being
female, by virtue of deriving from non-Christian, or "diabolic," religions and cultures,
and by virtue of being colonized or enslaved peoples who might rebel and use their
alleged magical power at any moment. Thus, in the Christian imperialist gaze, non-
Christian women and their mestiza daughters were sexualized, racialized, and demonized for the ostensibly religious crime of witchcraft, although they were often
tried in secular courts, where witchcraft was treated as a political crime.

Yet, while ecclesiastical and civil officials dismissed, discredited, exiled, or sometimes put to death nonwhite women charged with witchcraft, women themselves
used witchcraft as a means of subverting the sociosexual order sanctioned by religion
and enshrined in the colonial honor code as an ethical system.[19] Ruth Behar argues
that women used sexualized magic to control men and subvert the male order by
symbolically using their own bodies and bodily fluids as a source of power over
men. Accordingly, sexual witchcraft included the use of menstrual blood, wash water, pubic hair, and ensorcelled food to attract, tame, or tie men into submission or,
sometimes, to harm or kill a physically abusive or unfaithful husband or lover. In the
realm of sexualized magic, women developed a rich symbolic language and actions
that were as violent as men's beating of wives. Women's actions within this spiritual
domain represented a form of power.

If colonizing males thought of Indian women's bodies, both symbolically and materially, as a means to territorial and political conquest, women constructed and used
their bodies, both symbolically and materially, as instruments of resistance and sub-
version of colonial domination. Toypurina and the Chumash visionary placed their
bodies in the line of fire and organized and led others to do likewise. Other women
resisted in less visible, day-to-day practices: they poisoned the priests' food, practiced
fugitivism, worshipped their own deities, had visions that others believed and followed, performed prohibited dances and rituals, refused to abide by patriarchal sexual norms, and continued to participate in armed revolts and rebellions against the
missions, soldiers, and ranchos. Participants cited the priests' cruelty and repression
of traditional ceremonies and sexual practices among primary reasons for the attacks on the missions, for the assassination of the friar Andrés Quintana at Mission
Santa Cruz in 1812, and for the great Chumash *levantamiento* of 1824.[20]

Secularization of the missions after 1834 ended the systematic, day-to-day insti-
tutional assault on native peoples' sexuality. It did not, however, end the sexual violence against indigenous women in the ensuing eras of Mexican and Euro-American

rule. Although Albert Hurtado examines the violence toward native women in the second half of the nineteenth century and initiates an important discussion of Indian survival, the nature of Amerindian women's resistance and strategies of survival in the post-mission era remains largely uncharted terrain.[21]

That colonialism for all its brutal technologies and distorted narratives, could not completely destroy native women's historical autonomy is something native peoples have always known, but scholarly researchers are just beginning to learn.[22] Native oral traditions have preserved the histories, telling and retelling women's identities and re-membering across time, space, and generations. Through oral and visual traditions, and other means of communicating counter-histories, native women's power, authority, and knowledge have remained part of their peoples' collective memory, historical reality, and daily struggles of "being in a state of war for five hundred years."[23]

Certainly ideologies of resistance and social memory, as the recent wealth of Native American literature reveals, center women as pivotal figures in historical and contemporary resistance in their peoples' collective memory. Thus, Vera Rocha, the contemporary hereditary chief of the Gabrielinos, received the story of Toypurina and the Gabrielinos as a very young girl from her great-grandmother, who received it from her mother.[24] Rocha, in turn, transmitted the story to her children and grandchildren and, more recently, to the world in general in the form of a public monument—a prayer mound dedicated to Toypurina developed in conjunction with Chicana artist Judith F. Baca. Such histories remain archived in tribal, family, and individual memory, as well as in other texts—some written, most not.

The effort to reconstruct the historical agency of Amerindian women is insepa-rable from the effort to reconstruct the autonomy of the racially and culturally mixed women who, with their families, were recruited by the colonial state to colonize Alta California five years after the initial arrival of soldiers and missionaries in 1769. The second part of this chapter examines mestiza women's agency, and the record they left of it, within the contradictory roles they occupied as both dominated and dominating native subjects.

REPRODUCING THE COLONY: GENDER, SEXUALITY, AND THE FAMILY IN ALTA CALIFORNIA

> Settlers must be men of the soil, tillers of the field, accompanied by their
> families . . . of upright character . . . likely to set a good example to the heathen.
> —Teodoro de Croix, 1781,
> quoted in *Southern California Quarterly* 15, 1931

In Spain's New World empire, the central role of the conjugal family in consolidat-ing the conquest of new territory was rooted in methods initially developed during the wars of the reconquest of the Iberian peninsula from the Muslims.[25] First formulated in the charters of medieval Spanish towns, the role of the family in imposing Spanish hegemony was transplanted to the Americas in the form of social legislation and colonization policies such as the policy of domestic unity, or unity of residence.[26] Backed by royal decrees and a system of economic and political rewards and punishments, this policy was designed to solidify the development of the institution of Christian marriage and the patriarchal family and to reproduce Spanish-Catholic civilization in the colonies.

The arrival of single soldiers and priests in California in 1769 reproduced sociosexual conditions similar to those of Spain's earlier sixteenth-century conquests elsewhere. By 1772, fearing that the California settlements were on the verge of collapse and acknowledging the slow rate of local Amerindian conversions, Junípero Serra argued that the survival of the colony required the presence of "Spanish," meaning Hispanicized, women and families.[27] Thus, racially mixed soldier and settler families were recruited, outfitted, subsidized, and transported by the colonial state to populate Alta California and to reproduce Christian family life and society. Attracting families to the remote military outpost, however, was no easy matter. Serra first promoted intermarriage between soldiers and newly Christianized native women in California as a way to establish Catholic family life, to foster alliances between the soldiers and the Indians, and to curb the soldiers' sexual attacks against native women. To promote these families, Serra recommended that soldiers who married indigenous "daughters of the land" be rewarded with three kinds of bounty: a horse, farm animals, and land.[28]

In 1773, five newly converted Rumsien women married Catalán and mestizo soldiers at the Mission San Carlos de Borromeo, three married at San Luis Obispo, and three married at San Antonio de Padua. California's first mestizo families derived from these and similar unions at the presidios and missions. However, the intermarriage of soldiers with native women could neither meet the immediate need for families to populate the colony nor fulfill the civilizing mission assigned to sturdy Spanish families. To that end, between 1774 and 1781, colonial officials sent captains Fernando Rivera y Moncada and Juan Bautista de Anza on three modestly successful expeditions to recruit and bring to Alta California soldier, settler, and artisan *gente de razón* (Hispanicized) families from the northern provinces of Sonora-Sinaloa and Guadalajara. Subsequent attempts to recruit more families were decidedly unsuccessful, however. The Yuma rebellion of 1781, which closed the land route from Sonora, effectively arrested overland migration, and travel by sea was always perilous. During the decades of the 1780s and 1790s, colonial efforts to sentence convicts to California in lieu of other punishment and to bring settlers from Guadalajara also met with little success. Although a handful of families came with supply ships, most other new settlers were men.

The Wife of a Monterey Soldier, drawn in 1791 by the Spanish expeditionary artist José Cardero, is the earliest known image of a Hispanic woman in California. Efforts to recruit single women from Mexico met with little success throughout the colonial period, and most soldiers who married on the California frontier took Indian brides. *Courtesy Museo Naval, Madrid. Photograph courtesy Iris Engstrand.*

Governor Diego de Borica repeatedly sought to recruit single women as marriage, and thus sexual, partners for these men. However, viceregal authorities were unable to meet Borica's call in 1794 or his requests in 1798, first for "young healthy maids" (*doncellas*) and then simply for 100 women.[29] Instead, in 1800, with the help of the church, colonial officials shipped nineteen *niñas y niños de cuna* (foundlings)—ten girls and nine boys—to Alta California, where, according to Apolinaria Lorenzana, who arrived as a seven-year-old, they were "distributed like puppies" to various families.[30] With the exception of Apolinaria Lorenzana, all of the young women eventually married, though not without resistance.

The foundlings of 1800 were part of the last government-sponsored effort to recruit or promote colonizing families until the era of Mexican rule, when new invaders—Europeans and Euro-Americans—began arriving in California. Mexico responded by sending the Híjar-Padrés expedition of 1834, which arrived with forty-two families, including fifty children, plus fifty-five single men and thirteen single women.[31] Instead of soldiers, this expedition was comprised of teachers, artisans, farmers, and their families. By this time, "Anglos" from the United States had begun to intermarry with Californio "daughters of the land," descendants of California's first soldier-settler families.

Despite the scarcity of *hispanas* despite the church's promotion of intermarriage between soldiers and Christianized Indian women, despite the colonists' own racially mixed backgrounds, and despite the blurring of racial and ethnic distinctions, rates of intermarriage between the soldier-settler population and Amerindians in the Monterey area, where I have completed the research, were high only in the initial period.[32] Between 1773 and 1778, 37 percent of the soldier-settler marriages were with Christianized Amerindian women. For the entire colonial period, however, only 15 percent of all marriages in Monterey were interracial. As elsewhere in the Spanish colonial world, conquering and colonizing men in California seldom formalized their sexual relations with Amerindian women after the early stages of conquest, when there were fewer alternative mates and intermarriage held particular economic, political, and military dividends. To reproduce the colony in Alta California, women's race and ethnicity mattered as much as their procreative capacities.

The betrothal and marriage of María Antonia Isabela de Lugo to Ygnacio Vicente Ferrer Vallejo illustrate the interrelation between race and contractual marriage.[33] Lugo was betrothed to Vallejo, a soldier serving escort duty at Mission San Luis, on the day of her birth. The contract between Vallejo and Lugo's parents bound her to marry him when she reached menarche. On February 18, 1791, at the age of fourteen and a half, Lugo married Vallejo, by then forty years old and retired from military service. Vallejo had entered into a marriage contract with a family who, like himself, was classified as "Spanish" rather than as mestizo, mulato, coyote, pardo, or any other mixed-blood designation. Once married, he applied for an official decree of *legitimidad y limpieza de sangre* (legitimacy and purity of blood) for the Vallejo name. In 1806, after fifteen years of marriage, the family received the decree, which certified that the Vallejo bloodline was untainted by Jewish, African, or any other non-Christian blood.[34] Henceforth, the Lugo-Vallejo family, two of whose daughters married Euro-Americans while a third married a Frenchman, rested their prominence and high social standing, in good part, on their officially certified purity of blood. Thus, though historically, racially, and culturally related to indigenous and African peoples, the *gente de razón* soldiers and families articulated their own identity as "Californios"[35]

During the Mexican era, after 1821, an expansionist North American neighbor sent a new group of single, foreign males—Europeans and Euro-Americans—to California's shores.[36] Some came as individual wanderers, some as part of exploring expeditions, merchant capitalist ventures, or reconnaissance missions. Spain's earlier economic and political reforms and Mexico's independence from Spain in 1821 established the basis for an expanding economy and related developments that affected marriage and family life in California. The rise of private property in the form of large rancho grants, liberalization of colonization and trade policies, the secularization of the missions, the development of an agropastoral economy, and the increasing demand for imported goods established economic ties between Euro-American merchants and entrepreneurs and the landowning Californio families.

The intermarriage of daughters of the Californios to Euro-Americans and other foreigners who converted to Roman Catholicism and became naturalized Mexican citizens was, in many cases, the basis of these economic relationships.[37] From the early 1820s to the end of Mexican rule in 1846, intermarriages were celebrated between the daughters of families who controlled the economic and political power in California and the Euro-Americans, who would join in the overthrow of Mexican rule. These unions, which generally gave the Anglo husbands landed wealth (sometimes in the form of women's dowries, sometimes not) created still another group of mixed parentage. They also became the basis for the "old Spanish Californio family ancestry" claimed by Euro-American pioneers in narratives, memoirs, and histories of "Spanish California" published in the latter part of the nineteenth century, though often written in the wake of the U.S.-Mexican War and subsequent dispossession of the Californios.[38]

These narratives, many of which were commissioned and collected in the 1870s and 1880s by Hubert Howe Bancroft for his multivolume *History of California*, became the primary source for the interpretations of gender and gender relations, women's sexual and moral conduct, their racial characteristics, and the nature of the family that dominate subsequent histories of early California.[39] Descriptions of the patriarchal Spanish-Mexican family, reproductive patterns, and family size abound in these nineteenth-century narratives of Euro-Americans and elite Californios, produced within the conflicting ideologies of the prewar and postwar eras. Becom-

One of a series of pen-and-ink drawings produced by Emanuel Wyttenbach under the supervision of William Heath Davis, *A California Wedding Party of 1845* conveys some of the color and pageantry associated with marriage among the great rancheros. A successful merchant, Davis himself married into a Californio family in 1847. His bride, the sixteen-year-old María Estudillo, inherited part of her father's Rancho San Leandro, which added significantly to the couple's estates, in a pattern typical of unions between *hijas del país* and Yankees since early provincial days. *Courtesy California State Library.*

ing the authoritative social and cultural histories, the texts described California women as "remarkably fecund" and frequently commented that families were exceptionally large, with women bearing twelve, fifteen, and twenty children.[40] Women in California did, indeed, marry young, but the story is more complex. The study of marriage and the family in late eighteenth and early nineteenth-century California is far from complete.

Examining lists of colonizing expeditions, marriage investigations (*diligencias*), marriage records, baptismal records, and population censuses for 1790 and 1834 for Santa Barbara and Los Angeles, historian Gloria Miranda has charted differences between and changes in the traditional, essentially military community of the presidio and the less economically stable, more flexible community of the pueblo.[41] Numerous factors, including the stage of colonization, the paucity of eligible women, and the young age and frequent turnover of military personnel, contributed to the young age of first marriages in the presidios. They also contributed to the very low numbers of single women and to the continuation of arranged marriages among the *hispano* population. Widowhood was generally short-lived, and multiple serial marriages were common for women. By custom, as well as because of frontier conditions, both sexes attained adulthood at a chronically tender age, and marriage registers document girls marrying between the ages of thirteen and sixteen and boys marrying between sixteen and seventeen. Across the span of the colonial period, however, the average marriage age in presidial society was sixteen to seventeen years for women and twenty-seven years for men. And although the population of the pueblo was more stable and permanent than in the presidio, the greater diversity of the population and economic instability of Los Angeles delayed the age of marriage there. The average age of marriage for women in Los Angeles was twenty years, while men married in their early thirties.

Similarly, Katharine Meyer Lockhart concluded that a steady increase in wealth, particularly among the *pobladores* whose occupation was ranching, was a distinctive, positive feature that affected the demographic pattern at the pueblo of San José.[42] San José registered a steady two-year increase in women's average age at marriage and a small decrease for men across three generations.

During the Mexican period, the rising social and economic complexity of town life, the marked emergence of an increasingly diversified population of foreigners, and the decline in the prestige of the military establishment as the presidio brought California closer to the marriage patterns that had emerged much earlier in Spain's older frontiers. Thus, in the era after Mexican independence, marriage age increased slightly for women, the age gap between spouses decreased, and, with the immigration of foreigners, racial exogamy increased. Interestingly, the rate of intermarriage between Californio women and Euro-American and European men during the Mexican period in Monterey was 15 percent—the same rate of intermarriage recorded for Amerindian women and mestizo men during the colonial period.[43]

Despite the young age at marriage, families in California were considerably smaller than commonly thought, although there were regional variations. While Miranda found a provincial average of slightly more than three children per family in 1790 and a homogeneous pattern of three to four children across the forty-four-year span between the 1790 and 1834 censuses, Lockhart found an average of seven children per family in San José.[44] Although "for some Californians, having large families was considered a mark of status" and some members of affluent clans, including the De la Guerras, the Ortegas, and the Vallejos, had as many as thirteen and even nineteen children, this was not the norm in the province.[45] Similarly, demographic studies of colonial New Mexico and Texas have shown that, contrary to common belief, large families were not the norm in either of these two colonies.[46] Miranda and other scholars attribute small family size among married *gente de razón* couples to various factors, including high infant mortality rates, miscarriages, infertility, marital discord, the extended absence of husbands, and personal choice.

Miranda's and Lockhart's studies, and my own research in progress, reveal that age at marriage and family size of the mestizo population in colonial California are consistent with patterns identified for the borderlands region writ large and for parts of colonial Mexico and Latin America.[47] This was generally true for other patterns, including high incidence of female-headed households, concubinage, illegitimacy, adultery, and premarital sex. Across time, sexual patterns in California increasingly resembled the broader nineteenth-century postcolonial Mexican and Latin American world.[48]

The meaning of these patterns, which challenge conventional notions of marriage and the patriarchal extended family, as well as standard analytic categories, has yet to be fully interpreted. Analytic and interpretive categories that explain the larger differences between colonials and European patterns as well as internal differentiation remain elusive, and, at this juncture, questions more than answers are at the forefront of scholarly discussion. Certainly part of the problem besetting the development of interpretive models remains rooted in the difficulty of reconstructing the lives of subaltern subjects from written sources that often ignore or distort their existence. The evidence historians have developed thus for, however, illustrates that the patriarchal family—ostensibly the norm in colonial California—was always a highly contested realm.

CONTESTING FAMILIES:
WOMEN'S POWER, RESISTANCE, AND CONTRADICTIONS

I am a woman and helpless . . . [but] they will not close the doors of my own honor and birth, which swing open in natural defense and protection of itself.

—Eulalia Callis, 1786

Though few women and men who colonized Alta California in the latter third of the eighteenth century were literate, their voices and actions are inscribed in official and unofficial sources detailing the colonization of this remote outpost. Women's actions, if not often their words, appear in documents written largely by men, though sometimes penned in women's own hand and at other times written at their behest. These documents expose internal hierarchies, tensions, and contradictions in power relations among women and men as well as among women themselves. The following discussion of mestiza resistance is framed by the acknowledgement that, in the words of historian Florencia Mallon, "No subaltern identity can be pure and transparent; most subalterns are both dominated and dominating subjects, depending on the circumstances or location in which we encounter them."[49]

These sources reveal that women frequently contested Hispanic patriarchal norms and acted outside the cultural constructions of femininity that required of women

not merely chastity, if single, and fidelity, if married, but also demanded submissiveness, modesty, and timidity in order to affirm their sexual purity. During the period under study, some women in Alta California—from the high-born Eulalia Callis to the impoverished widow María Feliciana Arballo—consistently resisted and
defied patriarchal control of their social and sexual bodies. In some cases, they openly
defied the norms that were supposed to control them; in others, they strategically
used the idiom of honor to defend themselves, even as their actions violated the
honor codes of femininity.

We can only speculate what words and language the twenty-three-year-old, recently widowed Feliciana Arballo spoke to convince Juan Bautista de Anza, over Father Pedro Font's strenuous objections, to let her, a woman alone with two young
daughters and no male guidance or protection, accompany his overland expedition
from Sinaloa to Alta California in 1775–1776.[50] Arballo's husband had died after the
family signed up with the expedition to establish settlements on San Francisco Bay,
but before they had left Horcasitas. Throughout the journey, Font publicly castigated
and rebuked the widow Arballo and remonstrated De Anza for her presence. On the
freezing night of December 17, when the weary but jubilant colonists held a dance
to celebrate their safe crossing of the treacherous Colorado desert, Font, who was already angry because people were partying instead of praying, became incensed when
the young widow joined the party and began singing. "Cheered and applauded by all
the crowd," he wrote, "a very bold widow sang some verses that were not very nice."[51]
For these *poblador* families, whose subsidy upon becoming colonists allowed them rations for five years, the wages of sailors for two years, and free transportation to the
new colony, joining the expedition to Alta California signified a release from the grip
of poverty and misery in which the depressed economy of Sinaloa-Sonora sub-
merged them.[52] Arballo, however, did more than defy the priest. She subverted his
effort to shame her and control her behavior by inverting the positions, appropriat-
ing the public space, and performing within it.

At the other end of the social and economic spectrum, Eulalia Callis, La Gobernadora, also refused to abide the dictum of feminine submissiveness, timidity, and en-
closure in the home.[53] Like Arballo, Callis made private matters public and "created
a scandal" in February of 1785 by publicly accusing her husband, Governor Pedro
Fages, of infidelity and refusing to sleep with him. Fages denied her accusations, saying she fabricated his infidelity as a ploy to force him to relinquish his governorship
and return with her and their two children to Mexico. In her petition for legal separation, Callis stated that when she refused the advice of her priest and other men to
be *recogida* or *depositada* (sheltered or deposited in another's home) and continued to
accuse her husband publicly, she was arrested and, although ill, taken to Mission San
Carlos Borromeo, where she was kept incommunicado in a locked and guarded room
for several months. During her incarceration, Father de Noriega excoriated her from

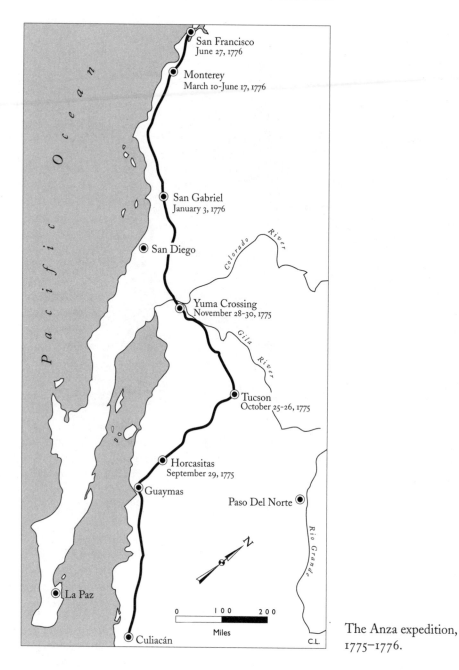

The Anza expedition, 1775–1776.

the pulpit and repeatedly threatened her with shackles, flogging, and excommunication. Callis, a wealthy woman from an influential family, was manipulating the idiom of gender-honor and notions of women's helplessness to defend her actions.

Historians of early California have dubbed Eulalia Callis the "notorious *gobernadora*," writing with tongue-in-cheek about Fages's domestic problems and alter-

A Californio woman grinds corn on a *metate* in a painting by Alexander Harmer, an American artist who in 1893 married the daughter of an old California family in Santa Barbara. On the ranchos, as in the towns, men typically spent their days on horseback or lounging about, while women, as a traveler observed in the 1840s, performed "most of the drudgery appertaining to housekeeping, and the cultivation of the gardens." *Courtesy Seaver Center for Western History Research, Natural History Museum of Los Angeles County.*

nately portraying Callis as a fiery, tempestuous Catalán woman or as a hysterical woman suffering postpartum depression.[54] Today, Callis's actions seem to have been more a strategy for survival. Callis, who was pregnant four times in six years, was all too familiar with the precariousness of life on the frontier. She gave birth to Pedrito in 1781, had a miscarriage at Arispe in 1782, traveled to California while pregnant with and was ill after the birth of María del Carmen in 1784, and buried an eight-day-old daughter in 1786. Thus her demand that the family return to Mexico City, her public denouncement of Fages, and her suit for ecclesiastical divorce can be reasonably interpreted as part of an overall strategy to ensure her own survival and that of her two remaining children.

Though from different ends of the social spectrum, and with attendant differences of power, Arballo and Callis refused to obey male authority and subverted gender-honor requirements that they be subservient, meek, and powerless. Both made private matters public and refused their respective priest's mandate of conduct. Both not only subverted the gender-honor code for women, they also undermined the Christianizing and "civilizing" mission by which *gente de razón* women were to be exemplar models of Spanish-Catholic womanhood's subservience to male authority. In Callis's case, her behavior further subverted the sociopolitical order that Spanish officials were attempting to impose on a racially and culturally mixed population of colonists, whom they already judged to be unruly, undisciplined, and disrespectful of authority.[55] Callis's actions, which carried the weight of her family's wealth and influence in Spain as well as her position as La Gobernadora, posed a particularly grave threat to the imposition of Spanish hegemony in the newly conquered territory. If the scarcity of *gente de razón* women and their importance to survival of frontier colonies liberalized some aspects of gender inequality, patriarchal structures nevertheless remained fundamentally unaltered and the technologies of rule enforced. Thus women's strategies of resistance, how they manipulated their circumstances, had to be carefully and subtly laid.

In view of the political and military imperative to populate Alta California with Christian families, officials of the colonial church and state consistently pressured women to marry, or, in the case of widows, remarry.[56] Despite the pressures, some women resisted entering the institution that gave them status in the community. Although the foundling girls of 1800 were brought explicitly as marriage partners for California soldiers, five of the ten girls informed the paymaster at Monterey in 1801 that they "did not want to receive suitors because they did not want to be burdened with marriage."[57] Apolinaria Lorenzana, the one *niña de cuna* who never married, tells us in her *testimonio* that although she had received a proposal of marriage as a young girl, "I refused his offer . . . because I was not particularly inclined toward that state [of matrimony] even though I knew the merits of that sacred institution."[58]

Instead, Lorenzana, who became known as *La Beata* (the pious one), entered a life of work and service in the missions as a *llavera*, *enfermera*, *cocinera*, and *maestra* (keeper of the keys/matron, nurse, cook, teacher). She maintained her independence, earned her livelihood by working for the Catholic Church, devoted her life to the "civilizing mission" the state assigned to mestiza colonists, and taught herself and others to write. A resourceful and intelligent woman, Lorenzana was respected and well-loved for her good works and selfless devotion to the health and well-being of Indians and mestizos alike. Lorenzana escaped the bonds of matrimony and control of her sexuality. As the *llavera* at Mission San Diego, however, her duties included policing the sexuality of the young neophyte women living in the mission compound by locking them in the *monjero* at nightfall and releasing them in the morning. She both resisted and enforced the control of women's sexuality and the sexual norms that Spanish colonial hegemony imposed in California.

The famed southern California ranchero Juan Bandini and his daughter Margarita, who, like her sisters, was celebrated for her beauty, ca. 1857. In domestic life among the Californios, women and children were expected to honor and respect the family patriarch, who, in turn, took pride in providing for the needs of wife and children, especially the protection of a daughter's honor. *Courtesy California Historical Society/Title Insurance and Trust Photo Collection, University of Southern California.*

Other women—both single and married mestiza women—contested patriarchal control of their sexuality by engaging in "scandalous" and illicit sexual activity.[59] During the period of conquest and settlement, women's sexual "transgressions" appear, in the records at least, to have been confined to adultery and *deshonra* (premarital sex). As California during the Mexican era evolved from a subsidized, military society to a more complex agropastoral, ranching, and market economy with more pronounced racial and social stratifications, cases of concubinage and prostitution were added to the list of mestiza women's illicit sexuality. Sexual violence, in the form of rape and incest, and sexually related violence—beating women to correct their sexual behavior—were present throughout.

Female and male sexuality in the Spanish colonial world was strictly regulated by the civil code, to say nothing of the moral code. Fornication, adultery, concubinage, prostitution, rape, incest, sodomy, bigamy, bestiality, and scandalous behavior were civil crimes for which perpetrators were prosecuted, and women were prosecuted more vigorously than men.[60] Moreover, since civil and canon law vested authority over a woman's sexuality in the male members of her family, the sexuality of a mother with a grown son, such as forty-year-old Josefa Bernal, was subject to her son's authority as well as to that of all other male relatives, whether living in the household or not. Bernal barely escaped being beaten by her twenty-five-year-old son Francisco when he found her in an adulterous relationship with Marcelo Pinto.[61]

It is clear that women's sexuality was also at risk within and without the family. An instance each of rape and incest appears in the colonial records, though a few more cases of rape, and a case of a teacher accused of molesting female students, were recorded during the Mexican period.[62] In this era, too, cases of concubinage, prostitution, and a significant increase in family violence, most specifically directed at women, appear in the records. Whether the low incidence of sexual violence toward mestiza women in colonial California was due to its nonexistence, to underreporting, or to the fact that most of the sexual violence was directed at Amerindian women has not yet been researched. What is clear is that across the eighty years of Spanish-Mexican rule, sexual violence and sexually related violence toward women became generalized throughout society. Some women responded with equal violence. Most, however, filed formal criminal charges against violent spouses in court.[63] Women had frequent recourse to the judicial system, and the records of Mexican tribunals contain cases that women filed in civil as well as criminal court, where they appear as both plaintiffs and defendants.

One approach to analysis of women's resistance during the Mexican period centers on the nineteenth-century narratives. Thus, Genaro Padilla finds that while Californio men's narratives remained embedded in patriarchal constructs, Californio women's narratives "voiced resistance to patriarchal domination that characterized social relations . . . and assertively figured themselves as agents in the social world they inhabited."[64] Women's narratives offered gendered perspectives that were critical of patriarchal constraints, affirmed women's presence in the public realm, and refuted the common assumption that Californio women welcomed the Euro-American conquest.

CONCLUSIONS

The construction of Amerindian and mestiza women's subjectivities in Alta California, as this essay has demonstrated, has historically been contested terrain. Most specifically, women's sexual and social bodies, their sexuality, their procreation, and the control of it have been the province of the patriarchal family, church, and state. Some women resisted, defied, and subverted patriarchal control of their sexuality within the family and without. From differing positions of power, as well as from contradictory locations, they carved out spaces, took actions, and fashioned responses within the family, which was at once a primary place of resistance, power, authority, and conflict.

The family was, and is, the most basic unit of sociopolitical organization and relations of power internally as well as externally. It was the primary place where women in eighteenth-and nineteenth-century Alta California constructed identity and subjectivity within the historical process of successive waves of conquest and colonialism, wherein mestizas were alternately part of the colonizing forces and part of the colonized peoples. In the Spanish colonial world, and particularly in new territories under conquest, the "Western" family, in its Spanish-Catholic incarnation, was deployed as a pivotal technology of rule. We are only now beginning to grapple with the complexities and contradictions of what that meant in the construction of "native" women's identities and subjectivities on the California homeland that was then, as it is now, contested space.

Engendering the history of Alta California, moving gender and the body to the center of historical inquiry, challenges us to rethink our conceptual, empirical, analytic, and interpretive categories.[65] It challenges us to question and reevaluate extant sources and our own assumptions as we approach them, and further summons us to expand the sources we use to study nonwritten text and other constructs of history. This chapter forms a small part of the larger feminist effort to engender and rethink history.

NOTES

1. Ana María Alonso, *Thread of Blood: Colonialism, Revolution, and Gender on Mexico's Northern Frontier* (Tucson: University of Arizona Press, 1995), 21.

2. Fray Junípero Serra to Antonio María de Bucareli y Ursúa, 21 May 1773, in Antonine Tibesar, ed., *Writings of Junípero Serra*, 4 vols. (Washington, D.C.: Academy of Franciscan History, 1955), 1: 363; Antonia I. Castañeda, "Sexual Violence in the Politics and Policies of Conquest: Amerindian Women and the Spanish Conquest of Alta California," in Adela de la Torre and Beatríz M. Pesquera, eds., *Building with Our Hands: New Directions in Chicana Studies* (Berkeley: University of California Press, 1993), 15–33; Antonia I. Castañeda, "Presidarias y Pobladoras: The Journey North and Life in Frontier California," in *Renato Rosaldo Lecture Series Monograph* 8 (1990–91): 25–54; Richard C. Trexler, *Sex and Conquest; Gendered Violence, Political Order, and the European Conquest of the Americas* (Ithaca: Cornell University Press, 1995); Albert L. Hurtado, "Sexuality in California's Franciscan Missions: Cultural Perceptions and Sad Realities," *California History* 71 (Fall 1992): 370–85; Albert L. Hurtado, *Indian Survival on the California Frontier* (New Haven: Yale University Press, 1988); Antonia I. Castañeda, "Amazonas, Brujas, and Fandango Dancers: Women's Sexuality and the Politics of Representation on the Borderlands," paper presented at the American Historical Association Annual Conference (January 1995); Virginia Maria Bouvier, "Women, Conquest, and the Production of History: Hispanic California, 1542–1840" (Ph.D. diss., University of California, Berkeley, 1995); Antonia I. Castañeda, "Presidarias y Pobladoras: Spanish-Mexican Women in Frontier Monterey, Alta California, 1770–1821" (Ph.D. diss., Stanford University, 1990).

3. See works by Ramón A. Gutiérrez: "Family Structures: The Spanish Borderlands" and "Sexual Mores and Behavior: The Spanish Borderlands," in Jacob Ernest Cooke, et al., eds., *Encyclopedia of the North American Colonies*, 3 vols. (New York: Charles Scribner's Sons, 1993), 2: 672–82 and 700–710; *When Jesus Came, the Cornmothers Went Away: Marriage, Sexuality, and Power in New Mexico, 1500–1846* (Stanford, Calif.: Stanford University Press, 1991); "Marriage and Seduction in Colonial New Mexico," in Adelaida R. del Castillo, ed., *Between Borders: Essays on Mexicana/Chicana History* (Los Angeles: Flor y Canto Press, 1990), 447–57; and "From Honor to Love: Transformation of the Meaning of Sexuality in Colonial New Mexico," in Raymond T. Smith, ed., *Kinship Ideology and Practice in Latin America* (Chapel Hill: University of North Carolina Press, 1984), 81–104.

4. See the following works by Deena J. González: *Refusing the Favor: The Spanish-Mexican Women of Santa Fe, 1820–1880* (New York: Oxford University Press, in press); "La Tules of Image and Reality," in de la Torre and Pesquera, eds., *Building with Our Hands*, 75–90; "Gender Relations: The Spanish Borderlands," and "Old Age and Death: The Spanish Borderlands," in Cooke and others, eds., *Encyclopedia of the North American Colonies*, 2: 406–412 and 780–82; and "The Widowed Women of Santa Fe: Assessments on the Lives of an Unmarried Population, 1850–1889," in Arlene Scandron, ed., *On Their Own: Widowhood and Aging in the American Southwest* (Chicago: University of Illinois Press, 1988), 45–64. See also the work of Asunción Lavrín: "Lo Feminino: Women in Colonial Historical Sources," in Francisco Javier Cevallos-Candau et al., eds., *Coded Encounters: Writing, Gender, and Ethnicity in Colonial Latin America* (Amherst: University of Massachusetts Press, 1994), 153–76; "In Search of the Colonial Woman in Mexico: The Seventeenth and Eighteenth Centuries," in Asunción Lavrín, ed., *Latin American Women: Historical Perspectives* (Westport, Conn.: Greenwood Press, 1978), 23–59; and "La vida feminina como experiencia religiosa: Biografía hagiografía en Hispanoamérica colonial," *Colonial Latin American Review* 2 (1993): 27–52; as well as Asunción Lavrin and Edith Couturier, "Las mujeres tienen la palabra: Otras voces en la historia colonial de México," *Historia Mexicana* 31 (1981): 278–313.

5. Rosaura Sánchez, *Telling Identities: The Californio Testimonios* (Minneapolis: University of Minnesota Press, 1995); Gyan Prakash, "Subaltern Studies as Postcolonial Criticism," *American Historical Review* 99 (1994): 1475–90; Florencia E. Mallon, "The Promise and Dilemma of Subaltern Studies: Perspectives from Latin American History," *American Historical Review* 99 (1994): 1491–1515, "Founding Statement: Latin American Subaltern Studies Group," *Boundary 2* 20 (Fall 1993): 110–21; Gayatri Chakravorty Spivak, "Can the Subaltern Speak?" in Cary Nelson and Lawrence Grossberg, eds., *Marxism and the Interpretation of Culture* (Urbana: University of Illinois Press, 1988), 271–313; Gayatri Chakravorty Spivak, "The Rani of Simur: An Essay in Reading the Archives," *History and Theory* 25 (1985): 247–72.

6. See Laura F. Klein and Lillian A. Ackerman, eds., *Women and Power in Native North America* (Norman: University of Oklahoma Press, 1995); Nancy Shoemaker, ed., *Negotiators of Change: Historical Perspectives on Native American Women* (New York: Routledge, 1995); Kevin Gosner and Deborah E. Kanter, eds., *Ethnohistory*, special issue, *Women, Power, and Resistance in Colonial Mesoamerica* 42 (Fall 1995); Greg Sarris, *Mabel McKay: Weaving the Dream* (Berkeley: University of California Press, 1994); Greg Sarris, *Keeping Slug Woman Alive: A Holistic Approach to American Indian Texts* (Berkeley: University of California Press, 1993); Greg Sarris, "'What I'm Talking about When I'm Talking about My Baskets': Conversations with Mabel McKay," in Sidonie Smith and Julia Watson, eds., *De/Colonizing the Subject: The Politics of Gender in Women's Autobiography* (Minneapolis: University of Minnesota Press, 1992); Carol Devens, *Countering Colonization: Native American Women in the Great Lakes Missions, 1630–1900* (Berkeley: University of California Press, 1992); Gretchen M. Bataille and Kathleen Mullen Sands, eds., *American Indian Women: Telling Their Lives* (Lincoln: University of Nebraska Press, 1984); Paula Gunn Allen, *The Sacred Hoop: Recovering the Feminine in American Indian Traditions* (Boston: Beacon Press, 1992); Paula Gunn Allen, *Grandmothers of the Light: A Medicine Woman's Sourcebook* (Boston: Beacon Press, 1991); Paula Gunn Allen, ed., *Spider Woman's Granddaughters: Traditional Tales and Contemporary Writing by Native American Women* (New York: Fawcett Columbine, 1989); Beatrice Medicine and Patricia Albers, eds., *The Hidden Half: Studies of Plains Indian Women* (Lanham, Md.: Uni-

versity Press of America, 1983); Victoria Brady, Sarah Crome, and Lyn Reese, "Resist! Survival Tactics of Indian Women," *California History* 63 (Spring 1984): 141–51; Rayna Green, *Native American Women: A Contextual Bibliography* (Bloomington: Indiana University Press, 1983).

7. Antonia I. Castañeda, "Marriage: The Spanish Borderlands," in Cooke and others, eds., *Encyclopedia of North American Colonies*, 2:727–38; Gutiérrez, *When Jesus Came*; François Giraud, "Mujeres y Familia en Nueva Espana," in Carmen Ramos Escandón, ed., *Presencia y transparencia: La mujer en la historia de México* (México, D.F.: Colegio de México, 1987, 61–77; Asunción Lavrín, ed., *Sexuality and Marriage in Colonial Latin America* (Lincoln: University of Nebraska Press, 1989), see especially the essays by Asunción Lavrín, Serge Gruzinski, Ann Twinam, Ruth Behar, Richard Boyer, and Thomas Calvo; Sylvia Arrom, *The Women of Mexico City, 1790–1857* (Stanford, Calif.: Stanford University Press, 1985); Patricia Seed, *To Love, Honor, and Obey in Colonial Mexico: Conflicts over Marriage Choice, 1574–1821* (Stanford, Calif.: Stanford University Press, 1988);

8. Klein and Ackerman, eds., *Women and Power in Native North America*, see especially Klein and Ackerman's introduction and essays by Victoria D. Patterson, Mary Shepardson, Sue-Ellen Jacobs, and Daniel Maltz and JoAllyn Archambault; Shoemaker, ed., *Negotiators of Change*, especially Shoemaker's introduction and essays by Lucy Eldersveld Murphy and Carol Douglas Sparks; Gosner and Kanter, eds., *Ethnohistory*, special issue, especially the essays by Alvis E. Dunn, Martha Few, and Irene Silverblatt.

9. Shoemaker, ed., *Negotiators of Change*, 7; Devens, *Countering Colonization*.

10. See Lucy Eldersveld Murphy, "Autonomy and the Economic Roles of Indian Women of the Fox-Wisconsin Riverway Region, 1763–1832," in Shoemaker, eds., *Negotiators of Change*, 72–89; Edward D. Castillo, "Introduction," in Edward D. Castillo, ed., *Native American Perspectives on the Hispanic Colonization of Alta California*, Spanish Borderlands Sourcebook 26 (New York: Garland Publishing, Inc., 1991), xvii–xlv; Eleanor Leacock and Richard Lee, eds., *Politics and History in Band Societies* (Cambridge: Cambridge University Press and Editions de la Maison des Sciences de I'Homme, 1982), especially the introduction and articles by Leacock and Lee; Mona Etienne and Eleanor Leacock, eds., *Women and Colonization: Anthropological Perspectives* (New York: Praeger, 1980), especially the articles by June Nash, Irene Silverblatt, and Robert Steven Grumet.

11. See Harry Kelsey, ed., *The Doctrina and Confesionario of Juan Cortés* (Altadena, Calif.: Howling Coyote Press, 1979), 112–16 and 120–23; Madison S. Beeler, ed., *The Ventureno Confesionario of José Señán, O.F.M.*, University of California Publication in Linguistics 47 (Berkeley: University of California Press, 1967), 37–63.

12. Hugo Reid, "Letters on the Los Angeles County Indians," in Susana Bryant Dakin, ed., *A Scotch Paisano in Old Los Angeles: Hugo Reid's Life in California, 1832–1852 Derived from His Correspondence* (Berkeley: University of California Press, 1939), app. B: 275.

13. Quotes in this paragraph are from Bouvier, "Women, Conquest, and the Production of History," 363–69.

14. Gutiérrez, "Sexual Mores and Behavior," 701.

15. "Ynterrogatorio sobre la sublevación de San Gabriel, 10 octubre de 1785," Archivo General de la Nación, Provincias Internas Tomo 1 (Californias): 120, Microfilm Collection, Bancroft Library, Berkeley, Calif.

16. Robert F. Heizer, "A Californian Messianic Movement of 1801 among the Chumash," *American Anthropologist* 43 (1941, reprint, 1962): 128–29. For discussion of the warrior

woman tradition, women's councils, religion, and spirituality as a source of women's power and resistance, and of women's cultural mediation and resistance in Native American history, see Elizabeth Salas, *Soldaderas in the Mexican Military* (Austin: University of Texas Press, 1990), 1–10; Clara Sue Kidwell, "Indian Women as Cultural Mediators," *Ethnohistory* 39 (Spring 1992): 97–107; Beatrice Medicine, "'Warrior Women'—Sex Role Alternatives for Plains Indian Women," in Medicine and Albers, eds., *The Hidden Half,* 267–80.

17. Heizer, "A Californian Messianic Movement of 1801 among the Chumash."

18. Antonia I. Castañeda, "Witchcraft on the Spanish-Mexican Borderlands," in Wilma Mankiller, Gwendolyn Mink, Marysa Navarro, Barbara Smith, and Gloria Steinem, eds., *The Reader's Companion to U.S. Women's History* (New York: Houghton Mifflin Company, in press).

19. Ruth Behar, "Sexual Witchcraft, Colonialism, and Women's Power: Views from the Mexican Inquisition," in Lavrín, ed., *Sexuality and Marriage in Colonial Latin America,* 178–206; Ruth Behar, "Sex and Sin, Witchcraft, and the Devil in Late Colonial Mexico," *American Ethnologist* 14 (February 1987): 344–54; Ruth Behar, "The Visions of a Guachichil Witch in 1599: A Window on the Subjugation of Mexico's Hunter-Gatherers," *Ethnohistory* 34 (Spring 1987): 115–38; see also Solange Alberro, "Herejes, brujas, y beatas: Mujeres ante el Tribunal del Santo Oficio de la Inquisición en la Nueva España," in Escandón, ed., *Presencia y transparencia,* 79–94; Henry Kamen, *Inquisition and Society in Spain in the Sixteenth and Seventeenth Century* (Bloomington: University of Indiana Press, 1985); Henry Kamen, "Notes on Witchcraft, Sexuality, and the Inquisition," in Angel Alcalá, ed., *The Spanish Inquisition and the Inquisitorial Mind* (Boulder, Colo.: Social Science Monographs, 1987), 237–47; María Helena Sánchez-Ortega, "Woman as a Source of 'Evil' in Counter-Reformation Spain," in Anne J. Cruz and Mary Elizabeth Perry, eds., *Culture and Control in Counter-Reformation Spain,* Hispanic Issues 7 (Minneapolis: University of Minnesota Press, 1992); Marc Simmons, *Witchcraft in the Southwest: Spanish and Indian Supernaturalism on the Rio Grande* (Lincoln: University of Nebraska Press, 1980).

20. Bouvier, "Women, Conquest, and the Production of History," 363–84; Edward D. Castillo, trans. and ed., "The Assassination of Padre Andrés Quintana by the Indians of Mission Santa Cruz in 1812: The Narrative of Lorenzo Asisara," *California History* 68 (Fall 1989): 117–25; Edward D. Castillo, "Introduction" and "The Native Response to the Colonization of Alta California," in Castillo, ed., *Native American Perspectives on the Hispanic Colonization of Alta California,* xvii–xlv and 423–40; Antonia I. Castañeda, "Comparative Frontiers: The Migration of Women to Alta California and New Zealand," in Lilian Schlissel, Vicki L. Ruiz, and Janice Monk, eds., *Western Women: Their Land, Their Lives* (Albuquerque: University of New Mexico Press, 1988), 283–300, especially 292–94; James Sandos, "Levantamiento! The 1824 Chumash Uprising," *The Californians* 5 (January–February 1987): 8–11; Bruce Walter Barton, *The Tree at the Center of the World: A Study of the California Missions* (Santa Barbara: Ross-Erickson Publications, 1980), 185; Sherburne F. Cook, *Conflict between the California Indian and White Civilization* (Berkeley and Los Angeles: University of California Press, 1976), 56–90.

21. Hurtado, *Indian Survival on the California Frontier.*

22. Sarris, "'What I'm Talking about When I'm Talking about My Baskets.'"

23. Gunn Allen, *Spider Woman's Granddaughters,* 2.

24. Author interview with Judith F. Baca, October 8, 1995, San Antonio, TX; Author interview with Vera Rocha, July 5, 1996, Baldwin Park, CA.

25. Heath Dillard, *Daughters of the Reconquest: Women in Castilian Town Society, 1100–1300* (New York: Cambridge University Press, 1984); Heath Dillard, "Women in Reconquest Castile: the Fueros of Sepúlveda and Cuenca," in Susan Mosher Stuard, ed., *Women in Medieval Society* (Philadelphia: University of Pennsylvania Press, 1976), 71–94; Salomé Hernández, "Nueva Mexicanas as Refugees and Reconquest Settlers, 1680–1696," in Joan M. Jensen and Darlis A. Miller, eds., *New Mexico Women: Intercultural Perspectives* (Albuquerque: University of New Mexico Press, 1986), 41–70.

26. José María Ots y Capdequi, *Instituciones sociales de la América española en el período colonial* (La Plata: Biblioteca Humanidades, 1934), 183–206.

27. Serra to Antonio María de Bucareli y Ursúa, Monterey, 24 August 1774, *Writings,* 2: 143; Serra to Bucareli, Monterey, 8 January 1775, *Writings,* 2: 203; Serra to Bucareli, Monterey, 30 June 1778, *Writings,* 3: 199.

28. Serra to Bucareli, Mexico City, 13 March 1773, *Writings,* 1: 325; Serra to Bucareli, Mexico City, 22 April 1773, *Writings,* 1: 341; Serra to Bucareli, Monterey, 24 August 1775, *Writings,* 2: 149, 151, and 153.

29. Branciforte al Governador, "Sobre envío de mujeres para pobladores," Orizaba, 25 enero de 1798, Archives of California, 14: 284, Bancroft Library; Salomé Hernández, "No Settlement without Women: Three Spanish California Settlement Schemes, 1790–1800," *Southern California Quarterly* 72 (Fall 1990): 203–33.

30. Memorias de Doña Apolinaria Lorenzana, "La Beata," marzo de 1878, Santa Barbara, Manuscript Collection, 1, Bancroft Library.

31. C. Alan Hutchinson, *Frontier Settlement in Mexican California: The Híjar-Padrés Colony and Its Origins, 1769–1835* (New Haven: Yale University Press, 1969).

32. Entries 3, 49, 50, 154, 180, 181, 182, 197, 290, 334, 387, 405, 528, 529, and 563, Libro de Matrimonios: Misión de San Carlos de Borromeo, vol. 1; Serra to Bucareli, "Report of the Spiritual and Material Status of the Five California Missions, 5 February 1775," *Writings,* 2: 237, 241. The findings for Monterey are consistent with those for Mexico. See Sherburne F. Cook and Woodrow Borah, *Essays in Population History: Mexico and the Caribbean,* 3 vols. (Berkeley: University of California Press, 1971–79), 1: 248–53. For early discussion of the racially and culturally mixed population that colonized California, see Jack Forbes, "Hispano-Mexican Pioneers of the San Francisco Bay Region: An Analysis of Racial Origins," *Aztlán* (Spring 1983): 175–189; Jack Forbes, "Black Pioneers: The Spanish-Speaking Afroamericans of the Southwest," in George E. Frakes and Curtis B. Solberg, eds., *Minorities in California History* (New York: Random House, 1971), 20–33, first published in 1966.

33. Charles Howard Shinn, "Pioneer Spanish Families in California," *The Century Magazine* (new series, v. xix), (1891): 377–89; Gloria E. Miranda, "Racial and Cultural Dimensions of Gente de Razón Status in Spanish and Mexican California," *Southern California Quarterly* 70 (Fall 1988): 265–78.

34. José María Estudillo, comandante de la compañia presidial, Información sobre nobleza de sange del Sargento Ignacio Vallejo y decreto concedido lo pedido, 20 julio 1807, Monterey, California, Archives of California, 16: 356; and Ynformación sobre la legitimidad y limpieza de sangre de Don Ignacio Vicente Ferrer Vallejo, padre del General Don Mariano Vallejo, 1806–1847, M. G. Vallejo Collection, Documentos para la Historia, Bancroft Library.

35. The origin and meaning of the term "Californio" remains unstudied. The earliest reference I have found to the use of this term is in the records of accounts of animals, crops, and the distribution of corn and wheat for the years 1782, 1784, and 1787 at Mission San Car-

los de Borromeo. However, it is unclear whether the term refers to neophyte Indians or to the soldier/settler population. See Copias de varios documentos en la Parroquia de Monterey. Parroquia de Monterey, C-C 24: 31, 34, Bancroft Library; Lisbeth Haas, *Conquest and Historical Identities* (Berkeley: University of California Press, 1995), 43. See also Genaro Padilla, *My History, Not Yours: The Formation of Mexican American Autobiography* (Madison: University of Wisconsin Press, 1993); Ramón A. Gutiérrez, "Unraveling America's Hispanic Past: Internal Stratification and Class Boundaries," *Aztlán* 17 (1986): 79–101.

36. Douglas Monroy, *Thrown among Strangers: The Making of Mexican Culture in Frontier California* (Berkeley: University of California Press, 1990); David J. Langum, *Law and Community on the Mexican California Frontier: Anglo-American Expatriates and the Clash of Legal Traditions, 1821–1846* (Norman: University of Oklahoma Press, 1987); David J. Weber, *The Mexican Frontier, 1821–1846: The American Southwest under Mexico* (Albuquerque: University of New Mexico Press, 1982); Leonard Pitt, *The Decline of the Californios* (Berkeley: University of California Press, 1966), 1–47.

37. For discussion of unions between Californio women and foreigners, see Sánchez, *Telling Identities;* Monroy, *Thrown among Strangers,* 158–61; Antonia I. Castañeda, "The Political Economy of Nineteenth-Century Stereotypes of Californianas," in Del Castillo, ed., *Between Borders,* 213–36.

38. Five of the eleven Californiana narratives from the Bancroft Collection are published in Rosaura Sánchez, Beatrice Pita, and Bárbara Reyes, eds., "Nineteenth Century Californio Testimonials," *Critica: A Journal of Critical Essays* (University of California, San Diego: Critica Monograph Series, Spring 1994). For analysis of the Euro-American narratives and the Californiano/Californiana counter-narratives, with a focus on the latter, see Genaro Padilla, "Recovering Mexican American Autobiography," and Rosaura Sánchez, "Nineteenth-Century Californio Narratives: The Hubert H. Bancroft Collection," in Ramón Gutiérrez and Genaro Padilla, eds., *Recovering the U.S. Hispanic Literary Heritage* (Houston: Arte Público Press, 1993), 153–78 and 279–92; Genaro Padilla, "Discontinuous Continuities: Remapping the Terrain of Spanish Colonial Narrative," in María Herrera-Sobek, ed., *Reconstructing a Chicana/o Literary Heritage: Hispanic Colonial Literature of the Southwest* (Tucson: University of Arizona Press, 1993), 24–36; Genaro Padilla, "Yo Sola Aprendí: Mexican Women's Personal Narratives from Nineteenth-Century California," in Susan Groag Bell and Marilyn Yalom, eds., *Revealing Lives: Autobiography, Biography, and Gender* (New York: State University of Press of New York, 1990).

39. Antonia I. Castañeda, "Gender, Race, and Culture: Spanish-Mexican Women in the Historiography of Frontier California," *Frontiers: A Journal of Women Studies* 11 (1990): 8–20.

40. Castañeda, "Gender, Race, and Culture"; Castañeda, "Political Economy of Nineteenth-Century Stereotypes"; Hubert Howe Bancroft, *California Pastoral, 1769–1848* (San Francisco: History Company, 1888), 305–34.

41. Miranda, "*Gente de Razón* Marriage Patterns."

42. Katharine Meyer Lockhart, "A Demographic Profile of an Alta California Pueblo: San José de Guadalupe, 1777–1850" (Ph.D. diss., University of Colorado, 1986), 114.

43. Miranda, "Hispano-Mexicano Childrearing Practices in Pre-American Santa Barbara." Twenty-six, or 15 percent, of the 170 Mexican women who married between 1822 and 1846 in Monterey married Euro-American or European men, see Castañeda, "Presidarias y Pobladoras: Spanish-Mexican Women in Frontier Monterey," 286–87, 291, fn. 1.

44. Lockhart, "A Demographic Profile of an Alta California Pueblo," 60–69.

45. Miranda, "Hispano-Mexicano Childrearing Practices," 309.

46. Alicia V. Tjarks, "Demographic, Ethnic, and Occupational Structure of New Mexico, 1790," *The Americas* 35 (July 1978): 45–88; Alicia V. Tjarks, "Comparative Demographic Analysis of Texas, 1777–1793," *Southwestern Historical Quarterly* 77 (January 1974): 291–338.

47. Miranda, "*Gente de Razón* Marriage Patterns"; Miranda, "Hispano-Mexicano Childrearing Practices"; Lockhart, "A Demographic Profile of an Alta California Pueblo." Two chapters of my manuscript in progress are based on demographic data that trace women in the marriage and birth (baptismal) records across the four presidios.

48. Castañeda, "Presidarias y Pobladoras: Spanish-Mexican Women in Frontier Monterey," 266–74; Lockhart also found low rates of illegitimacy in San José; see Lockhart, "A Demographic Profile of an Alta California Pueblo," 112–14. For family and household composition after 1848, which reveals rates of female-headed households consistent with the nineteenth-century pattern identified for parts of Mexico and Latin America, see Richard Griswold del Castillo, *La Familia: Chicano Families in the Urban Southwest, 1848 to the Present* (Notre Dame: University of Notre Dame Press, 1984); Barbara Laslett, "Household Structure on an American Frontier: Los Angeles, California, in 1850," *American Journal of Sociology* 81 (January 1975): 109–28.

49. Mallon, "The Promise and Dilemma of Subaltern Studies," 1511.

50. Herbert Eugene Bolton, trans. and ed., *Anza's California Expeditions,* 5 vols. (Berkeley: University of California Press, 1930), 4: 138, 428.

51. Ibid., 4: 428.

52. Ibid., 1: 228.

53. Ynstancia de Doña Eulalia Callis, Muger de Don Pedro Fages, governador de California, sobre que se le oyga en justicia, y redima de la opresión que padece, 23 August 1785, Archivo General de la Nación, Provincias Internas, 120: 66–81, Collection, Bancroft Library.

54. Bancroft, *History of California,* 1: 389–93; Irving Berdine Richman, *California under Spain and Mexico, 1535–1847* (Boston: Houghton Mifflin Co., 1911), 156–58; Charles C. Chapman, *A History of California: The Spanish Period* (New York: MacMillan Company, 1921), 398–400; Castañeda, "Presidarias y Pobladoras: The Journey North," 41–43, 54, fn. 103.

55. See Manuel Patricio Servín, "California's Hispanic Heritage: A View into the Spanish Myth," *Journal of San Diego History* 19 (1973): 1–9; Oakah L. Jones, Jr., *Los Paisanos: Spanish Settlers on the Northern Frontier of New Spain* (Norman: University of Oklahoma Press, 1979); Sidney B. Brinckerhoff and Odie B. Faulk, *Lancers for the King: A Study of the Frontier Military System of Northern New Spain, with a Translation of the Royal Regulations of 1772* (Phoenix: Arizona Historical Foundation, 1965); Max Moorhead, "The Soldado de Cuera: Stalwart of the Spanish Borderlands," in Oakah L. Jones, Jr., ed., *The Spanish Borderlands: A First Reader* (Los Angeles: Lorrin L. Morrison, 1974), 87–105; Leon G. Campbell, "The First Californios: Presidial Society in Spanish California, 1760–1822," in Jones, Jr., ed., *The Spanish Borderlands,* 106–18.

56. Bancroft, *History of California,* 1: 603–606; Castañeda, "Presidarias y Pobladoras: Spanish-Mexican Women in Frontier Monterey," 168–69, 203–204.

57. Castañeda, "Presidarias y Pobladoras: Spanish-Mexican Women in Frontier Monterey," 171–73; Hernández, "No Settlement without Women."

58. Lorenzana, "Memorias de Dona Apolinaria Lorenzana, La Beata," 45–46.

59. Castañeda, "Presidarias y Pobladoras: Spanish-Mexican Women in Frontier Monterey," 266–71.

60. Lavrín, "In Search of the Colonial Woman," in Lavrín, ed., *Latin American Women*, 35; Ots y Capdequi, *Instituciones sociales*, 250–51; Arrom, *The Women of Mexico City*, 65–70.

61. José Argüello a Fages, 26 noviembre de 1788, San Francisco, Trato ilícito entre un soldado y una muger casada, *Archives of California*, 4: 250.

62. Carrillo, 28 de noviembre de 1806, Santa Barbara, Causa de incesto, *Archives of California*, 16: 342–56; Antonio María Pico, Juez constitucional de primera nominación, 7 de mayo de 1845, San José Guadalupe. Causa criminal contra el vecino Mariano Duarte, maestro de escuela por tentativas de estupro en niñas de menor edad, *Archives of California*, 69: 139–42.

63. For Monterey, see Criminal Court Records, Mexican Archives of Monterey County, Office of the County Clerk, Salinas, Calif.

64. Padilla, *My History, Not Yours*, 26; Sánchez, *Telling Identities*; Richard Griswold del Castillo, "Neither Activist Nor Victim: Mexican Women's Historical Discourse—The Case of San Diego, 1820–1850," *California History* (Fall 1995): 230–43.

65. For feminist theories of gender, sexuality, and history, see: Joan W. Scott, ed., *Feminism and History* (New York: Oxford University Press, 1996); Deena J. Gonzalez, "A Resituated West: Johnson's Re-gendered, Re-racialized Perspective," in Clyde Milner III, ed., *A New Significance: Re-envisioning the History of the American West* (New York: Oxford University Press, in press); Ann-Louise Shapiro, ed., *Feminists ReVision History* (New Brunswick: Rutgers University Press, 1994); Kathleen M. Brown, "Brave New Worlds: Women's and Gender History," *William and Mary Quarterly* 50 (April 1993): 311–328; Susan Lee Johnson, "'A memory sweet to soldiers': The Significance of Gender in the History of the 'American West'," *Western Historical Quarterly* 24 (November 1993): 495–518; Antonia I. Castañeda, "Women of Color and the Rewriting of Western History: The Discourse, Politics, and Decolonization of History," *Pacific Historical Review* 61 (November 1992): 501–533; Joan W. Scott, "Experience," and Ana Maria Alonso, "Gender, Power, and Historical Memory: Discourses of Serrano Resistance," in Judith Butler and Joan W. Scott, eds., *Feminists Theorize the Political* (New York and London: Routledge, 1994), 22–40 and 404–425; Emma Perez, "Sexuality and Discourse: Notes from a Chicana Survivor," in Carla Trujillo, ed., *Chicana Lesbians: The Girls Our Mothers Warned Us About* (Berkeley: Third Woman Press, 1991), 159–84; Irene Silverblatt, "Interpreting Women in States: New Feminist Ethnohistories," in Micaela di Leonardo, ed., *Gender at the Crossroads of Knowledge: Feminist Anthropology in the Postmodern Era* (Berkeley, Los Angeles, Oxford: University of California Press, 1991), 140–74; Joan Wallach Scott, "Gender: A Useful Category of Historical Analysis," *American Historical Review* 91 (December 1986): 1053–75.

10

Serpent in the Garden

Environmental Change in Colonial California

William Preston

> [The Spanish] missions brought not only the cross but European cultigens, livestock, and habits of agriculture; they sought to convert the land as well as the natives, the one being essential to the other.
> —Stephen J. Pyne, Patricia J. Andrews, and Richard D. Laven,
> *Introduction to Wildland Fire,* 1996

The colonial processes initiated by the landing of Christopher Columbus in 1492 would inevitably and irrevocably spread throughout the Western Hemisphere and severely disrupt native peoples and their habitats. California's frontiers were eventually reached and breached by these alien forces that arrived in the form of European peoples and the organisms that accompanied, and often preceded, them. California's relative isolation and its physical geography proved insufficient as protection against these disruptive colonial invaders. Nevertheless, California's remote position and unique physical and cultural geography would greatly influence the timing, nature, and severity of the foreign onslaught. California—because of its distance from the initial European colonial emphasis in the Caribbean and Mesoamerica—was spared for 277 years the ravages of change that accompanied the founding of missions, presidios, and pueblos.

Despite this chronological respite from direct settlement, California was anything but an island of immunity from colonial influence during this interim. Sweeping ahead of the European settlers in space and time were powerful microscopic seeds of environmental and cultural change. Long before the foundations of Mission San Diego were established in 1769, a host of Old World (i.e., Europe, Asia, Africa) pathogens traveled along terrestrial and maritime pathways to penetrate California. These microbes were the first among a variety of alien processes that with time all but destroyed the intricate environmental accommodation that

Although the magnificent vista of Mount Tamalpais painted about 1870 by the American artist Gilbert Munger suggests a virginal landscape, it had in fact been managed and altered in various ways over the centuries. Long before European colonization, California Indians began to shape the natural world to their advantage through pruning, tilling, weeding, and especially burning. Their alteration of the environment was minor in comparison to that effected by the Hispanic invaders, however, who introduced plants, livestock, and land-use practices that radically transformed parts of California. *Courtesy anonymous collector.*

had evolved among the region's diverse assemblage of environments and peoples. Later, in 1769, Gaspar de Portolá and subsequent colonizers would augment these parasitic intruders with even more new germs and foreign organisms. Included among these later arrivals were the domesticated plants and animals that sustained the foreign invaders and the weeds and pests that plagued them. All these alien species would find inviting habitats somewhere within the complex and varied landscapes of California.

Also arriving with early settlers and their newly introduced species, was a cultural retinue of attitudes, values, and perceptions that had been formulated in the Old World and later modified in Latin America. Developed in a foreign land and ecological setting, these outlooks proved to be important companions of conquest and environmental change in California. Together, these invasive peoples, cultures, germs, plants, and animals would quickly and forever disrupt the evolutionary processes that had governed life and land in California since the end of the Ice Age, or Pleistocene Epoch. The colonial transformations of portions of California's environment were greater and more rapid than in most other New World continental locations.[1] The flora, fauna, and people that had composed the region's native life layer prior to 1492 were mostly unique to the New World and inordinately susceptible and vulnerable to the inadvertent and purposeful importation of Old World life forms and lifeways that created revolutionary environmental changes in California prior to 1848.

OLD WORLD VERSUS THE NEW WORLD:
THE GEOGRAPHY OF BIOLOGICAL INEQUALITY

> If a species evolves a superior adaptation to a given environment on one land mass, it may outcompete native organisms once it is transported to analogous ecosystems overseas.
>
> —Mark A. Blumler,
> "Invasion and Transformation of California's Valley Grassland," 1995

The profound consequences that Old World life forms and lifeways had on California prior to 1848 were in part functions of contrasting environmental and cultural settings. The Eastern and Western hemispheres, with their differing geographic attributes and particular evolutionary histories, produced a set of superior adaptations for the invading species, and crucial disadvantages for the colonized native species in California.[2] Owing to geographic chance, Old World landscapes generated a host of weeds that were not only capable of surviving transoceanic voyages but also were, on arrival in California, more competitive than indigenous species. Similarly, the microbial realm favored the Eastern Hemisphere, and the impacts of parasitic exchange were overwhelmingly more destructive to the New World than to the Old. As a whole, the effects of this geographic dichotomy were unidirectional in favor of the invader, and they were crucial to the environmental conquest of California.

The European adventurers departed from their lands of origin with biological advantages that were important weapons of imperialism. The geography of their Old World homeland and its long history of human occupation were instrumental to this unique biological inventory. Geographically, the Old World was blessed with the same basic range of tropical to arctic ecosystems as was the New World. However, most Old World ecosystems extended longitudinally over wider continental areas that offered greater climatic and ecological extremes for the adaptation of life forms. The land area was also extensive enough that environments such as Mediterranean ecosystems were able to withstand the extreme climatic fluctuations associated with the Ice Age. Of special significance was the geographical opportunity for biological interaction within and across these varied ecosystems. The crossroads of Africa,

Asia, and Europe, in particular, heightened the opportunities for long-term biological intercourse between these continents and enhanced the diversity and adaptive potential of Old World flora and fauna.

Moreover, for over one hundred thousand years, modern humans had evolved within this diverse Old World context. By the Neolithic period (ca. 10,000 B.C.), some Old World peoples had invented farming and were domesticating selected plants and animals, which, in turn, induced substantial biological and cultural changes.[3] The ensuing close and intimate association among humans, and especially their contact with domesticated animals, provided the catalyst for the development of deleterious parasites like smallpox, influenza, and measles. Old World peoples certainly suffered the epidemiological consequences of these microbial afflictions; however, by the eve of the European voyages of discovery, they were thoroughly experienced with these diseases and had acquired partial immunities to many of them.

In contrast, the relative potential for evolutionary adaptation and interaction of species in California and the Western Hemisphere in general was restricted by geography. New World continental ecosystems were longitudinally narrower and more isolated from one another by constricting land masses, such as the Isthmus of Panama. California was particularly insulated by its position on the western edge of a continent and by its eastern mountain and desert barriers. Thus, the enormous variety of plants and animals that did evolve in California were at a disadvantage when confronted with the older and more competitive species engendered in Old World habitats.

The history of humanity in the Western Hemisphere was also substantially different from that of the Old World, and this divergence had important bearing on the colonial transformations of California. The first peopling of the Western Hemisphere occurred long after their ancestors in the Old World had emerged, but prior to the evolution of the deadly parasites thought to be associated with the processes of domestication. In addition, the New World pioneers migrated in small groups through frozen Siberian landscapes that eliminated many of the Old World parasites that may have plagued them before they entered the Americas.[4] Eventually, some of the offspring of these immigrants also invented farming (in Mesoamerica and South America), but unlike their distant Old World ancestors, they domesticated very few animals and thus generated fewer deadly parasites. The Pre-Columbian inhabitants of California were far from disease-free, but owing to their ancestors' initial migratory and domestication histories, their parasitic tormentors were mild in comparison to the microbial destroyers that had evolved in the Old World.[5] Once these germs broke the bonds of their Old World habitat, as colonial stowaways, they proved disastrous to the Indians of California and their environment.

THE MAKING OF CALIFORNIA'S PRE-COLUMBIAN
LANDSCAPES AND ENVIRONMENTAL PERCEPTIONS

> The extremely rich, diverse, and apparently "wild" landscape that so impressed
> Europeans at the time of contact—and which traditionally has been viewed as
> a "natural, untrammeled wilderness" ever since—was to some extent actually a
> product of (and more importantly upon) [*sic*] deliberate human intervention.
> —Thomas C. Blackburn and M. Kat Anderson, *Before the Wilderness*, 1993

The early Spanish settlers failed to recognize and understand the critical role native
peoples played in fashioning their environments. Their European cultural heritage
had imbued the colonial immigrants with a sense of separation from the nonhuman
world and a certainty of their spiritual and economic sovereignty over all earthly
habitats and the non-Christians who inhabited them.[6] They failed either to recognize or to understand the ecological importance of people who were indelibly fused
culturally and spiritually to the land. This failure led to serious misconceptions and
tremendous environmental disruption.[7]

The early Hispanic settlers, and later the Americans (i.e., United States residents) who came to California, shared this European heritage and concluded that
California was a pristine "wilderness" shaped entirely by the hand of God. In their
minds they had discovered a "wild" landscape that was occupied only by a simple
people who effortlessly gathered the bounty of God's cornucopia and who were de-
serving candidates for acculturation.[8] Fortified by these assumptions and the motivations of empire, the Spaniards set out initially to improve this wilderness with the
preferred life forms and lifeways of their homelands. These colonial preferences and
misconceptions are aptly illustrated by the seventeenth-century naturalist Berabé
Cobo, who stated about the New World that "all the regions of the globe have contributed their fruits and abundance to adorn and enrich this quarter of the world,
which we Spaniards found so poor and destitute of the plants and animals most necessary to nourish and give service to mankind."[9]

The perceptions of the Europeans and the early Americans who succeeded them
were inaccurate to say the least. In reality, the physical surface and biological composition of California prior to 1492 was anything but a divinely crafted wilderness.
Instead of representing a Garden of Eden, it was, in fact, more of a garden of human
artifice, fashioned as much by human ingenuity as by divine intervention. In actu-
ality, in the words of Theodora Kroeber and Robert Heizer, "the white invaders
wrested from [the California Indians] a garden, not the wilderness it salved their
conscience to call it."[10] Through an intimate association that had matured over
thousands of years, the Indians of California had learned to interact with the land,
water, and life of nearly every portion of the state's non-human heritage. These

Chulamni hunters stalk their prey on the shores of San Francisco Bay in a lithograph
taken from a watercolor by the Russian artist Louis Choris, who in 1816 spent a month
here. Relying on animals for raw materials as well as for food, California Indians had an
enormous impact on faunal populations—especially those of large mammals, which were
significantly overhunted—until the natives' own numbers were reduced by protohistoric
and colonial plagues. From Louis Choris, *Voyage pittoresque autour du monde* (Paris, 1822).
Courtesy California Historical Society, FN-30511.

peoples for the most part were not farmers so much as domesticators, and in a number of important respects all had domesticated portions of their habitat in order to
induce greater subsistence.[11] Instead of relying on the axe, rake, or plow, they skillfully learned to prune, till, coppice, transplant, and burn California's vegetation in order to encourage a greater abundance of plant and animal foods and materials. The
land yielded its bounty to the ingenuity of native intervention and was substantially transformed in the process.[12]

The deliberate modification of the physical world by California's Pre-Columbian
peoples lasted for thousands of years and evolved into a relationship of accommodation. During the process, numerous habitats and species of plants became relatively dependent on human disturbance for maintenance, and the people, in turn, re-

lied on this plenitude and the animals it nurtured.[13] In essence, the Indians had merged with non-human processes and their sustained involvement was crucial to ecological stability.

At times the intense intervention in non-human processes by Indians resulted in depletions of important resources, especially the larger animals. The Indians hunted an impressive inventory of animals in California solely for survival. By late Pre-Columbian times, many of the larger species of animals were constrained demographically and spatially by the subsistence requirements of the native dwellers. Large game animals survived, but as marginal components of the landscape and the human diet. Unlike the disruptive consequences of colonial exploitation, however, the late Pre-Columbian depletions of certain animals and plant communities were not erosive to overall environmental health.[14] In all likelihood then, the California that Cabrillo and his fellow voyagers encountered in 1542 and 1543 was thoroughly modified, but the resource base remained virtually intact.[15]

The union of the human and non-human worlds in California was consciously recognized by all Indian peoples, and the reality was indelibly integrated into their world view.[16] To the California Indian, the material and human world shared an equal spiritual partnership "where abundance came with thrift and restraint—but also as a consequence of human disturbance."[17] The Indians recognized that the non-human world required their perpetual involvement to insure stability and order; however, the colonial invaders were oblivious to this dynamic relationship. The result was inadvertent and forced separation of the Indian from California's non-human world, and the initiation of irrevocable environmental disorder.

CALIFORNIA'S VULNERABLE ENVIRONMENTAL LINCHPINS AND ECOSYSTEMS

> Native Americans were the ultimate keystone species, and their removal
> has completely altered ecosystems, not only in the Intermountain West but
> throughout North America.
> —Charles E. Kay, "Aboriginal Overkill and Native Burning," 1995

California's humanized ecologies and landscapes proved inordinately vulnerable to the ecological repercussions of alien conquest. In comparison with most other continental regions of the Americas, California proved exceptionally susceptible and vulnerable to the organisms and cultural practices that were naturalized in the similar ecosystems found in Mediterranean and Near Eastern realms. Owing to the region's analogous physical setting and unique cultural susceptibility, the environmental responses to colonialism in California were more immediate and profound.

Due to their numbers and cultural ability to intensely modify California's physical world, the Indians were the most important organisms in California's Pre-Columbian ecology. They were the "keystone" species who were most responsible for structuring the landscapes of California and the linchpins on which the stability of the ecosystem depended.[18] The ability of the California Indians to sustain themselves and their role as the keystone species was predicated on maintaining their territorial sovereignty, high populations, traditional land-use practices, and religions founded in ecological equity. A change in any one or all of these crucial determinants would result in ecological imbalance and extreme disruption. Post-Columbian developments revealed the vulnerability of these human/environmental determinants and led rapidly to their virtual annihilation.

The exceptional rapidity and magnitude of the environmental changes wrought by colonialism were also conditioned by the nature of Pre-Columbian landscapes in California and their similarity to the Old World homelands of the colonists. It required more than 250 years of colonial expansion in North America before the Spaniards settled a land as similar to their original Mediterranean homeland as California was, with its climate of winter rainfall and summer drought and its analogous ecologies. As a consequence, no other colonial ecosystem of its size was more receptive to the biological weapons of conquest spawned in Europe's Mediterranean world. The greater adaptability of species originating in the more extreme and interactive Old World ecosystems provided ideal opportunities for them to spread rapidly and widely in this analogous environment.

The effects of the highly competitive Old World species were compounded by the extent of environmental changes the Indians had achieved before the colonial period. As a result of the extraordinary numbers and ingenuity of Indian peoples, California was one of the most altered precolonial landscapes in the Americas. The impact and magnitude of colonial disruptions thus were greater than if the land had been truly pristine.

PORTENTS OF PATHOGENS AND WEEDS
FROM CALIFORNIA'S PROTOHISTORIC PERIOD

> Old world disease did spread in advance of the mission frontier, destroying or altering the fabric of Indian society prior to sustained contact with Spaniards.
> —Daniel T. Reff, "Contact Shock in Northwestern New Spain," 1992

It is not clear precisely when California began to experience foreign-induced changes to its environment and native peoples. Conventional wisdom has it that colonial disruptions were initiated when the first Spanish mission was established at San Diego in 1769. Prior to that time, many authorities maintain, California was considered demographically and ecologically free of Old World influence and diseases.[19] The dearth of written accounts of California's long protohistoric period from 1519 to 1769, the region's late colonial occupation, and incorrect perceptions of the region's physical isolation have sustained this traditional view. Indeed, to this day, colonial images of California as an "island" persist in modern historical analysis. Moreover, the state's arid and topographic barriers have been perceived, incorrectly, as a *cordon sanitaire* against exotic contagion. Finally, the reluctance by some scholars to recognize the true importance of disease in the evolution of history has tempered inquiry into the possibilities of pre-mission pestilence in California. Existing archaeological and ethnographic materials derived from California's protohistoric period, therefore, have often been interpreted according to these traditional mindsets, thus preempting further research specifically devoted to the question of pre-mission disease. As a consequence, the prevailing attitude regarding California prior to 1769 is typified by the comment, "In California, nothing changed."[20]

The still-common notion that California remained isolated and aboriginally pristine before 1769 is becoming less tenable in light of epidemiological studies elsewhere in the Western Hemisphere. The view that exotic disease preceded settlement throughout the Western Hemisphere is emerging as more viable. In this context, if California's protohistory were indeed unchanged despite its proximity to disease sources and innate susceptibility, the region would have proved utterly anomalous to all the conditions governing colonial disease diffusion in the Western Hemisphere.[21]

The prospect that California somehow escaped exotic infestation for the 250 years of its protohistoric period is doubtful for a number of reasons. Native Californians were known to have been in contact with the indigenous human and nonhuman vectors—such as lice, mosquitoes, and fleas—inhabiting the diseased lands to the south and southeast. Furthermore, California natives were offered periodic opportunities for direct contamination from Europeans during visitations by Cabrillo, Drake, and Vizcaíno, as well as many other explorers. In light of general colonial epidemiological history, it would have been miraculous had these encounters occurred without the introduction of Old World bacteria and viruses into California.[22] Theoretically, the entry of just one episode of parasitic infection into California would have crippled severely the delicate environmental equation that hinged on the Indian as the keystone species.[23]

The delicate environmental balance that was maintained by Native American land-use practices was further disrupted by the early introduction of non-native species of weeds and grasses. It is not unreasonable to assume that some of the exploratory voyages along the coast of California, such as those of Cabrillo in 1542–1543 or Vizcaíno in 1602–1603, may have disseminated not only parasites but also alien seeds. Alien grasses, for example, seemed to have taken root sometime before the initial mission construction at San Diego in 1769. Specimens of exotic grasses (e.g. curly dock, red stem, and prickly sow thistle) have been found in the adobe bricks of some of the earliest missions and uncovered from excavations that predate 1769. The findings have been interpreted by some scholars as signifying a pre-mission presence of Mediterranean annuals in California.[24]

The invasive advantages of exotic weeds, in combination with the depletion of the California Indians by virulent disease, may account for the pre-mission colonizing success of these Old World flora. The composition and spatial properties of native grasses, sedges, herbs, and forbs were in large measure determined by native land-use measures, especially the intentional applications of fire. Many of the perennial bunchgrasses, for example, require periodic disturbances, such as burning, to grow vigorously and to reproduce competitively.[25] An interruption of these management procedures through the destruction of Indians by exotic contagion would have rendered the native grasslands more susceptible to encroachment and replacement by non-native weeds.[26]

The death of large numbers of Indians as a result of precolonial plagues also unleashed enormous imbalances among the animal communities. Recent findings challenge the misconception that has governed the conventional thinking about California's Pre-Columbian large-game inventory. The prevailing assumption was based on the enormous concentrations of both terrestrial and marine mammals that were documented for the colonial and early American periods (i.e., after 1848). This observed and documented menagerie was interpreted as a direct reflection of the Pre-Columbian landscape.[27] The supposition that Indians in California exploited large mammals without significantly reducing their range or numbers supported and reinforced this assumption.[28]

A revised view based on faunal analysis in western environments and recent archaeological evidence derived from within California reveals that the relationship between the Indians and large game differed significantly from the conventional wisdom.[29] Indeed, archaeological findings in California suggest that, like most Native Americans, the California Indians had a tremendous effect on the range and numbers of large game animals. As a result of human predation, the large marine and terrestrial mammals had been reduced to minor importance as nutritional sources for the natives during the centuries leading up to the colonial era.[30]

Events in California during the 250 years preceding missionization were destined to alter the Pre-Columbian equation between mammals and their human predators. The reported sightings by early explorers and settlers of abundant wild game reflect an already altered environment conditioned by precolonial impact. Juan Sebastián Vizcaíno's report that "there is much wild game, such as harts, like young bulls, deer, buffalo, very large bears, rabbits, hares, and many other animals" in the vicinity of Monterey in 1602 is typical of the observations recorded by nearly all visitors to California during the protohistoric period.[31] The superabundance of game also welcomed the first European settlers in 1769 and 1770. Various members of the

Portolá expedition reported numerous concentrations of large game (especially antelope, deer, and bears) throughout their journey. Indicative is the diary of Miguel Costanso, who saw "many herds of antelopes," and that of Fray Francisco Palóu, which noted "many deer."[32] According to the archaeological record and the demonstrated precedent in other North American locations, these sightings would have been unusual before the time of Columbus.

The explanation for the unusual presence of large game animals, prior to and after the time of missionization, is not surprising. Their populations simply irrupted as their chief predator, the California Indians, were reduced by protohistoric plague. Furthermore, colonial agencies, before and after 1769, dramatically reduced the constricting influence of the Indians on the animals, and their numbers continued to expand rapidly to unnatural proportions. In essence, the same colonial agencies that had proven so disastrous to the Indians provided a fertile setting for the nearly unfettered expansion of their former prey.

What effects the explosion in mammals may have had on flora and, in turn, what the impacts of introduced grasses had on animal life, during this early period, is difficult to discern. We do know, however, that the cultural and ecological changes initiated prior to 1769 in California were only the beginning. A dramatic upsurge in degree and type of environmental alteration would accompany foreign settlement after 1769.

HISPANIC SETTLEMENT AND HABITAT IMBALANCES: 1769–1848

> The successful exploitation of the New World by these people depended on their ability to "Europeanize" the flora and fauna of the New World.
> —Alfred L. Crosby, *The Columbian Exchange*, 1972

> From the plain we entered a hilly country, covered to the summits of the elevations with wild oats.
> —Edwin Bryant, *What I Saw in California*, 1848

The nature and degree of the environmental changes that were colonially induced in California prior to 1769 remain only vaguely understood. It is certain, however, that the precolonial disruptions were accomplished indirectly, without the permanent presence of the Spanish or their domesticated plants and animals. This would all change in 1769, when the floodgate of empire opened California to foreign settlement. The inadvertent arrival of pathogens, pests, and weeds combined with the purposeful introductions accompanying settlement to vastly accelerate environmental change.[33] For the first time, Old World species of both domestic livestock and crops

A Franciscan waters a garden of exotic flora at Mission Santa Barbara, 1892. Following Spanish settlement, the landscape of coastal California underwent an astounding metamorphosis, as introduced plants overwhelmed native perennials and annuals in much the same manner that the Spanish conquerors overwhelmed the native peoples. Within a generation or so, the indigenous grasses had largely given way to wild oats, mustard, and other invasive Mediterranean species. *Courtesy California Historical Society, FN-30505.*

were intentionally introduced, at the same time as the opportunities for the accidental entry of other organisms considerably expanded.[34] More crucial as a bridgehead for environmental transformation was the rapid colonial acculturation of the coastal Indians and the reduction of their population. The enforced changes in Indian lifestyles and their shrinking numbers progressively weakened their traditional relationship with California's physical world.[35] Once this reciprocal bond was disturbed, the environment became even more susceptible to the invasion and rapid establishment of the newly introduced flora and fauna.

The most immediate and widespread of the colonial impacts occurred within plant and animal communities.[36] These alterations were geographically most intense in the coastal one-sixth of California that fell under direct Spanish and later Mexican rule. Nonetheless, the Indians and landscapes lying beyond the northern and eastern frontiers of Hispanic control were also profoundly altered. The disruptions were transported to the interior by a variety of agents. Periodic Hispanic ex-

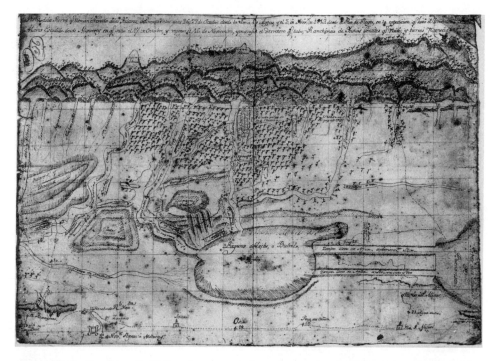

A map of the San Joaquin Valley, from approximately present-day Merced to Bakersfield,
prepared by Lieutenant José María Estudillo, who in 1819 entered the Tulare Lake
Basin by way of Mission San Miguel, *lower right,* to subdue uprisings among the Yokuts.
Spanish incursions into the interior of the province, which began in the early 1770s,
introduced alien pathogens, seeds, pests, and domestic animals that had far-reaching
consequences for the land and its people. *Courtesy Bancroft Library.*

peditions and parties of British and American trappers inadvertently disseminated
germs and forcefully removed or killed thousands of valley Indians. In addition,
runaway missionized Indians who found refuge in the interior often brought deadly
germs, exotic plants and animals, and new economic practices with them. Virulent
pathogens also arrived with nonhuman vectors such as mosquitoes to claim their human and, through association, environmental toll. Soon after 1769, feral livestock
found their way to these frontier lands or were abducted from the coast and integrated into the Indian economies of the Central Valley and elsewhere. All these
processes unleashed environmental changes of great, though unsystematically documented, magnitude.[37]

The physical and cultural manifestations of direct colonization set the stage for a
renewed surge of environmental modification that would encompass all of California. The most dramatic alterations anywhere in continental America occurred within
California's grasslands. Native grass species were virtually overwhelmed by the rad-

ical transformations in their environment.[38] In the southern two-thirds of California that was environmentally similar to the lands where they had originally spawned,
introduced weeds took root, flourished, and aggressively replaced native grasses.
Having evolved over a longer period in more extreme Mediterranean and Near
Eastern environments, the weeds—principally Mediterranean annuals—were simply better suited and more adaptive than many of the indigenous species to conditions in California.[39]

The rapid invasion by exotic species and replacement of native grasses was ensured
by a number of colonial conditions. Already at a biological disadvantage, the native
grasses were also forced to compete in an atmosphere marked by a severed relationship with the Indians of California and the encounter with vast new herds of domestic livestock and indigenous game. The majority of the invasive weeds had
evolved mutually with domestic livestock in the Old World, where they were first
domesticated. The native perennials and annuals, however, had evolved in a non-
pastoral setting and therefore were now at a biological disadvantage, especially when
grazing and periodic drought combined to weaken their competitive abilities.[40]

Being favored by inherent biological traits and colonially inspired conditions, the
exotic annuals spread like wildfire through California's grasslands. Species of Old
World annuals such as wild oats, ripgut, mustard, and filaree quickly became dominant near the coastal missions and began to spread inland.[41] Testifying to this remarkable dissemination are the frequent notations of exotic grasses (mostly wild
oats) encountered in the annals of early Americans who were exploring the interior
of California during the 1830s and 1840s. Zenas Leonard's account that "our course
lay through a large prairie covered with wild oats" during his party's transit of the
San Joaquin Valley in 1833 is typical of these sightings.[42] More evidence of the rapid
spread and preponderance of exotic species in some regions was their early integration into the diet of some interior Indians.[43]

The replacement of native grassland species by invasive flora seems to have occurred first on the south and central coasts and then spread into the San Joaquin Valley. By the time of the Gold Rush, the invasive Mediterranean annuals were pene-
trating the Sacramento Valley and the coast north of San Francisco. The momentum
of replacement initiated in the colonial era would carry over into the twentieth century and eventually Europeanize some 50 to 90 percent of California's grasslands.[44]

Paralleling the colonial transformation of the grasslands were more subtle but
profound alterations involving nearly every California habitat. These changes were
determined more by the destruction of Indian lifeways than by the appearance of aggressive foreign species. The weakening of the natives' function as keystone species,
because of murder, disease, and relocation, was the catalyst for most habitat modifications. The diverse mosaic of landscapes that had been structured and maintained
by native practices, especially the use of fire, slowly and progressively adjusted to the

Indians' removal from the ecological equation. In general, each major habitat responded by becoming more uniform in pattern and by losing some of the human-induced diversity.[45]

The habitat transitions triggered by colonial processes were incremental, but incessant. Brush and woods began to expand at the expense of grasses and open landscapes on the coast and in the interior. Chaparral communities adjusted to less frequent fires with encroachments onto the grasslands of the coastal valleys and the foothills of the Sierra Nevada.[46] The once-open understories of the coastal oak forests and the oak-grass woodlands cloaking the eastern margins of the Central Valley became tangled with the unmanaged growth of underbrush.[47] Similarly, at higher elevations where the open coniferous forests of the Coast Ranges and Sierra Nevada had once flourished, their fire-cleansed understories became crowded with brush, saplings, and litter.[48] These altered habitats would greet the American pioneers and be defined by them as the primordial condition of California's "wilderness." The tangled undergrowth and expanding woods also would impede the progress of Manifest Destiny and later threaten American lives and property with conflagrations.

Within each ecosystem, a gradual decline in the number, range, and diversity of many native species and habitats occurred when Indian intervention ceased. Grass species that are fire-dependent and were once important nutritional components of coastal Indians, such as chia and red maids, began to disappear, as did numerous varieties of useful bunchgrasses and other herbaceous plants.[49] Moreover, the vitality and productivity of many surviving species suffered from species-competition, microorganisms, and parasites that were no longer held in check by fire.[50]

Prior to colonial disruptions, many Indian groups intentionally worked to maintain a cover of vegetation on the drier slopes of habitats in southern California. Without their assistance, semi-arid landscapes often remained barren and exposed to the elements for longer periods after 1769. Unregulated livestock grazing and the colonial expansion of chaparral contributed to increased exposure and barrenness.[51] A representative and documented example of an early casualty of colonially induced erosion occurred on the west side of the San Joaquin Valley adjacent to the El Camino Viejo (i.e., the Los Angeles road). The once-rounded gulches that Spanish citizens observed on their treks between Los Angeles and San Francisco became steeply banked and eroded by the beginning of the American period.[52]

The purposeful addition of Old World animals and the unintended introduction of organisms into California also contributed to the alteration of vegetational patterns and of the land itself. The effects of the inadvertent importation and spread of exotic forms of microorganisms, insects, and vermin changed a variety of environmental components, particularly around the coastal settlements. These accidental introductions and their consequences would become more profound and evident during the American period, but the initial influence of domestic livestock would prove an immediate and powerful force in the new colonial ecology.

PROLIFERATION OF COLONIAL LIVESTOCK: 1769–1848

> They have stocked the country with such multitudes of cattle, horses, and other useful animals, that they have no longer the power to remove or destroy them.
> —William Shaler, *Journal of a Voyage between China and the North Western Coast of America Made in 1804,* 1935

With the exception of the transformation of the grasslands, most botanical adjustments to colonial interventions were gradual and were largely imperceptible until well into the American period. The general pattern of change experienced in the faunal communities of California was roughly parallel. Old World animals invaded numerous habitats, and indigenous animals experienced imbalances and adjustments. However, the pace of change was dramatically different from that of the vegetational community, and notice was immediate and unavoidable. Indeed, because of the disruptions unleashed by Hispanic settlement and faunal reproductive biology, some animal populations virtually exploded and quickly reached numbers and concentrations probably not achieved since the end of the Pleistocene Epoch.

The settlement of California required domestic animals for transport, policing, and sustenance. Fernando de Rivera y Moncada's overland expedition from Baja California in 1769, along with bringing general supplies, introduced 187 mules, 53 horses, and 204 head of cattle.[53] This was the first act in a process that would lead to the explosive numerical growth and spread of Old World animals. The agencies that were primarily responsible for this phenomenal growth and dispersal were the Hispanic settlement institutions, aided by the Indians themselves.

The continued importation and reproduction of domestic animals during the Spanish period (1769–1822) markedly increased the size and diversity of the inventories of mission livestock, eventually to include sheep, goats, pigs, and poultry. Official Spanish prohibitions against foreign trade and the constraints on private land concessions limited livestock expansion during the initial period. However, after 1822, new policies fostered by independent Mexico produced a surge in mission livestock numbers to take advantage of the burgeoning international trade in hides and tallow. Also, the eventual granting of approximately eight hundred ranchos by the late 1840s to Mexicans and foreigners alike greatly assisted in the dispersal of livestock to the Central Valley and other interior environments.[54]

The Indians contributed to the dispersal of livestock by rapidly incorporating them into their cultural and economic inventories. Indeed, the wholesale reorientation to the consumption of introduced animals became an essential ingredient for native survival.[55] This adaptation to eating livestock was in large measure necessary, owing to the environmental tumult triggered by colonialism and, in particular, the livestock's consumption of the grasses, nuts, and roots that the Indians had traditionally relied on for sustenance.[56]

Large cultural and ecological modifications ensued as a consequence of the relationship between the California Indians and livestock during the colonial period. The growing reliance on and preference for livestock, particularly by the non-mission Indians of the Central Valley and Sierran foothills, stimulated a quest for additional supplies. By the 1830s the natives' preferred method of acquisition was to raid the coastal settlements and ranchos and drive the livestock deep into the interior.[57] In addition to further aggravating the hostilities between the Indians and the coastal colonial settlers, this behavior also increased the degree and extent of environmental disruption. Valley Yokuts, and others, intentionally increased the concentrations of livestock in their own region and also served as middlemen for the trade in livestock with adjoining Indians, American horse traders, and New Mexican rustlers arriving from east of the Tehachapis.[58] As an outcome of the various agencies of dispersal, including feral migrations by cattle and horses in particular, by the time of the Gold Rush, Old World livestock was distributed over considerable portions of California. Regions in 1848 that were still mostly devoid of livestock were the northern portions of the coast and interior, the far eastern deserts, and the mountainous regions on the coast and in the interior, where predators such as lions and grizzly bears were numerous.[59]

The presence of enormous numbers of Old World livestock in California during the colonial era affected the state's ecosystems directly through grazing pressure and indirectly by provoking radical alterations in native land-use practices. In addition to accelerating the invasion of exotic grasses, livestock introduction forced nearly every plant community in affected areas to adjust to this new form of disturbance. In periods of drought, the forage depletion by excessive stock was often severe enough to threaten the livelihoods of even the colonials, who were forced to undertake the organized slaughter of tens of thousands of animals in attempts to preserve the range.[60]

Despite the toll taken by slaughter and drought, domestic and feral livestock continued to proliferate, and, combined with expanding numbers of native ungulates, they began to reshape the land itself. By the Gold Rush of 1848, the hills of southern California were sculptured with tier upon tier of terrace-like trails, and the plain of the Central Valley was in the words of one observer "furrowed with numerous deep trails, made by the droves of wild horses, elk, deer, and antelope."[61] The exposure of barren earth, where none had existed before, assisted in the colonial invasion of alien plants and drove the final nail into the coffin of Indian land-use practices that had fashioned the precolonial environment.

Native animal species were also forced to adapt to the new competitive environment on the range and to the floral disruptions created by hundreds of thousands of livestock. The exact consequences prior to 1848 are difficult to discern, but the processes of change attributable to livestock were set in motion and would eventually prove devastating to a number of native Californian habitats. The introduction

Cattle fill the landscape in an 1877 painting of a roundup on a southern California rancho by the English-born artist James Walker. Spanish colonizers brought livestock with them up from Mexico, the beginnings of the great herds that grazed the mission lands and, later, the vast ranchos that arose after secularization. Numbering in the hundreds of thousands by the 1840s, cattle not only shaped the economy and culture of provincial California, but played a profound role in altering native floral and faunal communities. *Courtesy California Historical Society; gift of Mr. and Mrs. Reginald Walker.*

of goats onto Santa Catalina Island in 1827 is a case in point. The habitat disturbance caused by these goats prior to 1848 is undetermined; however, their presence has been largely responsible for denuding much of the island, and primarily credited for the contemporary tally of forty-eight extinct native animal and plant species.[62]

A PROFUSE COLONIAL MENAGERIE: 1769–1848

> The deer, antelope and noble elk . . . were numerous beyond all parallel. In herds of many hundreds, they might be met, so tame that they would hardly move to open the way for the traveler to pass.
>
> —George C. Yount, quoted in Charles L. Camp, "The Chronicles of George C. Yount," 1923

The spectacular rise in the numbers and wide dispersal of Old World animals in California during the colonial era was matched by an irruption in the numbers of native game. Assessment of the colonial effects on some groups of animals such as insects, birds, and reptiles remains speculative, although considerably more is known about the consequences to certain aquatic and terrestrial game species. The great transformations that characterized the colonial era created a favorable environment for the expansion in numbers and territory of those animals that had once been targeted and depleted by Indian predation. The ecological imbalances and surge in the numbers of native animals triggered by the destruction of the Indians was also abetted by the presence of Old World animals. The combination of a vanishing Indian population and the widespread introduction and distribution of exotic fauna furnished a fecund environment where some species of animals flourished in numbers probably unknown in California since the Pleistocene Epoch.

Prior to the Columbian landfall, California harbored hundreds of thousands of Indians who possessed the ingenuity to restructure the faunal setting according to their needs. By the end of the colonial era in early 1848 and before the Gold Rush, largely because of virulent new diseases, California was relatively devoid of human predators. Indeed, the area supported fewer humans (perhaps 70,000 to 100,000) than at any time during the preceding millennium or two.[63] In contrast, the entry of humans from foreign lands during the same period was minimal in comparison and failed to balance the losses of more than 200,000 population experienced by the Indians. Indeed, by early 1848, colonialism in California had accounted for only about 7,000 Hispanic settlers and, at most, a few thousand additional foreign residents.[64] These settlers, especially in light of their land-use practices, did not fill the environmental niche of chief predator that had once been completely occupied by Indians. Instead, the colonial peoples relied on an alien economy that emphasized domesticated animals and plants for sustenance and, with the exception of some marine mammals, practically ignored the native species of game. Moreover, a substantial proportion of the surviving Indians diverted much of their attention from the traditional hunting of native species to the harvesting of Old World livestock, which further reduced the predation pressure on native game species.

Despite the range competition by livestock, and the associated habitat disruptions by colonialism in general, native game quickly expanded to extraordinary numerical heights. The aquatic and terrestrial landscapes of California were sufficiently lush to support millions of both native and Old World animals in the absence of traditional levels of predation. Ungulates such as deer, antelope, and elk also readily consumed the Mediterranean annual grasses that had spread among California's grasslands during the colonial period. These same grasses also provided the nutritional impetus for an explosion of rodent populations. Not only did rodents, such as ground squirrels, relish the foreign annuals, but they also preyed on the crops of wheat and barley introduced by the missionaries. This colonial by-product resulted in an environmental backlash that the settlers came to regret.[65]

An enormous herd of elk cross the Carquinez Strait in an illustration drawn by Emanuel Wyttenbach at the end of the nineteenth century under the direction of William Heath Davis. In his reminiscences, Davis recalled seeing as many as three thousand of the animals at a time crossing from Mare Island to the mainland in the early 1840s. Together with deer and antelope, elk populations rose rapidly in the colonial and provincial periods as their primary predator, Indians, declined. From William Heath Davis, *Seventy-Five Years in California* (San Francisco, 1929). *Courtesy California Historical Society, FN-30528.*

Like many of the Indians who shared their habitat, some of the larger mammals preyed on the nearly limitless supply of colonial livestock. The most notorious species among the carnivores that integrated the Old World livestock into their larder was the grizzly bear. With the chief predator, the Indians, undergoing a steep demographic decline during the colonial period, grizzly bears rebounded to fill this role and found their nutritional needs supplemented by the relatively easy pickings of Old World livestock. The colonial slaughter of thousands of livestock, especially after 1822 for the hide-and-tallow trade, significantly enhanced the comestibles of the grizzlies, which according to one observer "used to come by night to the ravines near the slaughter-corral where the refuse was thrown by the butcher.[66]

The colonial expansion in the number of grizzlies and their taste for domesticated livestock became a hindrance to settler and Indian alike. As late as the 1790s, missionaries were concerned about the livestock depletions caused by the depredations of grizzly bears and other predators. By the 1820s, however, the settlers' economic concerns diminished because the livestock were so plentiful that they could be slaughtered by colonials, Indians, and bears during most periods without significantly decreasing their abundance.[67]

The economic concerns presented by the growing number of grizzlies may have been redressed for the settlers by the superabundance of livestock, but grizzlies continued to menace the physical and economic health of the remaining California Indians. Without their traditional numbers and land-use practices, the surviving Indians were unable to reestablish a dominant relationship with the bears and increasingly fell victim of their attacks. The disruptions to the Indians' traditional food supply by domestic and feral livestock were also compounded because grizzly bears competed with humans for some of their most important resources. The problem was noted in 1841 by T. R. Peale, who observed that "the Indians and bear . . . thrash down the acorns, which is almost as effectively done by one as by the other."[68]

Documentation is unavailable, but it is reasonable to assume that overall numbers of game probably continued to rise during the colonial period as human numbers diminished within California. The rise in numbers was most pronounced in those areas of the coast and Central Valley that once nurtured the greatest concentrations of Pre-Columbian peoples.[69] Where Indian concentrations remained relatively high during the colonial period, game tended to continue to be more scarce. Documentation of this relationship is provided by Zenas Leonard, who entered the Tulare Lake Basin in 1834 and found that "here game is very scarce, owing to the numerous swarms of Indians scattered along in every direction."[70] Likewise, where Indian numbers fell precipitously, the presence of game was inordinately bountiful. George C. Yount also noted the correlation in 1833, when he visited the vicinity of present-day Benicia after a virulent epidemic of malaria. "The rivers were literally crowded with salmon, which, since the pestilence had swept away the Indians, no one disturbed."[71]

The new colonial settlers and foreign visitors harvested some of the aquatic and terrestrial game species and caused some depletion of selected species on a regional basis.[72] Despite these specific reductions, the overall presence of native game animals progressively increased and peaked in the late 1840s. The Gold Rush after 1848 would initiate a massive rise in harvesting and turn the growth curve of native game species downward.

In order to grasp the magnitude and spectacle of the multitudes of game that occupied California's land, water, and air during the colonial period one simply has to read any of the accounts made by settlers and visitors. No matter who made the observation or when, the commentators were impressed and enthusiastic about the exceptional quantities of California's colonial wildlife. Without exception, every inhabitant and visitor to California prior to 1848 would have concurred with Charles

Wilkes, who wrote in 1845 that "the variety of game in this country almost exceeds belief."[73] What Wilkes and his contemporaries failed to realize was that the impressive numbers and spatial dispersion of the game they marveled at was an abnormal consequence of prior colonial disruption.

HARVESTING INDIGENOUS ANIMALS, TREES, AND OLD WORLD CROPS

> Most of the fruits and vegetables of Europe have also been naturalized in California, where they come to great perfection.
>
> —William Shaler,
> *Journal of a Voyage between China and the North Western Coast of America*

In terms of degree and geographic extent, the most dramatic environmental alterations unleashed by foreign visitations and colonial settlement in California were products of inadvertent or indirect processes. Direct and conscious modifications by the newcomers were modest, in comparison, during the years 1769 to 1848. The colonists and visitors did open land for agriculture, cut trees, and harvest game, but in comparison to the consequences of their biotic introductions, such as weeds, livestock, and disease, as well as their role in fire suppression, the landscape modifications were minimal. Nonetheless, these relatively minor impacts were significant because they represented attempts by the foreign invaders to exploit the resource potential of California, and their conscious environmental and economic behavior would, from this time forward, govern the state's ecological destiny. Indeed, many of the extractive pursuits and intentional modifications initiated during the colonial period would evolve into enormous agencies of environmental change in California during subsequent periods.

Hunting

The early Hispanic settlers and foreign adventurers arrived in California to find an unbalanced landscape that was adjusting to the ecological disturbances triggered during the protohistoric period. One of the symptoms of ecological imbalance that was encountered, and actively exploited by the newcomers, was the abundance of large marine and land animals. Initially, these animals were hunted for subsistence, but after a brief interim, the predominant motivations for killing wildlife became international commerce and sport.

The first colonial intrusions along the coast required the Spaniards to supplement their diet by living off the land for a short time until their Old World animals and plants gained a foothold. They were able to shoot some animals and birds but were also forced to eat their own beasts of burden and small indigenous animals, such as ground squirrels and fish, generously provided by the Indians. This initial reliance on native wildlife was brief because of the rapid procreation of domestic livestock, and a taste for domestic meat over wild game.[74] Soon, subsistence hunting was rendered unnecessary and became a rarity among the Spanish and Mexican settlers.

Despite the availability of sufficient food from Old World animals, Hispanic colonists continued to act as catalysts for the harvesting of indigenous game for other purposes. As early as 1773, Spanish missionaries bartered with California Indians for sea otter pelts, and later it became standard colonial policy to encourage the Indians to kill these sea mammals for trading purposes. Once acquired by the Spanish, the prized pelts entered the trans-Pacific trade with China, in exchange for exotic commodities such as quicksilver.

Another commercial incentive for hunting during the colonial period was the international trade in cow hides and beef tallow. Given the presence of the burgeoning herds of elk, antelope, and deer, it was inevitable that these mammals, too, would be tapped for their skins and oils. Although a less significant source of hides and tallow than domestic livestock, such large game was periodically killed for these purposes, and consequently diminished first in the vicinity of the coastal settlements and later in the Central Valley.[75]

A greater colonial effect on native fauna was caused by foreigners arriving from lands beyond the limits of Spanish and Mexican imperial domination. California's bountiful terrestrial and aquatic wildlife attracted thousands of foreigners to the region during colonial times for profit and adventure. Fur-bearing animals enticed most of the early North American adventurers to travel overland to California, particularly between 1827 and 1842.[76] These trappers had a profound effect not only on the population of aquatic animals, such as beaver, river otter, and mink, but also on the larger mammals unlucky enough to be in the vicinity. The fur brigades subsisted almost entirely on wild game, and the trappers reduced the numbers and spatial distribution of elk, deer, antelope, and bear near their valley hunting grounds and annual rendezvous locales. The resulting slaughter was impressive, as noted by John Work, who reported a killing of 166 elk in only four days in January of 1833.[77] That the incentive for killing game went beyond the needs of subsistence or commercial profit is unquestioned, for nearly every foreign party that trooped through California during the colonial period fired indiscriminately on the animals of the air, sea, and ground, "let them be wanted or not."[78]

The fur brigades declined in the early 1840s due to their own success in decimating the fur-bearing animals throughout the Central Valley. In addition to nearly exhausting their prey, the trappers' own subsistence and sporting activities contributed to a regional depletion of large mammals in portions of the Sacramento Valley.[79] Despite the absence of trappers in the late 1840s, the hunting pressure was sustained by the increasing numbers of settlers located especially in the northern valley and on the southern coast. In spite of the constant predation in these and other locations, the influence of colonial hunting on land was insubstantial in comparison to that of the California Indians during late Pre-Columbian times. As a result, the numbers of non–fur-bearing land animals remained abnormally high, until the Gold Rush ushered in a new period of unparalleled slaughter and statewide faunal depletion.

The pattern of colonial influence on land animals was not duplicated for marine mammals. Because of the accessibility of California's productive coastal fringe, the behavior and reproductive biology of certain species, and the intensity of foreign exploitation, the degree of colonial impact on coastal life was more severe. As was true for the overland expeditions, the abundance of marine resources, particularly the otters and large pinnipeds such as fur and elephant seals, and sea lions, was the primary reason that numerous foreign vessels visited the shores of California during the colonial period. For the Russians, the sea life was bountiful enough to justify the eventual establishment of settlements and loading facilities at Fort Ross and Bodega Bay respectively. The sustained harvesting of marine mammals by foreigners is thought to have begun in 1741 with the voyage of Vitus Bering, who acquired sea otter pelts along the Northwest coast. From that time on, the Russians, Americans, and other foreigners unhesitatingly pursued these marine mammals for their skins and oils, over the objections of California's colonial authorities that they were poaching in Spanish, later Mexican, territory.[80] Despite the regulatory measures implemented after California statehood, some of these stocks of marine animals have yet to recover fully from colonial exploitation.[81]

Lumbering

Colonialism in California led to the elimination of many native forest-management practices and the unprecedented destruction of trees.[82] Hispanic, Russian, and American settlers harvested timber for their own immediate use and for trade. More important, however, they established the precedent for attitudes and practices that continue to have an enormous environmental impact.

Lumbering by Hispanic settlers in colonial California was modest. Wood was needed for a variety of structural and subsistence purposes. Trees were harvested around every mission and settlement as required, and, when locally unavailable, lumber was imported from impressive distances.[83] Nevertheless, as with their crops, animals, and weeds, Hispanic material culture had developed in the dry-land environments of the Mediterranean Basin. These Old World peoples had learned over time to cope with a scarcity of wood for building by adopting substitutes such as tile, rock, and adobe. Prior to the settling of California, the Spanish had modified their material needs somewhat in response to new conditions in the Americas, but Old World stylistic preferences endured and were basically intact by 1769. These cultural traditions, in combination with a limited equipment inventory, consisting only of axes, adzes, and whip saws, served to dampen the intentional Hispanic effect on the forests of California. With time, as the settlement infrastructure expanded, and as the use of wood gained greater acceptance, lumbering activities by Hispanic peoples along the coast increased, and commercial enterprises were launched.

The Russians and Americans, from more extensively wooded environments, were more dependent on lumber for housing and to replicate their accustomed culture. The Russian and American pioneers in Mexican California, like their Hispanic counterparts, regarded trees as objects unrelated to their spiritual existence. But they arrived bearing more sophisticated wood-working technologies and thus a greater potential for deforestation. Colonial tree-cutting by the Russians lasted for several decades, from about 1812 to 1841, but it was geographically restricted to the coastal forests around their settlement at Fort Ross and facilities at Bodega Bay, north of San Francisco.

Significant American lumbering in California began somewhat later, farther south in the Monterey and Carmel regions. Beginning in the early 1830s and over the next two decades, American lumbering activities spread north and south along the coast and accompanied American settlement eastward into the Sacramento Valley.[84] By the early 1840s, one of the principle agencies in the expansion of the industry was John Sutter, a Swiss immigrant. Over a decade, he initiated wood-cutting operations in vicinities ranging from Fort Ross in the west to the Mokelumne River on the southeastern edge of the Sacramento Valley. An effort initiated by Sutter in 1847 to construct a new saw mill on the American River at Coloma provided the fateful spark that in early 1848 ignited the Gold Rush and opened an era of unparalleled deforestion in California.

While the degree of overall deforestation in California was relatively minor during the colonial period, its consequences nonetheless gained the attention of some colonial administrators. Indeed, from the late 1830s onward, American lumbering and the increasing pace of tree-cutting around coastal settlements generated concern among Mexican colonial authorities. This concern ultimately led them to adopt a number of regulations designed to curtail tree-poaching by foreigners and the perceived negative impacts of deforestation. Neither the concern nor the regulations had much genuine effect, but they represented an early recognition that unrestrained harvesting of resources could backfire and lead to negative ecological repercussions.[85]

The change in colonial forestry practices, from a time when indigenous peoples governed California's forests to a time when Old World practices became dominant, occurred rapidly, but not smoothly, for native environments and inhabitants. The first encounter with colonial forestry practices often evoked shock and dismay among the surviving Indians. The degree of consternation displayed by some Native Californians is aptly conveyed by an account published in the 1870s, about the reaction of Yokuts, in the vicinity of the Kaweah Delta, to an episode of tree felling that "filled the Indians with more consternation and horror than any phenomena they have been privileged to witness before or since."[86] For the Indians of California as well as the colonial settlers, colonial logging was a perceptual and physical watershed in the use of forests. It represented a transition from a time when California Indians managed and harvested living forests to a time when settlers cut live trees but were still generations away from implementing effective tree-management and conservation practices.

Agriculture

In addition to their stylistic preferences, the colonial settlers of California possessed food and aesthetic tastes that were strongly conditioned by their ancestral geography. As they did with animals, the colonists preferred plants that had been originally domesticated in the Old World. Although supplemented by many New World species from Mesoamerica, the familiar plants still dominated their nutrition and ornamentation when Spanish settlers first arrived in California. The introduction of these floral domesticates, and the accompanying Old World agricultural practices, generated a variety of important environmental changes. Indeed, the introduction of domesticated plants served partially to augment the floral diversity of the region at a time when other colonial agencies were reducing species diversity. In addition, for the first time in California, west of the Colorado and Owens rivers, considerable modifications of land and water were required to ensure the colonists could raise domesticated crops.

The missionaries were the earliest and primary purveyors of agricultural experimentation in colonial California. The region proved ideal for their efforts, in part because the domesticated plants that thrived in the Mediterranean environments of the Old World did especially well in California. Nevertheless, unlike the Old World weeds, many of the domesticates, originating from both the Old and New Worlds, required artificial irrigation to flourish in California as they had in Spain and other dry-land settings throughout the Americas. In response to California's semiarid climate, and as a hedge against drought, water systems were established early, and they rapidly became prominent features of all mission landscapes.[87]

The digging of wells and diversion of streams for both domestic and irrigation purposes at the missions were the first large-scale hydrologic modifications in colonial California. In addition to irrigation, water was later impounded and diverted in both religious and secular settings for the grinding of grain and the milling of lumber.[88] The environmental and cultural consequences of these diversions are uncertain, but they probably changed the nature and availability of some aquatic resources important to the California Indians. Dams and reservoirs were unfamiliar to the Indians and, in some instances, were perceived by them as assaults on their spiritual well-being. The reaction of the Caymus, or Wappo, Indians to the plans to erect a dam on the Napa River in the 1830s by George Yount testifies to this. An Indian leader cautioned Yount that his dam was going to be erected on "the abode of the

Part of the water system at Mission Santa Barbara, drawn in the summer of 1847 by the American amateur artist William R. Hutton. Coming from lands with little rainfall and few rivers, Hispanic colonists had extensive experience in building waterworks, and their pioneer efforts on Spain's distant frontier initiated the hydraulic revolution that ultimately, more than any other agency, transformed the natural world in California. *Courtesy Huntington Library.*

tutelar & protecting spirit of the Caymus nation" and said the spirit was "bourn down with grief."[89] Yount reached a satisfactory accommodation with the Indians and completed his mill. Nevertheless, the pace and size of hydrologic constructions were increasing in California and so were the associated economic and psychological damages inflicted on the native peoples.

The control of water allowed the missions and pueblos to grow staples more reliably and to experiment with a profusion of plants. On his visit to Mission San Gabriel in 1830, George Yount described "vineyards, orchards and gardens alike planted not merely for the present but also for future generations to enjoy—Tropical fruits, and the productions of every clime were there and in rich profusion."[90] Yount's words were truly prophetic because the colonial agricultural legacy would, indeed, strongly influence the future of agricultural and water endeavors in California long after the Gold Rush.

A peak of about ten thousand acres of cultivated land was reached by the coastal missions and pueblos prior to secularization of the missions in 1834.[91] Acreage and irrigation works diminished in these vicinities after secularization, but the dispersal of agriculture into the interior of California was already in progress. The agencies of dispersal were the rancheros, American settlers, and the California Indians. Some of the rancheros and American settlers in the Sacramento Valley cultivated gardens, and in the case of John Sutter and others, planted fairly sizable farms. In spatial terms, the California Indians, who were either fugitives from the missions or, after secularization, landless refugees, dispersed domestic crops and agricultural knowledge, including irrigation techniques, especially into the interior valleys and deserts.[92]

Where colonial agriculture was practiced, the environmental impacts were many and varied. Colonial cultivation involved a replacement process whereby native ecosystems were removed to make room for exotic ecosystems composed of domestic plants and, if possible, artificial irrigation. The importation of seed crops and ornamental cuttings into California provided an additional avenue for the inadvertent introduction of exotic weeds and pests of unknown character.

Colonial agriculture also had significant consequences for the human relationship with California's diverse array of native flora and fauna. For the first time in California, people were forced by the colonial practice of agriculture to define some of the nondomestic, native flora and fauna as "weeds" and "pests" respectively. These weeds and pests were then attacked by the colonists as threats to their crops, and by extension, their livelihoods. On the other hand, some species of native flora and fauna took advantage of the disturbed cultivated environments and the availability of human-tilled forage. Herbaceous plants that flourished in water or disturbed ground invaded the fields, and animals, such as rodents and bears, often devoured the crops in defiance of eradication efforts.[93] Although only a small fraction of California was modified by colonial agricultural practices at the time of the Gold Rush, a process had been initiated that would ultimately modify tremendous portions of the state. This ongoing transformation of the landscape became a hallmark of its identity.

CONCLUSION

> Then, late in the scheme of things, one species that was to dominate and remake the entire land arrived on the scene.
> —Raymond F. Dasmann, *The Destruction of California*, 1965

The colonial invaders intercepted a process of human-induced environmental change that had been initiated when the first people journeyed to California millennia before the Columbian landfall. Like the Spanish, the first human inhabitants also transported foreign attitudes, technologies, and lifeways that were initially disruptive to

California's natural ecosystems. However, the environmental relationship of these newcomers matured with time and evolved into a mutual accommodation with the state's nonhuman heritage. Their foreign technologies, attitudes, and behaviors were naturalized to accommodate California's unique setting, and the landscapes, in turn, were restructured in response to the symbiosis of accommodation. Time and sustained human interaction with California's nonhuman processes created a landscape of mutual interdependence that was sustained by Indian ingenuity and numbers.

While restructuring much of the landscape according to their needs, the California Indians in late Pre-Columbian times had achieved a physical and spiritual integration with the nonhuman world. Periodically this relationship was severely disturbed by climatic fluctuations and resource depletions caused by human population pressure. However, new environmental accommodations were established on a bountiful resource base, and the changes were absorbed and reflected in the cultural and physical landscapes.

The native habitats of California nurtured dense populations of Indians and thrived under their stewardship. However, this environment also proved especially vulnerable to the disturbances that accompanied European colonialism. The Spaniards had emerged from an ecosystem that was similar to much of California but possessed inherent geographical and biological advantages. Like most European peoples, the Spanish had inherited a biological inventory that had evolved in the more ancient, diverse, and environmentally extreme settings of the Old World. Some of these exotic species were more competitive in California's analogous Mediterranean environments than was the native vegetation that they replaced. Also aiding in the successful naturalization of Old World plants and animals in the New World were the foreigners' own cultural attitudes and practices. The colonial invaders of California conquered the land as well as the people, fortified by their cultural traditions and religious beliefs of an innate sovereignty and superiority over all forms of non-Christian life, including the plants, animals, and native peoples.

Unbeknown to them, the colonists' Old World ancestors had also bequeathed to them a host of virulent pathogens that shared their vessels of exploration to the New World and California during its precolonial period. These microscopic invaders directly attacked the linchpins of ecological stability in California—the Indians. The unintended consequences of disease to native land-use practices triggered imbalances that rendered the environment increasingly susceptible to the encroachment of other foreign introductions, such as weeds. The settlement process, beginning in 1769, magnified the impacts of inadvertent pre-colonial changes and introduced intentional practices that multiplied and spread the environmental changes. The acculturation process and the domestic livestock that accompanied Hispanic settlement served further to corrupt and destroy the role of the California Indian as the keystone species.

Remarkably, the totality of environmental change in colonial California was initiated and sustained by just a few thousand foreign human beings. These foreigners quickly coopted the California Indians as the chief agency of ecological change despite being outnumbered by them. Indeed, as the colonial period progressed, the overall number of people dramatically declined in California, and yet the magnitude of environmental impact increased. The colonial pattern in California was extreme testimony to the vulnerability of New World peoples and landscapes to the human lifeways and biological products formulated in the Old World.

The environmental events in colonial California were roughly analogous to the initial peopling of the region toward the end of the Pleistocene Epoch. At that time, the ecologies of California were forced to adjust to the first arrival of humans and their accompanying attitudes and technologies. Ecological disruptions were manifested, but with time a less tumultuous accommodation was established as the newcomers became naturalized to their new home. Likewise, the colonial period introduced a whole new set of peoples, attitudes, organisms, and technologies. The ecological repercussions of these changes are still in progress, and naturalization among the contemporary inhabitants has yet to be achieved. The question is, will California have sufficient resources in the future for an environmental accommodation with more than thirty million people who still possess a colonial frame of mind?

NOTES

1. For assessments of the magnitudes of vegetational and faunal changes in California, see Elna Bakker, *An Island Called California* (Berkeley: University of California Press, 1984), 168; Mark A. Blumler, "Invasion and Transformation of California's Valley Grassland, a Mediterranean Analogue Ecosystem," in *Ecological Relations in Historical Times: Human Impact and Adaptation,* ed. Robin A. Butlin and Neil Roberts (Oxford: Blackwell Press, 1995), 310; and Richard N. Mack, "Temperate Grasslands Vulnerable to Plant Invasions: Characteristics and Consequences," in *Biological Invasions: A Global Perspective,* ed. James A. Drake, et al. (New York: John Wiley and Sons, 1989), 165; Raymond F. Dasmann, *California's Changing Environment* (San Francisco: Boyd and Fraser Publishing Co. 1981), 9–21. All references to "California" in this chapter, in keeping with common usage, refer specifically to Alta California, as distinct from Baja California. All references to the "New World" refer to North and South America, as well as to the Caribbean.

2. Blumler, "Invasion and Transformation of California's Valley Grassland"; Jared Diamond, "The Accidental Conqueror," *Discover* 10 (1989): 71–76; Mark A. Blumler, "Some Myths about California Grasses and Grazers," *Fremontia* 20 (1992): 22–27; and Alfred W. Crosby, *Ecological Imperialism: The Biological Expansion of Europe, 900–1900* (Cambridge: Cambridge University Press, 1986), 269–93.

3. William H. McNeill, *Plagues and Peoples* (Garden City: Anchor Books/Doubleday, 1976), 31–36.

4. Ibid., 25–30; Karl W. Butzer, "An Introduction to Current Geographical Research," in *The Americas Before and After 1492: Current Geographical Research, Annals of the Association of*

American Geography 82 (1992): 345–68; and Tom D. Dillehay, "Disease Ecology and Initial Human Migration," in *The First Americans: Search and Research,* ed. Tom D. Dillehay and David J. Meltzer (Boca Raton: CRC Press, 1991), 231–64.

5. Phillip L. Walker, Patricia Lambert, and Michael J. DeNiro, "The Effects of European Contact on the Health of Alta California Indians," in *Columbian Consequences: Archaeological and Historical Perspectives on the Spanish Borderlands West,* Vol. 1, ed. David H. Thomas (Washington: Smithsonian Institution Press, 1989), 349–64.

6. Lynn White, Jr., "The Historical Roots of Our Ecological Crisis," *Science* 155 (1967): 1203–1207; and Yi-Fu Tuan, "Discrepancies between Environmental Attitude and Behavior: Examples from Europe and China," *Canadian Geographer* 12 (1968):176–91.

7. Florence Shipek, "Kumeyaay Plant Husbandry: Fire, Water, and Erosion Management Systems," in Thomas C. Blackburn and M. Kat Anderson, eds., *Before the Wilderness: Environmental Management by Native Californians* (Menlo Park: Ballena Press Publications, 1993), 388.

8. M. Kat Anderson, "Native Californians as Ancient and Contemporary Cultivators," in *Before the Wilderness,* 151–54; Bev Ortiz, "Contemporary California Indian Basket Weavers and the Environment," in *Before the Wilderness,* 195; Thomas C. Blackburn and M. Kat Anderson, "Introduction," in *Before the Wilderness,* 18; and Theodora Kroeber and Robert F. Heizer, *Almost Ancestors: The First Californians* (San Francisco: Sierra Club, 1968), 24.

9. Bernabé Cobo, *Obras,* 2 vols. (Madrid: Atlas Ediciones, 1964), 1:420.

10. Kroeber and Heizer, *Almost Ancestors,* 24.

11. Blackburn and Anderson, in *Before the Wilderness,* 18. The use of the term *domestication* in this context is not traditional and does not mean the kind of domestication practiced by farming peoples in either the Old or New World.

12. Stephen J. Pyne, Patricia L. Andrews, and Richard D. Laven, *Introduction to Wildland Fire,* 2d ed. (New York: John Wiley and Sons, 1996), 608–9; Henry T. Lewis, "Patterns of Indian Burning in California: Ecology and Ethnohistory," in *Before the Wilderness,* 55–116; Jan Timbrook, John R. Johnson, and David D. Earle, "Vegetation Burning by the Chumash," in *Before the Wilderness,* 117–49; Helen McCarthy, "Managing Oaks and the Acorn Crop," in *Before the Wilderness,* 216–28; Florence Shipek, in *Before the Wilderness;* Harold H. Biswell, *Prescribed Burning in California Wildlands Vegetation Management* (Berkeley: University of California Press, 1989); Anderson, in *Before the Wilderness;* Bev Ortiz, in *Before the Wilderness,* and David W. Peri and Scott M. Patterson, "The Basket Is in the Roots, That's Where It Begins," in *Before the Wilderness,* 175–93.

13. James G. West, "Early Historic Vegetation Change in Alta California: The Fossil Evidence," in *Columbian Consequences,* Vol. 1, 334; Anderson, in *Before the Wilderness,* 155–56; McCarthy, in *Before the Wilderness,* 223; and Lewis, in *Before the Wilderness,* 69–70, 105–110.

14. Stephen W. Edwards, "Observations on the Prehistory and Ecology of Grazing in California," *Fremontia* 20 (1992): 3–11.

15. Anderson, in *Before the Wilderness,* 156.

16. Malcolm Margolin, ed., *The Way We Lived: California Indian Stories, Songs and Reminiscences* (Berkeley: Heyday Books, 1993), 95, 98; Leanne Hinton, *Flutes of Fire: Essays on California Indian Languages* (Berkeley: Heyday Books, 1994), 92; M. Kat Anderson and G. P. Nabhan, "Gardeners in Eden," *Wilderness Magazine* 45 (1991): 27–30; Wendell Berry, *Recollected Essays, 1965–1980* (San Francisco: North Point Press, 1981), 98; Matt Vera, "The Creation of Language, a Yowlumni Story," in *News From Native California* 7 (1993): 19–20; Anderson, in *Before the Wilderness,* 152–56; Blackburn and Anderson, *Before the Wilderness,* 19.

17. Anderson, in *Before the Wilderness*, 156.

18. Lewis, in *Before the Wilderness*, 113; Charles E. Kay, "Aboriginal Overkill: The Role of Native Americans in Structuring Western Ecosystems," *Human Nature* 5 (1994): 359–98.

19. Alfred L. Kroeber, *Handbook of the Indians of California* (Berkeley: California Book Company, 1925), 238–39; Sherburne F. Cook, *The Population of the California Indians 1769–1976* (Berkeley: University of California Press, 1976), 24; Sherburne F. Cook, "Historical Demography," in *Handbook of North Amercan Indians*, Vol. 8, *California*, ed. Robert F. Heizer (Washington: Smithsonian Institution Press, 1978), 91; and Robert H. Jackson, *Indian Population Decline: The Missions of Northwestern New Spain, 1687–1840* (Albuquerque: University of New Mexico Press, 1994), 55.

20. Raymond F. Dasmann, *The Destruction of California* (New York: The Macmillan Company, 1965), 33; William L. Preston, "Serpent in Eden: Dispersal of Foreign Diseases into Pre-Mission California," *Journal of California and Great Basin Anthropology* 18 (1996), 2–37; McNeill, *Plagues and Peoples*, 3–4; Jackson, *Indian Population Decline*, 116, 164.

21. It is widely acknowledged that demographic and environmental disruptions spread ahead of settlement in most areas of North America, including areas south and east of California before 1769. See Ann F. Ramenofsky, *Vectors of Death: The Archaeology of European Contact* (Albuquerque: University of New Mexico, 1987); and Henry F. Dobyns, *Their Number Become Thinned: Native American Population Dynamics in Eastern North America* (Knoxville: University of Tennessee Press, 1983); Daniel T. Reff, *Disease, Depopulation, and Culture Change in Northwestern New Spain, 1518–1764* (Salt Lake City: University of Utah Press, 1991), 86, 177–78, 234; Robert H. Jackson, "Epidemic Disease and Population Decline in the Baja California Missions, 1697–1834," *Southern California Quarterly* 63 (1981): 308–46; and Henry Dobyns, "Indian Extinction in the Middle Santa Cruz Valley, Arizona," *New Mexico Historical Review* 38 (1963): 163–81.

22. Preston, "Serpent in Eden"; Jon M. Erlandson and Kevin Bartoy, "Cabrillo, the Chumash, and Old World Diseases," *Journal of California and Great Basin Anthropology* 17 (1995): 153–73; Jon M. Erlandson and Kevin Bartoy, "Protohistoric California: Paradise or Pandemic," in *Proceedings of the Society for California Archaeology*, 304–309, ed. Judyth Reed (San Diego: Society for California Archaeology, 1996); and Harry Kelsey, "European Impact on the California Indians, 1530–1830," *The Americas* 41 (1984): 494–515.

23. Virulent epidemics of Old World germs (e.g., measles, smallpox, influenza, and malaria) in other colonial environments, and also in California after 1769, commonly killed from a quarter to over half (depending on the ailment) of those infected. See Ramenofsky, *Vectors of Death*, 171; and Sherburne F. Cook, "The Epidemic of 1830–1833 in California and Oregon," *University of California Publications in American Archaeology and Ethnology* 43 (1955): 322.

24. George W. Hendry, "The Adobe Brick as a Historical Source," *Agricultural History* 5 (1931): 110–27; West, "Early Historic Vegetation Change in Alta California," 335–48; S. A. Mensing and R. Bryne, "New Evidence for Pre-Mission Transformation of the California Grassland," *Abstracts of the American Association of Geographers*, 89th Annual Meeting, Atlanta, 6–9 April 1993.

25. Edwards, "Observations on the Prehistory and Ecology of Grazing in California"; Blumler, "Some Myths about California Grasses and Grazers," 24; Timbrook, et al., in *Before the Wilderness*, 138; Fred J. Kruger, G. J. Breytenbach, Ian A. W. MacDonald, and D. M. Richardson, "The Characteristics of Invaded Mediterranean-Climate Regions," in *Biological Invasions: A Global Perspective*, ed. James A. Drake et al. (New York: John Wiley and Sons, 1989), 203.

26. Edwards, "Observations on the Prehistory and Ecology of Grazing in California," 7.

27. Dasmann, *California's Changing Environment*, 6; Dale R. McCullough, *The Tule Elk: Its History and Ecology* (Berkeley: University of California, 1969), 15; Burney Le Boeuf, "History," in *The Natural History of Año Nuevo*, ed. Stephanie Kaza (Pacific Grove: Boxwood Press, 1981), 12. The use of the term "American" in this essay refers to individuals from the United States, and American "period" represents the period beginning with the Gold Rush of 1848.

28. Margolin, *The Way We Lived*, 95.

29. Throughout the American West numerous lines of evidence demonstrate that Native Americans were the major predators of large game and depressed their numbers impressively prior to colonial contact. Once destructive colonial consequences depleted the chief predator (i.e., the Indians) of the large game, the animals quickly irrupted territorially and numerically to a degree probably not experienced in North America since the termination of the Pleistocene Epoch. For authoritative accounts see Charles E. Kay, "Aboriginal Overkill and Native Burning: Implications for Modern Ecosystem Management," *Western Journal of Applied Forestry* 10 (1995): 125; D. K. Grayson, *The Deserts' Past: A Natural Prehistory of the Great Basin* (Washington: Smithsonian Institution Press, 1993); R. Daubenmire, "The Western Limits of the Range of the American Bison," *Ecology* 66:622–24; G. C. Frison, *Prehistoric Hunters of the High Plains*, 2d ed. (New York: Academic Press, 1991); Kay, "Aboriginal Overkill," 359–98.

30. W. R. Hildebrandt and Terry L. Jones, "Evolution of Marine Mammal Hunting: A View from the California and Oregon Coasts," *Journal of Anthropological Archaeology* 11 (1992): 360–401; Mark L. Raab, "An Optimal Foraging Analysis of Prehistoric Shellfish Collecting on San Clemente Island, California," *Journal of Ethnology* 12 (1992): 63–80; Jack M. Broughton, "Late Holocene Resource Intensification in the Sacramento Valley, California: The Vertebrate Evidence," *Journal of Anthropological Science* 21 (1994a): 501–14; Jack M. Broughton, "Declines in Mammalian Foraging Efficiency During the Late Holocene, San Francisco Bay, California," *Journal of Anthropology* 13 (1994b): 371–401.

31. Likewise, prior to Vizcaíno's voyage, explorers like Juan Rodríguez Cabrillo (1542–1543) and Francis Drake (1579) reported similar sightings. Herbert E. Bolton, *Spanish Exploration in the Southwest, 1542–1706* (New York: Charles Scribner's Sons, 1916), 91; Juan Páez, *Cabrillo's Log, 1542–1543: A Voyage of Discovery*, translated by James R. Moriarity and Mary Keistman (San Diego: Cabrillo Historical Association, 1968), 5; Robert F. Heizer, *Elizabethan California* (Ramona: Ballena Press, 1974), 92.

32. Miguel Costanso, "The Portola Expedition of 1769–1770," *Publications of the Academy of Pacific Coast History* 2 (1911): 77, ed. Frederick J. Teggart; Fray Francisco Palou, *Historical Memoirs of New California*, vol. 2, ed. Herbert E. Bolton (New York: Russell and Russell, 1966), 219; Pedro Fages, "Expedition to San Francisco Bay in 1770: Diary of Pedro Fages," ed. Herbert E. Bolton, *Publications of the Academy of Pacific Coast History* 2 (1911): 9; and Herbert E. Bolton, *Anza's California Expeditions*, vol. 2 (Berkeley: University of California Press, 1930), 347.

33. The Spanish settlement of California, with its emphasis upon *reducción* or *congregación* missions may have been assisted somewhat by the demographic and environmental conditions left over from the protohistoric period. See Jackson, *Indian Population Decline;* and Daniel T. Reff, "Contact Shock in Northwestern New Spain, 1518–1764," in *Disease and Demography in the Americas*, ed. John W. Verano and Douglas H. Ubelaker (Washington, D.C.: Smithsonian Institution Press, 1992), 272.

34. Bakker, *An Island Called California*, 168. Also see Blumler, "Invasion and Transformation of California's Valley Grassland," 310.

35. As the colonial infrastructure of missions, pueblos, and presidios expanded, authorities became ever more concerned that the fires set by Indians (mission and non-mission alike) would threaten not only their buildings and domestic livestock but also the acculturation process. According to Stephen Pyne and his fellow authors, "the fire problem and the social problem were one and the same"; Pyne et al., *Introduction to Wildland Fire*, 297. The concern over Indian burning climaxed in 1793, when Governor José de Arrillaga drafted a proclamation at Santa Barbara designed to "prohibit for the future . . . all kinds of burning, not only in the vicinity of the towns but even at the most remote distances"; quoted in Raymond C. Clar, *California Government and Forestry from Spanish Days until the Creation of the Department of Natural Resources in 1927* (Sacramento: California Division of Forestry, 1959), 8.

36. Dasmann, *The Destruction of California*, 61.

37. George H. Phillips, *Indians and Intruders in Central California, 1769–1849* (Norman: University of Oklahoma press, 1993); Sherburne F. Cook, "Colonial Expeditions to the Interior of California: Central Valley, 1800–1820," *Anthropology Records* 10 (1960): 238–92 (Berkeley: University of California Press); Sherburne F. Cook, "Expeditions to the Interior of California: Central Valley, 1820–1840," *Anthropological Records* 20 (1962): 151–214 (Berkeley: University of California Press). An account of a malaria epidemic that struck Central California from 1830 to 1833 and may have killed up to 75 percent of the native inhabitants in some places is found in Cook, "The Epidemic of 1830–1833 in California and Oregon," 322.

38. Bakker, *An Island Called California*, 168–69; Blumler, "Invasion and Transformation of California's Valley Grassland," 315, 324; Mack, "Temperate Grasslands Vulnerable to Plant Invasions," 165.

39. These adaptive advantages appear to validate that "Old World organisms are almost always 'superior' when the competition takes place in their home environment"; Alfred W. Crosby, *Ecological Imperialism*, 291.

40. The relative importance of domestic livestock in the replacement of native grasses by exotic annuals is a matter for debate. In some interior vicinities, such as the Central Valley, Mediterranean annuals seem to have arrived before the disturbances associated with livestock. The controversy also involves the composition of the original grassland habitats. For additional material addressing these issues, see H. F. Heady, "Valley Grassland," in *Terrestrial Vegetation of California*, ed. M. G. Barbour and J. Major (New York: John Wiley and Sons, 1977), 493–96, 500; Lyndon Wester, "Composition of Native Grasslands in the San Joaquin Valley, California," *Madroño* 28 (1981); Blumler, "Some Myths About California Grasses and Grazers," 23, 24, and "Invasion and Transformation of California's Valley Grassland," 319; L. T. Burcham, *California Range Land* (Sacramento: Division of Forestry, Department of Natural Resources, State of California, 1957), 90–104; West, "Early Historic Vegetation Change in Alta California," 334–37.

41. Blumler, "Some Myths about California Grasses and Grazers," 25; Heady, "Valley Grasslands," 497–98; Wester, "Composition of Native Grassland in the San Joaquin Valley," 231–41.

42. John C. Ewers, *The Adventures of Zenas Leonard* (Norman: University of Oklahoma Press, 1959), 88. For a substantial list of early pioneers in California who mention having seen substantial fields of wild oats, see Blumler, "Invasion and Transformation of California's Valley Grassland," 318.

43. Robert F. Heizer and Thomas R. Hester, "The Archaeology of Bamert Cave, Amador

County, California" (on file at Berkeley: University of California Archaeology Research Facility, 1973); Thomas J. Mayfield, *Indian Summer: Traditional Life Among the Choinumne Indians of California's San Joaquin Valley* (Berkeley: Heyday Books, 1993), 63.

44. Harold H. Biswell, "Ecology of California Grassland," *Journal of Range Management* 9 (1956): 21; Blumler, "Invasion and Transformation of California's Valley Grassland," 310; and Homer Aschmann, "Man's Impact on the Southern California Flora," in *Symposium Proceedings: Plant Communities of Southern California,* ed. June Latting (California Native Plant Society Special Publication No. 2, 1976), 42–43.

45. Blackburn and Anderson, *Before the Wilderness,* 19; and Robert Heizer, "Impact of Colonization on the Native California Species," *The Journal of San Diego History* 24 (1978).

46. Many observers have noted the expansion and increased density of chaparral environments since European colonization, but explanations regarding their continued persistence differ. See Timbrook, et al., in *Before the Wilderness,* 125–26, 146, and Homer Aschmann, *Symposium Proceedings,* 43–44.

47. Brooks D. Gist, *Empire out of the Tules* (Dexter MI: Thomson-Shore Inc., 1976), 195; and Lewis, in *Before the Wilderness,* 82, 86.

48. McCarthy, in *Before the Wilderness,* 223.

49. Timbrook, et al., in *Before the Wilderness,* 135–38; Blackburn and Anderson in *Before the Wilderness,* 19; Shipek, in *Before the Wilderness,* 380; Lewis, in *Before the Wilderness,* 70.

50. Shipek, in *Before the Wilderness,* 382. In a number of ecosystems, some species that had become dependent on natural and human-set fires for reproduction began to go into decline. See Lewis, in *Before the Wilderness,* 105–107.

51. The suppression of fire facilitated the spread of native species of chaparral that have moisture-absorbing roots and leaves that exude oils and other substances that inhibit the growth of annuals. The effect reduces the presence of annuals as ground cover and contributes to the barrenness of the more arid landscapes. See Shipek, in *Before the Wilderness,* 382, 383. The combined consequences of the extinction of native practices, livestock grazing, and expansion of the chaparral directly affected the health of top soils and interfered with the hydrologic cycle. Also owing to increased runoff and a reduced ability of the land to absorb moisture, groundwater levels have been documented to have changed in southern California. Groundwater change, in turn, has resulted in changes in plants dependent on the water and a loss of meadows and springs in some locations. See Shipek, in *Before the Wilderness,* 385; and West, "Early Historic Vegetation Change in Alta California," 343.

52. See Frank F. Latta, "Little Journeys in the San Joaquin" (Tulare: Frank F. Latta, 1937, on file at California State Library, Sacramento), 21. Depending on the environmental circumstances, floral invaders also served to protect the fragile skin of the land from erosive forces. The touted adaptability of Old World annuals allowed them to grow in a variety of disturbed conditions and served to protect barren soils that would have otherwise remained exposed. The "weeds, like skin transplants placed over broad areas of abraded and burned flesh, aided in healing the raw wounds that the invaders tore in the earth"; Crosby, *Ecological Imperialism,* 170. In addition, where native species no longer thrived, the exotic grasses quickly became the chief fodder for the livestock that sustained the imperial Spaniards and the foreigners who followed them to California.

53. David Hornbeck, *California Patterns: A Geographical and Historical Atlas* (Palo Alto: Mayfield Publishing Company, 1983), 55.

54. Ibid., 58; and John A Schutz, *Spain's Colonial Outpost* (San Francisco: Boyd and Fraser Publishing Company, 1985), 92. The number of livestock supporting the rancho system is un-

certain and assuredly fluctuated with droughts. Nevertheless, according to one assessment in 1848, "the present number is not much, if any, short of one million"; Edwin Bryant, *What I Saw in California* (Palo Alto: Lewis Osborne, 1967 [1848]), 445. Livestock within the mission system is enumerated by Robert H. Jackson and Edward Castillo, *Indians, Franciscans, and Spanish Colonization: The Impact of the Mission System on California Indians* (Albuquerque: University of New Mexico Press, 1995), 123–31; and Hornbeck, *California Patterns,* 55.

55. George H. Phillips, *The Enduring Struggle: Indians in California History* (San Francisco: Boyd and Fraser Publishing Company, 1981): 39.

56. Cook, "Expeditions to the Interior of California," 271.

57. The numbers of livestock carried off into the interior were not insignificant. Edwin Bryant in 1848 stated that "more than one hundred thousand can be distinctly enumerated, and that the total amount would probably be double that number"; Bryant, *What I Saw in California,* 434.

58. Phillips, *The Enduring Struggle,* 97, 160.

59. Bryant, *What I Saw in California,* 434; R. A. Thompson, *Historical and Descriptive Sketch of Sonoma County, California* (Philadelphia: L. H. Everts and Co., 1877); Ewers, *The Adventures of Zenas Leonard,* 122; McCullough, *The Tule Elk,* 20; and Aschmann, *Man's Impact on the Southern California Flora,* 42, 44.

60. A particularly poignant episode of range management occurred during the the droughts of 1807 and 1810, when seven or eight thousand horses were driven into the sea at Santa Barbara and Monterey respectively; Mariano Guadalupe Vallejo, "Ranch and Mission Days in Alta California," *Century Magazine* 41 (1890): 183–92. Also see *The Works of Hubert H. Bancroft, Volume 34, California Pastoral, 1769–1848* (San Francisco: The History Company, 1888), 338, 347.

61. Bryant, *What I Saw in California,* 302, 349.

62. Allan A. Schoenherr, *A Natural History of California* (Berkeley: University of California Press, 1992), 718. The ecological disruptions were especially acute and environmental damage the most severe during the periodic droughts that occurred prior to 1848. The droughts of 1795, 1820, 1828–1830, 1840–1841, and 1845–1847 were particularly damaging to the range. See McCullough, *The Tule Elk,* 15; and Burcham, *California Range Land.*

63. For a more accurate assessment of Indian depopulation in California, it is necessary to have an idea of the populations that existed prior to 1492. Unfortunately, demographically, very little is known about this period. The figures used here are derived from Cook, *The Population of the California Indians,* 43–44; Sherburne Cook, *The Conflict Between the California Indian and White Civilization* (Berkeley: University of California Press, 1976), 346, 357; and George H. Phillips, "Indians and the Breakdown of the Spanish Mission System in California," *Ethnohistory* 21 (1974): 291–302.

64. Hornbeck, *California Patterns,* 51; and Schutz, *Spain's Colonial Outpost,* 5.

65. E. R. Smith, "The California Ground Squirrel (Spermophilus beecheyi) Natural History and Control Policies with Economic and Ecological Ramifications" (M.A. thesis, Biology, San Francisco State University, 1980).

66. Vallejo, "Ranch and Mission Days in Alta California"; Tracy I. Storer and Lloyd P. Tevis, Jr., *California Grizzly* (Berkeley: University of California Press, 1955), 17, 129–30.

67. Zephyrin Engelhardt, *Santa Barbara Mission* (San Francisco: James H. Barry, 1923), 64; and Storer and Tevis, *California Grizzly,* 120.

68. John Cassin, "Mammalogy and Ornithology," in Charles Wilkes, *United States Ex-*

ploring Expedition During the Years 1838, 1839, 1840, 1841, 1842., vol. 8 (Philadelphia: Lea and Blanchard, 1858), 14; Storer and Tevis, *California Grizzly*, 82–90.

69. Scott W. Stine, "Hunting and the Faunal Landscape, Subsistence and Commercial Venery in Early California" (M.A. thesis, Geography, University of California, Berkeley, 1980), 50–53.

70. Ewers, *The Adventures of Zenas Leonard*, 120.

71. George C. Yount, quoted in Charles L. Camp, "The Chronicles of George C. Yount: California Pioneer of 1826," *California Historical Society Quarterly* 2 (1923):52.

72. For an assessment of the areas significantly affected by non–Indian hunting, see McCullough, *The Tule Elk*, 22, 26.

73. Wilkes, *Narrative of the United States Exploring Expedition*, vol. 5, 15. For descriptions of wildlife for a variety of locations and time periods, see Cook, "Colonial Expeditions to the Interior of California," 248, 252, 255, 258; Ewers, *The Adventures of Zenas Leonard*; Camp, "The Chronicle of George C. Yount"; John Work, *Fur Brigade to the Bonaventura: John Work's California Expedition, 1832–1833, for the Hudson's Bay Company*, ed. Alice B. Maloney (San Francisco: California Historical Society, 1945); Bryant, *What I Saw in California*; Jean F. La Pérouse, *The First Federal Expedition to California* (Los Angeles: Glen Dawson, 1959); C. M. Scammon, *The Marine Mammals of the Northwest Coast of North America* (San Francisco: John Carmany and Sons, 1874); William Shaler, *Journal of a Voyage Between China and the North Western Coast of America, Made in 1804 by William Shaler* (Claremont: Saunders Studio Press, 1935), 55; and John Bidwell, *Echoes of the Past: An Account of the First Emigrant Train to California* (Chico, Calif: Chico Advertiser, 1906).

74. For examples of the subsistence behavior of the early colonists, see Elliott Coues, *On the Trail of a Spanish Pioneer: The Diary and Itinerary of Francisco Garces*, vol. 1 (New York: Francis P. Harper, 1900), 241, 280; Costanso, *The Portolá Expedition of 1769–1770*, 14 and 101; and Eugene H. Bolton, *Fray Juan Crespi: Missionary Explorer on the Pacific Coast, 1769–1774* (New York: AMS Press, 1971), 239, 253. Indications of food preferences are found in A. Duhaut-Cilly, "Duhaut-Cilly's Account of California in the Years 1827–1828," translated by Charles F. Carter, *Quarterly of the California Historical Society* 8 (1929): 306–36.

75. A good account of the early sea-otter trade is found in Adele Ogden, *The California Sea Otter Trade, 1784–1848* (Berkeley: University of California Press, 1941). Notations of the use of wild terrestrial game for hides and tallow are located in Duflot de Mofrás, *Travels on the Pacific Coast*, 2 vols. (Santa Ana: Fine Arts Press, 1937), 257–58, and F. W. Beechey, *An Account of a Visit to California in 1826–1827* (San Francisco: Grabhorn Press, 1941). The diminishment of certain animals for hides and tallow was compensated somewhat by an increase in other native species that were drawn to the meat: "Abandoned on the hunting ground, bears, attracted by this prey, come from all sides to feed upon it"; Duhaut-Cilly, *Duhaut-Cilly's Account of California in the Years 1827–1828*, 241. For the specific geographical impacts on elk, see McCullough, *The Tule Elk*, 25–26.

76. The non-Hispanic land and sea forays were also largely responsible for the collision of imperial interests and the heightened international tensions that characterized the period. A more thorough account of fur brigade activities is found in Stine, "Hunting and the Faunal Landscape," 46.

77. Work, *Fur Brigade to the Bonaventura*, 28. He further enumerates that in the vicinity of the Marysville Buttes, "395 elk, 148 deer, 17 bears, & 8 antelopes have been killed in a month which is certainly a great many more than was required"; ibid, 31.

78. Ibid., 31. The desires and attitudes of the foreigners were aptly epitomized in 1847 by Edwin Bryant, who stated that "the hunting sportsman can here enjoy his favorite pleasure to its fullest extent." Bryant, *What I Saw in California*, 302.

79. Wilkes, *Narrative of the United States Exploring Expedition*, 183; and McCullough, *The Tule Elk*, 22, 26.

80. K. W. Kenyon, *The Sea Otter in the Eastern Pacific Ocean* (Washington: U.S. Department of the Interior, Bureau of Sport Fisheries and Wildlife, 1969), 135; and Ogden, *The California Sea Otter Trade*.

81. The magnitude of the marine harvest is nicely illustrated by colonial events on the Farallon Islands. By 1808, Yankee sealers were already harvesting Guadalupe fur seals on the islands in astonishing numbers. One American vessel is reported to have taken approximately 130,000 seals in a two-year period beginning in 1808 and another over 70,000 in three years. The marine bounty did not prove inexhaustible, as demonstrated by the Russians, who maintained a sealing station on the islands from 1812 to 1840. During the initial years the Russians were harvesting a yearly average of 1,200 to 1,500 Guadalupe fur seals, but by 1818 the annual yield had fallen to only two or three hundred. Carl L. Hubbs, "Back from Oblivion: Guadalupe Fur Seal: A Living Species," *Pacific Discovery* 9 (1956): 15. An assessment of colonial impacts on some marine species is found in Burney Le Boeuf, "Mammals," in *The Natural History of Año Nuevo*, 287–325. Recovery rates of some pinnipeds and otters are discussed in Terry L. Jones and William R. Hildebrandt, "Reasserting a Prehistoric Tragedy of the Commons: Reply to Lyman," *Journal of Anthropological Archaeology* 14 (1995):78–98.

82. Some Indian groups are reported to have used fire intentionally to attack older trees, but the practice was exceptional owing to the lack of economic necessity and the spiritual inhibitions to such behavior. See Anna H. Gayton, "Yokuts and Western Mono Ethnography," *Anthropological Records* 10 (Berkeley: University of California Press, 1948), 78; and Shipek, in *Before the Wilderness*, 387.

83. The construction of the fort, for example, between 1795 and 1800 at the entrance to San Diego's harbor, was accomplished with lumber shipped southward from the hillsides of Santa Barbara and Monterey. Clar, *California Government and Forestry*, 14. For the best account of the forestry practiced in California throughout the colonial period, also see ibid., 3–52.

84. A hallmark of American lumbering practices was the emphasis on the application of more efficient technologies, power systems, and commercialism. A series of water-powered saw mills was built by Americans immigrants beginning with one constructed for the authorities at Mission San Gabriel in 1822 or shortly thereafter; ibid., 15–18, 21–22, 25–26, 39, 42.

85. Mexican Minister of Interior Romero, quoted in ibid., 30. For a more detailed account of colonial forestry regulations, see ibid., 20, 30, 41–42.

86. Stephen Barton, "Early History of Tulare," Visalia *Weekly Delta* (July 2, 1874).

87. For more on mission irrigation, see Hornbeck, *California Patterns*, 51–53, and Norris Hundley, Jr., *The Great Thirst: Californians and Water, 1770s–1990s* (Berkeley: University of California Press, 1992), 42.

88. By 1815, most missions had small dams to impound water for irrigation and to power grist mills. The number of reservoirs increased during the colonial era and became commonplace in both religious and secular settings; Hornbeck, *California Patterns*, 53.

89. Camp, "The Chronicle of George C. Yount," 59.

90. Ibid, 43. Hispanic administration of water reflected Iberian custom and law. The predominant Hispanic custom, known as "Pueblo Water Right," lingered in California to influence the adjudication of water rights during the American Period; Hundley, *The Great Thirst,* 36–49.

91. Detailed accounts of the size and production of mission agriculture for various periods can be found in Frank Adams, "The Historical Background of California Agriculture," in *California Agriculture,* ed. Claude B. Hutchison (Berkeley: University of California Press, 1946), 10; Jackson and Castillo, *Indians, Franciscans, and Spanish Colonization,* 114–23; and Julia G. Costello, "Variability Among the Alta California Missions: The Economics of Agricultural Production," in *Columbian Consequences,* Vol. 1, 435–49.

92. Several accounts of Indian agriculture are noted in Bryant, *What I Saw in California,* 265, 314; Phillips, *Indians and Intruders,* 99–100; and Ewers, *The Adventures of Zenas Leonard,* 91, 95, 122.

93. See Storer and Tevis, *California Grizzly,* 61; and Smith, "The California Ground Squirrel."

11

Alta California's Trojan Horse

Foreign Immigration

Doyce B. Nunis, Jr.

In 1769, Spain undertook its last colonial initiative in the New World: the occupation of Alta California. Coincidental with the implementation of this final colonization endeavor was the growing rumble of discontent among English settlers along the eastern Atlantic seaboard of the continent. On the one hand, imperial Spain was extending its domain northward along the Pacific Coast, while colonial Americans were chaffing under British rule. The latter tension by 1776 would lead to the creation of a new nation, the United States; the coastal expanse coveted by Spain would eventually become the thirty-first state in that Union.

In establishing Alta California as a colony, Spain imposed on it certain restrictive policies. The province was forbidden to trade with any foreign vessels; foreigners were strictly prohibited from taking up permanent residence; manufacturing and agricultural diversity were not encouraged; and shipbuilding was prohibited without governmental license. Spanish colonial policy did support the development of farming and ranching, mainly as a means to make the colony self-sufficient in respect to basic foodstuffs. Annually, a supply ship from the Mexican port of San Blas brought essential goods and supplies that the colony could not produce, such as clothing, hardware, sugar, and the like, as well as military supplies for the four presidios erected for defensive purposes. Although Alta California was founded during the reign of Carlos III (1759–1788), the subsequent enlightened "Bourbon Reforms," instituted at the beginning of the nineteenth century to liberalize arcane restrictions that held Spanish colonies in a state of dependent economic bondage, had little impact in Alta California.[1]

Because Alta California was so far removed from Mexico, Spain had only limited success in recruiting colonists. To entice civilians, Spain had to offer each recruit basic clothing, food, and equipment, plus a promise of a plot of land and a pueblo

A daguerreotype portrait of Richard Henry
Dana, Jr., probably taken in 1840, at the time of
publication of his great book, *Two Years before the
Mast*. Though Dana later demeaned it as "a boy's
work," his narrative was a best seller, an evocative
and moving description of a sailor's lot at sea and of
life in California. In tight, luminous prose, Dana
wrote of the splendid climate and rich soil of this
distant Mexican province and of the "idle, thriftless
people" who occupied it—alerting his countrymen
to the promise of California, ripe for the picking,
and creating an American literary classic that is
as compelling today as when it was written.
*Courtesy National Park Service, Longfellow
National Historic Site.*

(town) lot for a home site. In addition, taxes were to be waived for a minimum of five
years.[2] However, under Spanish rule the colonial population of Alta California remained exceedingly small in respect to the vast size of the province. By 1820, settlers
numbered only about 3,270.[3]

The paucity of population was also due to the fact that the overland route from
Sonora, Mexico, a trail blazed by Juan Bautista de Anza in 1774–1775, which he used
the following year to bring the largest party of Mexican settlers to California—240
men, women and children—was severed by the bloody Yuma Indian uprising on the
Colorado River in 1781.[4] Thereafter, colonists had to cross the Sea of Cortez, then
trek overland through Baja California, or come by ship, the latter both expensive and
trying. By 1796, aware that Alta California remained grossly under-populated, Spain
decided to send convicts and orphans to the province as a means of augmenting the
number of settlers.[5] A few artisans were also recruited, but "on discovering that the
promises the authorities had made to them about rations and a bounteous life for
them [and] their families were hollow," they "quickly returned from whence they
came."[6] Another population stimulus came from the presidial soldiers, some of
whom married native or colonial women; when discharged from service, they usually became permanent residents.[7] However, the persistent sparsity of population,
spread out over so large a territory, later proved an added enticement for foreign immigration to the province.

Although the first foreigners to Alta California came as visitors, not immigrants,
they made a contribution to the eventual foreign immigration. The Frenchman

Jean-François de Galaup de la Pérouse, explorer and scientist, called at Monterey on September 15, 1786, with two vessels for a ten-day stay. His visit is vividly recorded in his journal, *A Voyage Round the World, in the Years 1785, 1786, and 1788*.[8] The expedition artist also left the first visualizations of life in Spanish California by depicting La Pérouse's reception at Mission San Carlos Borromeo in Carmel. Like other visitors to follow, La Pérouse was impressed by two distinctive California features. He observed that "the fertility of this land is almost beyond words . . . [and] the climate . . . does not differ greatly from our southern French provinces."[9] Such flattering comments began to project an attractive image that eventually would lure immigrants, particularly Americans, to Alta California. La Pérouse also noted that the expedition "enriched the gardens of the Governor and the missions with different seeds brought from Paris, which had kept perfectly and will provide them with added benefits."[10] This was the first gift that helped diversify the province's fledgling agriculture. Subsequent visitors would also present enrichment gifts.

The next foreign visitors anchored in San Francisco Bay, November 17, 1792, aboard *H.M.S. Discovery*, under the command of Captain George Vancouver. Cordially received, the British reprovisioned their vessel and at the same time paid a visit down the peninsula to Mission Santa Clara, thus seeing something of the countryside. The primary purpose of Vancouver's voyage was to survey the coastline, which he had carefully done on his passage south from Nootka Sound in present-day British Columbia.[11] On November 25, the *Discovery* sailed for Monterey, having been joined by its consort, *H.M.S. Chatham*, a few days earlier. Anchoring the following day, the two ships found their storeship, *H.M.S. Daedalus*, waiting.[12] The latter departed on December 29, while the other ships, delayed by weather and a fruitless search for two deserters, did not sail until January 15, 1793. Unhappily for the deserters, they were later caught and delivered to Vancouver during his last visit to Monterey in November 1794, en route to England.[13]

On Vancouver's second visit, which included calls at San Francisco, Monterey, Santa Barbara, and San Diego between September 17 and December 9, 1794, he was cooly received. The new governor strictly adhered to the firm Spanish policy that foreign ships were not welcomed in Spanish-controlled waters. However, the frigid reception did not deter Vancouver from his appointed charge: he continued to survey the coast southward. On departing San Diego, he surveyed the Baja California coastline as far south as Cape San Lucas. His task completed, Vancouver and his consort sailed for England.[14] On arriving home, he commenced preparing his copious journal for publication. It was published posthumously in 1798.[15]

The importance of Vancouver's visitations to Alta California is threefold. First, his nautical charts, maps, and geodetic surveys provided invaluable information for ship captains. This in turn eventually spurred maritime activity on the California coast. Second, his descriptions of the territory, complimentary in the extreme, reinforced

An engraving based on a drawing by the sailor and amateur artist John Sykes, *The Mission of St. Carlos, near Monterrey* was one of three pictures of California that appeared in George Vancouver's *Voyage of Discovery* (London, 1798). Vancouver's survey of the Spanish territory was full and thorough, and his book, which served as a guide for subsequent visitors, was the first publication illustrated with general views of this outpost of empire. To the left of the picture can be seen the half-built walls of the seventh and present-day mission church at Carmel. *Courtesy California Historical Society, FN-30519.*

La Pérouse's views. Third, his critical assessment of the province's pathetic military defenses emboldened foreign ship captains to call at California ports in defiance of Spanish policy; it also signaled foreign nations that the territory could easily be plucked with little prospect of opposition. In addition, Vancouver also presented a number of tangible gifts in California, mostly hardware, which were sorely needed and put to good use. A "handsome barrelled organ" was also presented to Fray Fermín Francisco de Lausén, president of the California missions.[16]

The first American vessel to call at a California port was the *Otter,* Captain Ebenezer Dorr commanding, in 1796. While the ship was anchored in Botany Bay, Australia, eleven convicts had stowed away in hopes of escaping their forced incarceration. Anxious to be rid of his unwanted passengers, Dorr dumped the ten men and a woman on the Carmel beach at gunpoint. When news of this action reached the California governor, he was irate. Faced with the first foreign immigrants, the governor had little recourse: he put the stranded men to work as carpenters and blacksmiths at a salary of nineteen cents a day. Much to his surprise, the former convicts proved hard-working and docile. Under orders, the governor reluctantly sent them to Spain the next year. He also sent along the first known maritime deserter, Irishman Joseph Burling, who had gone ashore at Santa Barbara the previous year.[17]

Rigid Spanish colonial policy, however, could not deter the increasing appearance of "Boston ships" off the California coast in the decade following the *Otter's* initial contact. Coastal waters abounded in sea otters, whose pelts brought a handsome price on the Canton market. The emergence of the sea-otter trade proved a boon to Spanish Californians. Bartering pelts for New England products and exotic Chinese goods, the coastal population, including the missionaries, obtained needed necessities and luxury items that enriched their living standard. At the same time a market was found for California hides, tallow, and cattle horns (for buttons), a harbinger of trade that would later flourish under Mexican rule. Any Yankee trader caught in this illegal coastal trafficking faced stiff penalties, ranging from incarceration in poorly maintained prison cells to confiscation of ship and cargo. But the settlers' whetted appetites for foreign goods and the extraordinary profits realized from the sea-otter trade proved worth the risk for most mariners. An additional benefit derived from this illicit trade was an increase in the number of maritime deserters who opted for life in Alta California, bringing with them their labor skills and knowledge of commerce.[18]

Spain's grip on Alta California, always tenuous at best, became a casualty of the Napoleonic Wars with the French invasion and conquest of Spain in 1808. By 1810 the annual supply ships from San Blas, so essential in the life of the province, were discontinued due to the lack of goods and money. Annual stipends for the missionaries and pay for the soldiery and the government were also suspended. Mexico could not afford to fill the void. Having become dependent on the annual ship and subsidies from Spain, factors that decidedly controlled the province, the California populace had little recourse—it turned to illicit trade with the "Boston ships" as a new "corner-stone in the edifice of [the] provincial economy." This profound shift literally changed the basis of life in the province: it fostered "the movement that eventually brought about the American occupation" of Alta California, namely the growing presence of Yankee maritime traders, many of whom became permanent residents.[19]

Three years before Spain fell victim to France's military prowess, the first Russian visitor, Nikolai Petrovich Rezanov, chamberlain to the czar, sailed into San Francisco Bay on the *Juno*, April 8, 1805. Dispatched to the Russian settlements in Unalaska on an inspection tour, Rezanov was appalled by the near-starvation he found in Sitka. To remedy the recurring problem of food shortages in the colony, he undertook the passage to Alta California in search of urgently needed foodstuffs. Cordially received by the governor, during his brief sojourn the Russian fell in love with Concepción Argüello, the fifteen-year-old daughter of the presidio commandant. Although they were bethrothed, marriage had to await the necessary clearances for an Orthodox Christian to marry a Roman Catholic. In the meantime, Rezanov was successful in obtaining supplies. His ship sailed on May 8 with a cargo of cereals, dried beans and peas, tallow, and dried meat. Unfortunately, on his return trip to Russia, Rezanov died during the overland journey.[20]

However, the knowledge that foodstuffs were plentiful and available in Alta California attracted Russian interest in establishing an agricultural base in northern California, where the climate was more conducive for agriculture than were the Russian colonies father north. As a result, in search of a proper site, Ivan Kuskov, an officer in the Russian-American Fur Company, landed in 1809 at Bodega Bay, north of San Francisco; he determined it to be a good harbor. Returning in 1812—Spain now completely under French dominion—he began the formal establishment of facilities at Bodega Bay and on a plateau eighteen miles to the north. There, a colony named Rus (later translated as "Ross" by Americans) was built. Ross became the agricultural base while Bodega Bay served as a post for the hunting of sea otter and seals by Aleut natives under Russian command.[21]

Russian timing proved advantageous. Spain, under French control, was helpless in thwarting the Russian-American Fur Company's intrusion on Spanish soil. Nor could Mexico respond: it was contending with a burgeoning independence movement launched in 1810 by Fathers Hidalgo and Morelos. Thus the Russians' illegal, squatter presence was challenged only by recurring protestations from the provincial governors. Lacking sufficient military manpower and resources to mount an aggressive threat, their remonstrations went for naught. Although precluded from active trade and communication with Alta California, the Russians later created new commercial opportunities after Mexico asserted its independence from Spanish rule.[22] In addition, after 1822 a more limited trade also developed between Ross and the San Francisco Bay area, mostly in bartering livestock for goods. The Russians also supplied more substantial items, notably building watercraft for missions Dolores and San José.[23]

In search of sea-otter pelts and seal skins, Russian-led Aleut hunters scoured coastal waters. One such party ran afoul of the authorities on September 19, 1814. Working from the mother ship, the *Ilem*, Vassili Tarakanoff and eleven Aleuts sent ashore to obtain a supply of fresh meat were captured at San Pedro and probably taken to Mission San Fernando. During their two-year imprisonment there, four of the Aleuts married local women and became Catholics and permanent residents. How many other Aleut hunters assimiliated in this fashion is unknown. Tarakanoff and his fellow captives at first labored as field hands. Later, Tarakanoff offered his skill as an ironmonger, hoping to forge metal ploughs to replace the arcane wooden ones in use at the mission. His efforts were to no avail: there was an iron shortage.

Undaunted, he was allowed to do carpentry. He built household and church furniture and was paid for his handicraft. Thereafter, he "was treated somewhat better." Subsequently, Tarakanoff and the remaining seven Aleuts were sent north, and from Mission Dolores, on November 1, 1816, they sailed for Bodega Bay.[24]

Russian contact also influenced California labor patterns. Aleut hunters caught poaching in coastal waters were placed in bondage labor. A French visitor to San Francisco in 1817 was struck by the "very well-made tables and benches" he saw in the officers' quarters at the presidio. On inquiry, he discovered they were the work of an Aleut captive. He caustically recorded: "So, in an establishment founded forty years ago by Spain, a savage from the Russian possessions was found to be the most skilled workman."[25]

In the twilight of formal Spanish rule, foreign maritime visitors continued to call at San Francisco. As was the custom of the day, each visitor recorded his impressions in a journal, all of which were duly published. The Russian-sponsored scientific expedition under the command of Lieutenant Otto von Kotzebue, commanding the *Rurik*, is a typical example.[26] Even the first French visitor to the bay, Camille de Roquefeuil, captain of the *Bordelais*, on a trading venture that brought him to San Francisco on three occasions during 1817 and 1818, recounted his experiences. [27] His visit also provided California with two of its earliest foreign immigrants, two Spaniards, José Fernandez, a passenger, and Antonio María Suñol, a seaman deserter. Both "became somewhat prominent and respected citizens of the province."[28]

Even the abortive privateer threat in the fall of 1818 from Hippolyte de Bourchard, commanding two vessels flying the Buenos Aires flag, made a contribution to population growth when one of its members, an American named Joseph Chapman, was captured. A skilled carpenter and millwright, Chapman received amnesty and became a highly useful citizen. He built the first mill in California at Mission Santa Ines and a second at Mission San Gabriel. For the latter, he also built a schooner for coastal trade.[29] His life in California became the prototype of other compatriots who followed. He became a Catholic, married a Californio, and received a land grant.[30]

With Mexican independence from Spain in 1821, Alta California became a province in the newly established nation. Mexican rule swept aside most of the previous restrictive Spanish policies that had hampered economic development, maritime trade, and foreign contact. One of the first things Mexico did was to open all its ports, including California, to foreign commerce.[31] Citizenship for foreigners, forbidden under Spanish rule, was for the asking: the naturalization process was fast and easy. By 1828, land grants could be obtained either through naturalization or by locating the title twenty-five miles from the coastline, presumably to discourage smuggling by foreigners and to use immigrants as buffers between the coastal settlements and hostile interior Indians.[32]

By the 1820s, California had been made known to the world by foreign visitors' published journals, including *Journal of a Voyage Between China and the North-Western Coast of America, made in 1804 by William Shaler*, the first American account, printed in 1808.[33] The more important of the Mexican-era journals were those of the British Captain Frederick W. Beechey, an 1826–1827 visitor, and his fellow countryman, Sir Edward Belcher, who came in 1836–1837. The latter contained the first detailed maps for the principal California ports.[34]

Under more relaxed Mexican rule, California maritime commerce flourished with the establishment of the hide-and-tallow trade by the 1830s. Originally sparked in 1822 by British businessmen in Peru, after 1828 it was dominated by American traders from New England, primarily Boston. Because of the complexity of the trade in respect to credit and collection, it was quickly recognized that it was essential to have resident traders at strategic places in California, namely San Francisco, Monterey, and Los Angeles. Although lacking a harbor comparable to the San Francisco Bay area, San Pedro provided a fairly safe anchorage to accommodate Los Angeles, which had one of the largest concentrations of cattle in its environs. These resident agents—at first British citizens like William E. P. Hartnell (1822) at Monterey and later American Alfred Robinson (1829), who was what might be called a floating agent—were the forerunners of others to come. And like them, most became permanent residents, Catholic converts, married Californio women, and acquired land grants.[35] Equally important, these resident traders were fair and honorable business men who won the confidence of the local populace.[36]

There is no question that prior to 1841 the majority of foreign immigrants reached California by ship, either as passengers or maritime deserters. Typical of the latter was the Englishman William A. Richardson, who bolted the whaleship that brought him to San Francisco in 1822. The governor granted him permission for permanent residence on condition that he teach his skills in the navigation arts and carpentry to young Californios.[37] Another, Michael White (1829), either English or Irish, built the first boatyard in California at Santa Barbara, which constructed the province's first two ships.[38] Maritime deserters' skills enhanced the local economy and labor pool.

The prospect of lucrative commercial enterprise in Mexican California proved attractive to a number of aspiring American entrepreneurs. As the hide-and-tallow trade was developing, two experienced trading ship captains decided on permanent residence in 1826, Henry D. Fitch in San Diego and John B. R. Cooper in Monterey. Both became Catholics and married into important local families.[39] In 1829, another American, Abel Stearns, who had resided in Mexico for several years, opted for settlement in Los Angeles. Already naturalized, he too, married into one of the leading southern California native families.[40] Another longtime trader-captain, Nathan Spear, took up residence in Monterey in 1831, later relocating to San Fran-

The adventurous and enterprising Yankee Abel Stearns arrived in California in 1829 and soon settled in Los Angeles, where he traded in hides and wines. Though disfigured in a brawl, *cara de caballo,* or Horseface, as he was nicknamed, won the hand of the beautiful Arcadia, one of the daughters of the famed ranchero Juan Bandini. Stearns, who became a great landowner as well as the leading merchant of southern California, possessed the handsomest house in El Pueblo, with a ballroom one hundred feet long. *Courtesy California Historical Society/Title Insurance and Trust Photo Collection, University of Southern California.*

cisco, where he became a major commercial figure. In 1838, he was joined by his nephew, William Heath Davis, who followed in his uncle's footsteps.[41] Thomas O. Larkin, recruited by his half-brother John B. R. Cooper, settled in Monterey in 1832 and became a dominant figure in subsequent Mexican California history. But unlike others, he married an American widow. Their union resulted in the birth of the first American child to be born in California. At the same time, Larkin retained his American citizenship and remained a Protestant.[42] Alpheus B. Thompson, another long-time ship captain, decided on Santa Barbara as his home in 1834.[43] These Americans became highly successful. Allied to important Californio families through marriage (except Larkin), they were exceedingly able businessmen who knew how to handle bookkeeping, purchasing, collection, and credit and who were conversant in Spanish, which gave them a decided advantage in the hide-and-tallow trade over the captains commanding the trading vessels. As permanent residents and Mexican citizens they exerted considerable influence over their respective local economies and played a major role in the province's overall economy.

A young American sailor, Richard Henry Dana, Jr., serving on the hide-and-tallow ship *Pilgrim,* left a graphic account of his experiences along the California coast in 1835 and 1836, in the heyday of that distinctive commerce. His famed book, *Two Years Before the Mast: A Personal Narrative of Life at Sea,* published in 1840, frequently alluded to two themes: the wonderful California climate and rich soil, and the many failings of Californios. These latter reflect his New England upbringing and bias against anything Spanish (or Mexican).[44] Californians in his view were "an

The Larkin House, built in the mid-1830s by the Massachusetts-born trader Thomas O. Larkin a few years after his arrival in California. Although Larkin used adobe bricks to construct the massive walls of his home, he incorporated conventional Yankee design features into it, blending Hispanic and American building traditions in a manner that typifies the cultural accommodation practiced by maritime immigrants of the 1820s and 1830s. *Courtesy California State Library.*

idle, thriftless people" who could "make nothing for themselves," not even wine. The men were "thriftless, proud, and extravagant, and very much given to gaming," while the women "had little virtue" and "their morality, of course, is not of the best."[45] Dana concluded his observations on California with a telling statement:

> Such are the people who inhabit a country embracing four or five hundred miles of sea-coast, with several good harbors; with fine forests to the north; the waters filled with fish, and the plains covered with thousands of herds of cattle; blessed with a climate, than which there can be no better in the world; free from all manner of diseases, whether epidemic or endemic, and with a soil in which corn yields from seventy to eighty fold. In the hands of an enterprising people, what a country this might be![46]

Later, Thomas Jefferson Farnham, in his *Life and Adventures in California*, echoed Dana. After presenting a glowing description of the richness of the California landscape and terrain, Farnham wrote: "But its miserable people live unconscious of these things . . . they sleep, and smoke and hum some tune of Castilian laziness, while surrounding Nature is thus inviting them to the noblest and richest rewards of honorable toil."[47] As for the Californians, they were "an imbecile, pusillanimous, race of men . . . unfit to control the destinies of that beautiful country."[48] Such commentary left an untoward legacy in California: the seeding of racism by Americans. The majority of seamen who frequented California ports were New Englanders who had been teethed on the Black Legend spawned during the terrible religious wars that swept Europe in the wake of the Reformation. To many Protestant English and Americans, Spaniards were a black-hearted, traitorous people, indolent, lazy, immoral, and depraved. That view was extended to Californios.

And yet there was a counterweight to this; many mariners and traders married Californio women. In Monterey, Dana noted "a number of English and Americans . . . who have married Californians, become united with the Catholic church, and acquired considerable property." Since the English and Americans had "more industry, frugality and enterprise than the natives, they soon get nearly all the trade into their hands."[49] But Dana saw a downside. Although these English and Americans were "more industrious and effective than Spaniards," their children were being brought up as Spaniards, "in every respect, and if the 'California fever' (laziness) spares the first generation, it always attacks the second."[50]

On the other hand, the Californio view of the foreigners in their midst was strikingly different. Those who became a part of the community through marriage, faith, and citizenship found total acceptance. Although racially prejudiced against the native Indian populace, which provided the basic labor in the province, Californios accepted the casual commercial ship and visitors with equanimity. They were tolerated with courtesy and welcomed so long as they did not breach the peace or give offense. Famed for their hospitality, Californios extended to foreign visitors the best that could be provided in way of food, drink, lodging, and entertainment. The missionary padres occasionally worried about the prospect of Protestant influence on the populace, but that worry never became an issue because the visitors were intent on business; they were not religious missionaries seeking converts.[51]

Another harmful byproduct of the hide-and-tallow trade was that by 1846, with formal American occupation of California, the Californios were faced with severe economic consequences from that commerce. Again, Dana pointed the finger at part of the cause. He candidly observed that his ship's cargo "consisted of everything under the sun . . . from Chinese fireworks to English cart-wheels," all to entice the gullible Californio elite, namely the ranchero dons and their wives, selling them goods "at an advance of three hundred percent upon the Boston prices."[52] As for the ladies, Dana recorded that the "fondness for dressing among the women is excessive, and is often the ruin of many of them." With abandonment, they "frequently made purchases at a rate which would have made a sempstress or waiting-maid in Boston open her eyes."[53]

Thus the trading ships brought a cornucopia of goods to entice the consumer-hungry elite Californios. Fashion dominated: each man tried to provide his spouse, as well as himself, with the best that was to be had, be it in clothing, jewelry, furniture, or what-have-you. It became the rage: no home was a real home without a canopied bed, even if it stood on a dirt floor.[54] There was no question, many items purchased were for show, not use. A classic example is the sale of three pianos, the first brought to California in 1844. Yet there was not a single person in all of Mexican California who knew how to play them.[55] Californio rancheros simply could not resist the new or the unusual in their buying sprees. Yankee traders exploited that gullibility with unashamed abandon.

As the hide-and-tallow trade began to weaken in the early 1840s, the Californios found themselves in increasing debt. Declining prices for hides and tallow, coupled with exhorbitant custom duties, greatly increased the cost of imported consumer goods. This final crunch necessitated the slaughter of more cattle for "California bank notes," as the sailors called cow hides.[56] As a result, prices were depressed. It was a harsh cyclical situation from which there was no escape. The economic distress was further compounded by gambling losses, for gambling was part of the Californio culture. When confronted with American rule after 1846, Californios found themselves with a tax burden placed on their extensive land holdings for the first time. Already in a debtor posture, this new demand, coupled with legal costs connected with proving land titles, wrought havoc to many Californios.[57]

Although there were adverse economic effects resulting from the hide-and-tallow trade, there was an often unnoted benefit. The hide-and-tallow ships brought with them books in their sea chests. Dana pointed this out. He came in contact with a fellow seaman who "was very fond of reading." As a result, the sailor was lent "some of the books we had in the forecastle, which he read and returned to us the next time we fell in with him."[58] Books became a decided element in trade, especially for a group of young northern Californios, some of whom had been educated at William Hartnell's *seminario,* taught by Father Patrick Short, a Picpus missionary expelled from Hawaii who arrived by ship at San Pedro in January 1832. The following year, he joined Hartnell's fledgling institution when it opened in Monterey. Subsequently, the college, which included a library, was relocated to Hartnell's nearby Alisal Rancho.[59] Some of Mexican California's young men were educated as a result of this pioneering, but all too brief, enterprise. Hartnell and Nathan Spear had already been tutoring select pupils privately, as were several other foreigners. As a result of these efforts, a group of Californios became relatively well educated. Their names dominate the history of the last decade of Mexican sovereignty: Juan Bautista Alvarado, José Antonio Carrillo, José Castro, Manuel Jimeno, and Pablo de la Guerra. Two other important figures were Mariano Guadalupe Vallejo and his brother Salvador. Vallejo had acquired a large library and named all of his children after some famous author or historical personality.[60]

But there was an impediment to book importation: the Catholic Church's opposition to books it had placed on the prohibited Index. This, however, did not preclude their clandestine importation. In 1831, the *Leonor*, under Captain Henry D. Fitch, reached San Francisco Bay. He had on board "several boxes of books, banned, of course, by the California clergy." By secret negotiations he traded them to young Vallejo for four hundred hides and ten kegs of tallow.[61] Vallejo in turn shared his new purchase with friends Alvarado and Castro under a pledge of utmost secrecy. Unfortunately, Castro inadvertently leaked the news to a lady friend, who proved indiscreet. All three men were summarily excommunicated. On appeal to Father Narcíso Durán, father-president of the Franciscan missions, and reputedly on the acceptance of a monetary gift, the ban was lifted. "I give you permission to read the prohibited books," Father Durán wrote, "even Voltaire, Telemachus, Rousseau, etc., and even the Protestant Bible, with the sole condition that they shall not be placed in the hands of irresponsible or non-intelligent people."[62] No doubt the successful challenge mounted by Californios against increasingly authoritarian Mexican rule in 1836, led by Alvarado and Castro, stemmed in part from the enrichment of their knowledge through education and books brought to California by trading ships.

Foreign immigration overland proved a more daunting and difficult challenge to the Californios than did welcoming and absorbing those who arrived by ship. The first step in the eventual realization of overland travel began in 1826, when trails westward were beginning to be explored by fur-trapping parties led by such famed trappers as Jedediah Smith, Sylvester and James Ohio Pattie (father and son), Ewing Young, and Joseph R. Walker. The first to reach southern California was Smith, who appeared with his small band at Mission San Gabriel in 1826. He returned the following year to a less than hospitable reception. Since he had no passport, he was incarcerated. On being freed, he rejoined his trappers and pushed northward, eventually reaching Fort Vancouver, the Hudson's Bay Company's main headquarters in the Pacific Northwest, located at the confluence of the Columbia and Willamette rivers. His retreat northward was not without cost. Only three trappers and Smith survived an Indian massacre at the Umpqua River in July 1828.

The Patties reached San Diego via northern Baja California as prisoners in 1827, both having been arrested for failing to have a passport. Sylvester died in captivity, but his son James, having brought some smallpox vaccine, was freed to vaccinate the populace. He remained as a translator until 1830, when he took ship to Mexico. Ewing Young and his band made an extensive trapping foray in 1829–1831, working out of Taos, New Mexico. A smaller group of that party, led by Young and including Christopher (Kit) Carson, reached Mission San Gabriel in 1830. The following year, a party of thirty-six, again led by Young, trapped the San Joaquin Valley and its rivers. In 1833, Young took his party into the Northwest, well into present-day Oregon, before again trapping the Sacramento, San Joaquin, and San Bernardino valleys. He returned to Los Angeles in the summer of 1834. During these same years, 1833–1834, Joseph R. Walker and his trappers discovered Walker's Pass across the southern Sierra Nevada range, visited Monterey, then left the province via the Sacramento Valley.[63]

These early fur trappers' exploits had a major effect on foreign immigration. First, they blazed the trails that would accommodate overland travel. It was this breed of "Mountain Men" who discovered and utilized what became known as the Oregon Trail. By their trapping in the Southwest, these same furmen stimulated the revival of the "Old Spanish Trail," an overland route from New Mexico to the Pacific Coast.[64] In 1829, Antonio Armijo, aware that American trappers had begun to use the long-closed trail, reopened that route of communication. Yearly thereafter, an annual caravan of packers made the trip to Los Angeles and its environs to trade New Mexican products for horses, mules, and cattle.[65]

The California Trail, from the Oregon country south to Sacramento, also was the handiwork of fur trappers. Equally important, experienced early trappers later served as overland guides to westbound immigrants. Another ancillary contribution was the resultant publicity the furmen's activities generated, ranging from detailed reports for the federal government, graphic accounts of their exploits published in newspapers, especially those on the frontier, and books such as Pattie's *Personal Narrative,* published in 1831.[66]

Finally, many of the furmen who traveled to California were captivated by it and became permanent residents. Most of these former trappers retained their American citizenship and eschewed naturalization, religious conversion, and intermarriage. Many of their names loom large in the territory's history: Job Dye, Isaac Graham, Isaac Sparks, Jonathan T. Warner, William Wolfskill, and Isaac Williams, to name a few.

As the American populace grew in numbers during the 1830s, it was inevitable the new arrivals would play a larger part in the political life of the province. This became an established fact in 1836, when Isaac Graham recruited a company of "Wood Sawyers & Hunters to the number of 50 to 60," dubbed Los Rifleros Americanos, who aided Alvarado and Castro in seizing power from the Mexican-appointed governor in 1836.[67] However, that support also contributed to the infamous "Graham Affair" in the early spring of 1840. Graham, along with some five dozen Americans and British, was arrested on charges of treason and packed off to Mexico to stand trial in Tepic. Through the intervention of American and British officials in Mexico, the prisoners were released. Some, including Graham, returned to California.[68] But the "Graham Affair" became a cause célèbre. Thomas J. Farnham, who was on the scene at the time, treated it extensively in his book, *Travels in California.*[69]

The lure of Mexican California gradually developed on the American western frontier, producing a trickle of overland immigration. Among the first to respond was a Swiss immigrant, John A. Sutter. Having failed in business and marriage, he fled Europe to New York in 1834. Journeying west to St. Louis, he visited Santa Fe with a trading party, then traveled overland to Oregon, took ship for Honolulu, later Sitka, before reaching San Francisco in 1839. He prevailed on the governor to grant him eleven leagues (48,400 acres) of land in and around the confluence of the Sacramento and American rivers at what is today the state's capital, Sacramento. Accompanied by some Hawaiian laborers recruited in the Islands, and guided by William Heath Davis, well-known resident American business agent in San Francisco, Sutter took possession of his land. In 1840 he began the construction of Sutter's Fort.[70] In the immediate years to come, with the advent of increased overland immigration, this would become California's first "Ellis Island." In addition, many new American arrivals sought land grants in the Sacramento Valley because of the protection afforded the region by Sutter's Fort and the foreign and Indian militia he maintained as a precaution against hostile Indian attack.

Preceding Sutter by three years as a permanent California resident was John Marsh. From 1833 to 1835, he had lived in Independence, Missouri, where he was a merchant. Facing failure and bankruptcy, in the summer of 1835, he fled to Santa Fe, where he remained for several months. In February 1836, he arrived in Los Angeles and petitioned the *ayuntamiento* (pueblo council) for a license to practice medicine. As proof, he offered his Harvard A.B. degree, printed in Latin, as testament to his medical qualifications. After some difficulty in having the degree translated, the council finally licensed him on February 25. Dissatisfied with life in the southland, he scouted the San Francisco Bay area for a possible rancho. For a time he was guest of fellow American Jacob P. Leese, who had settled in 1836. After reconnoitering the locale, he purchased for $500 José Noriega's Rancho Los Meganos, in present-day Contra Costa County, between Mt. Diablo and present-day Byron. On receiving title to the four leagues, Marsh renamed his property Rancho Pulpunes. He settled down to life as a ranchero.[71]

In 1840, Marsh was galvanized by the "Graham Affair." He was called to attend the prisoners, including Graham, who "was cut and bruised from head to toe." Appalled by the brutal treatment meted out to the prisoners, Marsh later dispatched a blistering letter to Commodore Thomas ap Catesby Jones and asked his complaint to be forwarded to Washington.[72] He wrote in part:

> The French and English protect their subjects and are consequently more respected, while our consul at Tepic and American Minister in Mexico are absolute ciphers. Our government thinks we are better able to take care of ourselves than the people of the other nations, and I am disposed to think there is some truth in the opinion. Be this as it may, in a year or two more we shall at least be able to protect ourselves in California.[73]

To further that end, he had already begun writing letters to his former Missouri friends urging them to immigrate to California. Sending his letters via Santa Fe to the Missouri frontier, he ultimately aimed to attract sufficient American settlers to

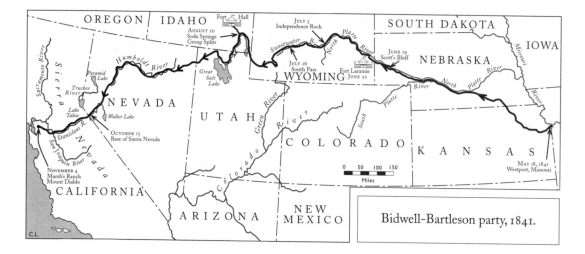

Bidwell-Bartleson party, 1841.

take actual possession of California, emulating their compatriots who had recently freed Texas from Mexican rule.[74]

As a direct result of Marsh's letters, the Western Emigration Society was formed in western Missouri in 1841 with an explicit purpose of recruiting immigrants for settlement in California. Although the recruitment drive was strongly opposed by frontier businessmen, the greatest discouragement came from Thomas J. Farnham. As recalled by John Bidwell, one of the first to join the Western Emigrant Society: "Just at this time [1841], and it overthrew our project completely—was published the letters of Farnham in the New York papers and republished in all the papers on the frontier at the instigation of the Weston [Missouri] merchants and others." In his volume, Farnham made no bones about his disdain for California and its Mexican rulers.[75]

But Bidwell was undeterred. He was the first to reach Sapling Grove, the rendezvous site, on May 9. Finally, by May 18, those who had determined to immigrate formally organized the party. This was the first planned overland immigration to California, a portent of what was to come. After adopting rules of conduct on the trail, the assembly elected John Bartleson as captain. Subsequently, the party was restyled the Bidwell-Bartleson party because Bidwell wrote the first published account of the company's overland trip. Fortunately for the greenhorns, the party attached itself to a Jesuit missionary band bound for the Northwest, guided by the experienced mountain man, Thomas Fitzpatrick, "Old Broken Hand."

The saga of the Bidwell-Bartleson party's westward trek need not be recounted, other than to note that at Soda Springs in present-day Idaho, the immigrants split into two groups: one bound for Oregon, the other California. The Bidwell-Bartleson party was forced to abandon their wagon and perilously made their way through the Sierra on foot. Fortune smiled, though; the party of thirty-two men and a

Called the "Prince of California Pioneers" by his biographer, John Bidwell crossed the Sierra Nevada and entered the broad expanse of the San Joaquin Valley in the autumn of 1841, one of the leaders of the first organized party of overland immigrants from the "States." In the vanguard of an ever-growing number of restless *norteamericanos* who would overrun the Mexican province, Bidwell subsequently acquired a vast rancho in northern California, mined for gold on the Feather River, and served as a United States Congressman. *Courtesy California State Library.*

woman with a baby daughter, reached Marsh's rancho in the shadow of Mt. Diablo on November 4, 1841.[76] One of the ironies of history was that this band of American immigrants was made welcome by Commandant General Mariano Guadalupe Vallejo. Although they lacked proper passports, he waived that formality. Subsequently, Vallejo and his brother Salvador became ardent enthusiasts for American immigration, since both were staunch admirers of democracy, typified, in their view, by the United States. They both later espoused the cause of an American takeover of California.[77]

Parallel with the Bidwell-Bartleson party was a like effort organized in Santa Fe. Two long-time American residents, John Rowland and William Workman, recruited a similar emigrant party. It may well be that Rowland had previously visited southern California several times, traveling with the annual trade caravan. To ensure their safety, the Workman-Rowland party traveled in tandem with the traders, the caravan totaling 134. The Workman-Rowland party—twenty-six men, four families, and servants (number unknown)—reached Tiburcio Tapia's Rancho Cucamonga in November, the exact date remains in dispute.[78] A message was dispatched to Los Angeles officials. Esteban Vigil, captain of the annual trade caravan, wrote, "I give you notice that a party of American merchants are coming, and with them are others who have the intention of residing in this country."[79] Rowland later reinforced this by stating that "The men with families come with the intention of establishing residence in this territory, and those have a trade to pursue same." The latter was important, for the party included two physicians, a tailor (Jacob Frankfort), musician, lawyers, gunsmith, engineer, mineralogist, naturalist, blacksmith, three carpenters, and two coopers.[80]

The successful, though harrowing, arrival of the Bidwell-Bartleson party in California was quickly made known on the Missouri frontier, as it was to the United States government. Ten of the original immigrants decided to return east in 1842 on horseback, led by Joseph B. Chiles and Charles Hooper. Using a variant of the Old Spanish Trail to Santa Fe, then via the Santa Fe Trail, they reached Independence, Missouri, in early September.[81] Their return would spark renewed interest in overland immigration. At the same time, Dr. Marsh informed Commodore Jones of the news:

> An event which will probably be regarded as of some importance in the future history of California, was the arrival in Nov. last year [1841] of an exploring party from the United States . . . they came in carriages to within about 200 miles of this place and probably would have come in them, the whole distance, had they [found] . . . the proper pass . . . their object was to see if California was indeed, the fine country it had been represented, and with the ulterior object of emigrating to it if it should meet their expectations. They were well received . . . and insured that all facilities will be afford them for the acquirement of lands.[82]

Although there was no immigration via the central or northern overland trails in 1842, a company of two hundred arrived in southern California from New Mexico, including forty foreigners who planned "to examine the country as a field for colonization." None of these, other than a few native New Mexicans, opted for permanent residence; the rest returned from whence they came.[83] However, the foreign resident population was increased by thirty-three who came by ship and elected to stay.[84]

In 1843, Chiles recruited and captained a party to Fort Laramie. There he met Joseph R. Walker, the experienced fur trapper, who joined as guide. Later the party split. Chiles took fifty-nine men, women, and children from present-day Boise to the Sacramento Valley by way of the Malheur and Pit rivers, thus opening a new trail. Walker pushed south and brought his group into the San Joaquin Valley via Walker's Pass.[85] A second party captained by Lansford W. Hastings, some 160 in number, departed Missouri for Oregon in 1842. Hastings, intent on going to California from the outset, led a party of fifty-three southward in the spring of 1843 along the established trail. En route, a goodly number defected on hearing that life in California was not an attractive prospect. Only sixteen or seventeen men and an unknown number of women and children reached Sutter's Fort.[86]

Sometime between 1843 and 1844, the journal John Bidwell kept of the 1841 pioneering overland trek was published either in Weston or Independence, Missouri.[87] This might well be called the first overland traveler's guide book. It certainly was used as such, since the only surviving copy, minus the title page, was brought to California by George McKinstry, Jr., an 1846 overland immigrant.[88] However, the journal had little or no impact on 1844 emigration, which consisted of only two parties. Andrew and Benjamin Kelsey, both members of the 1841 Bidwell-Bartleson party, later decided to move to Oregon, then changed their minds and returned south in 1844 to California with a company of thirty-six. The Stevens-Murphy party, led by Elisha Stevens, which included the large Murphy family, fifty men in all, plus women and children, followed the Bidwell-Bartleson route as best they could, but were more successful than their predecessor: they brought the first wagons across the Sierra, arriving safely at Sutter's Fort on December 3.[89]

Six civilian parties reached California overland in 1845. The first was led by Green McMahon, an 1841 overland pioneer, and James Clyman, a former trapper who kept a diary of the trip.[90] Originally the party went to Oregon, where most elected to settle. The rest followed McMahon and Clyman south to the Sacramento Valley in July. (One of the new arrivals, James Wilson Marshall, would earn fame for his gold discovery at Coloma in 1848.) A second Oregon contingent, forty-three in number, including a woman and three children, followed. The small Swasey-Todd party, twelve to thirteen men, using pack animals and horses, made it safely over the Sierra, as did the Grisby-Ide party, fifty men as well as families, totaling about one hundred in all. It proved to be the largest 1845 overland party. Two other smaller parties, one led by Solomon Sublette, with fifteen men, and a second Hastings contingent of ten travelers, also came to California.[91] The latter made it just in time, reaching Sutter's Fort on December 25. As for the Sublette party, it decided to return home.[92]

It is estimated that some 400 American emigrants came to California in 1845. Of that number, about 170 decided to become permanent residents.[93] However, these overland Americans were a new breed of settler. They came with their families when possible, remained United States citizens and Protestants, and if they arrived single, they often married fellow Americans. At the same time, some also acquired land grants, mostly in the Sacramento and San Joaquin valleys, an area that held little interest for Californios.

The sharp contrast between Spanish and Mexican California in respect to foreign immigration can be easily assayed. The first foreigner permitted to reside in Alta California was John Gilroy, an English seaman taken ill and left in San Francisco by the *Isaac Todd* in 1814, who lived out his days in and around the Monterey-Santa Cruz area. When Spanish rule ended in 1821, there were only seventeen foreigners residing in the entire province: five Americans, five Englishmen, three Irishmen, two Scotsmen, an Italian, a Portuguese, a Russian, and three blacks.[94] Under Mexican rule, by 1830 some 150 foreigners were residents; by 1835, that number doubled; by 1840, 380 are counted, and at the end of 1845, 680 foreigners are recorded.[95] The ma-

THE

EMIGRANTS' GUIDE,

TO

OREGON AND CALIFORNIA,

CONTAINING SCENES AND INCIDENTS OF A PARTY OF

OREGON EMIGRANTS;

A DESCRIPTION OF OREGON;

SCENES AND INCIDENTS OF A PARTY OF CALIFORNIA

EMIGRANTS;

AND

A DESCRIPTION OF CALIFORNIA;

WITH

A DESCRIPTION OF THE DIFFERENT ROUTES TO
THOSE COUNTRIES;

AND

ALL NECESSARY INFORMATION RELATIVE TO THE
EQUIPMENT, SUPPLIES, AND THE METHOD
OF TRAVELING.

BY LANSFORD W. HASTINGS,

Leader of the Oregon and California Emigrants of 1842.

CINCINNATI:

PUBLISHED BY GEORGE CONCLIN,

STEREOTYPED BY SHEPARD & CO.

1845.

Title page from Lansford Hastings's *Emigrants' Guide,* published in 1845 to promote settlement in California. Hastings, an Ohio-born lawyer who had visited the Mexican province two years earlier, proposed that overland travelers swing south of the Great Salt Lake on the "Hastings' Cut-Off" to save time. Following his advice in 1846, the Donner Party lost precious weeks wandering in the desert and, consequently, met disaster in the snows of the Sierra Nevada, nearly half of them perishing in their winter encampment. *Courtesy California Historical Society, FN-30522.*

jority were from the United States, but many nationalities had minority representation as reflected in the 1836 and 1844 censuses for Los Angeles, the only community raised to the legal status of *ciudad* (city) by the Mexican government.[96]

This foreign influx, as previously mentioned, augmented and enriched Alta California's labor force, bringing to it varied skills and talents, as well as founding and dominating the retail trades, including the introduction of retail branches. In addition, new commercial endeavors were launched that aided the province's economy. Innovations included viticulture, milling, ship construction, furniture manufacturing, blacksmithing—which led to the production of iron goods—distilleries, and especially lumbering.[97] The latter began in the early 1830s by independent American "sawyers," the contemporary name for today's lumberjacks. Thomas Larkin, who arrived with experience in sawmilling and lumbering, seized the opportunity and helped fashion the budding industry. Lumber and its byproducts became a profitable element in intercoastal trade and found a ready market in the Hawaiian Islands.[98]

The increasing presence of foreign nationals in California during the waning years of the Mexican period resulted in the appointment of resident consulate officials by the British, French, and United States governments. In 1842, James A. Forbes was appointed British vice-consul, taking office in October 1843; Louis Gasquet received his appointment in 1842 but did not reach California until mid-March 1845; he was succeeded by Jacob A. Moerenhaut in October 1846. Thomas O. Larkin was appointed American consul, taking up his formal duties in March 1844. He was the third consul appointed: the first, in 1837, died before he could embark for California; the second never took up his post.[99] Larkin's formal appointment, May 1, 1843, resulted in part from the abortive occupation of Monterey by American naval forces under Commodore Thomas ap Catesby Jones in October 1842, acting on the presumption that the United States and Mexico were at war.[100] Jones's seizure of Mexican California's capital without any resistance underscored Captain William Shaler's conclusion when he had paid a visit in 1804 with his ship, the *Lelia Byrd*: "The conquest of this country would be absolutely nothing; it would fall without an effort to the most inconsiderable force."[101]

With the election in 1844 of James K. Polk, who proclaimed America's "Manifest Destiny," Larkin was appointed "confidential agent," in modern parlance, a type of C.I.A. agent. The United States was troubled by the deep suspicion that France and Great Britain had aspirations on acquiring California as their territory. Secretary of State James Buchanan informed Larkin on October 17, 1845, that the United States "would vigorously interpose to prevent . . . [California] from becoming a British or French Colony." Furthermore, he continued, "whilst the President will make no effort and use no influence to induce California to become one of the free and independent States of this Union, yet if the People should desire to unite their destiny with ours, they would be received as brethren."[102]

A lithographic illustration, titled *Pass in the Sierra Nevada of California*, from John C. Frémont's epic *Report of the Exploring Expedition to the Rocky Mountains in the Year 1842, and to Oregon and North California in the Years 1843–'44* (Washington, 1845). A capable amateur scientist as well as a fearless adventurer, Frémont wrote engaging narratives of his travels, with the indispensable assistance of his wife, Jessie. His *Report* on his second and third expeditions not only served as a guide for immigrants but heated the passions of Americans eager to acquire a Pacific Coast empire. *Courtesy California Historical Society, FN-30518.*

Although unbeknown to the Californios, the year 1845 would prove a crucial one for Mexican California. In that year, two important United States government publications appeared: Charles Wilkes's *Narrative of the United States Exploring Expedition during the years 1838, 1839, 1840, 1841, 1842,* which included his account of the expedition's visit to California both by sea and land (an overland party from Oregon), and John Charles Frémont's report on his second expedition to the Far West, which included his first foray into California.[103] These two publications caught the attention of the American public, especially the politicians in Washington.

At the same time, events in California led to the armed overthrow of the province's last Mexican-appointed governor, General Manuel Micheltorena. Taking office in 1842, bringing with him an undisciplined and rowdy command of two hundred soldiers, Micheltorena and his *cholo* troops quickly alienated the Californio populace. They finally revolted in November 1844 and launched a campaign to rid the province of the governor and his despised soldiers. Sutter threw his support to Micheltorena and raised a company of one hundred American riflemen and one hundred loyal Indians to aid the embattled governor, who promised munificent land grants to those who came to his aid. In southern California, on the other hand, the entire foreign populace joined the rebels led by Pio Pico, José Castro, and Juan B. Alvarado. At the crucial confrontation between the two forces at the Battle of Cahuenga in February 1845, John Rowland and B. D. Wilson, members of the Workman-Rowland 1841 emigrant party, persuaded their fellow countrymen to abandon Micheltorena in the field. With the desertion of Sutter's company, Micheltorena surrendered two days later. He and his troops were force-marched to San Pedro, put on a chartered vessel, and sailed March 9 for Monterey to pick up the disposed governor's wife and additional soldiers. The ship departed on March 31, leaving behind fifteen to twenty previously discharged soldiers and a few others who wanted to remain.[104] Thus did actual Mexican rule in California come to an end. Pío Pico, a Californio, was chosen governor. Californios now ruled their native land, but their dominion was short-lived.

On the eve of the United States's war with Mexico, the American populace was festering under Mexican rule. There was a growing discontent among the newly arrived immigrants, who perceived Mexican laws as arbitary and repressive. Coming from a common law tradition, Americans found the Mexican justice system alien to their outlook.[105] Mexican law was designed to maintain the homogeneous, pastoral, and precommercial Californio society. This came into direct conflict with the atomistic and commercial-minded American immigrants, who wanted certainty and predictability in their daily transactions and who were not inclined to accept the conciliation and flexibility that characterized Mexican-California law. Rather than adhere to common law practice of enforcing a contract at any cost, the purpose of "Mexican civil litigation was to heal the breach in the community" without placing undue hardship on either disputant.[106] Because of the vastness of the territory, California's geographic isolation was largely responsible for the disparity between the written law and the system that actually developed in Mexican California. American immigrants disdained the paternalistic and benevolent dictatorial Mexican law, which worked to settle disputes locally and in an amicable fashion without any adherence to common law practice, notably the lack of trial by jury or writ of habeas corpus. There simply was little ground for reconciling the stark differences between the immigrants' legal outlook and that of the Californios.[107]

This situation became more acute after 1841 with the arrival of a new breed of immigrant. Most of these pioneers settled in interior areas eschewed by Californios. The resultant settlement pattern in effect fashioned American rural ghettos, segregated from the coast-bound Spanish-speaking community. Kindred souls tended to coalesce as a kind of protection of their way of life. Most new arrivals flaunted the requirement to make application for a passport, a kind of resident's visa. Intermarriage with the native populace was frowned upon, as was conversion to the Catholic

Church. Since the majority of the settlers after 1841 came as families, that binding unit reinforced the desire for isolation from the Californio community. These new immigrants were Americans, first, last, and always. That nativistic arrogance bred divisiveness and distrust between Californios and immigrant Americans.[108]

Reflecting on the growing discontent and disenchantment with Mexican law and rule, two American émigrés—John Marsh and Charles M. Weber—suggested to their compatriots that they begin to imitate their Texan counterparts and resist Mexican intrusions into their lives and property.[109] At the same time, some Californios, feeling little or no allegiance to Mexico, were openly debating whether to place California under the protection of France, Great Britain, or the United States. By the summer of 1846, unaware that war with Mexico had become a reality, and no doubt emboldened by the presence of John C. Frémont and his exploring brigade on a second visit to California, a group of American settlers in the Sacramento and Sonoma valleys commenced an armed revolt and unfurled a hastily lettered and drawn bear flag as a symbol of independence and liberty. This extraordinary movement, subsequently named the Bear Flag Revolt, led to the abortive establishment of the so-called California Republic, which lasted only a month, from June 10 to July 9, 1846. This mini-episode's success was due primarily to the active support rendered by Frémont and his troops. However, the effort was for naught when American naval forces formally occupied California's capital, Monterey, and took over the provincial government.[110] The latter achieved what the relatively small band of Bear Flaggers intended: to make certain California became a part of the United States. Ironically, the Mexican government's liberal policies respecting foreign nationals residing in California had proven to be Alta California's Trojan horse.

The historiography on the impact of foreign immigration on Alta California has been greatly enriched by a number of recent publications that are fully cited in the notes. Older studies, particularly the published journals of foreign visitors, are likewise cited in the notes. Two recent books are exceedingly important: David J. Langum, *Law and Community on the Mexican California Frontier: Anglo-American Expatriates and the Clash of Legal Traditions, 1821–1846* (1987), and Douglas Monroy, *Thrown among Strangers: The Making of Mexican Culture in Frontier California* (1990). They provide new insights into the relationship between Californios and foreign immigrants. A number of new biographies have added much to the understanding of foreign immigrants, and these are also cited in the endnotes. Although Mariano Guadalupe Vallejo has been treated in three biographies, there is a paucity of other Californio biographies. What is needed are more studies like Pearl R. Fibel, *The Peraltas: Spanish Pioneers and First Family of the East Bay* (1971). Exceedingly useful is *A Bibliography of Early California and Neighboring Territory Through 1846,* complied by Robert L. Santos (Turlock, Calif: Privately printed, 1992). For a general overview of sources pertinent to pre-1846 Alta California, see Doyce B. Nunis, Jr., and Gloria R. Lothrop, eds., *A Guide to the History of California* (Westport, Conn.: Greenwood Press, 1989), 3–34.

NOTES

1. For the impact of the "Bourbon Reforms" on trade and travel in Spanish America, with California being a notable exception, see John Lynch, ed., *The Spanish American Revolutions, 1808–1826* (Norman: University of Oklahoma Press, 1994).

2. An excellent example of this is found in Thomas Workman Temple II, "Supplies for the Pobladores," *Annual Publication Historical Society of Southern California* XV, Pt. 1 (1931): 121–34, and "Outfits of Soldiers, Settlers and Families," ibid., 146–47; Marion Parks, "Correspondence Pertaining to Reglamento and to Recruital of Pobladores," ibid., 135–42.

3. Hubert H. Bancroft, *History of California* (7 vols., San Francisco: A. L. Bancroft & Company, Publishers, 1884–1890), II: 392.

4. Herbert E. Bolton, ed. and trans., *Anza's California Expeditions* (5 vols., Berkeley: University of California Press, 1930), III and IV, passim. Also see Bolton, *Outpost of Empire: The Story of the Founding of San Francisco* (New York: Alfred A. Knopf, 1931).

5. Bancroft, *California*, I: 539, 605–606; II: 169; Salomé Hernández, "No Settlement Without Women: Three Spanish California Settlement Schemes, 1790–1800," in *Southern California's Spanish Heritage: An Anthology*, ed. by Doyce B. Nunis, Jr. (Los Angeles: Historical Society of Southern California, 1992), 309–38.

6. Douglas Monroy, *Thrown among Strangers: The Making of the Mexican Culture in Frontier California* (Berkeley and Los Angeles: University of California Press, 1990), 109–10.

7. An examination of Bancroft's "Pioneer Register" in his *California*, at the end of volumes II–V, attests to this eloquently.

8. The original French edition was published in Paris under the Imprimerie de la République in four volumes, 1797, followed by a second printing by Chez Plassan in 1798. The first English translation was published in London in 1799 by G. G. and J. Robinson, J. Edwards, and T. Payne. These are superceded by John Dunmore, trans. and ed., *The Journal of Jean-François de Galaup de la Pérouse, 1785–1788* (2 vols., London: The Hakluyt Society, 1955).

9. Ibid., I: 173.

10. Ibid.

11. W. Kaye Lamb, ed., *The Voyage of George Vancouver, 1791–1795* (4 vols., London: The Hakluyt Society, 1984), II: 486–91.

12. Vancouver's first California sojourn is recounted in ibid., 704–27, 737–46.

13. Ibid., 788; IV: 1417. Two other deserters from the *Daedalus*, the storeship, were also turned over by the Spanish authorities. Ibid., IV: 1416, n.2.

14. Ibid., III: 1062, 1114–22.

15. Vancouver died on May 12, 1798. His brother John completed the final manuscript, which was published in London by G. G. and J. Robinson, and J. Edward, three volumes plus atlas, in 1798. A second revised edition followed three years later (6 vols., London: John Stockdale, 1801).

16. Lamb, ed., *Voyage of George Vancouver*, III: 1110. The organ was taken to Carmel and today is on display at Mission San Juan Bautista in San Benito County. Ibid., 1. The pathetic military posture in Alta California is reflected in John P. Langellier and Daniel B. Rosen, *El*

Presidio de San Francisco: A History Under Spain and Mexico, 1776–1846 (Spokane, Wash.: Arthur H. Clark Company, 1996).

17. Bancroft, *California,* I: 538–40, and notes.

18. Robert G. Cleland, *A History of California: The American Period* (New York: The Macmillan Company, 1926), 1–21. Adele Ogden, *The California Sea-Otter Trade, 1784–1848* (Berkeley: University of California Press, 1941), provides solid treatment of this important early-nineteenth-century economic development. Also, see her study, "New England Traders in Spanish and Mexican California," in *Greater America: Essays in Honor of Herbert Eugene Bolton,* ed. by Adele Ogden and Engel Sluiter (Berkeley: University of California Press, 1945), 395–413. For the role of the missionaries, Sister Magdalen Coughlin, "Missionary and Smuggler: Acts of Disobedience or Civilization?" in *Some California Catholic Reminiscences for the United States Bicentennial,* ed. by Francis J. Weber (Los Angeles, 1976), 91–110.

19. Charles E. Chapman, *A History of California: The Spanish Period* (New York: The Macmillan Company, 1921), 438–39.

20. *The Rezanov Voyage to Nueva California in 1806 by Nikolai Petrovich Rezanov* (Reprint ed., Fairfield, Wash.: Ye Galleon Press, 1988), 11–64, offers his personal account. He died on March 1, 1807, at Krasnoyarsk in eastern Siberia. Ibid., 86. For his California romance, see Eve Iverson, "Nickolai Rezanov and Concepción Argüello: A Tale of Old California," *California Historian* 42 (Summer 1996): 6–15. Another first-hand account is found in *Langsdorff's Narrative of the Rezanov Voyage of Nueva California in 1806 by Doctor Georg H. von Langsdorff* (Reprint ed., Fairfield, Wash.: Ye Galleon Press, 1988), 17–143, a distillation from George Henrich von Langsdorff, *Remarks and Observations on a Voyage Round the World From 1803 to 1807,* trans. and annotated by Victoria J. Moessner, ed. by Richard A Pierce (Kingston, Ontario, and Fairbanks, Alaska: The Limestone Press, 1993), 2 vols. in one; for the California visit, 2: 84–129. The latter was originally published in German at Frankfort-on-the-Main, 1812, with an English translation in London, 1813–14, both editions in two volumes.

21. E[dward] O. Oliver Essig, "The Russian Settlement at Ross," *California Historical Society Quarterly* XII (September 1933): 191–209; Bancroft, *California,* II: 58–92, 294–320, 628–42; IV: 158–80; Adele Ogden, "Russian Sea-Otter and Seal Hunting on the California Coast, 1803–1841," *California Historical Society Quarterly* XII (September 1933): 217–39. An important collection of documents from Mexican archives has been published by W. Michael Mathes, ed., *La frontera Ruso-Mexicana, Documentos mexicanos para la historia del establecimiento ruso en California 1808–1842* (Mexico, 1990).

22. Basil Dmytryshyn and E. A. P. Grownhart-Baughn, trans and eds., *Colonial Russian America: Kyrill T. Khlebnikov's Reports, 1817–1832* (Portland: Oregon Historical Society, 1976), 108–16, provides an insight into this embryonic development. For example, the *Juno* in trading for foodstuffs offered in return Flemish and sail cloth, heavy woolens and cotton goods, leather boots, tempered saws and axes, as well as needles. Ibid., 114. In 1815 the brig *Ilem* offered Virginia tobacco, sugar, pewter ware, coffee, cotton stockings, wax candles, Chinese cloth, Bengal Calico, iron, and sailcloth. Ibid., 115.

23. The two vessels were built in 1823 and 1827. Essig, "The Russian Settlement at Fort Ross," 194–95.

24. Ivan Petroff, trans., Arthur Woodward, ed., *Statement of My Captivity Among the Californians by Vassili Petrovich Tarakanoff* (Los Angeles: Glen Dawson, 1953), 9–34. Bancroft, *California,* II: 308, has a garbled version and spells the name Tarakanof.

25. Charles N. Rudkin, trans. and ed., *Camille de Roquefeuil in San Francisco, 1817–1818* (Los Angeles: Glen Dawson, 1954), 14.

26. Originally published in German: *Entdeckungs-Reise in die Sü-See und nach der Berings-Strasse* . . . (3 vols., Weimar: Gebrüder Hoffmann, 1821); the first English translation, *A Voyage of Discovery, into the South Sea and Beering [sic] Straits* . . . , was published in London by Longman, Hurst, Rees, Orme, and Brown, three volumes, in 1821. An abridged edition followed that same year. The account by the expedition's artist, Lukovik Choris, with his drawings as illustrations, was published in Paris in 1822. One of the scientists, Adelbert von Chamisso, wrote another account, which appeared in volume one of the original German edition, later translated by George McElroy and published in *Overland Monthly* (March 1873), reprinted in August C. Mahr, *The Visit of the "Rurik" to San Francisco in 1816* (Stanford: Stanford University Press, 1932), and again as *A Sojourn in San Francisco Bay, 1816* (San Francisco: Book Club of California, 1936), with changes and corrections to the translation. A more scholarly edition of the latter is *A Voyage around the World with the Romanzov Exploring Expedition in the Years 1815–1818*, trans. and ed. by Henry Kratz (Honolulu: University of Hawaii Press, 1986), which is von Chamisso's full account of his adventures.

27. The original journal was published in Paris in 1823. That same year an abridged and crudely translated English edition was published in London. Rudkin, trans. and ed., *Roquefeuil in San Francisco*, offers a superior translation.

28. Bancroft, *California*, II: 288–89.

29. Ibid., 556, 568, 691; III: 140, 209, 363, 382.

30. Ibid., II: 757.

31. Sherman F. Dallas, "The Hide and Tallow Trade in Alta California, 1822–1846" (Ph.D. diss., Indiana University, 1955), 14.

32. W. W. Robinson, *Land in California* (Berkeley: University of California Press, 1948), 65–66.

33. Originally published in Philadelphia, it was reprinted by the Saunders Studio Press, Claremont, California, 1935.

34. Beechey, *Narrative of a Voyage to the Pacific and Bering's Straits* . . . (2 vols., London: Henry Colburn and Richard Bentley, 1831); a one-volume version was issued by the same publisher in 1832; Belcher, *Narrative of a Voyage Round the World* . . . (2 vols., London: Henry Colburn, 1843). Robert G. Cleland, *A History of California: The American Period* (New York: MacMillan Company, 1926), 91–107, was the first historian to point out how journals and travel accounts advertised California and influenced immigration, in a chapter aptly entitled, "Advertising and Immigration."

35. Dallas, "The Hide and Tallow Trade in Alta California," 75 ff.; Susanna B. Dakin, *The Lives of William E. P. Hartnell* (Stanford: Stanford University Press, 1949), is an excellent biography. For Robinson, see his *Life in California* (New York: Wiley & Putnam, 1846), with five reprint editions and even a paperback edition.

36. Antonio María Osio, *The History of Alta California: A Memoir of Mexican California*, trans. and ed. by Rose Marie Beebe and Robert M. Senkewicz (Madison: University of Wisconsin Press, 1996), 70, records that Robinson's integrity and honesty "won the widespread friendship of the inhabitants of the territory." Further praise for resident agents is expressed in ibid., 198.

37. Robert R. Miller, *Captain Richardson: Mariner, Ranchero, and Founder of San Francisco* (Berkeley: La Loma Press, 1995), details his life.

38. Michael C. White, *California All the Way Back to 1828,* ed. by Glen Dawson (Los Angeles: Glen Dawson, 1956), reprints a dictation given to Thomas Savage for H. H. Bancroft in 1877.

39. Bancroft, *California,* II: 765–66; III: 73–40. Ronald L. Miller, "Henry Delano Fitch, 1826–1848" (Ph.D. diss., University of Southern California, 1972), presents an overview of his California life. John Woolfenden and Amelie Elkinton, *Copper: Juan Bautista Rogers Cooper: Sea Captain, Adventure, Ranchero and Early California Pioneer, 1791–1872* (Pacific Grove, Calif: Boxwood Press, 1983), is an excellent biography.

40. Doris M. Wright, *A Yankee in Mexican California: Abel Stearns, 1798–1848* (Santa Barbara: Wallace Hebberd, 1977), documents Stearn's early life in Los Angeles.

41. William Heath Davis, *Seventy-Five Years in California,* ed. by Harold A. Small (San Francisco: John Howell-Books, 1967), describes in great detail the business affairs of Spear and himself in the Bay Area. Also, see Andrew F. Rolle, *An American in California: The Biography of William Heath Davis* (San Marino: Huntington Library, 1956). For concise biographies of Davis and Robinson, see Charles B. Churchill, *Adventures and Prophets: American Autobiographers in Mexican California, 1828–1847* (Spokane, Wash.: Arthur H. Clark Company, 1995), 19–69.

42. The best biography is *Thomas O. Larkin: A Life of Patriotism and Profit in Old California* by Harlan Hague and David J. Langum (Norman: University of Oklahoma Press, 1990). It supercedes the early study, Reuben C. Underhill's *From Cowhides to Golden Fleece: A Narrative of California, 1832–1858* (Stanford: Stanford University Press, 1939).

43. Bancroft, *California,* V: 746; D. Mackenzie Brown, ed., *China Trade Days* (Berkeley: University of California Press, 1947), 1–4. The latter is a selection of Thompson's commercial letters.

44. John H. Kemble, ed., *Two Years before the Mast. A Personal Narrative of Life at Sea* by Richard Henry Dana, Jr. (2 vols., Los Angeles: the Ward Ritchie Press, 1964), is the best edition. The original was published in New York by Harper & Brothers. Also see Churchill, *Adventurers and Prophets,* 93–114. Complementing Dana is William Dane Phelps ["Webfoot"], *Fore and Aft; or Leaves from the Life of An Old Sailor* (Boston: Nichols & Hale, 1871), and Briton C. Busch, ed., *Alta California, 1840–1842: The Journal and Observations of William Dane Phelps, Master of the Ship "Alert"* (Glendale, Calif: Arthur H. Clark Company, 1983). Churchill, *Adventurers and Prophets,* 71–89, provides an overview of Phelps, his book and journal.

45. Kemble, ed., *Two Years before the Mast,* I: 82, 171. David J. Langum, "Californios and the Image of Indolence," *Western Historical Quarterly* IX (April 1978): 181–96, provides a succinct treatment of the very points raised by Dana. Also, see Cecil Robinson, *With the Ears of Strangers: The Mexican American in Literature* (Tucson: University of Arizona Press, 1963), and his *Mexico and the Hispanic Southwest in American Literature* (Tucson: University of Arizona Press, 1977). David J. Weber, ed., *Foreigners in Their Native Land: Historical Roots of the Mexican Americans* (Albuquerque: University of New Mexico, 1973), provide insights into this supposed California trait of laziness, as does James D. Hart's *American Images of Spanish California* (Berkeley: Friends of the Bancroft Library, 1960). Important articles are Harry Clark, "Their Pride, Their Manners, and Their Voices: Sources of the Traditional Portrait of the Early Californians," *California Historical Quarterly* 53 (Spring 1974): 71–82; Raymund A. Paredes, "The Mexican Image in American Travel Literature, 1813–1869," *New Mexico Historical Review* 52 (January 1977): 5–29, and his article "The Origins of Anti-Mexican Sentiment in the United States," *New Scholar* 6 (1977): 130–65.

46. Kemble, ed., *Two Years before the Mast*, I: 171–72.

47. The Farnham quote is from his *Life, Adventures and Travel in California* (New York: Cornish, Lamport, 1852), as quoted in Cleland, *A History of California*, 98.

48. Thomas J. Farnham, *Travels in California* (Reprint of 1844 ed., Oakland: Biobooks, 1947), 148.

49. Kemble, ed., *Two Years Before the Mast*, I: 88.

50. Ibid., 172.

51. Osio, *The History of Alta California*, ed. and trans. by Beebe and Senkewicz, 70, 198; Monroy, *Thrown among Strangers*, 110–12, details Californio-Indian relations. Sir George Simpson, *Narrative of a Voyage to California in 1841–42* (Reprint ed., San Francisco: Private Press of Thomas C. Russell, 1930), 125, wrote: "Among the light-hearted and easy-tempered Californians, the virtue of hospitality knows no bounds. They literally vie with one another in devoting their time, their homes, and their means to the entertainment of a stranger." For other Franciscan outlooks, see Zephyrin Engelhardt, *The Missions and Missionaries of California* (4 vols., San Francisco: James H. Barry Company, 1912–1915), III: 317; IV: 106–107, 114.

52. Kemble, ed., *Two Years before the Mast*, I: 82–83.

53. Ibid., 84.

54. Sir George Simpson, in his *Narrative of A Voyage of California in 1841–42*, 119, caustically made note of this: " . . . the beds appear to be the grand point of attraction, and embody all the skill and taste of the female of the families, though the farther that one advances south the lines and the lace, and the damask and the satin, and the embroidery , serve only to enshrine more populous and lively colonies of Las Pulgas [fleas], decidedly the best-lodged, and as we found to our cost not the worst-fed, denizens of California."

55. Erastus D. Holden, "California's First Pianos," *California Historical Society Quarterly* XIII (March 1934): 34–37. Vallejo bought one.

56. Dallas, "The Hide and Tallow Trade in Alta California," 163–69; Kemble, ed., *Two Years before the Mast*, I: 82–85, 88 .

57. Leonard Pitt, *The Decline of the Californios* (Berkeley and Los Angeles: University of California Press, 1966), traces the Californios' sad demise. However, he omits to take note of their extravagance prior to 1846, which helped lead them to become debtors.

58. Kemble, ed., *Two Years before the Mast*, I: 91.

59. Harold C. Whelan, SS. CC., *The Picpus Story* (Pomona: Apostolate of Christian Renewal, 1980), 104–11.

60. It should be noted that of the ill-fated Padrés-Híjar party, which came to California from Mexico in 1834, most of the 250 in number on the roster, including a school teacher, were well-educated.

61. Doyce B. Nunis, Jr., *Books in Their Sea Chests: Reading along the Early California Coast* (Sacramento: California Library Association, 1964), 8–9; Nellie Van de Grift Sánchez, *Spanish Arcadia* (Los Angeles: Powell Company, 1929), 226–30.

62. Durán's letter is found in Mariano Guadalupe Vallejo's "Recuerdos Historicos y Personales tocante a la Alta California," III: 109–17, ms., Bancroft Library, University of California, Berkeley.

63. The travels of Smith, the Patties, Young, and Walker are detailed in Robert G. Cleland, *This Reckless Breed of Men: The Trappers and Traders of the Southwest* (New York: Alfred A. Knopf, Publisher, 1963). *The Californios versus Jedediah Smith, 1826–1827: A New Cache of Documents*, ed. by David J. Weber (Spokane, Wash.: Arthur H. Clark Company, 1990), casts

new light on Smith's two California visits. For an insight into James O. Pattie, see Churchill, *Adventurers and Prophets,* 143–57.

64. LeRoy R. Hafen and Ann W. Hafen, *Old Spanish Trail: Santa Fe to Los Angeles* (Reprint ed., Lincoln: University of Nebraska Press, 1993), provides an overall history.

65. Ibid., 155–94; Eleanor Lawrence, "Mexican Trade Between Santa Fé and Los Angeles, 1830–1848," *California Historical Society Quarterly* X (March 1831): 27–39.

66. Doyce B. Nunis, Jr., "The Fur Men: Key to Westward Expansion," *The Historian* XXIII (February 1961): 157–90.

67. Alfred Robinson to Bryant & Sturgis, December 18, 1836, Alfred Robinson Papers, California Historical Society, San Francisco; Doyce B. Nunis, Jr., *The Trials of Isaac Graham* (Los Angeles: Dawson's Book Shop, 1967), 21–22.

68. Ibid., 22–33; Bancroft, *California,* IV: 2–35.

69. Farnham, *Travels in California,* 57–110, 124–39.

70. Richard Dillon, *Captain John Sutter: Sacramento Valley's Sainted Sinner* (Reprint ed., Santa Cruz; Western Tanager Press, 1981), 19–106, originally published under the title *Fool's Gold: A Biography of John A. Sutter* (New York: Coward-McCann, Inc., 1967). For a revisionist view of the life of Sutter, see Kenneth N. Owens, ed., *John Sutter and a Wider West* (Lincoln: University of Nebraska Press, 1994).

71. George D. Lyman, *John Marsh, Pioneer* (New York: Charles Scribner's Sons, 1930), 193–223; Robert G. Cowan, *Ranchos of California* (Fresno: Academy Library Guild, 1956), 47.

72. Lyman, *John Marsh, Pioneer,* 237–40.

73. Dated November 24, 1842, ms., Bancroft Library.

74. Lyman, *John Marsh, Pioneer,* 237–40.

75. Doyce B. Nunis, Jr., ed., *The Bidwell-Bartleson Party: 1841 California Immigrant Adventure* (Santa Cruz: Western Tanager Press, 1991), 9.

76. Ibid., 15. Bidwell's complete journal is reprinted in this source.

77. The Vallejos' views are detailed in Alan Rosenus, *General M. G. Vallejo and the Advent of the Americans* (Albuquerque: University of New Mexico Press, 1995) Rosenus observes: "Vallejo was extremely partial to American political thought. He was also impressed by the talented, sometimes unpredictable immigrants . . . From the early 1840s on, his desire to make California a part of the United States became his most urgent political goal." Ibid., xiv.

78. Ignacio Palomares to Santiago Argüello, December 2, 1841, Departmental State Papers, Bernicia Prefectura y Juzgada, III: 100, Bancroft Library. Bancroft, *California,* IV: 227, holds the party "arrived at San Gabriel in early November."

79. Letter to the Prefect of Los Angeles, October 15, 1841, San Diego Archives, 279, Bancroft Library; Juan B. Alvarado to José Castro, December 6, 1841, Vallejo Documents, X: 383, Bancroft Library.

80. "Lista de los que acompanan al Ser. que suscribe en su lleguda al territorio de Alta California," by John Rowland, February 26, 1842, Prefecture Records of Los Angeles, 1840–1850, Los Angeles County, Huntington Library, San Marino. An English translation is in the Los Angeles County Recorder's Office, Hall of Records, Los Angeles.

81. Nunis, ed., *The Bidwell-Bartleson Party,* 141.

82. Letter dated November 24, 1842, quoted in ibid., vi.

83. Bancroft, *California,* IV: 343–44.

84. Ibid., 341.

85. Ibid., 392–95.

86. Ibid., 389–90.

87. Nunis, ed., *The Bidwell-Bartleson Party,* 3–7, discusses the problem of the publication date.

88. This copy is in the Bancroft Library.

89. Bancroft, *California,* IV: 444–47.

90. Charles L. Camp, ed., *James Clyman, Frontiersman* (Portland: The Champoeg Press, 1960), 65 ff.

91. Bancroft, *California,* IV: 572–79.

92. Doyce B. Nunis, Jr., "The Enigma of the Sublette Overland Party, 1845," *Pacific Historical Review* LVII (January 1959): 331–49.

93. Bancroft, *California,* IV: 587.

94. Ibid., II: 247, 283, 444, 478–79, 739 781; III: 757.

95. Ibid., V: 524, 588.

96. Los Angeles was raised to the status of a city on May 25, 1836. Author's copy of a facsimile of the proclamation. See J. Gregg Layne, "The First Census of the Los Angeles District," *Quarterly Historical Society of Southern California* VIII (September–December 1936): 81–99, which records fifty foreigners: twenty Americans; four English, five French, three Portuguese, two Africans, one each from Canada, Curaçao, Germany, Ireland, Italy, Norway, and Scotland; Marie E. Northrop, "The Los Angeles Padron of 1844," ibid., XLII (December 1960): 36–417, lists sixty-one foreigners: thirty-one Americans, five English, eight French, three each from Peru, Portugal, and Spain, two from Chile and Germany, one each from Columbia, Italy, and the Philippine Islands. In another census, 1829, compiled by Guillermo Cota, fifty-three foreigners are enumerated: twenty-six Americans, five English, six French, three each from Portugal, Peru, Spain, two each from Chile, Scotland, and Germany, one Italian. Thomas W. Temple, II, "Some Notes on the 1844 Padron de Los Angeles," ibid., 422.

97. Mercantile Trust Company of California, "Beginnings and Development of Trade on the Pacific Coast of North America," *Monthly Review* XI, Pts. 6–9 (January–April 1923): 10–12, 39, 41, 56–61, 78–79; Iris A. Wilson, "Early Southern California Viticulture," *Quarterly Historical Society of Southern California* XXXIX (September 1957): 242–50.

98. Hague and Langum, *Thomas O. Larkin,* 44, 62, 64–66, 78–79; Sherwood D. Burgess, "Lumbering in Hispanic California," *California Historical Society Quarterly* XLI (September 1962): 237–48.

99. Ernest A. Wiltsee, "The British Vice Consul and the Events of 1846," *California Historical Society Quarterly* X (June 1931): 99; Abraham P. Nasatir, "The French Consulate in California, 1845–1856," ibid., (September 1932): 203–207; Hague and Langum, *Thomas O. Larkin,* 97–99.

100. Bancroft, *California,* IV: 289–329; George M. Brooke, Jr., "The Vest Pocket War of Commodore Jones," *Pacific Historical Review* XXXI (August 1962): 217–34.

101. Quoted in Cleland, *History of California,* 470–82, which reprints Shaler's complete description of California.

102. George P. Hammond, ed., *The Larkin Press* (10 vols., Berkeley and Los Angeles: University of California Press, 1951–1968), 4: 44–45.

103. Wilkes's *Narrative* was published in five volumes plus atlas in Philadelphia by Lea and Blanchard. The California portion has been reprinted in *Columbia River to the Sacramento* (Oakland: Biobooks, 1958). Frémont's *A Report of the Exploring Expedition to Oregon and North California in the Years 1843–44,* was published in Washington, D.C., by the Gov-

ernment Printing Office. It is reprinted in full in Donald Jackson and Mary Lee Spence, eds., *The Expeditions of John Charles Frémont* (3 vols., Urbana: University of Illinois Press, 1970–1984), I: 426–806.

104. Bancroft, *California*, IV: 455–512.

105. David J. Langum, *Law and Community on the Mexican California Frontier: Anglo-American Expatriates and the Clash of Legal Traditions, 1821–1846* (Norman: University of Oklahoma Press, 1987), treats this complex issue in masterful fashion.

106. Ibid., 131.

107. Monroy, *Thrown among Strangers*, attempts to seek an "understanding of the complex interactions of . . . two antithetical cultures," (xiii) that is, between the Californio natives and Anglo immigrants, whom he refers to as "elites." The latter were bent on exploitation of both the Indian and Latino population, in his view.

108. Some of the more established pre-1840 immigrants, notably Thomas O. Larkin, were not too pleased with the new arrivals. An important discussion of the impact of the post-1840 immigrants is detailed in John A. Hawgood, "The Pattern of Yankee Infiltration in Mexican Alta California, 1821–1846," *Pacific Historical Review* 27 (February 1958): 27–37.

109. For their immigrant recruitment activities, see Lyman, *John Marsh, Pioneer*, 237, 242, 262–67, and James Shebl, *Weber! The American Adventure of Captain Charles M. Weber* (Lodi, Calif.: San Joaquin Historical Society, 1993), 44–51.

110. The most current treatment of the Bear Flag Revolt is found in Neal Harlow, *California Conquered: War and Peace on the Pacific, 1846–1850* (Berkeley and Los Angeles: University of California Press, 1982), 85–114. Also, see Barbara R. Warner, *The Men of the Bear Flag Revolt and Their Heritage* (Spokane, Wash.: Published by the Arthur H. Clark Company for the Sonoma Valley Historical Society, 1996.)

12

War in California, 1846–1848

Lisbeth Haas

INTRODUCTION

The most recent and thorough account of the Mexican-American War in California has been written by Neil Harlow in his book *California Conquered*, published in 1982. Harlow provides the background to war and carries the story of American conquest through 1850, when California was admitted to the Union. Harlow's book offers the first complete story of the war since Hubert Bancroft's large and substantive history was published in 1886.[1] Like Bancroft, Harlow relies on a wealth of primary sources. Though Harlow focuses his story around the American military leaders who led the conquest of the territory, he also discusses the Californios' role in the war, and takes their resistance to the American occupation seriously.

Nevertheless, historians in general have yet to produce a literature that investigates in a sustained manner the strategies Californio leaders and citizens developed to thwart the American takeover and that examines their goals and objectives in waging a resistance that lasted for six months and enabled them to reoccupy for a time Los Angeles, Santa Barbara, and San Diego. In most war accounts, Californios are invisible, or their involvement and commitment, ideas, and intentions are dismissed. With the exception of Harlow and a few others, historians have poorly portrayed Californios guerrilla-type tactics of war that involved surprise attack and quick retreat, or they have argued that Californios were too politically divided to effectively resist.[2]

Yet it took hundreds of troops under Stockton, Frémont, Kearny, Gillespie, and Mervine to reestablish American control of southern California from late September 1846 to early January 1847. The story behind this has remained relatively unexplored in part because few historians, including Harlow, have used Spanish language sources in writing their histories. Moreover, a frequently quoted Californio source gives the impression that Californios were indifferent to the American occupation and cession of land. That source is a mistranslation that has María de las An-

United States troops cross the San Gabriel River on the afternoon of January 8, 1847, in a watercolor by William Meyers, a gunner on the U.S.S. *Dale*. The Americans, commanded by Commodore Robert Stockton and General Stephen Kearny, quickly vanquished the Californios and then advanced on Los Angeles for the final engagement of the war. Though the *Dale* was in Mexican waters at the time of the battle, Meyers was not on the scene, and as in his other depictions of military engagements in California, he relied on eyewitness accounts in composing his watercolors. *Courtesy Franklin D. Roosevelt Library, Hyde Park, N.Y.*

gustias de la Guerra saying "the conquest of California did not bother the Californians, least of all the women." If accurately translated, her statement should read "the taking of the country did not please the Californios at all, and least of all the women."[3] Genaro Padilla is the only author to offer a detailed account of Californios' reflections on the war, the daily resistance waged by women and men, and their changing perceptions of American society and political structure. This he did by examining almost one hundred narrative histories spoken or written by Californios during the 1870s.

If Californios are rarely at the center of war accounts, native peoples in California, who were still the vast majority of the population, are entirely absent, unless their presence is simply noted without being studied. One has to look at primary sources, or comb accounts of Indian history, in order to situate the war's effect on California Indians. We know that some joined the American battalions as scouts, a few worked for and others worked against Californios. The majority remained neutral, intent upon not becoming involved in a war between two nations interested in acquiring Indian land and labor. We know little of Indian peoples' experiences during the war except that the presence of ever larger numbers of settlers and soldiers meant that their conditions of life grew worse, their autonomy was sharply reduced, and their interactions with settler society became ever more heavily policed.[4]

Much of what we do know has been written as biography or is contained in the diaries, letters, autobiographies, and testimonies of the war's participants. The largest number of historical accounts and biographies document the lives and actions of American participants, many of whom also wrote vivid first-hand accounts of their experiences.[5] Published works on and by Californios are far less extensive, but a few have begun to be published and others are available in manuscript form.[6] These recent historical works, combined with primary accounts, make it possible now to begin to develop a more complete portrait of the war as a military, political, and social event that dynamically shaped the new state and the lives of its Mexican, American, and Indian populations.

THE WAR AT A GLIMPSE

War between the United States and Mexico, the immediate causes for which stemmed from the United States' annexation of Texas, was declared on May 13, 1846, and it ended with the Treaty of Guadalupe Hidalgo on June 30, 1848. But preludes to the war in California began as early as 1842. These heightened the Californios' sense of caution against an American government and American immigrants who proved capable of, if not intent upon, defying the political sovereignty of their territory. When the war with Mexico was announced in California by U.S. naval officer Commodore John Drake Sloat on July 7, 1846, Californio forces had already been fighting against Americans to retake the Sonoma area from a group of settlers instigated by U.S. Army officer John C. Frémont, who had illegally imprisoned Californio officials, seized governmental and private property, occupied Sonoma and its surroundings, and declared California the "Bear Flag Republic," independent of Mexico. After Sloat's announcement of war, these settlers were brought into the United States Army as the California Battalion under Frémont.

The U.S. Navy forces and the California Battalion took Monterey and San Francisco, and the Californio forces moved south to join with others to protect the capital of Los Angeles. The Americans followed them, occupying every presidio and pueblo to San Diego as they went. After Los Angeles fell to the American forces in mid-August 1846, Californios regrouped themselves under a new command. They retook the whole of southern California by the end of September, and engaged in battles and skirmishes to maintain the south through early January 1847.

Californio forces were always outnumbered and militarily overpowered by American volunteers, soldiers, sailors, and their superior weapons. The Pacific Squadron, the land army under Frémont, and the U.S. Army under Stephen Kearny, who arrived in December 1846, presented a formidable enemy that ultimately prevailed. Californios signed the Treaty of Cahuenga on January 13, 1847, in which they pledged to put down their arms and were, in turn, promised the full exercise of their civil liberties and property rights while the territory was occupied by the United States. Seven American military officers governed California from its occupation in July 1846 to its admission as a state in 1850. They were instructed to respect and adhere to Mexican law when it did not conflict with American objectives. Land speculation and continuous immigration into the territory during the occupation hinted at the momentous changes that would occur after the treaty of Guadalupe Hidalgo ceded California, Arizona, New Mexico, parts of Nevada, Utah, and Colorado, and an enlarged area of Texas to the United States. At the war's end Mexico's national territory had been reduced by half, and the conditions of life for Californios and Native Americans within the ceded territories were drastically transformed. Having established this chronology of the war and its aftermath, let me turn to a more detailed discussion of the preludes to war.

PRELUDE TO WAR AND THE BEAR FLAG REPUBLIC

On October 19, 1842, Commodore Thomas Jones sailed into Monterey harbor, seized Mexican ships anchored there, and sent Captain James Armstrong into Monterey with a summons for the governor to surrender, declaring the intention of the United States to occupy Lower and Upper California (the latter embraced the present states of California, Nevada, Utah, and part of Colorado). Jones commanded the U.S. Pacific Squadron. If war between the United States and Mexico were declared, he was under orders to seize and hold every port in California from San Francisco to San Diego. Jones received word that war with Mexico was imminent. He anticipated a conflict with British fleets when he arrived in Monterey Bay, since it was also rumored that Mexico had ceded California to Great Britain in partial repayment of British loans. Instead of encountering hostilities, the Pacific Squadron took the population of Monterey by complete surprise. The pueblo was not equipped to defend itself. With 29 soldiers and 25 others who could bear arms, Californio forces were no match to the 160 men Jones would march ashore. Nor were the eleven cannons protecting the Monterey presidio able to defend the pueblo against Jones's eighty cannons.

That same night, former Governor Juan Bautista Alvarado sent a commission of Californios to Jones's ship to discuss the terms of surrender. The treaty they drew up ceded control of the district of Monterey, an area extending from San Juan Bautista

Monterey in 1842 as depicted by the lithographer Charles Gildemeister, working from an original drawing by an unidentified artist. Commissioned by the prominent American trader Thomas O. Larkin, the print shows the sweep of the town from the old presidial chapel, *far left*, to the custom house. That October, when Commodore Thomas ap Catesby Jones sailed in and demanded that Mexican authorities surrender the California capital, Larkin served as interpreter. *Courtesy Oakland Museum of California; gift of Mrs. Emil Hagstrom.*

to San Luis Obispo. Though Jones had demanded possession of both Californias, the surrendered land was enough to enable his forces to occupy the presidio and pueblo of Monterey. After signing the treaty the following morning, Jones's men went ashore. Marching six abreast to the tunes of "Yankee Doodle" and "The Star-Spangled Banner," they took over the presidio as Californio soldiers evacuated the fort.[7] Jones read a proclamation to the citizens of Monterey in which he announced that they could exercise their full civil liberties, and would be protected by the "stars and stripes . . . henceforth and forever."[8] All the while, of course, Jones lacked any official information about whether the two countries were indeed at war.

While the Californios capitulated militarily instead of risking a battle in which they had no chance, Alvarado sent word for help to California's recently appointed Governor Manuel Micheltorena in Los Angeles. Micheltorena immediately began to organize a resistance to the American forces. He urged all Californios to drive their cattle to the interior and take up arms to defend their territory. He ordered the military officers in each presidio to similarly encourage citizens to prepare for conflict. Micheltorena also requested troops from Mexico to defend the territory. The governor was two hours into his march north to Monterey when he received an official apology from Commodore Jones, who declared he had made a mistake and withdrawn his forces. The occupation had lasted less than two days. On October 21, 1842, Jones's secretary had found correspondence in Monterey that confirmed Mexico was neither at war with the United States nor intended to give California to England.

Jones was temporarily recalled for this unwarranted aggression. He would, however, return to Alta California as commodore of the Pacific Fleet at the end of the war. His willingness to risk his position to secure California for the United States was acknowledged with appreciation by a government that had attempted to acquire California, Texas, and New Mexico through diplomatic channels as early as 1822.[9] Commodore Jones's instructions to occupy California in the case of war was consistent with U.S. policy as defined in the Monroe Doctrine of 1823, which declared the United States' intentions of keeping all European powers from gaining new colonies or politically intervening in the nations of the Western Hemisphere. The doctrine was frequently invoked in official discussions about California. In late October 1845, for example, President Polk stated in a cabinet meeting, and recorded in his diary that, "the people of the United States would not willingly permit California to pass into the possession of any new colony planted by Great Britain or any foreign monarchy."[10] Senator Thomas Hart Benton, an expansionist and the father-in-law of John C. Frémont, added that it was his opinion that American settlers on the Sacramento River would ultimately hold California for the United States.

Severing California from Mexico and annexing it to the United States was one of the main objectives of the Polk administration, and it appears that the United States government provided covert leadership to organize American immigrants in California to revolt and declare an independent republic, as Americans had done in Texas.[11] Certainly the immigrants who arrived in California after 1841 were likely prospects for this action. Unlike earlier immigrants who learned Spanish, adopted Catholicism, established close ties with the population, and sought the status of naturalized citizen or legal residence, later immigrants most often remained illegal settlers who resided on the margins of California's social and political life. Many of them believed themselves superior to the Californio and Indian populations, expressing their right to the land in conjunction with their notions of white racial superiority. As Reginald Horsman argues, "by 1850 the emphasis was on the American Anglo-Saxons as a separate, innately superior people who were destined to bring good government, commercial prosperity" and Christianity to less civilized peoples.[12]

Californios had long fought to create and protect their political autonomy in territorial affairs and would not allow either Mexico or the United States to erode their sovereignty without significant resistance.[13] Even those who sympathized with the United States's republican system and democratic ideals would express a strong sense of having been deceived by Americans whose race ideas were pervasively expressed against them during the war and occupation. Though Californios had a history of conflict over power between the northern and southern parts of the territory, they had joined forces in November 1844 against Governor Micheltorena and the Mexican soldiers who arrived under his command to protect California, but were known for pillaging instead. After ejecting Micheltorena from the territory in February 1845, prominent figures among the rebels assumed authority over the government. In a spirit of compromise between north and south, Pío Pico from Los Angeles became governor, and General José Castro from the vicinity of Monterey became military commander of the territory. But political antagonisms between Californios had not abated. When war broke out with the United States, Pico was rumored to be planning an attack against Castro. War caused them to again join their forces instead. Indian peoples in California made strategic use of these tensions to increase their raids against Californio ranches and pueblos, and were successful in keeping Californio society from expanding beyond the coastal area. Drawing on long-standing enmity between Indian peoples and Californios, the United States would benefit by making a few, limited alliances with Indians during the war.

The U.S. government was confident that California would become part of the United States at some future date, and began to send expeditions to explore the region during the 1840s. In the summer preceding the war, Captain John C. Frémont of the Topographical Corps led a large group of frontiersmen and a few scientists through Mexican territory, including parts of the present states of New Mexico, Colorado, Utah, and California, allegedly to determine, among other things, a route for a railroad to the Pacific, terminating either in California or in the Oregon Country.[14] Frémont, who had led a previous expedition through northern California and was familiar with American settlements there, reached California at the end of December.

Frémont arrived during a period of extreme tension between Mexico and the United States, and between Californios and the American settlers. The U.S. Congress had voted to annex Texas that December. Months earlier, during the late summer of 1845, Governor Pico had already sent out a call for Californios to prepare to defend themselves against the United States. Californios and the Mexican government feared the dangers posed by the hundreds of American immigrants who had taken up residence along the Sacramento River and north of San Francisco Bay. Orders arrived from Mexico City to stop American immigration into California. In an attempt to eliminate Sutter's Fort as a gathering point for foreigners, Mexico sent envoy Andrés Castillero with instructions to purchase it for the Mexican government. In early November 1845, General Castro and Castillero went to the fort to persuade John Sutter to sell, but he rejected the offer. While there, Castro attempted to establish amicable relations with the immigrants. He told them they could stay in the territory if they obeyed its laws, settled only in Sonoma or New Helvetia (the territory surrounding Sutter's Fort), and applied within three

Probably painted in San Francisco in 1852, William S. Jewett's romantic portrait of John C. Frémont conveys the popular contemporary image of the young Army officer— dashing, bold, defiant, courageous. Frémont helped focus national attention on California through his writings and, later, played an important role in the conquest of the province. *Courtesy National Portrait Gallery, Smithsonian Institution.*

months for a permit to reside in the territory on the condition that they leave if their permits were denied.

Frémont arrived among these immigrants near Sacramento in the middle of January 1846, and proceeded south to Monterey. He stayed in Monterey with the American counsel and merchant Thomas O. Larkin, from whom he purchased supplies. Larkin and Frémont both asked General Castro to give Frémont permission to stay in California to rest his men and animals before proceeding to Oregon. Castro qualified his consent by stating that the Americans needed to remain in the valley of the San Joaquin River, far away from Mexican pueblos and ranchos along the coast. In defiance of this order, Frémont and sixty armed men traveled in and camped near the settlements at San José, Santa Cruz, and Salinas Valley. As they traveled, the Californios' accusations against them mounted.[15]

Upon receiving these reports of aggression and the persistent, unauthorized presence of armed Americans, José Castro ordered Frémont to leave the province immediately. Frémont's response was belligerent. He camped his men on a small plateau between the Salinas and the San Joaquin valleys overlooking the principal road to Monterey and the pueblo of San Juan Bautista. Raising the American flag, he invited conflict. As Castro prepared to remove them by force, Frémont abandoned camp on the night of March 9, 1846, and headed for the Sacramento Valley, where he found American settlers fearful that they would be expelled from the territory and convinced that Castro had encouraged bands of Yokuts and Miwok Indians to attack them.[16]

Frémont meandered toward Oregon in late April, but five days before war was declared between the United States and Mexico (on May 13, 1846), he received an urgent and confidential message from a courier that sent him back to California. By May 29, Frémont had established a camp north of Sutter's Fort, which became the center of activity for the Americans who organized the Bear Flag incident. On June 10, eleven of these men left Frémont's camp to take some 170 horses from Castro's soldiers, who were driving them to join forces Castro was massing in Santa Clara. The Americans were perhaps responding to their fears that Castro was organizing a military campaign to force them to leave the territory. Perhaps they were inspired to act by Frémont's insistence that they could, indeed, establish an independent republic. Their illegal seizure of government horses was the first act of the Bear Flag incident. Having seized the horses, they decided also to take the military garrison at Sonoma. With twenty men and a body of recruits that grew as they rode, they headed to the garrison.

General Mariano Guadalupe Vallejo was awakened by these men and informed that he was under arrest. Aware that he did not have troops at the garrison or other means to restrain the men and defend his family and the town, Vallejo surrendered and invited three negotiators into his home. As he formulated the articles of capitulation, his captors drank the brandy Vallejo offered. The articles contained three paragraphs, one of which Vallejo wrote in Spanish. This paragraph emphasized that Vallejo's motive for peaceful capitulation was to protect the lives of his family members, and the lives and interests of all the inhabitants under his jurisdiction. For literary critic Genaro Padilla, this paragraph symbolized Vallejo's resistance "within a confined, and dangerous, rhetorical space."[17] Prohibited by the articles from taking up arms for or against the invaders, General Vallejo should have remained free. But he and a captain, a colonel, and Vallejo's son-in-law were taken prisoner, and would remain locked up in extremely harsh conditions for the next few months. In the days that followed, the mayor of Sonoma and other prominent Californios were similarly jailed.

That same Sunday morning the Americans occupied Sonoma and made a flag with a bear and a star, hoisted it at the fort, and brought together citizens from the pueblo and vicinity to proclaim the Bear Flag Republic of Independent California.[18] In a crude formulation of their position, they told the citizenry, "as enemies we will kill and destroy you! but as friends we will share with you all the blessings of lib-

The guidon carried by the American frontiersmen who in June 1846, following their capture of Sonoma, proclaimed the Republic of California. Joseph Warren Revere of the U.S. Navy secured the guidon the following month, when American forces occupied the town, and later presented it to the Society of California Pioneers. Along with the original Bear Flag, it was destroyed in the fire of 1906. *Courtesy California State Library.*

erty."[19] The Bear Flaggers took horses from Vallejo and others, and "borrowed" flour, meat, and other goods from the storerooms of many citizens without offering compensation.

In a letter to Thomas Larkin, the United States consul in Monterey, Governor Pío Pico protested this act, stating that a "great number (multitude) of North American foreigners have invaded the frontier, encamping in the Plaza of Sonoma. . . . Personal rights have been attacked, well-established social contracts broken, the sacred soil of another nation profaned and, in short, the leader of the multitude of foreigners, William B. Ide, by insulting libel, urged them to a separation from the Mexican Union."[20] Rosalía Vallejo de Leese elaborated on the event. Frémont, she stated, arrived some days after this incident. On June 20, on hearing that Californios under Captain Padilla were approaching Sonoma to rescue the citizens, he forced her to write Padilla to stop him. Stating that he would "burn our houses with us inside of them if I refused to address Padilla in the manner he wishes me to do," Vallejo de Leese acquiesced. "In the family way," she explained, "I had no right to endanger the life of my unborn baby." She decried their thieving and aggressive manner in Sonoma, and closed her account by describing her means of resistance, which was to keep the memory of the incident alive, and to refuse to learn English. "Those hated men inspired me with such a large dose of hate against their race," she passionately recalled, "that though twenty-eight years have elapsed since that time,

I have not yet forgotten the insults they heaped upon me, and not being desirous of coming in contact with them, I have abstained from learning their language."[21] While significant for the war, the incident was perhaps even more important for creating great resentment and bitterness against the Americans on the part of Californios.

THE WAR

Californios under Castro engaged in skirmishes against the Bear Flaggers immediately, and the citizens of Sonoma began a quiet, but sustained, resistance that spread throughout the territory once the war was announced and the formal occupation of California began.[22] As Juan Bautista Alvarado explained about the political and judicial authorities who fled to the hills and organized the resistance, we "loved our country most dearly because we had only been able by dint of immense sacrifice to maintain it at the level of contemporary civilization."[23] Alvarado, like almost all of the Californio elite, spoke favorably of the American constitution and democratic government, but he, like many others, was not willing to accept an occupation that was unconditional and beyond Californio power to control.

This resistance gathered momentum when American forces planted their flag and declared possession of California, which happened in early July, under the command of Commodore Sloat, naval commander of the Pacific Squadron. Upon hearing of the early battles of the war, he carried out his long-standing instructions to seize California before another power did, a policy that had similarly motivated Commodore Jones almost five years earlier. On July 2, 1846, Sloat sailed into Monterey and learned of the Bear Flag incident from United States Navy Commander John Montgomery, who had pledged the government's neutrality. On July 7, 1846, Sloat raised the American flag and sent word to General Castro and Governor Pío Pico to surrender. He sent Commander Montgomery to occupy San Francisco Bay and the town of Yerba Buena, and enlisted 350 men who had been acting under the auspices of the Bear Flag Republic into the California Battalion under Frémont.[24] The would-be republic dissolved with the American occupation.

With the northern part of the state secured by Sloat and Montgomery, and the impending arrival of Commodore Stockton, who sailed into Monterey Bay on July 15 to take over the leadership of the Pacific fleet in California from Sloat, General Castro began a retreat southward to join his forces with those of Governor Pico. On July 16, Governor Pico issued orders in Santa Barbara that all citizens of the territory, whether native-born or naturalized, take up arms. He sent for ammunition from Baja California. Acting under orders from Pico, Abel Stearns, a southern California ranchero, threatened to fine rancheros who did not join the defense. Pico's force of 100 men joined Castro's 160 men, and they marched to Los Angeles to protect the capital. Their former inter-regional tensions "turned to nearly unanimous animosity toward the common enemy."[25]

Leaving behind enough men to secure their hold on the north, the American forces followed Castro south. Frémont arrived at San Diego harbor in late July. Town officials refused his request to hoist the American flag, so Frémont's men raised it themselves, and a contingent of forty-eight Americans remained in San Diego after Frémont began his march north to Los Angeles. Stockton sailed from Monterey on August 1. He stopped in Santa Barbara to raise the American flag and leave a small occupation force, and anchored at San Pedro on August 6. Though General Castro sent word to Stockton that they should not fight but discuss the terms of a truce instead, Stockton refused anything short of Californios' declaring the territory independent of Mexico and under American protection. Castro and Pico had already rejected this alternative.

On August 9, as Stockton was marching towards Los Angeles, Castro, then camped outside of the city with his men, composed a mournful farewell to Californios and went south to Sonora, where he would ceaselessly petition the Mexican government for arms and soldiers to retake California. That same evening, Pico similarly wrote a proclamation of farewell that emphasized California's inadequate defense. He stayed in hiding on Teodosio Yorba's rancho south of Los Angeles until September 7 when he escaped to Baja California. From there, he also endlessly petitioned the Mexican government for money, arms, and troops to restore California to Mexico.[26]

An advance American contingent arrived in Los Angeles on August 11 to find the streets deserted and government buildings ransacked of their documents and furniture by government officials who had fled with the Californio troops to the hills surrounding the city. Stockton marched into Los Angeles two days later. With Castro and Pico gone and the major ports occupied by American troops, he decreed that both Californias belonged to the United States and proclaimed himself commander-in-chief and governor. In the days that followed, Californio troops were rounded up in northern and southern California and then released on parole after they promised not take up arms again for the duration of the war. Government was to be conducted through the same institutions and laws as during the Mexican period, and Stockton declared that the citizens of California should meet and elect their officials. But the military occupation stood in the way of the smooth operation of elective government. The city had a curfew, soldiers searched and seized goods in private homes, and citizens' freedom of association was limited.[27] With these conditions in place, the troops under Stockton and Frémont returned to Monterey and Sonoma, respectively, and left Archibald Hamilton Gillespie in charge of Los Angeles.

The Americans returned north with a false sense of victory. In the following month Los Angeles, Santa Barbara, San Diego, Santa Inés, and San Luis Obispo, and surrounding lands were retaken by a Californio army composed of both soldiers and civilians. They had gathered together at ranchos outside the cities and beyond easy surveillance, and built a force under José María Flores. Simultaneously, the citizens of Los Angeles banded together under the leadership of Sérbulo Varela and Flores to force Gillespie out of Los Angeles by the end of September. On September 29, Gillespie signed the Articles of Capitulation, which called for an exchange of prisoners and ensured his safe retreat to a ship in San Pedro harbor.[28] Flores, Andrés Pico, and José Antonio Carrillo led the resistance. Flores called the departmental assembly into session. On October 26, 1846, they elected Francisco Figueroa as president of the California territory and Flores as commander-in-chief and governor, with Manuel Castro appointed military commander in the north. Flores declared a state of siege and issued a proclamation in early November that required all male citizens between the ages of fifteen and sixty, whether born in California or naturalized, to appear for military duty at the first warning, under penalty of death as a traitor. To fund the war the government rescinded Pío Pico's order to sell the California missions.[29]

The Californios' tactics of resistance incorporated a broad sector of the population. They moved their cattle and other livestock from the coast so that the American troops would not be able to use the cattle for meat, but left enough for the Californio forces, who traveled without supplies because they could rely on the citizenry. When Stockton withdrew American troops from Sonoma, Yerba Buena, San José, San Juan Bautista, and Monterey to send them south to quell the counterattack, paroled Californios similarly left for the countryside to join the resistance. Women hid Californio soldiers at great risk to their families, pleaded for the lives of their loved ones, and prepared the ground for negotiations that would leave the Californio citizenry able to exercise their civil rights once the hostilities had ended. They engaged in small, but daily, acts of resistance, and criticized Californio leaders José Castro and Pío Pico for leaving the country rather than defending it.[30]

These acts enabled the outnumbered and overpowered Californio army to maintain its hold for months, even as a concerted American force was preparing a counter-offensive. Gillespie's ship stayed in San Pedro harbor after he was ousted from Los Angeles, and he was soon joined by another American warship on October 6. A battalion of vigilant Californios kept them close to the harbor. On October 14, Stockton and Frémont sailed south from San Francisco to Monterey. Frémont began his overland march to Los Angeles, with a battalion of 430 men. Some had come on his original exploration party or were emigrants who continued to arrive on sailing vessels or via the Overland Trail. Frémont's men generally furnished their own equipment, ammunition, and uniforms, and drove three hundred head of cattle. A company of Indian scouts traveled with them. They included Wallawallah and Delaware Indians from the Columbia River in Oregon territory, and Miwok and

Yokuts from the Sacramento Valley. Part of the company encamped without fires some three miles in advance of the battalion and the rest remained some distance to the rear, according to Fremont, "so that no traveler on the road escaped falling into our hands."[31] Frémont's battalion was formidable, and Californios were largely relegated to skirmish with contingents of the troops when the opportunity arose, such as at the battle of La Natividad, near San Juan Bautista on November 16. Though Californios had inferior weapons, at this encounter they outnumbered the contingent of Americans and suffered fewer casualties.

Stockton sailed to San Pedro harbor and then moved on to San Diego with approximately 750 men. Though his numbers and armaments would have permitted him to retake Los Angeles, the resistance appeared sufficiently strong to make him wait for the reinforcement by Frémont and Kearny's forces. Though he occupied the center of town, American forces did not control the countryside. From San Diego, Stockton sent men into Baja California for horses, cattle, and sheep, built fortifications, and fended off attacks by Californios. In the meantime, General Stephen Kearny marched overland to California from New Mexico, which he had occupied after the outbreak of the war with Mexico. He brought a relatively small contingent to California, though supporting troops, called the Mormon Battalion, would follow.[32]

The biggest battle of the war was fought at San Pascual on December 6 as Kearny's tired and unprepared troops approached San Diego. Because the gunpowder of most of Kearny's men was wet, much of this confrontation involved hand-to-hand combat that was favorable to Californios, who were famous for their horsemanship and more equipped with lances and muskets than rifles. Americans suffered significant casualties, with eighteen dead and seventeen wounded. Californios reported eleven injuries and no deaths.

The final battles of the war involved about five hundred Californio forces at the San Gabriel River, outside of Los Angeles, on January 8 and January 9, 1847. They fought against Stockton's troops, while the battalions of William Mervine, Kearny, and Frémont were marching towards Los Angeles to converge on the city at once. Though the battles of San Gabriel and La Mesa (also known as the Battle of Los Angeles) were fought on two consecutive days, relatively few casualties resulted, with about twelve Americans wounded and three Californios killed.[33]

Waging the war was very costly to Californios. The relatively few deaths were deeply felt among the small population that was closely interconnected through family and extended kin relations, and for whom victory remained out of reach. For decades, they had not been able to stem the tide of American immigration, control the California Indian frontier, or secure monetary aid, arms, and soldiers from Mexico, despite the constant appeals of General Castro and former Governor Pío Pico. After the lost battle of Los Angeles, and with doubts growing rapidly among soldiers

The illustrious ranchero and Californio patriot Andrés Pico, who on a cold December morning in 1846 led his men to victory at San Pascual, beating the weary dragoons of General Stephen Kearny in one of the bloodiest battles of the war in California. The following month, realizing further resistance was futile, Pico surrendered the country to John C. Frémont in the Treaty of Cahuenga. *Courtesy California Historical Society/Title Insurance and Trust Photo Collection, University of Southern California.*

and the civilian population about the feasibility of continued fighting, Californios sought a truce. General Flores and men among his ranks left for Sonora, as negotiators went to Stockton's camp to determine the conditions for peace.[34]

The war in California ended with the Treaty of Cahuenga, signed on January 13, 1847. The articles of capitulation provided every citizen with the same rights as United States citizens. Californios were all guaranteed the protection of their life and property and the right to unhindered movement and travel, and the men pledged that they would not take up arms again for the duration of the war with Mexico. They were also guaranteed that they would not have to take an oath of allegiance to the United States until a treaty of peace was signed between the two nations.

Though fighting ended in Upper California, both Californias had been objects of interest to the United States government. Stockton announced as early as August 17, 1846, that the United States had taken possession "of Upper and Lower California" and declared these separate territories under the possession of the United States as a single territory.[35] He ordered a military blockade of the Pacific ports of Mexico in August 1846, and the disruption of commerce in the Gulf of California, sending some of his fleet to occupy Baja California. In September 1846, just as the resistance to the American occupation was being organized in Upper California, an American warship landed in the harbor of La Paz, Lower California, seized a number of Mexican vessels, which they put into the service of the United States, and secured a pledge of neutrality from Governor Colonel Francisco Palacios Miranda. The governor had little choice. For two years he had been left without any military or naval resources. With neutrality secured and a resumption of hostilities in Upper California, Stockton's men went back to Alta California. Only after peace was finally secured in January 1847 did Stockton order his troops to resume the blockade of Mazatlán, and to occupy Baja California.[36]

When the naval occupation of the Baja Peninsula began in July 1847, the invaders did not encounter resistance. And the annexation of Baja California was initially sought in the armistice talks that began in late August 1847. Perhaps in part for that reason, by September a significant resistance had been organized by Captain Manuel Piñeda. Battles, skirmishes, and raids against American troops persisted in Lower California until the end of the war on May 30, 1848, when the United States agreed by treaty to evacuate, rather than to annex, Baja California. Over five hundred residents of that territory were given asylum and United States citizenship for their support of the occupation. These refugees were transported to the United States by retreating American vessels.[37] Most of the refugees were from among the landowning and political elite, and had family connections among elite Californios. They were provided with limited compensation by the United States government for their losses as they left the territory. Others continued to claim land in Baja California, as did María Amparo Ruiz de Burton, and would wage long and retracted battles to retain that land in the American period.[38]

THE TREATY OF GUADALUPE HIDALGO

The Treaty of Guadalupe Hidalgo ceded the territories of Alta California and New Mexico to the United States (these territories contained land in the present states of Arizona, Nevada, Utah, and Colorado). Together with the loss of Texas, Mexico's national territory was reduced by half at the war's end. In the initial treaty negotiations that began as early as September 1847, Mexico was only willing to cede that part of California that extended from Monterey northward. Its reluctance led the United States to drop its demands for Lower California, though President Polk, in his annual message to Congress in December of 1847, promised never to give either of the Californias back to Mexico. The United States remained firm in its demand for Upper California. Mexico initially sought a compromise by establishing the border two leagues north of the port of San Diego, to retain that valuable harbor on the Pacific, but the United States succeeded in proving that San Diego had been a part of Alta California from the first Spanish exploration of the area. The international boundary was established one marine league south of the southernmost point of the bay of San Diego.[39] In compensation, the U.S. paid fifteen million dollars for this land and met other financial obligations to Mexico.[40]

Of the treaty's twenty-three articles, four defined the rights of Mexican citizens and Indian peoples in the territories. Articles 8 and 9 outlined Mexican citizens' rights of residence, property, and citizenship. Free to continue to live in the ceded territories as either United States or Mexican citizens, their property was to be "inviolably respected" whether or not they assumed citizenship or continued their residence as Mexicans in the United States. If property was sold, the proceeds were free of taxation. All persons had to declare their intent of citizenship within one year or they would be assumed to have elected to become United States citizens. These new citizens, Article 9 reads, "shall be incorporated into the Union of the United States and be admitted, at the proper time (to be judged by the Congress of the United States) to the enjoyment of all the rights of citizens of the United States according to the principles of the constitutions."[41]

Article 10 guaranteed that "all grants of land made by the Mexican government . . . shall be respected as valid."[42] The article also enabled citizens to continue the process to clear their titles under terms defined by Mexican law. The most severe consequence of the treaty for Californios was that the president asked the U.S. Senate to strike this article, arguing that property rights were already guaranteed in Article 8 of the treaty. However, one of the first acts of Congress after California was admitted to the Union in 1850, was to pass the California Land Act (1851). Each Spanish and Mexican land grant had to be reviewed and approved by a land court and the U.S. attorney general before legal title could be acknowledged. Rancheros had to submit to the land court a map of their ranchos and all the documents that proved legitimate title. The land had to be surveyed using American techniques of measurement. Litigation over these ranchos took an average of seventeen years. The land court often approved the grants, but the attorney general of the United States just as often sent them back rejected. Many cases went as far as the U.S. Supreme Court. In the meantime, California state law enabled squatters to preempt uncultivated land for which title had not yet been confirmed. If the grant was accepted and patented, the grantee had to pay squatters for the cost of their improvements on the land.

Most titles were ultimately confirmed, but only a handful of ranchero families still possessed their lands when their titles had cleared. In the relatively cash-scarce economy of California, lawyers, land speculators, surveyors, new immigrants with ready cash, and squatters ended up owning or claiming all or portions of almost every rancho in the state. As long as titles were unconfirmed, the new owners held their portions in shares-in-common, but this did not stop the ranchos from being bought and sold on paper one or more times before their titles were secured. Once confirmed, the land was legally divided at a rapid pace. Land speculation had already begun before the war. In commenting on a report about the "laws and precedents" pertinent to land titles, Military Governor Richard Mason observed in early 1850 that "much of what would probably constitute the public domain had been acquired by speculators who would endeavor to dispose of it to settlers at an exorbitant profit."[43] Rancheros, U.S.

The Indian Chefo gathers his family about him in a photograph probably taken in the late nineteenth century. When California passed from Mexican to American rule, Indians were accorded even less protection under law than previously, with no right of title to the lands they occupied. Living on the periphery of society, openly hunted down and killed in mining days, their numbers declined precipitously. *Courtesy California Historical Society, FN-30500.*

Army and Navy personnel, and the newest immigrants who arrived for the Gold Rush were speculating in town lots and on rancho lands. Miners and others who arrived for the Gold Rush gained the passage of land laws that favored the squatter, speculator, and farmer, after mounting intense political pressure upon the declaration of statehood.[44] Some Californios, like José Castro and Antonio María Osio, left California and returned to Mexico. The vast majority remained in the territory, living on ever smaller pieces of rural land, or moving into the old pueblos where it was easier to hold on to a small parcel of land.[45]

California Indians were even less protected by the treaty. While all Indians in Mexico were made citizens by law in 1826, few California Indians had been able to exercise their rights of citizenship during the Mexican period. Interpretations of their rights generally placed them among Indians discussed in Article XI of the treaty. This article begins by stating that "A great part of the territories which, by the present treaty, are to be comprehended for the future within the limits of the United States, is now occupied by savage tribes." The treaty map identified the largest area of ceded land as "*Apacheria.*" This reference included from 160,000 to 180,000 Indians.[46] The article declared the United States responsible for policing and controlling those tribes, and preventing their raids into Mexico, especially protecting the states of Chihuahua, Sonora, and Sinaloa.

The article was written at the request of Mexican negotiators, who felt they needed the provision to get northern states whose populations were sharply against cession of the territory to accept the treaty. This article denies all land rights to Indian peoples who had not exercised their rights of citizenship by stating that "when providing for the removal of the Indians from any portion of the said territories, or for its being settled by citizens of the United States . . . special care shall then be taken not to place its Indian occupants under the necessity of seeking homes." Though some California Indian peoples, such as the Tapai and Ipai near San Diego, ultimately won the right to hold dual nationality status because their lands were divided by the border, the great majority of California Indians living within or near Mexican society held their village lands in a usufructory manner (their land rights extended to the use of the land, but did not confer legal title).[47]

A U.S. Senate committee confirmed the federal government's right to declare indigenous lands public domain and to take possession of them "as the absolute and unqualified owners." "The Indian," the committee stated, "had no usufructory or other rights therein which were to be in any manner respected."[48] Land speculators, squatters, and settlers would also seek Indian lands and state law offered these lands to the speculator, who dispossessed whole villages with impunity.[49]

PUBLIC MEMORY AND HISTORY

Historical accounts and public records of the military and civil resistance to the American occupation by Californios are rare. Few names from Mexican California are known. Likenesses of Pío Pico and Mariano Vallejo, the two most prominent, stand as civic monuments that record a memory of their presence and activity in Mexican California. Towns and cities may also record a name or two of a local Californio, rarely if ever connecting it to political history or a more substantive account of the colonial and Mexican past, the war, and statehood. This absence of representation in public memory contrasts quite sharply to the public monumentalization of Sutter's Fort, the Bear Flag republic, and the figures of Montgomery, Stockton, Frémont, Kearny, Sloat, and Polk. Other American men are remembered locally. Their stories play a part in forging the pioneer and patriotic history that so commonly pushes out other versions of the past in public commemoration.[50] But the relative absence of Californios and Indians in public memory is also the result of their demographic, political, cultural, and economic losses that began during the occupation in 1846.

This near erasure of Californios and California Indians from public memory is reinforced in much of the scholarship, which is organized around the American in-volvement in California to the near exclusion of other groups. In sharp distinction to the numerous biographies of American military men who were involved in the war, biographies of California leaders, and female and male citizens who were highly affected by and involved in the war, have yet to be written. But the material exists to write about the war from Californio perspectives and according to the experiences of individuals and particular groups. Many of those primary sources are recorded in Norman E. Tutorow's annotated bibliography, *The Mexican-American War.* Tutorow lists narratives of Californios, describes the collections at the Bancroft, Huntington, and California State libraries, and at Santa Barbara Mission, and points to the official papers and other documents left by Castro, Mariano Guadalupe Vallejo, and many other Californio governmental and military officials.[51]

These same archives must be searched in systematic ways for material on Indian history. Indian perspectives on the war and occupation must be brought to the fore. How was the war interpreted and responded to by each group? Did it change the na-ture of Indian-white relations? The territorial dispossession of most Indian societies in California shortly after the war needs to be thoroughly examined and Indian re-sponses carefully studied.

We need to understand, in short, the many sides to this conflict and to investigate it through Spanish as well as English-language documents. This would begin to pro-vide a fuller accounting of the war and its consequences for the entire population of California. We also should push our understanding of American involvement in the war beyond the history of generals, their policies, and military action. We need to un-derstand more fully who these soldiers were on both sides of the battlefield. What were their hopes, their aims and aspirations, and how did these change during the course of the war? What were the goals and aspirations of the citizens who sup-ported either side?[52] We need to know more about the response of Californios who were for and against the American invasion, and of those foreigners who had settled in California and who fought on the Californio side, or turned their affiliations back to the United States during the war. We need to have new studies of the war that also reexamine the Bear Flag incident to see how and why the men and women who had recently settled in this territory were willing and able to take up arms.

A social history of the occupation and war would begin to explain how people lived through the period and how they were changed by this political event. It would bridge two periods in time, raise and answer new questions about society and politics. The newest studies of wars show them to be important to understanding the formation of patriotic legends and state histories, of gender, ethnic, and race relations, and of the po-litical ideas that pervade post-war society. Future studies of the Mexican-American War should take a broader view that takes into account the various sectors of society and the whole spectrum of persons and relationships that were affected by it.

NOTES

1. Neal Harlow, *California Conquered: War and Peace on the Pacific, 1846–1850* (Berkeley: University of California Press, 1982). Hubert Bancroft, *History of California*, Volume V, 1846–1848 (San Francisco: The History Co., 1886). Few books have been written on the war in California. Most of the literature consists of articles on battles and books on particular individuals. Perhaps the war in California is not well researched because the war with Mexico has been, according to Robert W. Johannsen, virtually forgotten by the nation. See his article "America's Forgotten War," *Wilson Quarterly* (Spring 1996): 96–107.

2. In Sally C. Johns's article "Viva Los Californios! The Battle of San Pasqual," *Journal of San Diego History* (Fall 1973): 1–13, she presents a well-researched essay that provides a vivid portrait of the Californios' resistance. In contrast, see Kenneth Johnson, "The Battle of San Pasqual" *Pacific Historian* 20 (Winter 1977): 368–73; Frank J. Polley, "Americans at the Battle of Cahuenga" *Historical Society of Southern California, Annual Publication* (1894): 47–54; Corinne King Wright, "The Conquest of Los Angeles" *Historical Society of Southern California Publications* (Spring 1919): 18–25.

3. Genaro Padilla, *My History, Not Yours* (Madison: University of Wisconsin Press, 1993), 149. María de las Angustias de La Guerra Ord, *"Ocurrencias en California,"* 1878, ms, Bancroft Library, University of California, Berkeley. The translation is entitled *Occurrences in Hispanic California*, translated and edited by Francis Price and William Ellison (Washington, D.C.: Academy of American Franciscan History, 1956), 59.

4. On neutrality and a brief account of the war years, see George Harwood Phillips, *Chiefs and Challengers: Indian Resistance and Cooperation in Southern California* (Berkeley: University of California Press, 1975), 61, and James Rawls, *Indians of California: The Changing Image* (Norman: University of Oklahoma Press, 1984), esp. 82–105.

5. Though not exhaustive, the titles below are some of the richest sources of information. See Mary Lee Spence and Donald Jackson, eds., *The Expeditions of John Charles Frémont: The Bear Flag Revolt and the Court-Martial* (Urbana: University of Illinois Press, 1973), vol. II; Allan Nevins, ed., *John Charles Frémont: Narratives of Exploration and Adventure* (New York: Longmans, Green, and Co., 1956); Simeon Ide, *Who Conquered California? The Conquest of California by the Bear Flag Party, and a Biographical Sketch of the Life of William B. Ide* (Glorieta, N. Mex.: Rio Grande Press, 1967); Philip St. Geo. Cooke, *The Conquest of New Mexico and California: An Historical and Personal Narrative* (Albuquerque: Horn and Wallace, 1964); Harlan Hague and David Langum, *Thomas O. Larkin: A Life of Patriotism and Profit in Old California* (Norman: University of Oklahoma Press, 1990); George P. Hammond, ed., *The Larkin Papers: Personal, Business, and Official Correspondence of Thomas Oliver Larkin, Merchant and Consul in California*, 10 vols. (Berkeley: University of California Press, 1951–68).

6. Padilla's *My History* was extremely useful, as was Antonio María Osio, *The History of Alta California: A Memoir of Mexican California*, translated by Rose Marie Beebe and Robert Senkewicz (Madison: University of Wisconsin Press, 1996). Also see Rosalía Vallejo de Leese, "History of the Bear Party," ms, 1874, Bancroft Library; Juan Avila, "Notas Californianas" ms, 1878, Bancroft Library; Juan Bautista Alvarado, "Historia de California, 1876," ms, Bancroft Library.

7. See C. L. Higham, "Songs of the Mexican War: An Interpretation of Sources," *Journal of the West* 28 (July 1989): 16–23.

8. Harlow, *California Conquered*, 9, and see Gene A. Smith, "The War that Wasn't: Thomas ap Catesby Jones's Seizure of Monterey," *California History LXVI* (June 1987): 105–13.

9. See Frederick Merk, *Manifest Destiny and Mission in American History: A Reinterpretation* (New York: Alfred A. Knopf, 1963). Seymor V. Conner and Odie B. Faulk focus on the short-term causes for the war in *North America Divided: The Mexican War, 1846–1848* (New York: Oxford University Press, 1971) and Thomas B. Jones criticizes that perspective, emphasizing the long-term goals of United States foreign policy in his article "Mexican War Scholarship: The Connor-Faulk Assessment" *The Journal of Mexican American History* 5 (1977): 103–24. Also see Wayne Cutler, et al., eds., *Essays on the Mexican War* (College Station: Texas A & M University Press, 1986). For a study of contemporaneous Mexican perspectives on American expansionism, see Gene M. Brack, *Mexico Views Manifest Destiny, 1821–1846: An Essay on the Origins of the Mexican War* (Albuquerque: University of New Mexico Press, 1975).

10. Allan Nevins, ed., *Polk: The Diary of a President, 1845–1849* (New York: Longmans, Green, and Co., 1952), 19 (entry of Friday, 24 October 1845).

11. See John A. Hawgood, "John C. Frémont and the Bear Flag Revolution: A Reappraisal" *Southern California Quarterly* 44 (June 1962): 67–96. Historians have disagreed about how far Polk was willing to go for California. In "California History Textbooks and the Coming of the Civil War: The Need for a Broader Perspective of California History," *Southern California Quarterly* 56 (Summer 1974): 159–74, Ward M. McAfee asks whether Polk deceitfully pushed Mexico into a war to acquire California, or whether, by sending John Slidell to negotiate with Mexico, he was honestly attempting to reach a peaceful settlement. For more on this debate, see Richard R. Stenburg, ed., "President Polk and California: Additional Documents" *Pacific Historical Review* 10 (June 1941): 217–19, and Glenn W. Price, *Origins of the War with Mexico: The Polk-Stockton Intrigue* (Austin: University of Texas Press, 1967), who argue that California was a principal cause for the war, while Justin H. Smith, *The War with Mexico* (1919, reprinted Gloucester, Mass., 1963), and Eugene I. McCormac, *James Polk: A Political Biography* (Berkeley, 1922), argue that Polk would have sacrificed California to avoid war if the Texas boundaries were settled.

12. Reginald Horsman, *Race and Manifest Destiny* (Cambridge, Mass.: Harvard University Press, 1981), 2, and esp. chapters 7 and 8. Robert Walter Johannsen examines the meaning of the war to many Americans in his *To the Halls of the Montezumas: The Mexican War in the American Imagination* (New York: Oxford, 1985). John Edward Weems explores the race ideas and experiences of the common soldier in the Mexican War in his *To Conquer a Peace: The War Between the United States and Mexico* (1974, reprinted College Station: Texas A & M University Press, 1988).

13. Before the war Californio political leaders held differing views on their allegiance to Mexico. See Hague and Langum, *Larkin*, 117, and Harlow, *California Conquered*, 89.

14. Merk, *Manifest Destiny*, 77. Adrian George Traas emphasizes the importance of the topographical engineer to expansion; see his book *From the Golden Gate to Mexico City: The U.S. Army Topographical Engineers in the Mexican War, 1846–1848* (Washington, D.C.: United States Army publ., 1993).

15. Hague and Langum, *Larkin*, 120–21. They were accused of attempted rape (see Osio, *The History*, 223), and of horse theft and insulting, belligerent attitudes towards the population (see Harlow, *California Conquered*, 61–73).

16. George Harwood Phillips, *Indians and Intruders in Central California, 1769–1849* (Norman: University of Oklahoma Press, 1993), 133.

17. Padilla, *My History*, 56–60.

18. On the whole incident, see Ide, *Who Conquered California?*; Hawgood, "John C. Frémont"; and James L. Brown, *Dissension in Arcady: The Bear Flag Revolt* (Cambell, Calif.: The Academy Press, 1978).

19. Padilla, *My History*, 58.

20. Pío Pico, from Santa Barbara, June 29, 1846, in "Governor Pico's Protest Against the Action of the Bear Flag Party" in *Historical Society of Southern California Publications* 10 (1916): 129–30.

21. Vallejo de Leese, "History of the Bear Party."

22. Osio, *The History*, 230–34.

23. Juan Bautista Alvarado, "History of California," 1876, ms, Bancroft Library, 5: 219–22, and quoted in David Weber, ed., *Foreigners in the Native Land: Historical Roots of the Mexican Americans* (Albuquerque: University of New Mexico Press, 1973), 129–30.

24. On the role of the United States Navy in the California war, see Oakah L. Jones, Jr., "The Pacific Squadron and the Conquest of California, 1846–1847," *Journal of the West* (April 1966): 187–202, and on American military action in the war, also see John D. Tanner, Jr., "Campaign for Los Angeles—December 29, 1846, to January 10, 1847" *California Historical Society Quarterly* XLVIII (September 1969): 219–41.

25. Douglas Monroy, *Thrown among Strangers: The Making of Mexican Culture in Frontier California* (Berkeley: University of California Press, 1990), 177, and Harlow, *California Conquered*, 143.

26. See "Pío Pico's Correspondence with the Mexican Government, 1846–1848," *California Historical Society Quarterly* XIII (March 1934): 99–149.

27. Harlow, *California Conquered*, 149–54; Hague and Langum, *Larkin*, 148.

28. Hubert H. Bancroft translates the text of the rebels, entitled *Pronunciamiento de Varela y otros Californios contra los Americanos*, in his *History*, 5:310 n; also see Monroy, *Thrown among Strangers*, 178.

29. Harlow, *California Conquered*, 161–63 and 193–94.

30. See Osio, *The History*, 235–36; Padilla, *My History*, 114–20, 125–30; Spence and Jackson, eds., *The Expeditions*, 236–37.

31. Spence and Jackson, eds., *The Expeditions*, 235.

32. Harlow, *California Conquered*, 172–73.

33. Ibid., 211; Hague and Langum, *Larkin*, 155; Juan Avila, "Notas Californianas," ms, Bancroft Library.

34. See Juan Avila, "Notas Californianas."

35. See Doyce B. Nunis, Jr., *The Mexican War in Baja California: The Memorandum of Captain Henry Halleck* (Los Angeles: Dawson's Book Shop, 1977), 18–19.

36. Nunis, ed., *The Mexican War*, 24.

37. Ibid., 26–27, and 60. Also see Kenneth M. Johnson, "Baja California and the Treaty of Guadalupe Hidalgo," *Journal of the West* (April 1972): 328–47.

38. Ruiz de Burton's book, *The Squatter and the Don* (Houston: Arte Público Press, 1992, initally published in 1885), represented her last effort to plead for the land rights of elite Californios.

39. Richard Griswold del Castillo, *The Treaty of Guadalupe Hidalgo: A Legacy of Conflict*

(Norman: University of Oklahoma Press, 1990), 38–40; also see David M. Pletcher's *Diplomacy of Annexation: Texas, Oregon, and the Mexican War* (Columbia: University of Missouri Press, 1973).

40. Griswold del Castillo, *The Treaty*, 179–99.

41. Ibid., 189–90.

42. Ibid., 189–90, and 45–48.

43. Harlow, *California Conquered*, 290; Hague and Langum, *Larkin*, 176–98; and see Beverly E. Bastian, "'I Heartily Regret That I Ever Touched a Title in California': Henry Wager Halleck, the Californios, and the Clash of Legal Cultures," *California History* LXXII (Winter 1993/94): 310–23.

44. One of the first and still highly informative studies of this process is presented by Leonard Pitt in *The Decline of the Californios: A Social History of the Spanish-Speaking Californians, 1846–1890* (Berkeley: University of California Press, 1966).

45. Osio, *The History*, 247–48. On land loss and its political, social, and cultural ramifications see Albert Camarillo, *Chicanos in a Changing Society: From Mexican Pueblos to American Barrios in Santa Barbara and Southern California, 1848–1930* (Cambridge, Mass.: Harvard University Press, 1979); Richard Griswold del Castillo, *The Los Angeles Barrio, 1850–1890* (Berkeley: University of California Press, 1979); and, for a recent text that examines Californio and Indian society through Spanish and American conquests, see Lisbeth Haas, *Conquests and Historical Identities in California* (Berkeley: University of California Press, 1995), and the previously cited work of Monroy, *Thrown among Strangers.*

46. Griswold del Castillo, *Treaty of Guadalupe Hidalgo;* Oscar Martínez, *Troublesome Border* (Tucson: University of Arizona Press, 1988), 53–79, 57.

47. One person's history that vividly depicts this dilemma is presented in Florence Shipek's, *Delfina Cuero* (Menlo Park, Calif.: Ballena Press, 1991); and see Shipek's history of land policy in, *Pushed into the Rocks: Southern California Indian Land Tenure, 1769–1986* (Lincoln: University of Nebraska Press, 1987).

48. See Robert Heizer, ed., *Report of Special Federal Concern About the Conditions of California Indians, 1853–1913: Eight Documents* (Socorro, N.Mex.: Ballena Press, 1979), 65.

49. See Rawls, *Indians of California*, parts II and III.

50. See John Bodnar, *Remaking America: Public Memory, Commemoration, and Patriotism in the Twentieth Century* (Princeton: Princeton University Press, 1992), especially 120–37.

51. Norman E. Tutorow, comp. and ed., *Mexican-American War: An Annotated Bibliography* (Westport: Greenwood Press, 1981), 42, 46–47, and John Parish, "California Books and Manuscripts in the Huntington Library," *Huntington Library Bulletin 7* (April 1935): 36–58, summarize the manuscripts in the Huntington Library related to the Mexican War. Genaro M. Padilla also lists narrative accounts in *My History*, 271–72.

52. A more recent literature brings social history to the study of the Mexican War. On soldiers' experiences and their ideas and attitudes, see James M. McCaffrey, *Army of Manifest Destiny: The American Soldier in the Mexican War, 1846–1848* (New York: New York University Press, 1992), and Samuel J. Watson, "Manifest Destiny and Military Professionalism: Junior U.S. Army Officers' Attitudes Toward War with Mexico, 1844–1846," *Southwestern Historical Quarterly* 99 (April 1996): 466–98. On the cultural history of war photos, as this was the first war with a photographic record, see Martha A. Sandweiss, Rick Stewart, and Ben W. Huseman, *Eyewitness to War: Prints and Daguerreotypes of the Mexican War, 1846–1848* (Fort Worth: Amon Carter Museum/Washington D.C.: Smithsonian Institution Press,

1989), and Thomas R. Kailbourn, "The View from the Ojo de Agua: A Daguerreian Relic of Saltillo, Mexico, ca. 1847," *Southwestern Historical Quarterly* 95 (October 1991): 221–31. On the Irish soldiers who deserted and became heroes in Mexico, see Robert Ryal Miller, *Shamrock and Sword: The Saint Patrick's Battalion in the U.S.-Mexican War* (Norman: University of Oklahoma Press, 1989), and Marc Cramer, "The Fighting Irish of Mexico," *Americas* 48 (March–April 1996): 20–27.

Picturing California

Anthony Kirk

The images of early California that illuminate the pages of this volume are a well-spring of information and delight. Encompassing the widest range of artistic expression—from mysterious and fiercely beautiful pictographs to lyrical and wondrously evocative nineteenth-century landscape views—they enlarge our understanding of a long-lost world, vividly illustrating the firsthand observations of early explorers as well as the scholarly studies of modern historians. Speaking to us across the ages, the pictures tell of a world once fresh and new on the far western reaches of the American continent, of the rhythms of life played out by vital and vigorous civilizations, of the clash of empires on Pacific shores.

The Indian peoples who entered this virgin land sometime before the end of the last Ice Age produced the first pictorial art in California as many as two thousand years ago, when they began to paint designs on secluded rock outcroppings. Their imagery, which comprised both simple monochromatic symbols and complex multicolored designs, reached a highpoint among the Chumash, whose startling and brilliant art (figure 2) is believed to have been associated with religious ceremonials, some of them incorporating the use of the hallucinogen datura. The Chumash chiefly made use of geometric elements in the creation of their pictographs, but like other California Indians, they also incorporated figures of humans, beasts, reptiles, and insects into designs, suggesting that whatever supernatural visions may have animated their creative impulses, they were also powerfully influenced by the natural world about them.

The Spanish navigators who sailed dangerous seas to explore California's wild and windswept shores similarly composed pictorial images that reflected their relationship to this fabled land—a relationship entirely different from that of the native peoples, whose lives moved with the very pulse of nature itself. Like the French, English, and Russian voyagers who followed in their wake, the Spanish used art to advance imperial ambitions. The primary imagery of discovery was cartography, the making of maps to further subsequent exploration and settlement. Though the simple *derroteros*, or charts, produced by Vizcaíno and other early explorers evoke no real sense of place, some of the decorative and highly finished maps of the eighteenth century invite us to picture California much as the Spanish did more than two centuries ago. Suggestive of the evolving Hispanic understanding of this new land is the recently rediscovered *Plano del Puerto de Sn Francisco* (figure 3), a striking cartographic representation that seamlessly blends realism with abstraction. Drawn in 1776 by José de Cañizares, the pilot who the previous year had accompanied Captain Juan Manuel de Ayala on the first Spanish reconnaissance of the most magnificent of California estuaries, it incorporates discoveries made on a second survey that October. A seminal image of one of the defining natural landmarks of the Golden State, it portrays the Hispanic presence of presidio and mission with two tiny icons—outposts of empire nearly lost in a vast and largely unknown landscape, on which appear symbolic representations of countless trees, some of them, as indicated by the map's legend, *colorados*, or redwoods.

As international interest in Spain's distant province mounted over the decades, increasing numbers of European explorers came to anchor off the California coast. The passionate pursuit of knowledge that characterized the Enlightenment was the principal inspiration of many of these voyagers, though hopes of advancing trade relations and, not infrequently, imperial ambitions also underlay their visits. In seeking to add to the rapidly growing body of "natural philosophy," navigators and scientists devoted themselves to observing, measuring, collecting, and cataloguing, embracing in their investigations the wide-ranging interests of the age. The creation of a useful visual record was often fundamental to the success of their endeavors, and in an era when photography was unknown, artists played an essential role in these grand enterprises.

The earliest known European images of California to emerge from direct observation are two ornithological drawings, pictures of a California thrasher and a pair of California quail, executed in Monterey in 1786 by Jean-Louis-Robert Prevost, one of the artists who accompanied the famed French navigator Jean-François de Galaup, Comte de La Pérouse, on his final, ill-fated voyage to the South Sea. Of the two pictures, published eleven years later in the posthumous *Voyage de La Pérouse autour du monde,* the latter (figure 1) is the more engaging. It shows a male and female of the species posed on the brow of a hill, the pair characteristically active and alert, and in the best tradition of expeditionary art, the illustration is both aesthetically pleasing and accurately drawn.

Subsequent voyagers added to this founding pictorial record, directly and indirectly documenting the course of empire in this golden land. In picturing California, expeditionary artists preserved their impressions of flora and fauna, native peoples, Hispanic institutions, and the land itself. To assist in the advance of geographical knowledge—so crucial to mariners and, potentially, to military men—draftsmen frequently made careful topographical studies of landfalls, headlands, and harbors. John Sykes, a young master's mate and amateur artist who sailed with George Vancouver to California in the early 1790s, created a vast visual record of the far-flung Pacific coastline. Typical of his work is *View of Monterrey* (figure 4), a subtly rendered watercolor that shows the adobe walls of the royal presidio nestled in the lee of pine- and oak-studded rolling hills. Upon the expedition's return to England, the most significant images were copied by a professional artist and later appeared, together with a series of sailing charts, as engravings in the atlas to Vancouver's *Voyage of Discovery to the North Pacific Ocean and Round the World* (1798). The three volumes of Vancouver's narrative, which portentously concluded that the sole consequence of the Spanish settlement of California was to throw "irresistible temptation in the way of strangers to trespass over their boundary," was similarly enlivened with drawings from Sykes's brush, including three illustrations of Monterey and environs. These images—which, like the work of other artists discussed here, can be found scattered through the present volume—gave European and American readers their first glimpse of the California landscape and the tenuous Hispanic presence of presidio and mission.

Throughout the age of exploration,the astonishing variety of wildlife in this North American Eden attracted the attention of naturalists and artists alike. Although the scientists who accompanied the great Spanish navigator Alejandro Malaspina to Monterey in the autumn of 1791 recorded a wide range of birds, quadrupeds, and fish, it was the former that captivated José Cardero, the expedition's unofficial artist. Cardero, who had shipped with Malaspina as a cabin boy and was described by his superiors as "a simple amateur, not devoid of taste or artistic feeling," produced a series of handsome ornithological drawings that are the oldest extant color images of California by an expeditionary draftsmen. In picturing California, Cardero, like Jean-Louis-Robert Prevost before him, captured the wild beauty of the California quail (figure 5), carefully preserving the appearance of what a century and a half later would become the state bird.

Though wildlife and floral specimens were usually drawn on the spot or soon thereafter, the first representation of the state flower, the golden poppy, was completed years after it was collected in the autumn of 1816 by Adelbert von Chamisso, the naturalist with the Russian South Sea exploring expedition commanded by Otto von Kotzebue. The specimen obtained at San Francisco by Chamisso, who named the flower in honor of the ship's surgeon, Johann Friedrich Eschscholtz, ultimately entered the botanical collections of the Royal Academy of Berlin. Drawn and engraved by Friedrich Guimpel, this emblematic California flower, *Eschscholzia cali-*

fornica, with its vivid yellow petals, appeared as a hand-colored illustration (figure 6) in the 1820 compilation of recent Royal Academy acquisitions, *Horae Physicae Berolinensis,* printed in Bonn.

Like the distinctive flora and fauna of California, the native inhabitants of Spain's distant province drew the attention of expeditionary artists. Typically, though, their approach was strictly scientific, and as suggested by the work of José Cardero, Georg Heinrich von Langsdorff, and others, they focused on elements of dress and decoration and ethnic features rather than on the essential humanity of their subjects. In sharp contrast to these images are the watercolors produced by two Russians: Louis (Ludwig) Choris, who, like Adelbert von Chamisso, arrived in California in 1816 with Otto von Kotzebue, and Mikhail Tikhanov, who two years later visited Monterey and Bodega Bay with the around-the-world expedition of V. M. Golovnin. Tikhanov's beautiful and highly finished watercolor *Balthalzar* (figure 7), which shows a young Coast Miwok or Kashaya Pomo in both profile and full-face, is not only rich in ethnographic detail but suggestive of the boy's complex inner life. Though more loosely rendered, Louis Choris's brooding portrait of a man from the Guimen tribelet, *Indian of California* (figure 8), is the more evocative of the two likenesses, the deep and powerful humanity of Indian eyes shining brightly across the centuries.

Although José Cardero made drawings of a presidial soldier and his wife as early as 1791, the Hispanic settlers who held California for Spain and, later, Mexico never received the close artistic attention bestowed on the native peoples. One of the more striking images of Old California, however, illustrates the provincial dress of the pastoral period. The work of an unidentified artist who in 1837 accompanied Abel Du Petit-Thouars to Monterey, *Costume de la Haute Californie* and *Dame de Monterey* (figure 9) are among the brilliant hand-colored lithographs that appear in the magnificent folio atlases to the French explorer's travel narrative. In pose and costume, the pair reveal the elegance, color, and grace of elite Californio society, which so captivated Richard Henry Dana and other travelers of the 1830s and 1840s.

Chiefly concerned with creating accurate visual documents, the artists who visited this Pacific Eden when the banners of Spain and Mexico floated overhead rarely concerned themselves with high aesthetic intentions. A notable exception was Richard Beechey, a young midshipman on the British vessel of discovery H.M.S. *Blossom,* which came to anchor in California waters in the autumn of 1826. The son of the prominent London portrait painter, Beechey, in the course of two visits, produced a series of striking watercolors that are not only carefully observed and accurately drawn but are wonderfully evocative of the lyrical beauty of provincial California, suggesting the artist's own enchantment with a bright and sunny land. Typical is *The Mission of San Carlos, Monterrey* (figure 10), executed in January 1827, before the winter rains had begun to turn the landscape green. Enlivened with picturesque details, such as the Californio watching a group of Indians gambling, it is a splendid depiction of a mission in its heyday, when the Franciscan establishments were the great economic institutions of the province.

The commander of the *Blossom*, Midshipman Beechey's half-brother Frederick, lamented, like Vancouver before him, the lack of development in California, warning "that this indifference cannot continue; for either it must disappear under the present authorities, or the country will fall into other hands." But though the British coveted California, as did the French, the Russians had already taken action to seize and hold part of this Spanish possession, constructing in 1812 a fortified village, later known as Ross, on a coastal bluff some seventy miles north of San Francisco. Among the few images of this isolated outpost is a watercolor, (figure 11) by Il'ia Voznesenskii, a Russian scientist who arrived at the settlement in 1840 and spent a year investigating the natural history and Indians of the region. Made as a gift for Alexander Rotchev, the governor of the colony, the picture shows the fort, a scattering of farm buildings and workshops just outside the stockade, and to the right, beyond the road, the wooden houses where Russians, Aleuts, and Kashaya Pomo lived. Well-observed and crisply rendered, like all of Voznesenskii's work, it is a charming and picturesque vision of Russian California.

In the summer of 1841—the same year the Russians would sell Ross and retreat north to Alaska, abandoning old dreams of empire—the first exploring expedition from the United States, the Wilkes Expedition, entered California. Among the members of a detachment that traveled overland from the Oregon country and down the Sacramento Valley was the artist Alfred T. Agate, who produced the earliest known drawings of the interior of the Mexican province. Completed from field sketches shortly after Agate returned to New York, *South Branch of the Clamet* (figure 12) depicts an incident in which two Indians were discovered watching the exploring party from a high outcrop of lava rocks. In Agate's handsome watercolor, the rich riparian growth bordering the Klamath River contrasts strongly with the soft earth tones of the dry upland plain, which teemed with herds of antelope, while in the distance can be seen Mt. Shasta and, to the right, the towering barren cinder cone that Wilkes thought "the most remarkable object in this place."

American interest in California mounted swiftly in the years following Wilkes's visit, culminating in the Bear Flag Revolt and the Mexican War, which brought west numerous men with a talent for drawing. Among the artists who pictured the province in this momentous era was the unidentified maker of the delicate watercolor *California Regiment in Camp* (figure 13). One of several drawings by different hands in the journal of Lieutenant John McHenry Hollingsworth, a Maryland native who planned on settling in California, it shows the smartly attired soldiers of Company I of the First New York Volunteers at Monterey in the spring of 1847.

Also swept westward by the winds of Manifest Destiny was William R. Hutton, paymaster's clerk to the United States volunteer troops. A surveyor by training and a talented amateur artist, Hutton produced dozens of drawings during his California years, among which *San Francisco in 1847* (figure 14) is particularly fine. Looking across Yerba Buena Cove from Rincon Point, it shows the scattered village bathed in the warm light of the setting sun, a moment of quiet grace before the dawning of the American era in which the discovery of gold would swiftly change the face of Old California.

Picturing California

A Folio

Figure 1 · Jean-Louis-Robert Prévost, *Male and Female California Quail*. From Jean-François de Galaup, Comte de La Pérouse, *Voyage de La Pérouse autour du monde*, 1797. *Courtesy California Historical Society, FN-30508.*

Figure 2 · Painted Cave, Santa Barbara County, ca. 1000–1780. *Courtesy Santa Barbara Museum of Natural History. Photograph by George Stoll.*

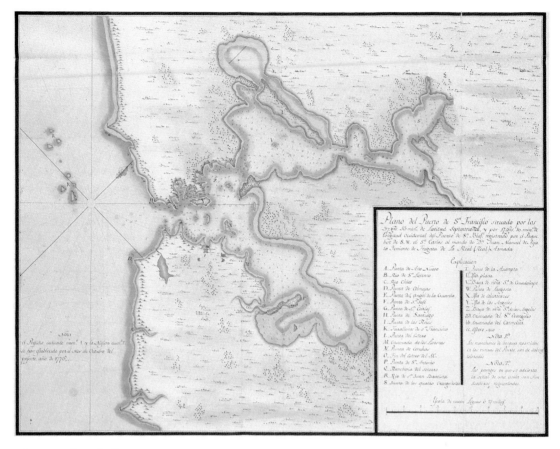

Figure 3 · José de Cañizares, *Plano del Puerto de Sn Francisco*, 1776. *Courtesy Bancroft Library.*

Figure 4 · John Sykes, *View of Monterrey*, ca. 1792. *Courtesy Bancroft Library.*

Figure 5 · José Cardero, *California Quail*, 1791. *Courtesy Museo Naval, Madrid. Photograph courtesy Iris Engstrand.*

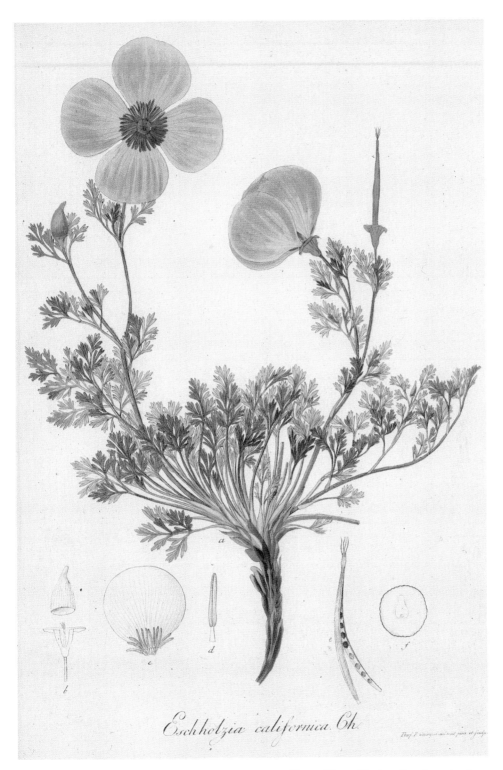

Eschholzia californica. Ch.

Figure 6 · Friedrich Guimpel, *Eschholzia californica.* From *Horae Physicae Berolinensis*, 1820.

Figure 7 · Mikhail T. Tikhanov, *Balthalzar*, 1818. *Courtesy Art Research Museum, St. Petersburg, Russia. Photograph courtesy Anchorage Museum of History and Art.*

Figure 8 · Louis Choris, *Indian of California*, 1816. *Courtesy Oakland Museum of California; Museum Donors Acquisition Fund.*

Figure 9 · Unidentified artist, *Costume de la Haute Californie* and *Dame de Monterey*. From Abel Du Petit-Thouars, *Voyage autour du monde sur la frégate la Vénus, pendant les années 1836–1839: Atlas pittoresque*, 1841. *Courtesy Bancroft Library*.

Figure 10 · Richard Beechey, *The Mission of San Carlos, Monterrey,* 1827. *Courtesy Autry Museum of Western Heritage, Los Angeles.*

Figure 11 · Il'ia Voznesenskii, *View of Ross,* 1841. *Courtesy Peter the Great Museum of Anthropology and Ethnography, St. Petersburg, Russia. Photograph courtesy Anchorage Museum of History and Art.*

Figure 12 · Alfred T. Agate, *South Branch of the Clamet*, 1842. *Courtesy Bancroft Library.*

Figure 13 · Unidentified artist, *California Regiment in Camp*, 1847. *Courtesy California Historical Society.*

Figure 14 · William R. Hutton, *San Francisco in 1847*, 1847. *Courtesy Huntington Library.*

Contributors

M. KAT ANDERSON is an ethnoecologist with the National Plant Data Center, Natural Resources Conservation Service, Department of Environmental Studies, University of California at Santa Cruz. She has a Ph.D. from the University of California, Berkeley, in wildland resource science. Her special research interest is the analysis of ancient wildlands harvesting and management techniques that meet human needs and allow for the coexistence of other life forms. She is co-editor of *Before the Wilderness: Environmental Management by Native Californians.*

MICHAEL BARBOUR is a plant ecologist who has been a faculty member of the University of California, Davis, since 1967. He has a Ph.D. in botany from Duke University. His research interests have focused on determining critical environmental requirements for such California vegetation types as tidal salt marsh, coastal dune, desert scrub, and high mountain conifer forest. He is a co-author or co-editor of several standard textbooks: *Plant Biology, Terrestrial Plant Ecology* (3 editions), *North American Terrestrial Vegetation* (2 editions), *Terrestrial Vegetation of California* (2 editions), and the chapter "North American Vegetation" in the recently published first volume of *The Flora of North America.*

ANTONIA I. CASTAÑEDA, a Chicana feminist historian, teaches in the department of history at St. Mary's University, San Antonio, Texas. Her research and teaching interests focus on gender, sexuality, and women of color in California and the Borderlands from the sixteenth to the twentieth century. Her current projects include a cultural history of Indo- and Afro-mestizas in colonial Alta California, a bilingual critical edition of nineteenth-century Californiana narratives, and a cultural history of Tejana farm workers.

IRIS H. W. ENGSTRAND, professor of history at the University of San Diego, received her Ph.D. from the University of Southern California, where she specialized in the history of California, Latin America, and the American West. Dr. Engstrand has received numerous awards and fellowships, including an Award of Merit from the California Historical Society, a Haynes Foundation Fellowship at the Huntington Library, and a Fulbright Research grant to Spain. She is the author of fifteen books, including *San Diego: California's Cornerstone; Spanish Scientists in the New World: The Eighteenth Century Expeditions;* and *Joaquín*

Velázquez de León: Royal Officer in Baja California. She has translated and edited the diary of José Mariano Moziño as *Noticias de Nutka: An Account of Nootka Sound in 1792.*

MICHAEL GONZÁLEZ received his Ph.D. from the University of California, Berkeley. He now teaches United States history, California history, and Chicano history at the University of San Diego.

RAMÓN A. GUTIÉRREZ is a professor of ethnic studies and history at the University of California, San Diego, and the founding chair of the Ethnic Studies Department and the Center for the Study of Race and Ethnicity at UCSD. Trained as a Latin Americanist, with interests in those portions of the United States that were once under Spanish colonial rule, Gutiérrez is best known for his book, *When Jesus Came, The Corn Mothers Went Away: Marriage, Sexuality and Power in New Mexico, 1500–1848,* and for his numerous articles and anthologies on race relations in the U.S. Southwest.

LISBETH HAAS is an associate professor of history at the University of California, Santa Cruz. Her book *Conquests and Historical Identities in California, 1769–1936* (University of California Press, 1995) won the 1997 Elliott Rudwick prize from the Organization of American Historians for a history of ethnic and racial minorities in the United States. She is currently writing *An Illustrated History of California* for Oxford University Press.

STEVEN HACKEL, a graduate of Stanford and Cornell universities, is assistant professor of history at Oregon State University. A former fellow of the Institute of Early American History and Culture in Williamsburg, Virginia, he is completing a book on Indian-Spanish relations in colonial California. His examination of politics in the California missions, "The Staff of Leadership: Indian Authority in the Missions of Alta California," appeared in the April 1997 issue of *The William and Mary Quarterly.*

ANTHONY KIRK completed his doctorate in history, with a specialization in American cultural history and art history, at the University of California, Santa Barbara. Dr. Kirk is a historical consultant in Santa Cruz, California. He is the author of *Founded by the Bay: The History of Macaulay Foundry, 1896–1996* (1996), and he has recently completed a book-length manuscript entitled "Visions of a Golden Land: California Art and Artists from the Age of Exploration to the Great Earthquake and Fire of 1906."

DOUGLAS MONROY is professor of history and director of the Hulbert Center for Southwest Studies at The Colorado College. A native of Los Angeles and a graduate of Hollywood High School and the University of California, Los Angeles, he presently lives in Colorado Springs with his two children. He is the author of *Thrown Among Strangers: The Making of Mexican Culture in Frontier California* (an Organization of American Historians prize winner) and *Born by the Rivers: The First Great Migration and the Creation of Mexican Los Angeles,* both from the University of California Press.

DOYCE B. NUNIS, JR. is distinguished professor emeritus of history, University of Southern California. He has written and edited fifty books and numerous articles. Since 1962, he has been editor of the *Southern California Quarterly,* published by the Historical Society of Southern California. He is a Fellow of the California Historical Society and the Historical Society of Southern California, as well as the recipient of CHS's Henry Raup Wagner Medal. He was decorated with the Order of Isabel the Catholic by King Juan Carlos I for his scholarly contributions to the history of Spain in Alta and Baja California.

RICHARD J. ORSI is professor of history at California State University, Hayward. A graduate of Occidental College in Los Angeles, he received his doctorate from the University of Wisconsin, Madison. He is the co-author (with Richard B. Rice and William A. Bullough) of *The Elusive Eden: A New History of California,* 2d ed., (McGraw-Hill, 1996), and co-editor (with Alfred A. Runte and Marlene Smith-Baranzini) of *Yosemite and Sequoia: A Century of California National Parks* (1993). He is nearing completion of another book, "A Railroad and the Development of the American West: The Southern Pacific Company, 1860–1930." Since 1988, he has been editor of *California History,* the quarterly of the California Historical Society.

WILLIAM PRESTON is a professor of geography at California Polytechnic University, San Luis Obispo, where he was honored with an "Outstanding Teacher Award." He holds a Ph.D. in geography from the University of Oregon and is the author of *Vanishing Landscapes: Land and Life in the Tulare Lake Basin.* His current research interests include pre-mission epidemiology, Indian resource ecology, and environmental alteration in California. Results of these efforts have been published in geographical, anthropological, and historical journals.

JAMES A. SANDOS, professor of history at the University of Redlands, earned his Ph.D. from the University of California, Berkeley, in 1978 where he studied with Woodrow Borah. Within the framework of Borderlands history, he has had an ongoing interest in Indian-white relations in California since 1769. Sandos's publications include "Junípero Serra's Canonization and the Historical Record," *American Historical Review,* XCIII, 1253–1269, which won the Hubert B. Herring Prize for Best Article in Latin American Studies in 1988, and *The Hunt for Willie Boy: Indian-hating and Popular Culture* (University of Oklahoma Press, 1994, joint with Larry E. Burgess), which won the Gustavus Myers Center Award for an Outstanding Book on the Subject of Human Rights in North America in 1994.

WILLIAM S. SIMMONS, professor of anthropology and former chair of the Department of Anthropology, is dean of the Division of Social Sciences at the University of California, Berkeley. Educated at Brown University (B.A., 1960) and Harvard University (Ph.D., 1967), Professor Simmons is an authority on the native peoples of North America, with a particular focus on California and New England. He currently is engaged in field research with the Maidu of Lassen and Plumas counties and with Professor Kent Lightfoot is writing a book on the Spanish, Mexican, Russian, and American frontiers in California.

MARLENE SMITH-BARANZINI has been the associate editor of *California History* since 1990. She is co-author (with Howard Egger-Bovet) of a children's U.S. history series, including *Book of the American Indians* (1994), *Book of the American Colonies* (1995), *Book of the American Revolution* (1994), *Book of the New American Nation* (1996), and the forthcoming "Book of the Civil War," published by Little, Brown. She is co-editor (with Richard J. Orsi and Alfred A. Runte) of *Yosemite and Sequoia: A Century of California National Parks* (1993). She is completing a new introduction to *The Shirley Letters* (Heyday Books, forthcoming).

VALERIE WHITWORTH is a language arts educator and a science writer who has had a lifelong interest in Native American cultures and the natural landscape. She has an undergraduate degree in English and history from the University of California, Berkeley, and graduate degrees from the University of California, Davis, and DQ University, Davis, the only non-reservation college in the United States devoted to the education of Native Americans. She has been a teacher at every level—primary, secondary, college—for twenty years, and she has also functioned as an independent consultant on adult literacy, teacher training, and the diagnosis of causes of reading difficulties in children. She is currently working on a book, "The History of DQ University."

Index

DESIGNER: Terry Bain
COMPOSITOR: Integrated Composition Systems, Inc.
TEXT: 11/14 Adobe Caslon
DISPLAY: Adobe Caslon Regular, Italic and Small Caps
TEXT PRINTER: Malloy Lithographing, Inc.
COLOR PRINTER: Southeastern Printing, Inc.
BINDER: Malloy Lithographing, Inc.